Schaffhausen

Konstanz

NORTHERN
SWITZERLAND

Winterthur

ZÜRICH

St Gallen

Rüti

**Northern Switzerland**
Pages 138–161

**Zürich**
Pages 162–179

Zug

ern
ne)

Stans

Sarnen

Altdorf

Bad Ragaz

Klosters

Chur

EASTERN
SWITZERLAND AND
GRAUBÜNDEN

Andermatt

Zillis

CENTRAL
SWITZERLAND
AND TICINO

Mesocco

St Moritz

Locarno

Bellinzona

Lugano

| 0 kilometres | 50 |
|---|---|
| 0 miles | 50 |

**Central Switzerland
and Ticino**
Pages 210–243

**Eastern
Switzerland
and Graubünden**
Pages 180–209

EYEWITNESS TRAVEL

# SWITZERLAND

# EYEWITNESS TRAVEL

# SWITZERLAND

Main Contributors **Adriana Czupryn,
Małgorzata Omilanowska
Ulrich Schwendimann**

**DK**

LONDON, NEW YORK,
MELBOURNE, MUNICH AND DELHI
www.dk.com

**Produced by** Hachette Livre Polska sp. z o.o., Warsaw, Poland

**Editors** Teresa Czerniewicz-Umer, Joanna Egert-Romanowska

**Designer** Paweł Pasternak

**Cartographers** Magdalena Polak, Olaf Rodowald
**Photographers** Wojciech and Katarzyna Mędrzakowie,
Oldrich Karasek
**Illustrators** Michał Burkiewicz, Paweł Marczak

**Contributors**
Małgorzata Omilanowska, Ulrich Schwendimann,
Adriana Czupryn, Marek Pernal, Marianna Dudek

**For Dorling Kindersley**
**Editor** Lucilla Watson
**Consultants** Gerhard Brüschke, Matthew Teller
**Translator** Magda Hannay
**Production Controller** Louise Minihane

Printed and bound in China.

First American edition, 2005

15 16 17 18 10 9 8 7 6 5 4 3 2 1

Published in the United States by DK Publishing,
375 Hudson Street, New York, NY 10014

**Reprinted with revisions 2008, 2010, 2013, 2015**

Copyright © 2005, 2015 Dorling Kindersley Limited, London
A Penguin Random HouseCompany

Published in Great Britain by Dorling Kindersley Limited.

A catalog record is available from the Library of Congress

ISSN 1542-1554
ISBN 978 1 4654 2681 9

MIX
Paper from
responsible sources
FSC™ C018179
www.fsc.org

---

**The information in this
DK Eyewitness Travel Guide is checked regularly.**
Every effort has been made to ensure that this book is as up-to-date as possible at
the time of going to press. Some details, however, such as telephone numbers,
opening hours, prices, gallery arrangements and travel information, are liable to
change. The publishers cannot accept responsibility for any consequences arising from
the use of this book, nor for any material on third party websites, and cannot
guarantee that any website address in this book will be a suitable source of travel
information. We value the views and suggestions of our readers highly. Please write to:
Publisher, DK Eyewitness Travel Guides, 80 Strand, London WC2R 0RL, UK,
or email: travelguides@dk.com.

Front cover main image: The Santuario della Madonna del Sasso, Locarno

◀ A pretty cobbled street in the town of Brienz, in the Bernese Oberland

# Contents

## How to Use
This Guide **6**

The tower of the Gothic Cathédrale
St-Nicolas, in the town of Fribourg

---

# Introducing
# Switzerland

## Discovering
Switzerland **10**

## Putting Switzerland
on the Map **16**

## A Portrait of
Switzerland **20**

## Switzerland Through
the Year **34**

The Piazza Grande in Locarno, lined with
shops, cafés and restaurants

Lake Lucerne, at the geographical and historical heart of Switzerland

Panel from the 1513 altarpiece in the Église
des Cordeliers, Fribourg

Münster St Vinzenz,
in Bern *(pp62–3)*

# HOW TO USE THIS GUIDE

This guide helps you to get the most from your visit to Switzerland. *Introducing Switzerland* maps the country and sets it in its historical and cultural context. Features cover topics from wildlife to geology. The eight sections comprising *Switzerland Region by Region*, three of which focus on Bern, Geneva and Zürich, describe the main sights, with photographs, maps and illustrations. Restaurant and hotel listings, and information about winter sports and many other outdoor activities, can be found in *Travellers' Needs*. The *Survival Guide* contains practical tips on everything from using the Swiss rail network to choosing the best times of year to visit Switzerland.

## Bern

A separate section is devoted to Switzerland's capital city. Each of Bern's main sights is shown on the map of the city centre and described in numerical order.

**Sights at a Glance** lists key places of interest.

**A locator map** shows where you are in relation to other areas of the city.

### 1 City Map

For easy reference, sights are numbered and located on a map. The main streets, bus stations, railway stations and tourist offices are also shown.

**A suggested route** for a walk is marked by a broken red line.

### 2 Street-by-Street Map

This gives a bird's-eye view of the key areas described in each section.

### 3 Detailed Information

All the sights in each city are described individually. Addresses and opening hours are given for each sight, and if there is an admission charge, this will be indicated. The key to symbols is on the back flap.

## 1 Introduction

An overview of the history and character of a major city or region of Switzerland is given here.

## Switzerland Region by Region

In this book, the country is described in eight chapters, three of which focus on Switzerland's major cities and five on its distinctive regions. The map on the inside front cover shows this regional division. The sights listed are shown and numbered on the *Regional Map* at the beginning of each chapter.

## 2 Regional Map

This shows the main road network and gives an illustrated overview of the whole region. All sights covered in the chapter are numbered and there are useful tips on getting around.

**Each area** of Switzerland is identified by colour-coded thumb tabs corresponding to the map on the inside front cover.

## 3 Detailed Information

All towns, villages and other places to visit are described individually and listed in order, following the numbering given on the *Regional Map*. Each entry also contains practical information such as museum opening times.

**Story boxes** explore some of the region's historical and cultural subjects in detail.

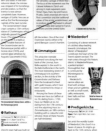

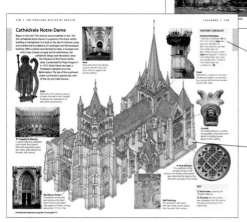

**A Visitors' Checklist** provides a summary of the practical information you need to plan your visit.

## 4 Switzerland's Top Sights

These are given two or more full pages. Historic buildings are often dissected so as to reveal their interiors. Stars indicate sights that visitors should not miss.

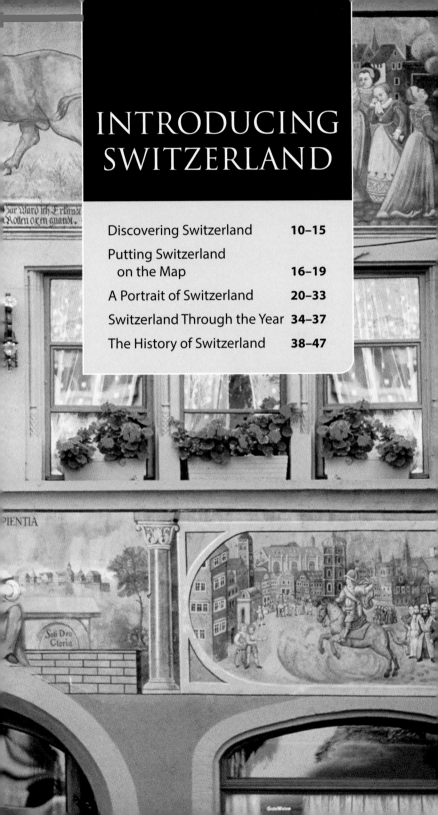

# INTRODUCING SWITZERLAND

# DISCOVERING SWITZERLAND

The following tours have been designed to see the best of Switzerland while keeping travel to a minimum. Firstly, there are three two-day tours that take in the country's most significant cities: Zürich, Bern and Geneva. These itineraries can be combined to form a six-day tour, and additional suggestions are made for those who wish to extend their trip.

Next, come a three-day and a four-day tour. The former is a short tour of Italian-speaking Canton Ticino, the latter a tour of predominantly French-speaking Western Switzerland that starts (or finishes) in Geneva. Lastly, a six-day tour focuses on Switzerland's best-known features: its spectacular mountains and charming historic towns.

**The attractive town of Fribourg**
Nestled on the River Sarine, Fribourg boasts charming streets lined with well-preserved Gothic houses.

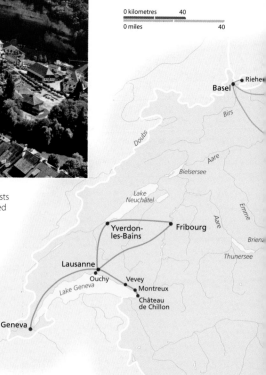

## Four Days in Western Switzerland

- Enjoy the laid-back charm of lakeside **Montreux** and **Vevey**.

- Admire the **Château de Chillon**, one of Europe's most evocative castles.

- Wander the cobbled streets of **Fribourg**, renowned for its Gothic architecture.

- Relax at a spa in **Yverdon-les-Bains**, home to one of Switzerland's largest and oldest spa complexes.

- Explore **Lausanne**, a historic university town on Lake Geneva that is renowned for its lively cultural scene.

**Luzern's Chapel Bridge**
Dating from the 14th century, Luzern's wooden footbridge is the oldest in Europe.

## Six Days of Mountains and Cities

- Admire the works of Picasso and other 20th-century artists at the Rosengart Collection in historic **Luzern**.

- Ride the world's steepest cog railway to one of the country's most famous peaks, the **Pilatus**.

- Explore the splendid art galleries and museums of **Basel**.

- Take a revolving cable car to the summit of the **Titlis** mountain, or hop aboard the world's first double-decker, open-topped cable car and marvel at the **Stanserhorn**.

- Stroll through beautiful **Schaffhausen**, with its Gothic, Renaissance and Baroque architecture.

- Stay in romantic **Stein am Rhein**, Switzerland's most beautiful small town.

- Admire the Benedictine monastery of **Kloster Einsiedeln**, one of the finest examples of Baroque architecture in the world.

### Key

— Four Days in Western Switzerland

— Three Days in Italian-Speaking Switzerland

— Six Days of Mountains and Cities

## Three Days in Italian-Speaking Switzerland

- Visit **Ascona**, which was once home to Europe's intellectuals and artists.

- Spend some time in the historic, palm tree-filled city of **Locarno**.

- Stroll along the shore of chic **Lake Lugano** to the traffic-free village of **Gandria**.

- Take a memorable rail trip on the historic narrow-gauge **Centovalli Railway**.

- Visit **Bellinzona**, home to not one but three castles – together they are recognized as a UNESCO World Heritage Site.

- Marvel at the **Matterhorn**, Switzerland's best-known mountain peak.

## Two Days in Zürich

*Switzerland's financial centre, Zürich is an attractive lakeside city with fine buildings, pretty cobbled streets and a lively cultural scene.*

- **Arriving** Zürich airport is 10 minutes by train from Zürich's main station, the Hauptbahnhof. From here, there are excellent countrywide connections.
- **Moving on** Zürich to Bern takes about 90 minutes by car, a little less by train.

### Day 1

Start the day with a stroll along **Bahnhofstrasse** *(p168)*, with its high-end shops and one-off boutiques. Then, cross the river to Zürich's Old Town, the medieval heart of the city, and window-shop as you wander the cobbled pedestrianized streets of **Niederdorf** *(p171)*. A short boat trip around the **Zürichsee** *(p173)* provides views of the impressive **Grossmünster** *(pp170–71)*, with its stunning 20th-century stained-glass windows. Back on shore, stop for a late lunch at the restaurant next door to the renowned **Kunsthaus** *(pp174–5)*, before admiring the gallery's fine permanent collection and great temporary shows. After dinner, if you still have some energy, try the lively bar scene in **Zürich West** *(p177)*.

Zürich's Old Town, as seen from the top of the Grossmünster

### Day 2

Spend the morning getting acquainted with Switzerland's history, from the prehistoric era to the present day, at the extensive **Landesmuseum**, or National Museum *(pp166–7)*. Return to Bahnhofstrasse and visit **Globus** *(p179)*, Zürich's main department store, where the Swiss specialities for sale in the food hall make for a tasty lunch. If you need to relax, spend the afternoon enjoying coffee and cake at one of the city's famed cafés, while watch and clock enthusiasts can admire the assortment of timepieces at the **Uhrenmuseum Beyer** *(p168)*.

> **To extend your trip…**
> Just 30 minutes away, in **Winterthur** *(pp160–61)* are the Museum Oskar Reinhart and the Kunstmuseum, both showcasing art from the 19th and 20th centuries, including works by Monet, Van Gogh and Picasso.

## Two Days in Bern

*Switzerland's capital is also one of its most attractive cities. Small and easy to get around on foot, much of the medieval centre is closed to traffic, making strolling a delight.*

- **Arriving** Bern is about 90 minutes by rail from Zürich. Basel airport, small but with frequent connections to main European cities, is just over an hour away.
- **Moving on** Geneva is less than 2 hours away by train.

### Day 1

Pass the morning wandering around Bern's medieval **Old Town** *(pp56–7)*. Admire the façade of the **Rathaus** *(p64)* and visit the splendid late-Gothic cathedral, the **Münster St Vinzenz** *(p62–3)*. Make sure you see – and hear – the **Zytglogge** *(p59)*, Bern's famous clock tower and once the city's western gate.

The iconic Zytglogge clock tower, at the end of Marktgasse, in Bern

From the river, see the impressive **Bundeshaus** *(pp58–9)*, the seat of Switzerland's government, before heading back to the 13th-century **Marktgasse** *(p59)*, lined with restaurants and cafés, for lunch. While away the afternoon in Bern's splendid art gallery, the **Kunstmuseum** *(pp60–61)*, with 3,000 paintings spanning from the 14th to the 20th centuries.

### Day 2

Just east of the city is **Bear Park** *(p64)*, a forested natural park that is home to Bern's famous brown bears. The Bern Show, in the nearby tourist office, presents a visual history of the city, while the beautiful Rosengarten provides a scenic view of the Old Town. After a bite to eat, head south of the river to the Museum District. Check out modern art at the **Kunsthalle** *(p64)*, the impressive stamp collection at the **Museum für Kommunikation** *(p65)*, or the displays of Alpine wildlife at the **Naturhistorisches Museum** *(p65)*.

> **To extend your trip…**
> The lakes of **Thunersee** *(pp78–9)* and **Brienzersee** *(p82)* surround **Interlaken** *(p79)*. From here, take a rack railway or cable car to the **Jungfraujoch** *(p83)*, where the Jungfrau, Mönch and Eiger form a stunning ridge.

For practical information on travelling around Switzerland, see pp296–301

## Two Days in Geneva

*In a splendid location on the shores of Europe's largest lake, Geneva is a dynamic and cosmopolitan city.*

- **Arriving** Geneva's international airport is located 6 km (4 miles) northwest of the city.
- **Moving on** Transfer to the city is just 6 minutes by train and 15 minutes by bus.

### Day 1

From the tourist office on Pont de la Machine, walk along the quay to the lakeside **Jardin Anglais** (p101). Continue on for views of the iconic **Jet d'Eau** (p101). Retrace your steps and head for Geneva's **Old Town** (pp100–1), stopping at the 12th-century **Cathédrale St-Pierre** (pp102–3) and the oldest house in the city, **Maison Tavel** (p104), now a museum that tells the story of daily life in Geneva from the 14th to the 19th centuries. Stop for lunch somewhere on **Place du Bourg-de-Four** (p103), then admire the ethnographic collection at the **Musée Barbier-Mueller** (p104).

### Day 2

Head out of the city to Avenue de la Paix for a guided tour of the **Palais des Nations** (p105), the European seat of the United Nations. Afterwards, visit the nearby **International Red Cross and Red Crescent Museum** (p105), which houses moving displays centred on global humanitarian issues. In the afternoon, take a boat trip on **Lake Geneva** (pp122–3). Disembark at **Lausanne** (pp116–21) for a bite to eat, then return to Geneva by train or boat.

> **To extend your trip...**
> The buzzing university city of Lausanne, with its great lakeside position, elevated Old Town and fine Gothic **Cathédrale Notre-Dame** (pp118–19), is worth an extended visit.

Eating alfresco on Piazza della Riforma in Lugano

## Three Days in Italian Switzerland

*Experience the piazzas and palm trees of a very different Switzerland.*

- **Arriving** Milan's Malpensa airport is a 90-minute drive from Lugano, canton Ticino's largest city. From Zürich, the scenic train trip takes less than 3 hours.

### Day 1: Lugano

Spend a day in the Italian-style city of **Lugano** (pp216–17), on the lake of the same name. The small church of **Santa Maria degli Angioli** (p217) features stunning Renaissance frescoes by Bernardino Luini. Enjoy a lazy lunch at a pavement café in **Piazza della Riforma** (p216), then take the funicular up to the village of **Monte Brè** (p215) for fantastic views. If energy levels permit, walk along the lake to **Gandria** (p215), a small village on the hillside, before heading back to Lugano.

### Day 2: Bellinzona, Locarno and Ascona

Head to the enchanting **Lake Maggiore** (pp220–21), stopping in **Bellinzona** (pp224–5), home to three castles, together UNESCO-listed, then go on to **Locarno** (pp218–19). Wander along the tree-lined lake, then go through **Piazza Grande** (p218) and up to the cobbled Old Town, with its cafés and boutiques, for lunch. Next, take the funicular to the 16th-century church of

**Madonna del Sasso** (p219) and admire the view. After, go to **Ascona** (p221), a chic resort that once drew artists and thinkers. From here, take a boat to **Brissago** (p220), home to a small botanical garden. Stay overnight in either Ascona or Locarno.

### Day 3: Centovalli and Italy

Travel by train from **Centovalli** (p222) to Domodossola, in Italy, and enjoy the stunningly scenic trip. Once in Italy, take another train to the village of Stresa, on the west side of Lake Maggiore, and see the Borromean Islands. Return to Locarno by boat.

> **To extend your trip...**
> Travel by train to **Zermatt** (p93) for breathtaking views of the **Matterhorn** (p94). Stay overnight in Zermatt, then go on to Lake Geneva, picking up the four-day tour of Western Switzerland (p14) for a wonderful week's trip.

The imposing UNESCO-listed Castello di Montebello in Bellinzona

The medieval Château de Chillon, on the eastern shore of Lake Geneva

## Four Days in Western Switzerland

*Predominantly French-speaking, Western Switzerland boasts diverse landscapes, lakes and vineyards, plus a rich collection of atmospheric towns and internationally famous cities.*

- **Arriving** Both Geneva and Zürich airports are ideal entry points into Western Switzerland. From each, good road and rail networks make getting around easy.

### Day 1: Geneva
Pick a day from the Geneva city itinerary on page 13.

### Day 2: Vevey and Montreux
Travel to the lakeside resorts of Vevey and Montreux. The trip is lovely, especially in the summer, when the hillsides are lush with vines. Charming **Vevey** (p124) has attracted many celebrities over the years, including Charlie Chaplin and artist Oskar Kokoschka. Wander along the lakeshore, through the historic quarter and on to the Musée Jenisch, which houses a large number of Kokoschka's works, plus a superb collection of prints by European artists from the 16th century. Next, head to **Montreux** (pp124–5), famous for its annual jazz festival. Glitzier than Vevey, Montreux has many large *belle époque* hotels offering views across the lake and the Alps beyond.

### Day 3: Château de Chillon and Fribourg
From Montreux, take a leisurely 45-minute walk along the lake to the enchanting medieval **Château de Chillon** (pp126–7). Set on a rocky spur on the eastern shore of Lake Geneva, this castle is a very popular site, so get there early to avoid the crowds. There's plenty to see here: the Aula Magna, with its 15th-century ceiling; the richly painted Grand Burgrave Hall; the frescoed chapel and the subterranean vaulted prison. Next, travel to the university city of **Fribourg** (pp130–31), on the River Sarine. The train journey takes about 75 minutes, with a change in Lausanne. Drivers can take the scenic A12 road. Do not miss the 16th-century Hôtel de Ville, the Cathédrale St-Nicolas and the Rue d'Or, with its fine Gothic houses.

### Day 4: Lausanne and Ouchy
Journey back to Lake Geneva and **Lausanne** (pp116–21), one of the country's most attractive cities. Spreading upwards from the lake, Lausanne is so steep that there is a one-line metro to haul residents uphill. Your first stop should be the impressive 12th-century **Cathédrale Notre-Dame** (pp118–19). Afterwards, wander through the steep and atmospheric Old Town. The **Palais de Rumine** (p117), now home to five museums, is well worth a visit. After lunch in the Old Town, head north of the city centre to the **Fondation de l'Hermitage** (p120), a villa housing a fine collection of French Impressionist art. The surrounding park is landscaped with exotic trees. On the outskirts of Lausanne is the pretty lakeside village of **Ouchy** (p121), location of the popular Olympic Museum. The village's tree-lined promenade is a good spot to relax and watch life pass by. Head back to Geneva.

#### To extend your trip...
En route from Fribourg, take in **Yverdon-les-Bains** (p132). Home to one of the country's largest spa centres, it's the perfect place to unwind after a day's sightseeing.

The fine Gothic features of the Cathédrale Notre-Dame, Lausanne

## Six Days of Mountains and Cities

*This tour combines breathtaking mountain scenery and beautifully preserved medieval and Gothic towns.*

- **Arriving** After landing in Zürich, head to **Luzern** (pp236–43), a 30-minute drive or 45-minute train journey away. Luzern will be your base for two nights.

### Day 1: Luzern and Vitznau
Take a guided tour of Luzern's pretty **Old Town** (pp238–9). See the **Chapel Bridge** (p236), the oldest wooden bridge in Europe, the **Jesuit Church** (p237) and the Renaissance **Rathaus** (p240). Lovers of

modern art should head to the **Rosengart Collection** *(p236)*, and everybody should seek out the fascinating **Swiss Transport Museum** *(pp242–3)*, packed with almost every mode of mechanized transport. After lunch, take the boat – a steamer, if you're lucky – to the small resort of **Vitznau** *(p229)*, and ride a train up to the summit of the Rigi massif for some truly terrific views. Return to Luzern for the evening.

### Day 2: Pilatus
The destination of the day is **Pilatus** *(pp232–3)*, one of Switzerland's most famous peaks. The journey from Luzern can involve a boat trip, a cable car or a cog railway – or all three – and, depending on your route, can take much of the day. The cog railway, which runs only in the summer, is the steepest in the world, with a gradient of 48 per cent. Expect spectacular views of Lake Lucerne from the summit. Return to Luzern.

### Day 3: Stans or Engelberg
Tiny **Stans** *(p233)* is a 20-minute drive or train journey from Luzern. Stroll through its pretty historic district, then go to the summit of the Stanserhorn by funicular railway and the world's first double-decker, open-top cable car. Alternatively, around 45 minutes by train from Luzern is the village of **Engelberg** *(p233)*, which lies at the foot of the Titlis. From Stand, just above Engelberg, a rotating cable car lifts you to the peak at a dizzying height of 3,239 m/10,627 ft.

Next, travel to Basel. The trip takes around 1 hour 45 minutes by car; it is longer by train, since it involves a change in Luzern.

### Day 4: Basel
Stroll around the historic centre of **Basel** *(pp142–51)*, along the banks of the Rhine. Pick up some treats for a picnic lunch from the daily market in the Marktplatz, then head to the **Münster** *(pp148–9)*, a medieval cathedral with 14th-century crypt frescoes and remains of Romanesque and Gothic sculpture. The **Rathaus** *(p143)*, with its restored deep-red façade, appears much as it would have in 1600. The **Kunstmuseum** *(pp150–51)* has a prestigious collection of art from the 15th to the 20th centuries. If contemporary art is more to your taste, head to the **Kunsthalle** *(p146)*. Spend the night in Basel.

### Day 5: Riehen, Schaffhausen and Stein am Rhein
Take the tram to **Riehen** *(p154)*, northeast of Basel, to admire the 19th- and 20th-century art (including works by Van Gogh, Picasso, Matisse and Rothko) at the Fondation Beyeler. Return to Basel for lunch, then head east to **Schaffhausen** *(pp184–5)*. By train or car, the trip takes around 90 minutes. If time permits, stop off in **Baden** *(pp158–9)*, one of the oldest spa towns in Switzerland. Schaffhausen, like so many Swiss towns, is beautifully preserved, and its cobbled streets are lined with fine examples of Gothic,

The bright red façade of Basel's eyecatching Gothic town hall

Renaissance, Baroque and Rococo architecture, as well as 16th- and 17th-century fountains. Journey on to nearby **Stein am Rhein** *(p186)*, just 20 minutes away, for the night. Said to be Switzerland's most beautiful small town, it is a delight for lovers of architecture, chock-full as it is of medieval and Renaissance buildings.

### Day 6: St Gallen
Head east to **St Gallen** *(pp188–91)*, around an hour by car and an hour and a half by train. A university town of some importance, St Gallen was the centre of lacemaking in the 1800s. Admire the medieval half-timbered houses in the historic centre, then head to the **Textilmuseum** *(p188)*, with its fine collection of lace and embroidery from Switzerland and abroad. St Gallen's main attraction is undoubtedly the magnificent cathedral *(pp190–91)* and its stunning Baroque library, the **Stiftsbibliothek** *(p188)*; both are UNESCO World Heritage Sites. Head back to Zürich. The trip takes around an hour by car or train.

> **To extend your trip...**
> En route to Luzern from Zürich, stop at **Kloster Einsiedeln** *(pp230–31)*. This Benedictine abbey is one of the finest examples of Baroque architecture in the world. From Zürich, the train trip is about an hour.

Beautiful view of Lake Lucerne and Mount Pilatus from the Rigi massif

# Putting Switzerland on the Map

Located in the Alpine region of central Europe, Switzerland is a landlocked country covering some 41,300 sq km (15,950 sq miles) and inhabited by 8 million people, 23 per cent of whom are non-Swiss. It borders Germany to the north, Austria and Liechtenstein to the east, Italy to the south, and France to the west and northwest. Switzerland consists of three distinct geographical regions, which stretch across the country southwest to northeast: the Jura mountains, covering a small area in the northwest; the Mittelland, a central plateau, and the Alps in the south and east. The capital city is Bern.

Colmar

Freibu
Breisg

Rhine

A35

A5

Mülheim

Mulhouse

419 ✈

A98

Basel
(Basle)

A3

18 Birs

A2

Aarau

St-Ursanne

A16 Delémont

Olten

A

Doubs

A36

Besançon

N57

JURA

6 Solothurn

Aare

A5

Langenthal

La Chaux-
de-Fonds

Biel (Bienne)

5

A1

Burgdorf

Wolhusen

Bielersee

A6

F R A N C E

Doubs

Neuchâtel

10

Lake
Neuchâtel

Bern (Berne)

10

D72

Pontarlier

10

A5

A1

✈

Aare

Champagnole

Yverdon-les-Bains

9

1

Fribourg
(Fryburg)

Thun

Brienz

A6

Thunersee

Brienze

A12

Bulle

Spiez

Interlaken

Lausanne

A9

Vevey

11

Zweisimmen

Kandersteg

A1

Lake Geneva (Lac Léman)

Nyon

5

21

Aigle

B e r n e s e    A l p s

Brig

Thonon-
les-Bains

A9

Sion

Sierre

9

Simplon
Pass

✈

Geneva

A40

Rhône

A9

P e n n i n e    A l p s

21

Grand St
Bernard Pass

27

I T A L Y

Sc

Aosta

A5

Issogne

Valnontey

Biella

Cuorgne

Ivrea

A4

## Europe

FINLAND

NORWAY

SWEDEN

ESTONIA

LATVIA

North
Sea

DENMARK

LITHUANIA

UNITED
KINGDOM

NETHERLANDS

GERMANY

POLAND

BELARUS

REP. OF
IRELAND

BELGIUM

CZECH REP.

UKRAINE

FRANCE

SWITZERLAND

AUSTRIA

SLOVAKIA

HUNGARY

ROMANIA

Atlantic
Ocean

SLOV.

CROATIA

BOSNIA
HERZ.

SERBIA

BULGARIA

PORTUGAL

SPAIN

ITALY

ALBANIA

GREECE

MOROCCO

ALGERIA

TUNISIA

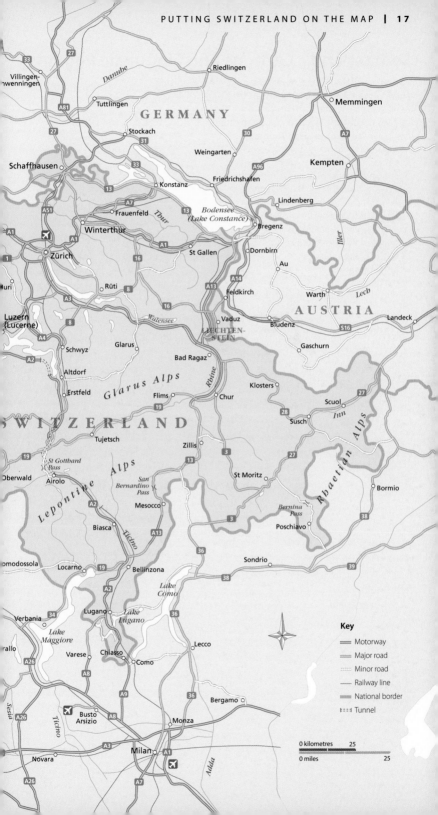

# Switzerland's Cantons and Linguistic Regions

Switzerland is divided into 26 cantons, six of which (Appenzell-Ausserrhoden, Appenzell-Innerrhoden, Basel-Landschaft, Basel-Stadt, Nidwalden and Obwalden) are known as half-cantons but operate as full cantons. Each canton has its own constitution, legislation and financial autonomy. The country is divided into three main linguistic regions. While German predominates in northern, eastern and central Switzerland, French is spoken in the west, and Italian in the south. Valais, or Wallis, has distinct French- and German-speaking regions. Romansh is the language of a small minority of people in Graubünden, where German and Italian predominate.

**Swiss Cantons**

| | | | |
|---|---|---|---|
| | **Western Switzerland** | AG | Aargau |
| JU | Jura | ZH | Zurich |
| NE | Neuchâtel | | **Eastern Switzerland and Graubünden** |
| VD | Vaud | | |
| FR | Fribourg | SH | Schaffhausen |
| GE | Geneva | TG | Thurgau |
| | **Mittelland, Bernese Oberland and Valais** | AR | Appenzell-Ausserrhoden |
| | | SG | St Gallen |
| SO | Solothurn | AI | Appenzell-Innerrhoden |
| BE | Bern | GL | Glarus |
| VS | Valais | GR | Graubünden |
| | **Northern Switzerland** | | **Central Switzerland and Ticino** |
| BS | Basel Stadt | ZG | Zug |
| BL | Basel Land | LU | Luzern |

| | |
|---|---|
| SZ | Schwyz |
| UR | Uri |
| TI | Ticino |
| NW | Nidwalden |
| OW | Obwalden |

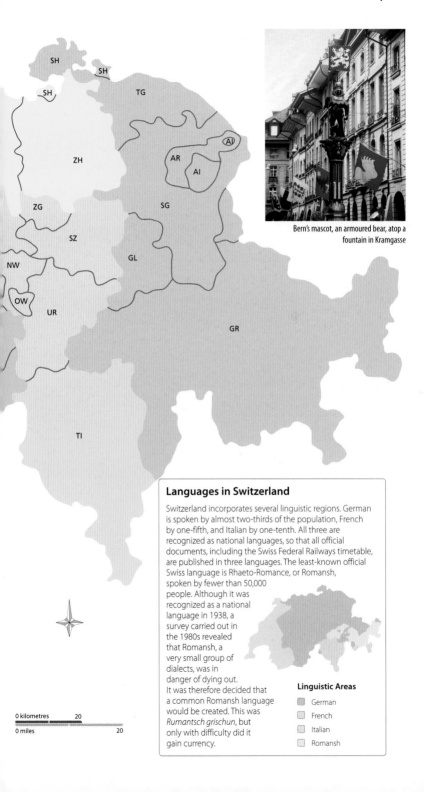

Bern's mascot, an armoured bear, atop a
fountain in Kramgasse

## Languages in Switzerland

Switzerland incorporates several linguistic regions. German
is spoken by almost two-thirds of the population, French
by one-fifth, and Italian by one-tenth. All three are
recognized as national languages, so that all official
documents, including the Swiss Federal Railways timetable,
are published in three languages. The least-known official
Swiss language is Rhaeto-Romance, or Romansh,
spoken by fewer than 50,000
people. Although it was
recognized as a national
language in 1938, a
survey carried out in
the 1980s revealed
that Romansh, a
very small group of
dialects, was in
danger of dying out.
It was therefore decided that
a common Romansh language
would be created. This was
*Rumantsch grischun*, but
only with difficulty did it
gain currency.

### Linguistic Areas

- German
- French
- Italian
- Romansh

0 kilometres 20

0 miles 20

# A PORTRAIT OF SWITZERLAND

A landlocked country in the cultural and geographical heart of Europe, Switzerland has a distinct character and dynamism. While the country is admired for the beauty of its Alpine environment, its people are respected for their industry and technical ingenuity, as well as their social responsibility and direct democratic system of government. It is also one of the world's richest countries.

Switzerland has virtually no natural borders. The Alpine mass of which it mostly consists extends eastwards into Austria, westwards into France, and southwards to form valleys that run down to Lombardy, where the border straddles several lakes. Although Switzerland's northern border follows the course of the Rhine, even here it crosses this natural feature, bulging out around Basel and taking in a mosaic of German and Swiss enclaves around Schaffhausen.

This mountainous country has engendered a robust spirit of independence and enterprise and a zealous work ethic in its population. Both Catholic and Protestant, and with diverse cultural roots, the Swiss are remarkable for their strong sense of unified nationhood. Switzerland's national character has also been moulded by its neutrality. Having avoided many of the major conflicts that shaped the culture of other European nations, Switzerland stands at a slight remove from the wider world.

Switzerland today is a prosperous and highly industrialized nation with a cosmopolitan lifestyle. On the one hand, it is forward-looking and innovative. On the other, it is traditional and conservative, valuing stability above change, with a keenness to maintain cultural continuity and links with the past.

The Aletsch Glacier seen from the Eggishorn, whose peak reaches 2,927 m (9,603 ft)

◀ The Swiss Open Air Museum Ballenberg, near Brienz

Biel/Bienne, the Bielersee and St Petersinsel, seen from Boezingenberg, in the Jura mountains

## Population, Language and Religion

The Jura mountains, in the north, and the Alpine region, to the south, are sparsely populated. The highest population density, and most of the country's industrial activity, is in the central Mittelland, concentrated in and around the capital Bern, and also in the lakeside cities of Geneva, Lausanne, Luzern and Zürich.

Switzerland's linguistic and religious divisions are also distinctive. The German-speaking population inhabits the northern slopes and valleys of the Alps and a large section of the Mittelland plateau. The northern shores of Lake Geneva, the gentle slopes of the Jura mountains and the western

Alps are inhabited by French-speaking Swiss. Italian is spoken south of the main Alpine ridge, while the Romansh-speaking minority inhabits a few isolated high mountain valleys in the east. German is spoken by two-thirds of the population, French by one-fifth, Italian by one-tenth and Romansh by less than 1 per cent. Switzerland is almost equally divided between Protestant and Catholic, these religions crossing linguistic divides. The population also includes a small number of Jews and Muslims.

Divisions between French, Italian and German speakers, and between Protestants and Catholics, which have dogged the unity of the Confederation throughout its history, are still tangible today.

### Democracy in Action

Switzerland is a federal republic consisting of 26 cantons. With its own tax, legal, fiscal and educational systems, each canton is virtually an independent state, enjoying considerable autonomy within the Swiss Confederation.

Traditional folk costume of the Fribourg region

The country is governed by a Federal Assembly, a bicameral parliament consisting of a directly elected Federal Council and a Council of States, whose delegates represent the individual cantons. Switzerland's main political parties are the

Regatta on Lej da Silvaplana in Graubünden

Swiss People's Party, the Social Democrats, the Free Democrats and the Christian Democrats. Certain major issues are decided directly by the people, by referendum. Voting, on matters ranging from the national speed limit to concerns of strictly local relevance, takes place at national, cantonal and communal level.

## The Economy

The Swiss economy is based on banking and international trade, the service industries, manufacturing, agriculture and tourism. Standards of living are high, unemployment is low and per capita income is one of the highest in the world.

Alpine festival in Beatenberg, on the Thunersee

The country's major exports are precision machinery, clocks and watches, textiles, chemicals and pharmaceuticals. Chocolate and dairy products, including cheese, are also major exports.

Although only 5 per cent of the population is engaged in agriculture, this sector of the economy enjoys a privileged status, with some of the highest subsidies in the world. This is not only of benefit to farmers but, since it contributes to the preservation of Switzerland's picturesque landscape, it also supports the country's hugely important tourist industry.

Livestock accounts for almost three-quarters of Swiss farming, and dairy farming and agriculture for one quarter. More than a third of the country's cheese production is exported, chiefly in the form of Emmental and Gruyère.

## Arts and Sciences

A highly cultured country, Switzerland plays a leading role in the arts, hosting such important events as the Lucerne Music Festival, the Montreux Jazz Festival and the Rose d'Or

television awards. Art Basel is the world's premier contemporary art fair, and the Kunsthaus in Zürich is a national art gallery with collections of international importance.

The best-known of all Swiss intellectuals is the philosopher Jean-Jacques Rousseau (1712–78), who was born in Geneva but spent most of his life in France. Other important Swiss writers include the German-born dramatists Max Frisch (1911–91) and Friedrich Dürrenmatt (1921–90). Hermann Hesse (1877–1962), who was born in Germany, became a Swiss citizen and wrote many of his greatest works in Switzerland. Many Swiss artists and architects have also won international recognition.

Cattle returning from mountain pastures, in the Schwarzenburg region

Among the most prominent is the architect Le Corbusier (1887–1965), who was born and grew up in La-Chaux-de-Fonds, but who is more closely associated with France, and the sculptor and painter Alberto Giacometti (1901–66), a native of Graubünden, who spent nearly all his adult life in Paris. Although he retained his German citizenship, the artist Paul Klee (1879–1940), who was born near Bern, is treated as Swiss. Other notable Swiss artists include the painter Ferdinand Hodler (1853–1918), the sculptor Jean Tinguely (1925–91) and the polymath Max Bill (1908–94).

Since the 1930s, Switzerland has produced several architects of international renown. Mario Botta (b. 1943) designed the Museum of Modern Art in San Francisco, and Jacques Herzog and Pierre de Meuron are the architects who designed the world's largest steel structure, the 2008 Olympic Stadium in Beijing.

Switzerland also has a tradition of excellence in the sciences. It was in Bern that Albert Einstein developed his theory of relativity, and to date an impressive number of 25 Swiss citizens have won Nobel prizes. The Federal Institute of Technology in Zürich and the prestigious European Centre for Nuclear Research near Geneva have put Switzerland at the forefront of scientific research.

*Clearing*, an installation by Gillian White, depicting the links between art and nature

## Traditional Activities

A sport-loving nation, the Swiss make the most of their Alpine country. Skiing, snowboarding, sledging and skating are popular winter sports. Kayaking, rafting, hiking and a host of other active summer sports have a large following among the Swiss.

Certain rural areas are home to distinctive types of sport. These include *Schwingen*, an Alpine form of wrestling, *Hornussen*, a ball game played with long, curved bats, and cow fights *(combats des reines)*, staged in the canton of Valais. Yodelling and alphorn-playing are also an integral part of the Alpine way of life. However, many young town folk, regardless of region, are deeply indifferent to these traditional activities, as they are to the *Waffenlauf*, a long-distance race run by competitors dressed in uniforms and carrying rucksacks and rifles on their backs.

Contestants in a *Schwingen* match, a Swiss form of wrestling

## Environmental Issues

The Swiss have a punctilious approach to preserving their natural environment. Two examples of this are a remarkably developed and well-coordinated public transport system, and a scrupulous and proactive approach to recycling waste.

Swiss Guards at a ceremony at the Vatican in Rome

Switzerland is the first country to have made compulsory the fitting of catalytic converters to cars, and national regulations concerning the emission of toxic gases and other substances are among the most stringent in the world. Such consideration towards the environment has had a measurable effect on the quality of life in Switzerland. Even in towns or cities the size of Luzern, Bern or Zürich, the rivers and lakes are so clean that it is perfectly safe to swim in them.

Most Alpine plants and many wild animals are protected by law, and certain animals, such as the ibex, wolf and bear, have been reintroduced. Forests, which cover about a third of the country, are also protected. Forestry is tightly regulated and logging of large areas, which heightens the risk of landslides and avalanches, is forbidden. Switzerland is a signatory to the 1999 Alpine Convention, drawn up together with eight other Alpine nations to protect the Alpine environment from the harmful effects of tourism and motorized transport.

## Switzerland on the World Stage

Although it is a neutral country, Switzerland maintains a citizen army to defend its borders. National service is compulsory. However, except in time of war, the Swiss army has no active units and no top general, although regular training takes place. The last mobilization occurred during World War II. Today, the only Swiss mercenaries are the Swiss Guards, who defend the Vatican and act as the papal bodyguard in Rome.

The European headquarters of the UN and the world headquarters of the International Red Cross are based in Geneva, and Switzerland sees its role in international affairs as a largely humanitarian one.

Kayaking on the Valser Rhine in Graubünden

# The Swiss Alps

About two-thirds of Swiss territory consists of Alpine and sub-Alpine areas. At lower elevations up to 1,500 m (5,000 ft), agricultural land and deciduous trees predominate. These give way to coniferous forest, which above 2,200 m (7,200 ft) in turn gives way to scrub and Alpine pastures. At altitudes above 3,000 m (9,800 ft), mosses and lichens cover a desolate rocky landscape, above which are snowfields, glaciers and permanently snow-covered peaks. While snow and rainfall increase with altitude, the Alpine climate is affected by two seasonal winds, the cold, dry easterly *bise* and the warm southerly *Föhn*, which brings clear, sunny skies then rainfall to the western Alps.

**Meadow and pasture** cover almost half of Switzerland. Wild clover and campanula grow abundantly in the high meadows of the Bernese Oberland.

**Glacial lakes**, formed by the melting of glaciers, are a common sight in the Alps. The Bachalpsee, near which rises the Wetterhorn, lies at the heart of a particularly scenic part of the Swiss Alps.

**Mosses and lichens** cling to the surface of rugged crests and precipitous scree-filled gorges.

**Scrub**, including dwarf mountain pine, as well as rhododendron and alder, cover the transitional zone between the forests and the high mountain peaks. At this altitude the growing season, from June to August, is brief.

**Lush vegetation** thrives on sheltered slopes and along gulleys cut by mountain streams.

**High Alpine meadows** provide lush summer grazing for cattle.

## Mountain Landscape

*The Alps are cut through by deep valleys, terraces, cols and gorges. To the south of the Alps lies the canton of Ticino, which enjoys a Mediterranean climate. To their north are the long limestone sub-Alpine ranges, whose sheer rockfaces merge into the flatter Mittelland, central Switzerland's relatively low-lying plateau.*

**Forests** in Switzerland are closely monitored and protected. Clearing hillsides, which increases the danger of avalanches, is forbidden.

**Alpine streams** flowing through dense pine forests are a part of the extraordinarily beautiful scenery in the Swiss National Park.

Spruce predominates in forests at higher altitudes

## Alpine Plants and Animals

In spring Switzerland's high Alpine meadows are covered with a carpet of flowers, including aster, edelweiss, campion, and several species of gentian. Most Alpine flowers are protected and it is forbidden to pick them. Alpine wildlife includes ibex and chamois, marmot, alpine hare, golden eagle, bearded vulture, and the rarely seen European lynx. Several species of these animals, including those that have been reintroduced, are also protected.

**Edelweiss**, the symbol of Switzerland, grows among rocks at altitudes up to 3,500 m (11,500 ft). It has star-shaped flowers and woolly leaves.

**Alpenrose**, a species of rhododendron, grows mostly at altitudes of 2,500 m (8,200 ft). Its flowers create large areas of dense colour.

**Gentian** grows mainly in rock crevices and in woodlands. Its roots are used in the pharmaceutical industry.

**The Alpine ibex** lives above the treeline for most of the year. A species of wild goat, it is extremely agile over mountainous terrain.

**The chamois**, a goat antelope, frequents regions between wooded mountainsides and the snowline. Agile and shy, it is seldom seen at close range.

**The marmot** lives in burrows in Alpine meadows. When disturbed, it emits a piercing, high-pitched whistle.

**Areas of grassland**, like this one around the Schwarzsee, a lake at the foot of the Matterhorn, provide summer grazing for sheep. Thick snow covers these pastures during winter.

# Formation of the Alps

About 70 million years ago, the Adriatic Microplate began to drift northward, colliding with the rigid European Plate. While the oceanic floor that lay between them was forced downwards, the Adriatic Microplate was thrust upwards, creating the Alps. This upheaval, which continued until 2 million years ago, caused the upper strata of rock to fold over on themselves. The older metamorphic rocks, thrust up from the substratum, thus form the highest part of the Alps, while the more recent sedimentary and igneous rocks make up the lower levels. The action of glaciers during successive ice ages then scoured and sculpted the Alps, giving them their present appearance.

**The Matterhorn**, carved by the action of ice, is the most distinctive and best-known of Switzerland's peaks. Lofty and awe-inspiring, it rises to a height of 4,478 m (14,691 ft).

**The Aletsch Glacier**, in the Bernese Alps, covers about 86 sq km (33 sq miles) and is about 900 m (2,952 ft) deep. It is the largest glacier in the Alps.

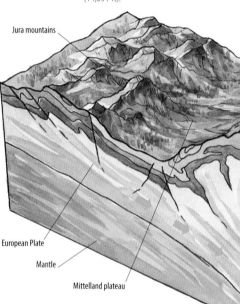

Jura mountains

European Plate

Mantle

Mittelland plateau

## Alpine Glaciers

Vestiges of the Ice Age, Alpine glaciers continue their erosive action. As they advance, they scour valley floors and sides, carrying away rocks which are ground and then deposited as lateral and terminal moraines. Glacial lakes fill basins scooped out by glaciers. Hanging valleys were created when glaciers deepened the main valley.

Snowfield

Hanging valley

Glacial lake

Tongue of glacier

Lateral moraine

Karst spring

Terminal moraine

Medial moraine

Crevasses

**The Jura mountains**, consisting of fossil-rich marl and limestone, are relatively low. They feature caves, sinkholes and underground streams. Because of their exceptionally well-preserved strata, the mountains gave their name to a geological period, the Jurassic.

## The Swiss Alps

Apart from those in the eastern part of the canton of Graubünden, the Swiss Alps, like the French Alps, belong to the Western Alpine Group, which in turn consists of ten separate ranges. This part of the Alpine range has the highest and steepest peaks and most contorted geological formations. It is also where Switzerland's landscapes of snow and ice are at their most breathtaking. The Valais Alps contain many of Switzerland's most impressive peaks, including the Matterhorn and Dufourspitze, which at 4,634 m (15,203 ft) is the country's highest mountain. The southern Alps lie in the canton of Ticino. The eastern Alps contain the Swiss National Park.

**Key**

| | |
|---|---|
| | Western Alps |
| | Eastern Alps |
| | Southern Alps |
| | Swiss upland |
| | Jura mountains |

Western Alps

Southern Alps

Direction of tectonic thrust

Adriatic Plate

Mantle

## Alpine Landscape

*Shaped by the action of ice, the landscape of the Alps was created during a succession of ice ages that occurred 600,000 to 10,000 years ago. During periods of glaciation, the ice sheet was up to 2,000 m (6,500 ft) thick. Typical of the glacial landscape are sharp ridges, steep gullies, flat-bottomed valleys carved out by advancing glaciers, glacial lakes and hanging valleys with waterfalls creating streams.*

**The Swiss National Park** is situated in the Rhaetian Alps, which form part of the Eastern Alpine Group. Its pristine Alpine landscape, covering 170 sq km (66 sq miles) in Graubünden, ranges from evergreen forest to desolate rocky areas and permanent snow at high altitudes.

# Swiss Architecture

Serene Romanesque abbeys, lofty Gothic cathedrals, lavishly decorated Baroque churches and town houses with painted façades all form part of Switzerland's architectural heritage. For most of its history, however, Swiss architecture reflected various European influences – German in the north and east, French in the west, and Italian in the south – without developing a distinctive style until the mid-20th century. Swiss vernacular architecture, however, has always been distinctive. It is epitomized by the Alpine chalet, of which there are several local variants.

**Painted façade** of a fine 16th-century town house in Stein am Rhein, Schaffhausen.

## Romanesque (10th–12th Centuries)

As elsewhere in western Europe, the flowering of the Romanesque style in Switzerland was due largely to the diffusion of religious orders, which spearheaded a renewal in religious architecture. Romanesque buildings are characterized by massive walls, rounded arches, groin vaulting, and a restrained use of decorative carving. Among the finest examples of the style in Switzerland are the Benedictine monastery at St Gallen, the Münster zu Allerheiligen in Schaffhausen, and its culmination, Basel's remarkable Münster.

**The Grossmünster** in Zürich, begun in the 11th century, was stripped of its interior decor during the Reformation.

**The Romanesque crypt of Basel's** 12th-century Münster

## Gothic (13th–15th Centuries)

Characterized by pointed arches, ribbed vaulting and flying buttresses, the Gothic style emphasizes vertical perspectives, with stained-glass windows admitting light to lofty interiors and decoration on towers and portals. Fine examples of Swiss Gothic architecture include the Cathédrale St-Pierre in Geneva and Cathédrale de Nôtre-Dame in Lausanne, both of French inspiration, and the Münster in Bern, in the German Gothic style. Important Gothic secular buildings include the Château de Vufflens and Château de Chillon, and Bellinzona's three castles, Montebello, Sasso Corbaro and Castelgrande.

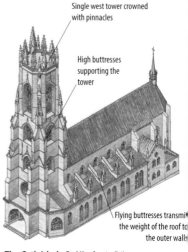

Single west tower crowned with pinnacles

High buttresses supporting the tower

Flying buttresses transmit the weight of the roof to the outer walls

**The Cathédrale St-Nicolas** in Fribourg, built in the 14th and 15th centuries, exemplifies the High Gothic style.

**The Château de Chillon**, built by the Dukes of Savoy on an islet near Montreux, is one of the finest extant examples of Gothic fortified architecture in Switzerland.

## Renaissance (15th–16th Centuries)

Coinciding with the Reformation, the Renaissance reached Switzerland in the late 15th to early 16th centuries. The style is most clearly seen in secular buildings, such as town halls, mansions with arcaded courtyards and fine town houses, like those in Bern. While the Gothic style tended to persist in the country's German-speaking regions, Renaissance influence was strongest in central and southern Switzerland.

**The Rathaus** in Luzern, completed in 1606, is built in the style of a Renaissance Florentine palazzo but its mansard roof reflects Swiss traditions.

**The Collegio Pontificio di Papio** in Ascona, built around 1584, has a fine Renaissance arcaded courtyard with a double tier of beautifully proportioned arches.

## Baroque (17th–18th Centuries)

The end of the Thirty Years' War in 1648 was marked by a renewal in building activity in Switzerland. In the country's Catholic regions many new churches were built, and older ones remodelled, in the Baroque style. Characterized by extensive ornamentation, painted ceilings, scrollwork and gilding, the Baroque in Switzerland came under foreign influences and has north Italian and south German variants. The finest examples of Baroque architecture in Switzerland are the Klosterkirche in Einsiedeln, completed in 1745, and St Gallen Cathedral, completed in 1768.

**The Klosterkirche** at Einsiedeln has an ornate gilt and polychrome ceiling typical of the Baroque style.

St Gallen Cathedral, a fine example of Swiss Baroque architecture

## The Swiss Chalet

Characteristic of Switzerland and other adjacent Alpine areas, the chalet was originally a herdsman's house. Although there are many regional variations, the chalet is typically built of timber, generally to a square plan, and is covered with a low-pitched roof made of wood, slate or stone. The roof usually projects both at the eaves and at the gables, and the gable end is sometimes filled with a triangular area of sloping roof. Many chalets also have balconies, which may be fronted with decoratively carved railings.

**Doors** of wooden houses are of panel construction, and are usually covered with decorations and reinforced with ornamental metalwork.

Half-timbered chalet at the Open Air Museum Ballenberg

**Rural house** typical of the Bern region of the Mittelland during the Baroque period. The roof is designed to enable it to withstand heavy coverings of snow.

# Tunnels and Railways

The building of Switzerland's renowned railways, tunnels and viaducts began in the mid-19th century, driven by the needs of a precociously industrialized economy and made possible by the technological advances of the age. As track was laid along seemingly inaccessible mountain routes, tunnels were driven beneath mountains and viaducts built to span deep valleys. By the end of the 19th century, narrow- and full-gauge rail networks, including rack-and-pinion track on the steepest inclines, covered the country. While part of the rail network caters for visitors, it is used mainly by modern express, intercity and high-speed trains.

**An intercity train** of Swiss Federal Railways crosses the River Sarine on the Grandfey viaduct, in the Fribourg region.

| 0 kilometres | 50 |
| 0 miles | 50 |

**The funicular train** from Mülenen takes visitors up the Niesen, whose peak rises to 2,362 m (7,749 ft). From the summit there is a magnificent view of the Thunersee, Spiez and the Jungfrau range.

**Key**

—··— Major railway

—— Minor railway

···· Rail tunnels

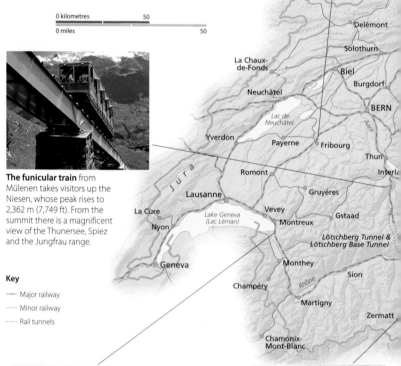

Basel
Delémont
Solothurn
La Chaux-de-Fonds
Biel
Burgdorf
Neuchâtel
**BERN**
*Aare*
*Lac de Neuchâtel*
Yverdon
Payerne
Fribourg
Thun
Interla
Romont
Gruyères
Lausanne
*Jura*
Vevey
Gstaad
La Cure
*Lake Geneva (Lac Léman)*
Montreux
Nyon
*Lötschberg Tunnel & Lötschberg Base Tunnel*
Geneva
Monthey
Sion
Champéry
*Rhône*
Zermatt
Martigny
Chamonix-Mont-Blanc

**An intercity train** on a main line that opened in 1996. Skirting Lake Geneva, it passes near the beautiful Château de Chillon.

**The Glacier Express** crosses 291 bridges and viaducts and runs through 91 tunnels on its scenic route between Zermatt and St Moritz.

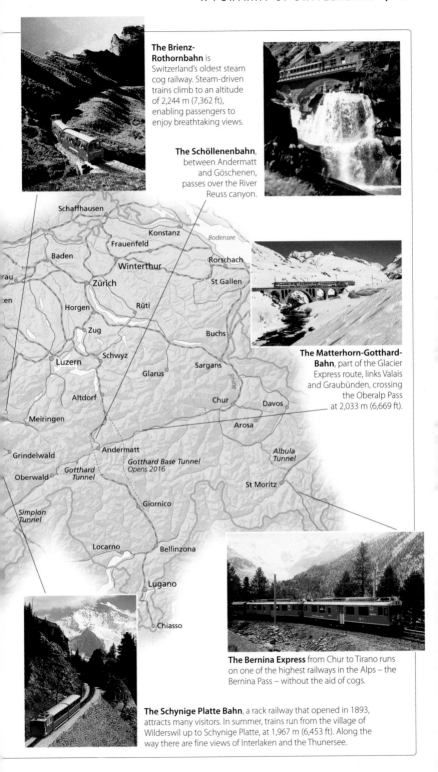

**The Brienz-Rothornbahn** is Switzerland's oldest steam cog railway. Steam-driven trains climb to an altitude of 2,244 m (7,362 ft), enabling passengers to enjoy breathtaking views.

**The Schöllenenbahn**, between Andermatt and Göschenen, passes over the River Reuss canyon.

**The Matterhorn-Gotthard-Bahn**, part of the Glacier Express route, links Valais and Graubünden, crossing the Oberalp Pass at 2,033 m (6,669 ft).

**The Bernina Express** from Chur to Tirano runs on one of the highest railways in the Alps – the Bernina Pass – without the aid of cogs.

**The Schynige Platte Bahn**, a rack railway that opened in 1893, attracts many visitors. In summer, trains run from the village of Wilderswil up to Schynige Platte, at 1,967 m (6,453 ft). Along the way there are fine views of Interlaken and the Thunersee.

# SWITZERLAND THROUGH THE YEAR

The Swiss enjoy a great variety of festivals. These range from colourful spectacles in which entire towns, cities and villages take part, to sophisticated art, music and film festivals, some of which are internationally famous. Among these are the Lucerne Festival of classical music and Bern's International Jazz Festival.

While the country unites to celebrate its origins on National Day (1 August), a large proportion of popular festivals, such as Bern's onion fair in November, have a more local, though no less historic, significance. Many folk festivals, particularly those ushering in the arrival of spring, have pagan roots, and in mountain villages cows are honoured in ceremonies that mark the spring and autumn transhumance – the seasonal movement of livestock.

Between December and March, the country also hosts many winter sports events, including several world championships.

Chalandamarz, a children's spring festival in the Engadine on 1 March

## Spring

The early spring is a time of transition. As the winter sports season nears its end, cold dark days begin to brighten and the first of the spring festivals, at which winter is ritually despatched, take place. Open-air voting sessions resume, cows are ceremonially taken up to their summer pastures, and in the Valais the first cow fights of the year are held.

### March

**International Jazz Festival** (March–May), Bern. Major three-month festival of blues, jazz and gospel music.

**Chalandamarz** (1 March), villages all over the Engadine. Children's spring festival, with costumed parades.

**Engadine Ski Marathon** (2nd Sunday in March). Major cross-country skiing marathon run from Maloja to S-chanf with about 13,000 participants.

**International Motor Show** (March), Geneva. Prestigious annual event.

**Verbier Xtreme** (mid-March). Daredevil off-piste skiing and boarding, Verbier.

**Basel World** (3rd week in March), Basel. Watch and jewellery fair.

**Snow and Symphony** (late March–early April), St Moritz. World-famous orchestras and soloists present a series of 20 concerts of classical music and jazz.

**Oesterfestspiele** (around Easter), Luzern. Festival of Easter music.

### April

**Sechseläuten** (3rd Monday in April), Zürich. Spring festival with parade of medieval guilds and the ritual burning of Böögg (Old Man Winter).

**Lugano Festival** (mid-April–June), Lugano. Classical music concerts.

**Fête de la Tulipe** (mid-April–mid-May), Morges. Colourful tulip festival.

**Fête du Soleil** (late April–May), Lausanne. Carnival with bands and markets.

**Combat des Reines** (mid-April–May), Valais. Traditional cow fighting takes place in four Swiss valleys – Heremence, Herens, Anniviers and Bagnes.

**Landsgemeinde** (last Sunday in April), Appenzell Innerrhoden. Open-air cantonal voting session.

### May

**Landsgemeinde** (1st Sunday in May), Glarus. An open-air cantonal voting session conducted by a show of hands.

**International Rowing Regattas** (late May), Luzern. World-class rowing races on the Rotsee.

Traditional cow fights, held in Valais in spring

## Average Daily Hours of Sunshine

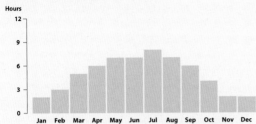

**Sunshine Chart**
July is the sunniest month, but May, June and August also feature sunny weather. The cloudiest months are in winter, from November to January.

Dancers in traditional costume at a summer folk festival in Appenzell

## Summer

In mountain villages summer is celebrated with a host of folk festivals, with much eating, drinking and merriment. Elsewhere, the first of many open-air events, including music festivals and summer sporting events, takes place. At the height of summer, Swiss National Day (1 August) is celebrated in every town and village with bonfires and fireworks.

### June

**Alpaufzug** (mid-June), across the Alps. Cows, adorned with flowers, are herded to high Alpine meadows, while celebrations are held in villages.
**Art Basel** (mid-June), Basel. Major international contemporary art fair in leading galleries across the city.

Participant in the Fêtes des Vignerons, Vevey

**Jazz Ascona** (late June), Ascona. The music of New Orleans, in the largest jazz event outside the USA.
**William Tell** (late June–mid-September), Interlaken. Open-air performances of Schiller's play about the Swiss hero.

### July

**Open-Air Rock and Pop Music Festival** (early July), St Gallen.
**Montreux Jazz Festival** (July), Montreux. Festival of jazz blues, rock, reggae and soul music. Free concerts on the promenade.
**Avenches Opera Festival** (6–21 July). World-class opera productions at the 6,000-seat Roman amphitheatre.
**Swiss Open** (mid-July), Gstaad. International men's tennis tournament.
**Moon and Stars** (mid-July), Locarno. Rock and pop music in the city's Piazza Grande.

### August

**National Day** (1 August), throughout Switzerland. Celebrations, with fireworks, music, street illuminations and lantern processions, marking the birth of the Swiss Confederation in 1291.
**Fêtes de Genève** (early August), Geneva. Music, street theatre, firework displays and sport.
**International Film Festival** (early August), Locarno. Some 7,000 spectators enjoy outdoor viewings on Europe's biggest cinema screen.
**Street Parade** (either of the first two weekends in August), Zürich. Huge open-air gathering of almost a million techno-music fans.
**Inferno Triathlon** (mid-August), Jungfrau region. Bike and run 5,500 m (18,045 ft) uphill, then swim 3,100 m (2 miles) to cool off.
**Lucerne Festival** (mid-August–mid-September), Luzern. The famous festival of classical music, with international orchestras, conductors and soloists.

Celebrations on National Day in Oberhofen, on the Thunersee

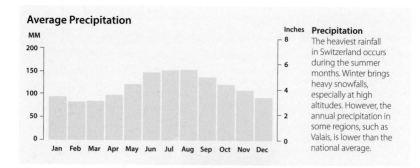

## Average Precipitation

**Precipitation**
The heaviest rainfall in Switzerland occurs during the summer months. Winter brings heavy snowfalls, especially at high altitudes. However, the annual precipitation in some regions, such as Valais, is lower than the national average.

## Autumn

When the trees on the Alpine hillsides start to take on autumnal colours and the vines are heavy with ripe grapes, it is time to give thanks for the harvest. Colourful agricultural fairs are held across the country; chestnut and wine festivals take place everywhere and the cows are returned to their barns, where they will spend the winter.

### September

**European Masters** *(early September)*, Crans Montana. Switzerland's premier golfing event, a highlight of the PGA European tour.
**La Bénichon** *(mid-September–October)*, Canton Fribourg. Festival of thanksgiving.
**Knabenschiessen** *(2nd weekend in September)*, Zürich. Shooting contest for boys and girls aged 12–16.
**Wine Festival** *(late September)*, Neuchâtel. The largest of its kind in Switzerland. Others are held throughout the country.
**Fête de la Désalpe** *(last Saturday in September)*, across the Alps. Celebrations as cows decorated with flowers are brought down from their summer grazing in the high Alpine meadows.

### October

**Combats des Reines** *(early October)*, Martigny. Cow fighting in the Roman amphitheatre, the ultimate winner being proclaimed Reine des Reines (Queen of the Queens).

Festivities marking the return of cows from their Alpine pastures

**Autumn Fair** *(early October)*, Basel. Switzerland's largest and longest-established food fair and funfair runs for two weeks.
**La Bénichon** *(3rd Sunday in October)*, Châtel-St-Denis. Harvest thanksgiving, with procession in traditional dress.

**Älplerchilbi** *(October–early November)*, Obwalden and Nidwalden. Folk festival with alphorns and yodelling.

### November

**Expovina** *(first two weeks of November)*, Zürich. Fair, with wine tastings, at which wines imported from all over the world are put on display on ships moored along Bürkliplatz.
**Räben-Chilbi** *(2nd Saturday in November)*, Richterswil. Young people carrying lanterns made of turnips join in a procession.
**Bach Festival** *(two weeks in early November)*, Lausanne.
**Gansabhauet** *(mid-November)*, Sursee. Ancient harvest festival rite in which blindfolded contestants try to behead a dead goose with a blunt sword.
**Zibelemärit** *(4th Monday in November)*, Bern. Onion fair, with confetti battle and other festive activities marking the beginning of winter.

September Wine Festival, Neuchâtel

## Average Temperatures

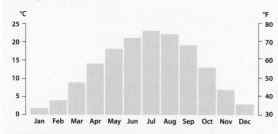

**Temperatures**
Temperatures are highest in June, July and August, though they rarely exceed 30° C (86° F). The coldest month is December, when temperatures often drop below freezing.

Ice sculptures at the World Snow Festival in Grindelwald

## Winter

Advent, Christmas and the Feast of St Nicholas are the main focus of fairs and festivals in December. New Year is exuberantly celebrated throughout the country. In some parts of Switzerland it is marked twice, first in accordance with the current Gregorian calendar, and again according to the older Julian calendar. This is also the season of a variety of winter sports events, from ice hockey and curling to horse racing on ice. Between New Year and mid-March, countless carnival balls, folk festivals with masquerades and fancy dress keep spirits up through the cold winter months. They culminate in Fasnacht, a three-day festival held in many parts of Switzerland, which precedes Lent.

Carnival participant, in devil's costume

## December

**St Nicholas Day** *(on or around 6 December)*, all over Switzerland. Parades and fairs celebrating Santa Claus' arrival.
**Fête de l'Escalade** *(1st Sat in December)*, Geneva. Festival commemorating the Duke of Savoy's failed attempt to capture Geneva in 1602.
**Spengler Cup** *(late December)*, Davos. World ice-hockey tournament.
**New Year's Eve** *(31 December)*, villages of Appenzell. Masked characters with cowbells usher in the New Year.
**New Year's Eve** *(31 December)*, Verbier. The biggest, wildest outdoor rave in the Alps with hours of fireworks broadcast live on TV.

## January

**Vogel Gryff** *(mid- to late January)*, Basel. Three-day folk festival involving a lion, a griffin and Wild Man of the Woods.

**Coppa Romana** *(mid-Jan)*, Silvaplana. Europe's largest open-air curling contest.
**World Snow Festival** *(mid-January)*, Grindelwald. Fantastic ice-sculpture contest, held on a natural skating rink.
**Hot-Air Balloon Week** *(late Jan)*, Château d'Oex. Week-long spectacle as the skies fill with colourful hot-air balloons.
**Cartier Polo World Cup on Snow** *(late January)*, St Moritz. Polo played on the frozen lake at St Moritz.

## February

**Roitschäggättä** *(week before Ash Wednesday)*, Lötschental. Nocturnal parades by men wearing grotesque masks.
**White Turf** *(1st half of February)*, St Moritz. International horse races held on the frozen lake.
**Fasnacht** *(February or early March)*, Basel. Major spring carnival lasting three days and three nights, with thousands of costumed figures playing drums and piccolos. Also celebrated around the same time in Luzern, Bern and other towns.

### Public Holidays

**New Year's Day** (1 Jan)
**Good Friday** (Karfreitag, Vendredi Saint)
**Easter Monday** (Ostermontag, Lundi de Pâques)
**Ascension Day** (Himmelfahrt, Ascension)
**Whit Monday** (Pfingstmontag, Lundi de Pentecôte)
**National Day** (1 Aug)
**Christmas Holiday** (25 & 26 Dec)

# THE HISTORY OF SWITZERLAND

The history of Switzerland began in 1291, when three small cantons formed an alliance against their foreign overlords, the Habsburgs. As other cantons joined, the alliance expanded, but there followed centuries of instability, with bitter conflict between cantons and religious groups. It was not until 1848 that a central government was established and that modern Switzerland was born.

## Helveti and Rhaetians

From about 500 BC, the lands that now comprise Switzerland were settled by two peoples: the Rhaetians, possibly an Etruscan people who settled in a small area in the east; and the Helveti, a powerful Celtic tribe, who settled in the west. The Helveti established several small townships here, including La Tène, near Neuchâtel.

## From Roman to Frankish Rule

By 58 BC both Helvetia and Rhaetia, as they were known, were incorporated in the Roman Empire, the Helveti becoming allies of the Romans against warlike tribes to the north. Under Roman rule Aventicum (Avenches), capital of the Helveti, became a Roman province. Other towns with villas were built, agriculture flourished and new roads were laid out. In AD 260, Helvetia and Rhaetia were once again attacked by Germanic tribes. While the eastern region was taken by the Alemani, driving the Rhaetians into the hinterland, the western region was seized by Burgundians. In 401 the Romans abandoned their Alpine province.

By the 6th century, the Swiss territories of the Alemani and Burgundians had been taken by the Franks. These lands were later incorporated into Charlemagne's Holy Roman Empire, and in 843 they were divided between his grandsons.

## Alliance of the Cantons

In 1033, Burgundy was reunited within the Holy Roman Empire. However, as imperial power declined, feudal dynasties came to prominence. The most powerful was that of the Habsburgs. In 1291, the free peasants of the Forest Cantons of Schwyz, Uri and Unterwalden formed an alliance against Habsburg power, their delegates meeting in Rütli Meadow to swear their mutual allegiance. This was the nucleus of what later became the Swiss Confederation. In the 14th century they were joined by the cantons of Luzern, Zürich, Glarus, Zug and Bern. In their attempts to break the Confederation, the Habsburgs suffered crushing defeats in a succession of battles with the Confederates, who eventually won their independence in 1499.

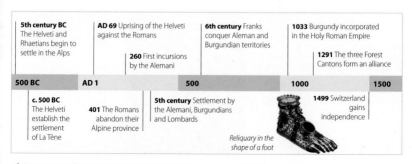

| **5th century BC** The Helveti and Rhaetians begin to settle in the Alps | **AD 69** Uprising of the Helveti against the Romans | **6th century** Franks conquer Aleman and Burgundian territories | **1033** Burgundy incorporated in the Holy Roman Empire |
| | **260** First incursions by the Alemani | | **1291** The three Forest Cantons form an alliance |

| 500 BC | AD 1 | 500 | 1000 | 1500 |

| **c. 500 BC** The Helveti establish the settlement of La Tène | **401** The Romans abandon their Alpine province | **5th century** Settlement by the Alemani, Burgundians and Lombards | **1499** Switzerland gains independence |

*Reliquary in the shape of a foot*

◄ Representatives of the three Forest Cantons swearing the oath of allegiance on Rütli Meadow in 1291

# The Struggle for Independence

In 1291, on the death of Emperor Rudolf I, representatives of the cantons of Schwyz, Uri and Unterwalden decided to form an alliance against the power and tyranny of the Habsburgs. The oath of mutual allegiance that they swore at Rütli Meadow in August that year laid the foundations of the Swiss Confederation. The wars that the Confederates fought against the Habsburgs and the Burgundians in the 14th and 15th centuries demonstrated the superiority of agile peasant troops over heavily armed knights. The Swiss also became renowned for their valour as soldiers and were sought after as mercenaries throughout Europe.

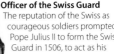

**Officer of the Swiss Guard**
The reputation of the Swiss as courageous soldiers prompted Pope Julius II to form the Swiss Guard in 1506, to act as his bodyguards and to protect the Vatican.

**Battle of Dornach (1499)**
Confederate soldiers launched a surprise attack on troops commanded by Heinrich von Fürstenberg, who was killed in the battle.

**Mercenary troops** sent by Charles VII of France to aid the Habsburg cause march on Basel.

**Battle of Morgarten (1315)**
The army of Duke Leopold of Habsburg suffered a crushing defeat when it fought against peasant Confederate forces at the Battle of Morgarten.

**Shield of Schwyz**
Originally plain red, as here, the shield of Schwyz was later charged with a white cross. A red cross on a white ground became the Confederation's emblem.

**Confederate soldiers** at the foot of a tower rally behind a banner with the emblem of Basel.

**Crossbow**
The crossbow was the basic weapon in the Swiss army's arsenal.

Defensive walls around Basel

**William Tell's Arrow**
According to legend, William Tell was sentenced to death by the Austrian bailiff Hermann Gessler for refusing to acknowledge Habsburg power, but won a reprieve by shooting an apple off his son's head with his crossbow. William Tell later killed Gessler.

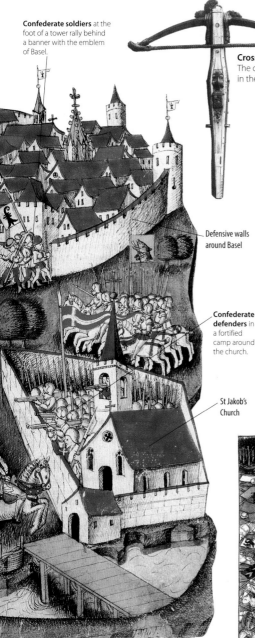

**Confederate defenders** in a fortified camp around the church.

St Jakob's Church

### Battle of St Jakob

*In 1444, at the request of the Habsburg king Friedrich III, Charles VII of France sent a 20,000-strong army of mercenaries to Switzerland. In their fortified camp at St Jakob, on the River Birs, near Basel, defenders of the Confederation put up a heroic defence but were slaughtered.*

**Battle of Laupen (1339)**
After the siege of Bern, the armies of Bern and Luzern give thanks to God for their defeat of the Duke of Burgundy and his ally, the canton of Fribourg.

Defeat of the Swiss at the Battle of Marignano (1515)

## The Peak of Territorial Power

Emboldened by independence, yet surrounded by territories held by the Habsburgs and other powers, the Swiss Confederation attempted to secure and expand its territory to the north, east and south. In 1512, Confederate troops conquered Lombardy, occupying Locarno and Lugano. However, their stand against combined French and Venetian forces at Marignano in 1515 ended in defeat, after which Switzerland abandoned its policy of expansion and moved towards military neutrality. The Confederation itself, however, continued to grow, Fribourg and Solothurn joining in 1481, Basel and Schaffhausen in 1501 and Appenzell in 1513. The cantons now numbered 13.

## The Reformation

The great religious and political movement to reform the Roman Catholic Church originated in Germany in the early 16th century and quickly spread throughout western Europe. At the vanguard of the Reformation in Switzerland were the humanist Ulrich Zwingli (1484–1531), who was active in Zürich, and Jean Calvin (1509–64), who led the movement in Geneva. While the urban cantons embraced the Reformation, the poorer and more conservative cantons of central Switzerland remained faithful to Catholicism. Despite this rift, the cantons remained loyal to the Confederation throughout the wars of religion that swept through Europe in the 17th century.

## Prosperity and Industry

The Swiss Confederation's independence from the Austrian Empire was formally recognized by the Peace of Westphalia, which ended the Thirty Years' War (1618–48). Switzerland did not take part in the conflict, and this contributed to a boost in the country's economy.

During the war Switzerland had in fact played a key role in trade throughout Europe, and the arrival of refugees, particularly Huguenots, revitalized Switzerland's textile industry. Industrial expansion continued in

Burning of religious paintings, in response to Zwingli's preaching against the worship of images

| 1500 | 1550 | 1600 | 1650 | |
|---|---|---|---|---|

**1515** Battle of Marignano. The Confederation declares neutrality

**1525** Zwingli's reforms accepted by the church authorities in Zürich

**1559** Jean Calvin founds the Calvin Academy in Geneva

**1680s–1690s** The brothers Jakob and Johann Bernoulli, at Basel University, lay the foundations of the theory of probability and integral calculus

**1684** Peace of Westphalia guarantees Switzerland's neutrality

Louis XIV and representatives of the Swiss Confederation

William Tell victorious over the dragon of the French Revolution, a symbol of Swiss resistance

the 18th century, when the weaving of silk, linen and cotton became mechanized, while clockmaking, introduced to Switzerland by French and Italian refugees in the 16th century, became one of the country's most important industries.

### The Helvetic Republic

The principles of the French Revolution were supported by Switzerland's French-speaking regions, but this was a threat to the stability of the Confederation. In 1798, having conquered northern Italy, and wishing to control routes between Italy and France, Napoleon invaded Switzerland. Under Napoleon the 13 cantons of the Confederation were abolished and replaced with the short-lived and unpopular Helvetic Republic.

The Swiss Confederation, as it was now known, was restored in 1803, although it remained under French control until the fall of Napoleon in 1815.

### The Swiss Confederation

Six further cantons – St Gallen, Graubünden, Aargau, Thurgau, Ticino and Vaud – joined the Confederation in 1803, and Valais, Neuchâtel and Geneva in 1815. Internal religious hostilities continued, however, and in 1845 seven Catholic cantons formed a military alliance known as the Sonderbund. Condemned as unconstitutional by the Protestant cantons, this led to civil war, and the defeat of the Catholic faction by Protestant forces.

A new constitution was drawn up in 1848, transforming what had until then been a loose confederation of cantons into a union ruled by a Federal Assembly in Bern, which was chosen as the Swiss capital. National unity was, however, tested again in 1857, when Prussia threatened to take the canton of Neuchâtel. The 100,000-strong Swiss army sent to the Rhine border repelled Prussian ambitions.

The Swiss army bound for the Rhine to defend Neuchâtel in 1857

**1723** Leonhard Euler, founder of modern mathematics and author of almost 900 publications, graduates at Basel

**1815** Napoleon is defeated. Congress of Vienna reaffirms the eternal neutrality of the Swiss Confederation

**1857** The Confederation repels Prussia's attempt to take the canton of Neuchâtel

Henri Dunant

| 1750 | 1800 | 1850 | 1900 |
|------|------|------|------|

**1798** Invasion by the French. Establishment of the Helvetic Republic

French grenadier

**1847** Civil war and defeat of the Sonderbund

**1864** Henri Dunant founds the International Red Cross in Geneva

**1848** The new constitution establishes central government

# Economic Growth

As early as the 17th century, Switzerland already had active textile and clockmaking industries, the foundations of which were laid by Huguenot refugees from France. By the second half of the 18th century, aided by its neutrality in international politics, the growing affluence of the middle classes and long periods of domestic peace, Switzerland was becoming as industrially advanced as other countries in Europe. Swiss economic growth accelerated in the 19th century, when the textile industry was mechanized and exports increased. This was also a boom period for precision engineering and the chemicals industry. Swiss foods, including Philippe Suchard's chocolate, Henri Nestlé's powdered milk and Julius Maggi's stock cubes, became international brands.

**Excited crowds** gather around the Egyptian-style statue personifying industry.

**Allegory of Justice**

**The Swiss Pavilion at the Great Exhibition of 1851**
The 270 exhibits in the Swiss Pavilion included textiles and lace, clocks and watches, and pharmaceuticals. There was also a model of Strasbourg Cathedral made by Jules Leemann, a sculptor from Bern.

**A locomotive**, symbol of modern technical achievement.

**Women workers** operating belt-driven machinery.

**An entrepreneur** presenting his products to interested merchants.

**Invention of the Telegraph**
The first electric telegraph was built by the physicist Georges-Louis in Geneva in 1774.

**Development of the Railway Network**
Zürich's imposing Hauptbahnhof, or central station, was built in 1867.

### Clock- and Watchmaking
The Swiss clock is a symbol of accuracy and reliability.

## St Gotthard Pass

The gateway over the Alps between central and southern Switzerland, the St Gotthard Pass lies at 2,108 m (6,919 ft) above sea level. On one of the main transport routes between Germany and Italy, it is also one of Europe's crucial arteries. With international funding of 102 billion Swiss francs, work on building a tunnel and a railway line beneath the pass began in 1871. It opened to traffic in 1882.

Allegory of Industry

### Poster for St Moritz
From the 19th century, the popularity of Swiss resorts and tourist regions began to grow rapidly.

### Driving a mail waggon
over the pass was arduous, sometimes dangerous and, because of heavy snow, possible only in summer.

### Road Through the Alps
In the 19th century Switzerland's dramatic Alpine scenery began to attract numerous visitors.

**Italian workers** who were employed to drill the tunnel staged a strike in 1875. Intervention by the army eventually brought a return to work.

**A group of clients**, including a German visitor wearing a coat with a fur collar, and an American donning a wide-brimmed hat.

## Apex of Industrial Development
*This monumental fresco in the Musée d'Art et d'Histoire in Neuchâtel (see p135) portrays the achievements of Swiss industry in the 19th century. Through allegory the painting depicts the environment in which Swiss industry consolidated its position in the international market.*

### Swiss Chocolate
Among Swiss chocolate manufacturers whose brands became known worldwide in the 19th century was Philippe Suchard (1797–1884).

First assembly of the League of Nations, Geneva, in 1920

## World War I

At the outbreak of World War I, maintaining its neutrality was one of Switzerland's principal concerns. Relations between French- and German-speaking Swiss deteriorated, as both linguistic groups supported opposing sides in the war. However, appeals for national unity averted the danger of open conflict.

By 1915, some 100,000 Swiss troops had been mobilized to guard the country's frontiers. As the war went on, Switzerland embarked on a wide-ranging aid programme for some 68,000 prisoners of war and refugees. Political asylum seekers who had come to Switzerland included many heads of state and political figures, including the Bolshevik leader Lenin and the Russian revolutionaries Trotsky and Zinoviev.

The revolutionary socialist ideas that they brought fomented unrest among Swiss workers, which culminated in the General Strike of 1918. The strike was quickly broken by the army but, as a result of their action, the workers won proportional represen-tation, improved welfare and a 48-hour working week.

## The Interwar Years

In 1920 Switzerland voted to join the newly formed League of Nations and, in tribute to the country's neutrality, Geneva was chosen as the organization's headquarters.

While the 1920s had been a period of prosperity, Switzerland, like the rest of Europe, fell prey to the Depression of the early 1930s. Also at this time, Switzerland's pacific stance and democracy were threatened by Nazi and Fascist sympathizers among its population.

By the late 1930s, as war seemed imminent, Switzerland's economy accelerated, fuelled partly by the booming arms industry in which the country was involved and by the fact that Swiss banks now played an important role in international finance.

General Henri Guisan, Commander-in-Chief of the armed forces, at the outbreak of war in 1939

**1901** Henri Dunant, founder of the International Red Cross, receives the first Nobel Peace Prize to be awarded

**1918** General Strike and introduction of the 48-hour week

**1934** Carl G Jung, founder of analytical psychology, becomes head of the Department of Psychology at Zürich University

**1960** Professor Auguste Piccard's son Jacques reaches a record depth of 10,911 m (35,800 ft) in the Pacific Ocean in a bathysphere designed by his father

| 1900 | 1910 | 1920 | 1930 | 1940 | 1950 |
|------|------|------|------|------|------|

**1914–18** Switzerland maintains neutrality during World War I

**1920** Switzerland joins the League of Nations

**1922** The Simplon Tunnel opens

**1939–45** Switzerland maintains neutrality during World War II

*Drilling the Simplon Tunnel*

Swiss artists and scientists were also coming to prominence. Among them were the artists Paul Klee (1879–1940) and Alberto Giacometti (1901–66), the architect Le Corbusier (1887–1965) and the psychologist Carl G Jung (1875–1961).

## World War II

In 1940, with Nazi Germany to the north and east, France under German occupation to the west and Fascist Italy to the south, Switzerland was surrounded. Invasion seemed inevitable, collaboration with Germany was suspected and the advantages of submitting to Germany were even contemplated. General Henri Guisan, Commander-in-Chief of the Swiss army, responded by assembling his officers on Rütli Meadow, birthplace of the Confederation, in 1291. Here he reaffirmed Switzerland's neutrality and demanded that all officers renew their vows of allegiance to the Confederation.

Although Switzerland was not directly drawn into World War II, it played a part in the conflict. The country acted as a secret meeting place between leaders of the Allied and Axis powers and set up anonymous bank accounts for German Jews. Swiss banks also provided currency for the purchase of military equipment and exchanged gold pillaged by the Germans for currency needed by the Third Reich.

## Postwar Years to the Present

Unlike all other European countries, Switzerland remained untouched by the

Demonstration in 1963 by women demanding the right to vote in national elections

upheaval of war and detached from the postwar new world order. It was not until 1971 that women won the right to vote in federal elections, and the country continues to reject membership of the European Union, although popular opinion is divided on this issue. Switzerland did, however, vote to join the United Nations in 2002. In line with increasing globalization, Switzerland has softened its isolationist stance, and its relations with the EU remain at the top of the political agenda.

In 1996, the country was rocked by the "Nazi Gold" scandal, when it was alleged that Swiss banks were holding gold looted by the Nazis and the assets of Jews who had perished in the Holocaust. Under strong US pressure, in August 1998 Switzerland agreed to pay $1.25 billion in compensation to families of Holocaust victims and to certain Jewish organizations – leaving a severe impression on the national psyche.

*Diego* by Alberto Giacometti

Poster for Swiss membership of the European Union

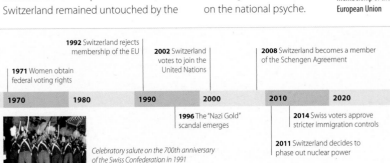

*Celebratory salute on the 700th anniversary of the Swiss Confederation in 1991*

# SWITZERLAND REGION BY REGION

# Switzerland at a Glance

From the snowbound Alps and verdant Jura mountains to the more densely populated plateau of the Mittelland that lies between them, Switzerland offers a wealth of different impressions. It has no coastline but the shimmering waters of its large, clean lakes amply make up for this. Picturesque mountain villages and atmospheric medieval towns of its remoter areas contrast with the cosmopolitan cities of Bern, Zürich, Lausanne, Luzern and Basel. For many, the Alps, which offer unrivalled skiing and other winter sports, as well as a pristine natural environment, are the country's greatest attraction. South of the Alps, the canton of Ticino is a different world, with a lively Italian culture and a warm Mediterranean-style climate.

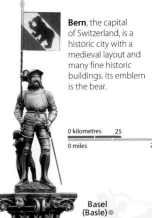

**Bern**, the capital of Switzerland, is a historic city with a medieval layout and many fine historic buildings. Its emblem is the bear.

0 kilometres    25

0 miles    25

Basel (Basle)

**Lausanne**, on the north side of Lake Geneva, is a vibrant cultural centre. The cathedral, in the medieval city centre, is one of Switzerland's most important Gothic buildings.

St-Ursanne

Olten

Langenthal

La Chaux-de-Fonds

Biel/Bienne

Bielersee

Neuchâtel

Lake Neuchâtel

Bern (Berne)

**BERN**
(See pp52–69)

Fribourg (Fryburg)

Thun

B

Brienz

**WESTERN SWITZERLAND**
(See pp112–137)

Lausanne

Lake Geneva (Lac Léman)

Mü

Kandersteg

**MITTELLAND, BERNESE OBERLAND AND VALAIS**
(See pp70–95)

Geneva

**GENEVA**
(See pp96–111)

Sion

**Geneva** enjoys a magnificent setting on the largest lake in the country. A city with a cosmopolitan culture, it is the headquarters of over 250 international organizations and NGOs.

**The Matterhorn** is the most distinctive and dramatic peak in the Swiss Alps. The resort of Zermatt lies in a valley at the foot of the mountain.

◄ Oberhofen Castle, on the shore of the Thunersee

**Schaffhausen**, the capital of Switzerland's northernmost canton, has an atmospheric medieval town centre. The Munot, a Renaissance fortress in the east of the city, towers over the Rhine.

**Zürich**, on the River Limmat, is Switzerland's largest city, and the centre of Swiss banking and trade in gold. The central landmark of the Old Town is the imposing twin-towered Grossmünster.

**Val Bregaglia** is one of Graubünden's many scenic Alpine valleys. Surrounded by granite peaks and containing a variety of rock formations, it is regarded as a rock-climber's paradise.

● Schaffhausen

● Konstanz

NORTHERN
SWITZERLAND
(See pp138–161)

● Frauenfeld

*Bodensee*
*(Lake Constance)*

Zürich ● ● Winterthur

**ZURICH**
*(See pp162–179)*

● Muri

Luzern
(Lucerne)

*Walensee*

● Glarus

Bad Ragaz ●

● Stans

● Altdorf

● Erstfeld

Chur ● Klosters ●

iringen

**EASTERN
SWITZERLAND AND
GRAUBÜNDEN**
*(See pp180–209)*

● Arosa

delwald

● Zillis

**CENTRAL
SWITZERLAND
AND TICINO**
*(See pp 210–243)*

Mesocco ●

Val
Bregaglia ●

● St Moritz

● Maggia

● Locarno

*Lake
Maggiore*

● Bellinzona

● Lugano

**The Hofkirche** is one of Luzern's many fine buildings. This charming city, set on Lake Luzern and surrounded by mountains, is the cultural capital of central Switzerland.

**Bellinzona**, the capital of Ticino, owes its importance to its strategic position. It is the starting point of roads leading to the St Gotthard and San Bernardino passes.

# BERN

With a picturesque setting on the River Aare and fine buildings lining the cobbled streets of its medieval centre, Bern is one of the most beautiful of Switzerland's historic towns. Although it is the Swiss capital, it retains the atmosphere of a provincial town. Bern is also a university city, the seat of the Federal Assembly and the headquarters of several international organizations.

Bern lies on a narrow, elevated spit of land set in a sharp, steep-banked bend of the River Aare. It was founded by Berthold V, Duke of Zähringen, in 1191, and its coat of arms features a bear. According to legend, the duke decided to name the new settlement after the first animal that he killed in the next hunt: this was a bear (*Bär*), and the duke duly named the town Bärn. After the demise of the Zähringen dynasty, Bern became a free town. Growing in power and prosperity, it joined the Swiss Confederation in 1353.

After a fire destroyed its timber buildings in 1405, the town was rebuilt in stone. It is from this period that the appearance of Bern's beautiful Old Town largely dates.

In 1528 the Bernese declared themselves in favour of the Reformation, and supported the Protestant cause. By the 16th century, Bern, led by a prosperous nobility, was a powerful city-state that, in the 17th and 18th centuries, further expanded its territory through the annexation of surrounding lands. Invaded by Napoleonic forces in 1798, Bern lost some of its territories but remained important enough to be chosen as the federal capital in 1848.

In the 20th century and into the 21st, Bern has continued to expand. Today, with a mostly German-speaking population, it is Switzerland's political and educational hub, and the base of major industries. Its historic Old Town is a UNESCO World Heritage Site.

The Rathaus, Bern's town hall, dating from the 15th century and with later alterations

◀ Splendid stained-glass window in the Münster (Cathedral), Bern

# Bern at a Glance

With many of its streets restricted to pedestrians and public transport, Bern's compact Old Town (Altstadt) is both easy and pleasant to explore on foot. Set on a narrow rocky ridge, the Old Town stretches from the Nydeggbrücke, in the east, to the Käfigturm, a tower that was originally a city gate, in the west. The main artery through the Old Town is Marktgasse, lined with old houses that have been converted into shops. The museums in the Kirchenfeld district, on the opposite bank of the Aare, are easily reachable on foot via the Kirchenfeldbrücke.

Statue of Samson subduing a lion, dating from 1545, on the Samsonbrünnen, a fountain in Kramgasse

Münster St Vinzenz, featuring Switzerland's tallest church tower

The 550-year-old Untertor Bridge over the River Aare in Bern

0 metres 400
0 yards 400

ERWEG
BREITENREINSTRASSE
NORDRING
WYTTENBACHSTRASSE
SCHLÄFLISTRASSE
SPITALACKERSTRASSE
GREYERZSTRASSE
VIKTORIARAIN
SPITALACKER
VIKTORIASTRASSE
KORNHAUSSTRASSE
GOTTHELFSTRASSE
BLUMENBERGSTRASSE
SPITALACKERSTRASSE
VIKTORIASTRASSE
SONNENBERG- STRASSE
SCHÄNZLISTRASSE
RABBENTAL- STRASSE
ALTENBERG
ALTENBERGSTRASSE
ALTENBERGSTRASSE
ARGAUERSTALDEN
Kornhausbrücke
WTTESTRASSE
BRUNNGASSHALDE
Untertorbrücke
KORN-HAUS-PLATZ
POSTGASSHALDE
RATHAUSGASSE
POSTGASSE
Nydeggbrücke
CTG
KRAMGASSE
GERECHTIGKEITSG
JUNKERNGASSE
MÜNSTERGASSE
CASINO-PLATZ
ALTSTADT
SCHIFFLAUBE
AARSTRASSE
WASSERWERKGASSE
MURISTALDEN
KIRCHENFELDBRÜCKE
DALMAZIQUAI
KOLLERWEG
HELVETIA-PLATZ
MARIENSTRASSE
THUNSTRASSE
HELVETIASTRASSE
BERNASTRASSE
HALLWYLSTRASSE
DUFOURSTRASSE
KIRCHENFELD
CKE
KIRCHENFELDSTRASSE

## Sights at a Glance

1. Universität
2. *Kunstmuseum pp60–61*
3. Bärenplatz
4. Bundeshaus
5. Marktgasse
6. Zytglogge
7. Kramgasse
8. *Münster St Vinzenz pp62–3*
9. Münstergasse
10. Erlacherhof
11. Gerechtigkeitsgasse
12. Rathaus
13. Bear Park
14. Kunsthalle
15. Schweizerisches Alpines Museum
16. Museum für Kommunikation
17. Bernisches Historisches Museum
18. Schweizerisches Schützenmuseum
19. Naturhistorisches Museum

Figures of the Wise and Foolish Virgins on the Münster's main portal

**For keys to symbols** *see back flap*

# Street-by-Street: The Old Town

With long cobbled streets lined with red-roofed houses and picturesque arcades, Bern's Old Town (Altstadt) is the best-preserved historic town centre in Switzerland. The layout of its streets, which are punctuated by colourfully painted fountains, has remained largely unchanged since the early 15th century. This was also the period when the Münster and the Rathaus, two of its great landmarks, were built. While the western district of the Old Town is filled with shops and busy street markets, the older eastern district has a more restful atmosphere.

**❺ Marktgasse**
The main axis through the western part of the Old Town begins at the Käfigturm (Prison Tower). This tower was the city's western gate in the 13th and 14th centuries.

**Kornhaus**
Now a cultural centre, this 18th-century granary was built over large vaulted wine cellars that currently house a restaurant.

**Französische Kirche** is the oldest church in Bern.

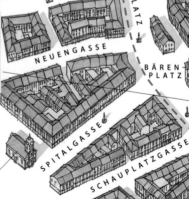

**❸ Bärenplatz**
This square overlies the spot where a moat once ran, along Bern's west side.

**Heiliggeistkirche** is Switzerland's finest Protestant church.

**Bundesplatz**
The Bundeshaus, with its paintings of historical events, overlooks this square.

SPEICHERGASSE

WAISENHAUSPLATZ

ZEUGHAUSGASSE

NEUENGASSE

MARKTGASSE

BÄREN-PLATZ

SPITALGASSE

SCHAUPLATZGASSE

BUNDES-PLATZ

| 0 metres | 100 |
| 0 yards | 100 |

**⑫ Rathaus**
The town hall is fronted by a double staircase and a Gothic loggia that leads through to the main entrance.

**⑪ Gerechtigkeitsgasse**
This is the eastern section of the main axis through the Old Town. The house at no. 68 is the Weavers' Guild, the façade featuring a gilt griffin. Another striking landmark is a fountain with a statue of Justice.

**Locator Map**
*See pp54–5.*

**⑧ ★ Münster St Vinzenz**
The most striking feature of Bern's Gothic cathedral is the magnificent central portal, surrounded by painted figures.

**⑨ Münstergasse**
On Tuesday and Saturday mornings the arcades along this street are filled with a bustling street market.

**Key**

— Suggested route

**⑦ Kramgasse**
The main axis through the Old Town is continued by Kramgasse. This street begins at the Zytglogge, the clock tower marking the western limit of the oldest part of the Old Town.

**⑥ ★ Zytglogge**
From 1191 to 1250 the clock tower was the city's western gate, and it was later used as a prison. Its elaborate chimes begin at four minutes before the hour.

# ❶ Universität

Hochschulstrasse 4.

Although the University of Bern was founded in 1834, the city's academic traditions go back to the 16th century. In 1528 a theological school was established, and it occupied a former Franciscan monastery that stood on the site of the Casino on what is now Casinoplatz.

In 1805 the school became an academy, which in turn was elevated to the status of university, its premises still being the former monastery.

As the university grew, with increasing numbers of students and the addition of new faculties, larger premises were required. These were built in 1899–1903, on the embankment of the Grosse Schanze (the Great Rampart) that formed part of Bern's 17th-century defence system. This is now the main university building and is a monumental structure in an eclectic mixture of the Neo-Renaissance and Neo-Baroque styles.

# ❷ Kunstmuseum

*See pp60–61.*

# ❸ Bärenplatz

This elongated esplanade has the appearance of a wide street rather than a square, particularly because it is seamlessly continued by another square, Waisenhausplatz, on its north side. Only a fountain marks the division between the two.

Bärenplatz (Bear Square) is named after the bear pit once located here, while Waisenhausplatz (Orphanage Square) owes its name to the former orphanage, in a fine Baroque building that is now the police headquarters.

Both squares were laid out on the course of the moat that was dug on the western side of the town in 1256. On the east sides of both squares stand the Dutch Tower and the **Käfigturm** (Prison Tower). The Käfigturm has a steeply pitched roof with

The Bundeshaus, surrounded by colourful autumn foliage

a slender lantern tower topped by a spire. It was incorporated into a wall that was built to the west as Bern expanded, and was the town gate from 1250 until 1350. From 1643 to 1897 the tower was used as a prison, and since 1999 it has served as a centre of political discourse, being the venue for political seminars, meetings with politicians and exhibitions.

On its southern side Bärenplatz adjoins Bundesplatz, an esplanade dominated by the Bundeshaus. Bundesplatz is lined with cafés, and a fruit and flower market is held here on Tuesday and Saturday.

**🚇 Käfigturm**

Marktgasse 67. **Tel** 031 322 75 00. **Open** 8am–6pm Mon–Fri, 10am–4pm Sat.

# ❹ Bundeshaus

Bundesplatz 3. **Tel** 058 322 90 22. 🖼 11:30am & 3pm Mon–Sat (also 2pm early Jul–late Aug). 🔳 **parlament.ch**

The imposing seat of the Federal Assembly stands on a cliff overlooking the Aare valley. Although it faces north onto Bundesplatz, its most attractive aspect is from the south – from Monbijoubrücke, a bridge on the Aare.

The Bundeshaus (parliament building) was designed by W H Auer in a bold Neo-Renaissance style, and completed in 1902. The central part of the building contains a spacious domed hall. The hall is decorated with paintings illustrating important events in Swiss history; the dome has stained-glass panels featuring the emblems of

### Ferdinand Hodler (1853–1918)

One of the most outstanding Swiss painters of his time, Ferdinand Hodler was born in Bern but spent most of his life

Self-portrait by Hodler

in Geneva. He initially produced exquisitely realistic landscapes and portraits but later became a leading exponent of Symbolism. Often allegorical, his Symbolist paintings have a haunting beauty and typically feature groups of stylized, symmetrically arranged figures. Hodler was also well-known for his monumental wall paintings. His late work, which has a more spontaneous style, anticipated the development of Expressionism.

Switzerland's regions and cantons, and stained-glass windows with allegories of justice, education, public works and defence. The main assembly hall, in the south wing, is decorated with paintings depicting delegates of the cantons of Uri, Schwyz and Unterwalden swearing the oath of alliance on Rütli Meadow (see p39).

Visitors are able to listen to debates from the public gallery. You can tell when parliament is in session by the flag flying from the Bundeshaus.

The Bundeshaus is flanked by two other government buildings. That to the east was designed by Auer and built in 1892, and the building to the west was designed by F Studer and built in 1857.

The Bundesterrasse, a wide promenade behind the Bundeshaus, offers a panoramic view of the Alps. A funicular near the western side of the Bundeshaus takes visitors down to the bottom of the Aare valley.

The Käfigturm, the former gate at the western end of Marktgasse

## ❺ Marktgasse

Laid out in the 13th century, as the town expanded westwards, Marktgasse runs east to west from the Zytglogge, the original town gate, to the Käfigturm, the later gate.

Marktgasse is now the centre of Bern's shopping district, and the arcades lining it are filled with shops, restaurants and cafés. Marktgasse also has two Renaissance fountains: the **Anna-Seiler-Brunnen**, which commemorates the woman who founded Bern's first hospital, in 1354, and the **Schützenbrunnen** (Marksman Fountain).

At its eastern end Marktgasse forms a right angle with Kornhausplatz, which follows the line of the earliest town walls. On this square is the macabre **Kindlifresserbrunnen** (Ogre Fountain), with an ogre eating an infant.

Off the northwestern side of Kornhausgasse stands the **Französische Kirche** (French Church). Built in the 12th century as part of a monastery, it is the oldest church in Bern. It was taken over by French Protestants, most of them Huguenot refugees, in the 17th century.

## ❻ Zytglogge

Marktgasse. **Tel** 031 328 12 12.
🕐 Apr–Oct: 2:30–3:20pm daily (also 26–31 Dec). 🏛

Also widely known as the Zeitglockenturm, the tower is Bern's central landmark. It was the town's west gate from 1191 to 1250, when it was superseded by the Käfigturm. Rebuilt after the fire of 1405, the Zytglogge was then used to imprison prostitutes.

Its astronomical clock was made by Caspar Brunner in 1527–30. The clock contains mechanical figures, including bears and a crowing cock, that begin their procession on the clock's east face at four minutes before the clock strikes the hour.

The guided tour allows visitors to observe the clock's mechanism at close quarters, see the rooms in the tower and admire the view.

Restaurant in an arcade on Kramgasse

## ❼ Kramgasse

With Gerechtigkeitsgasse, its eastern extension, Kramgasse marks the main axis of Bern's early medieval town plan, which was laid out in the late 12th century. Both sides of Kramgasse are lined with fine historic buildings and guild houses fronted by long arcades.

Also on Kramgasse are three fountains: the **Zähringer-brunnen** (1542), with a bear in armour holding the standard of Berthold von Zähringer, Bern's founder; the **Simsonbrunnen** (1545), with a figure of Samson subduing a lion; and the unadorned **Kreuzgassbrunnen** (1778). At Kramgasse 49 is the **Einsteinhaus**, where the great German physicist and mathematician Albert Einstein lived from 1903 to 1905 and where he began to develop the theory of relativity while working at the patent office. Einstein's apartment is now a museum, displaying his writing desk and other objects from his time in Bern.

Clock face on the Zytglogge

🏛 **Einsteinhaus,**
Kramgasse 49. **Tel** 031 312 00 91. **Open** Mar–Oct: 10am–6pm daily; Oct–mid Dec: 10am–5pm Tue–Fri, 10am–4pm Sat. 🏛 🌐 **einstein-bern.ch**

# ❷ Kunstmuseum

Bern's Museum of Fine Arts houses a collection of over 3,000 paintings of international importance. Spanning the 14th to the 20th centuries, it includes Early Renaissance paintings, 16th- and 17th-century Old Master paintings, and 19th- and 20th-century French paintings, including works by Delacroix, Manet, Monet, Cézanne, Braque, Gris, Picasso, Klee and Kandinsky. Swiss artists, among them Ferdinand Hodler and Albert Anker, are well represented.

**Ice on the River**
This winter landscape of broken ice carried downstream by a wide river was painted in 1882 by the French Impressionist Claude Monet.

**★ The Chosen One**
Consisting of an alignment of stylized figures, this painting by Ferdinand Hodler, dating from 1893–4, is typical of the artist's mature style. He called this method of painting Parallelism.

Main entrance

## Gallery Guide

*The collection of Old Master paintings is displayed in the basement. The 19th-century paintings are exhibited on the ground floor and the 20th-century collection occupies the first floor.*

**★ The Temptation of St Anthony by Demons**
This painting by the 16th-century Bernese artist Niklaus Manuel Deutsch is one of a pair. Its pendant depicts the temptation of St Anthony by women.

*For hotels and restaurants see pp248–55 and pp264–75*

**Dans un Jardin Meridional**
This rare 1914 garden fantasy by Pierre Bonnard (1867–1947) is a splendid example of his love for intense colour.

**VISITORS' CHECKLIST**

**Practical Information**
Hodlerstrasse 8–12. **Tel** 031 328 09 44. **Open** 10am–9pm Tue, 10am–5pm Wed–Sun. 🖼 🖥 📷
W **kunstmuseumbern.ch**

First floor

★ **Ad Parnassum**
Paul Klee produced this painting at a time when he was fascinated with Pointillism, painting with small dots of pigment.

**Blue Horse**
This painting by Franz Marc reflects the artist's fondness for the colour blue and his love of horses, to which he ascribed great spirituality.

Ground floor

**Drunken Doze**
The museum's large collection of paintings by Picasso includes works from his early Blue Period, including this portrait.

Basement

**Key**
- ☐ Old Master paintings
- ☐ 19th-century paintings
- ☐ Modern paintings
- ☐ Temporary exhibitions

# ❽ Münster St Vinzenz

A splendid example of the German-influenced late Gothic style, Bern's Münster is the most recent of Switzerland's great Gothic cathedrals. The architect was Matthäus Ensinger of Strasbourg, who designed it as a three-aisle basilica with fan vaulting, side chapels and a tower. Work on the cathedral began in 1421 and continued into the 16th century. It was not, however, until 1893, when the spire was added, that the building was finally completed. Exactly 100 m (328 ft) high, the Münster is the country's tallest church and largest ecclesiastical building. The tower is still inhabited by tower-keepers.

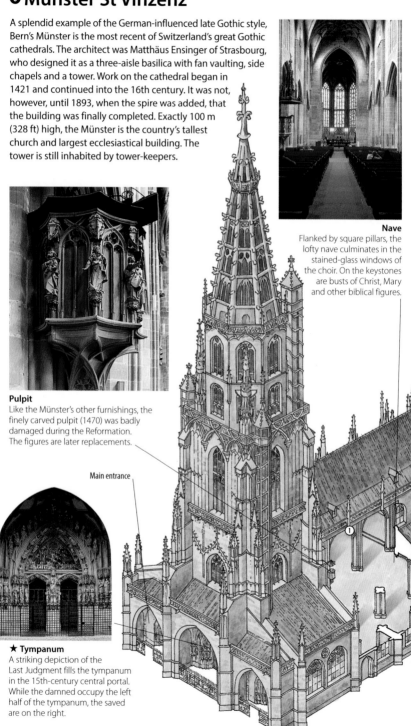

**Nave**
Flanked by square pillars, the lofty nave culminates in the stained-glass windows of the choir. On the keystones are busts of Christ, Mary and other biblical figures.

**Pulpit**
Like the Münster's other furnishings, the finely carved pulpit (1470) was badly damaged during the Reformation. The figures are later replacements.

Main entrance

**★ Tympanum**
A striking depiction of the Last Judgment fills the tympanum in the 15th-century central portal. While the damned occupy the left half of the tympanum, the saved are on the right.

## VISITORS' CHECKLIST

**Practical Information**
Münsterplatz. **Tel** 031 312 04 62.
**Open** winter: 11:30am–4pm Sun,
noon–4pm Mon–Fri, 10am–5pm
Sat; summer: 11:30am–5pm Sun,
10am–5pm Mon–Sat. 📷 for
groups & tower.

★ **Stained Glass**
The choir is lit by stained-glass
windows (1441–50). The central
panel depicts Christ's Passion
and Crucifixion.

## KEY

① **The rib vaulting**, by Daniel
Heintz, dates from the 1570s.

② **Flying buttresses** transmit the
weight of the roof outwards and
downwards to the outer walls.

## 9 Münstergasse

Running parallel to Kramgasse,
Münstergasse links Theaterplatz
with **Münsterplatz**, which is
lined with arcaded buildings.
On Tuesday and Saturday
mornings (and Thursday
from April to October),
this square is filled with
a busy meat and cheese
market. During Advent,
it is replaced by a large
Christmas market.

At the junction of
Münstergasse and
Theaterplatz stands the
**Stadt- und Universitäts-
bibliothek**, the City and
University Library. This
18th-century building
stages exhibitions of
books and manuscripts on
the history of Bern and on
literary subjects.

At the point where
Münstergasse joins Münsterplatz
stands the **Mosesbrunnen**
(1791), a fountain with the
figure of Moses holding the
Ten Commandments. He points
to the second of them, which
forbids idolatry, a stricture that
was one of the main tenets of
the Reformation.

On the Münster's south side
is the Münsterplattform, a
terrace with trees and Baroque
pavilions from which there are
beautiful views over the Aare.

Figure of Moses on the
Mosesbrunnen

### 📖 Stadt- und Universitäts-
bibliothek
Münstergasse 61. **Tel** 031 631 92 11.
**Open** 8am–7pm Mon–Fri,
8am–noon Sat.

Colourful flags along Münstergasse

## 10 Erlacherhof

Junkerngasse 47. Closed to visitors.

East of Münsterplatz,
Münstergasse is continued
by Junkerngasse, a street
once inhabited by Bern's
wealthiest citizens.

At no. 47 is the **Erlacherhof**,
a Baroque mansion built by
Hieronymus von Erlach, mayor
of Bern, and completed in
1752. It is designed
in the French style,
with wings set at
a right angle to
the main building,
enclosing a grand
courtyard. To the rear
is a formal garden, also
in the French style.

The Erlacherhof is
now the official residence of the
mayor of Bern and the seat of
the city's government.

## 11 Gerechtigkeits-
gasse

Some of the oldest and most
beautiful arcaded buildings in
Bern line this street. Many of
them were built as guild houses,
and their façades are heavily
decorated with motifs reflecting
the relevant trade.

Gerechtigkeitsgasse, or Street
of Justice, also has a fountain,
the **Gerechtigkeitsbrunnen**,
which features a figure
personifying Justice.

In the side alley at no. 31
is the Berner Puppen Theater
(see p67), a puppet theatre
that stages shows for children
and also produces puppet
plays for adult audiences.

At its eastern extremity,
Gerechtigkeitsgasse leads to
Nydeggasse. This is where a
castle stood, probably about
100 years before Berthold V
chose the location as a secure
spot on which to establish a
new town (see p53). In the late
15th century the castle was
replaced by a small church, the
**Nydeggkirche**, and in the 19th
century a stone bridge, the
**Nydeggbrücke**, was built
over the deep gorge of the
Aare, connecting the Old Town
with Bern's eastern district.

The Rosengarten with a view of Bern Old Town

## ⓬ Rathaus

Rathausplatz 2. **Tel** 031 633 75 50. 📁
8:30am–noon & 1:15–5pm Mon–Thu.

The seat of the canton and city of Bern's legislative assemblies since it was built in 1406–16, the Rathaus is an attractive building with an elegant Gothic façade (see illustration on p53).

Since the 15th century the Rathaus has undergone major restoration, and the ground floor was completely rebuilt in 1939–42. However, it still retains its authentic Gothic character, making it typical of Bernese architecture. The building is fronted by a double staircase with balustrades decorated with tracery. Beneath the balustrades are a pair of stone reliefs featuring human figures. On the loggia at the top of the staircase are a clock and statues set on canopied consoles.

Near the Rathaus stands the **Kirche St Peter und Paul**, a Catholic church in the Neo-Gothic style, completed in 1858.

One of the pair of stone reliefs on the façade of the Rathaus

## ⓭ Bear Park

Bärengraben. **Open** 8am–5pm daily.

Brown bears, indelibly associated with Bern since the town was founded in 1191 (see p53), were kept in pits (Bärengraben) on the far side of the Nydeggbrücke, across the river from the Old Town's eastern extremity, from the early 16th century.

The bears now enjoy a forested 6,000-sq-m (64,590-sq-ft) modern park, opened in 2009. Sloping down from the old bear pits to the river, it has numerous caves and pools that provide the bears with a truly natural environment.

Next to the old bear pits, in a former tram depot, is one of the town's two helpful tourist offices, where there is also a restaurant serving local cuisine and beer brewed on the premises. The tourist office also presents the **Bern Show**, a visual history of Bern told through a model of the city, slides and spoken commentary.

A steep path from the old bear pits leads up to the **Rosengarten**. Laid out on a hillside, with a scenic view of the Old Town across the Aare, this rose garden contains over 200 varieties of roses.

### 🎦 Bern Show

Am Bärengraben. Grosse Muristalden.
**Tel** 031 357 15 25. **Open** Mar–May: 10am–4pm daily; Jun–Sep: 9am–6pm daily; Oct: 10am–4pm daily; Nov–Feb: 11am–4pm Fri–Sun. Show (in English) every 20 mins.
**W** baerenpark-bern.ch

## ⓮ Kunsthalle

Helvetiaplatz 1. **Tel** 031 350 00 40.
**Open** 11am–6pm Tue–Fri, 10am–6pm Sat–Sun. 📷
**W** kunsthalle-bern.ch

Kirchenfeldbrücke leads from Casinoplatz, in the Old Town, over the Aare to Helvetiaplatz, on the south bank of the river, where many of Bern's museums are located.

The Kunsthalle, a building in the Modernist style, was founded in 1918 and has retained its prominence as a showcase for modern art. It has no permanent collection but stages a continuous programme of exhibitions. Past events include one-man shows of the work of such artists as Paul Klee, Alberto Giacometti and Henry Moore. Details of upcoming shows here are available from the Kunsthalle itself and from Bern's tourist offices.

Landscape by Alexandre Calame, Schweizerisches Alpines Museum

## ⓯ Schweizerisches Alpines Museum

Helvetiaplatz 4. **Tel** 031 350 04 40.
**Open** 10am–5pm daily (to 8pm Thu).
📷 **W** alpinesmuseum.ch

Through videos, photographs, dioramas, models and paintings inspired by the Alps' magnificent scenery, the museum describes the Alps' geology, topography, climate and natural history, and documents all aspects of human activity in the mountains.

The displays include a graphic explanation of how glaciers are formed, how they are melting, and a model of the Bernese Oberland. Separate sections are devoted to various aspects of Alpine life, including transport, industry, tourism and winter sports. The daily life and culture of Alpine people are also described, as are modern concerns for environmental protection.

One exhibit in the section devoted to the history of mountaineering is *The Climb and the Fall*, parts of two dioramas by Ferdinand Hodler illustrating the conquest of the Matterhorn *(see p58)*.

Mural, Bernisches Historisches Museum

### ⑯ Museum für Kommunikation

Helvetiastrasse 16. **Tel** 031 357 55 55. **Open** 10am–5pm Tue–Sun. 🚻 **W** mfk.ch

The history of the human endeavour to communicate over long distances is compellingly presented at the Museum of Communication. The displays span the gamut from bonfires to satellites, and multimedia presentations usher the visitor into the complex world of modern telephone exchanges and state-of-the-art mail-sorting systems.

The museum also holds one of the world's largest collections of postage stamps. Numbering over half a million, they include such rarities as an 1840 Penny Black. A programme of temporary exhibitions complements the museum's permanent displays.

### ⑰ Bernisches Historisches Museum

Helvetiaplatz 5. **Tel** 031 350 77 11. **Open** 10am–5pm Tue–Sun. 🚻 ♿ **W** bhm.ch

Laid out on seven floors of a Neo-Gothic building reminiscent of a medieval fortified castle, the artifacts displayed at Bern's Museum of History are highly diverse.

Among the most interesting exhibits here are some of the original sandstone figures from the west front of the late Gothic Münster *(see pp62–3)* and a spine-chilling depiction of the Dance of Death, a copy of a 16th-century monastic wall painting.

The pride of the museum, however, is its collection of 12 Burgundian tapestries, the oldest of which date from the 15th century. Among the most notable is the Millefleurs-tapisserie (Thousand Flowers Tapestry), which once belonged to Charles the Bold, Duke of Burgundy.

Other sections are devoted to archaeology, with displays of Stone Age, Ancient Egyptian, Roman and Celtic artifacts. Exhibits of coins and medals and of items of armour can be seen, as well as a spectacular collection of Islamic artifacts. A scale model of Bern as it was in 1800 is also on show.

### ⑱ Schweizerisches Schützenmuseum

Bernastrasse 5. **Tel** 031 351 01 27. **Open** 2–5pm Tue–Sat, 10am–noon & 2–5pm Sun. **W** schuetzenmuseum.ch

The origins of the Swiss Rifle Museum go back to 1885, when the participants in a shooting festival decided to create a rifle section within the Bernisches Historisches Museum. The pieces now form a museum collection in their own right.

Consisting of a vast array of guns, the collection illustrates the history of firearms from the early 19th century. Also on display are cups, medals and other trophies awarded at shooting festivals.

### ⑲ Naturhistorisches Museum

Bernastrasse 15. **Tel** 031 350 71 11. **Open** 2–5pm Mon, 9am–5pm Tue, Thu & Fri, 9am–6pm Wed, 10am–5pm Sat–Sun. 🚻 **W** nmbe.ch

With roots going back to the early 19th century, Bern's Museum of Natural History is one of the oldest museums in Switzerland.

It is best known for its numerous dioramas in which stuffed animals are shown in re-creations of their natural habitats. There are sections devoted to the reptiles, birds and mammals of Africa, Asia and the Arctic, but the most impressive displays are those focusing on the wildlife of the Alps. Also on view is the stuffed body of Barry, a St Bernard famous for his feats of mountain rescue in the 19th century *(see p88)*. The museum also has a large collection of Alpine minerals and fossils.

A manually operated telephone exchange, Museum für Kommunikation

# ENTERTAINMENT IN BERN

Bern's vibrant cultural scene offers entertainment of every kind, from ballet to jazz and in styles ranging from the classic to the avant-garde. The city's many cultural centres host a varied programme of art and photography exhibitions as well as other cultural events. Classic plays presented at the Stadttheater are complemented by fringe productions staged in many small independent theatres. While the prestigious Bern Symphony Orchestra makes the city a focus of the classical music repertoire, Bern also has a long-standing tradition of hosting major jazz and rock festivals. Like those of many other capital cities, the streets and squares of Bern are enlivened by street musicians. Bern is also well endowed with nightclubs.

## Information and Tickets

The best source of information on entertainment and cultural events in Bern is the city's tourist office, **Bern Tourismus**. *Bern Aktuell*, a free guide available at the tourist office, gives listings of mainstream events in German, French and English. The Thursday edition of *Berner Zeitung*, the daily newspaper, includes *Agenda*, a supplement with entertainment listings in German.

Tickets for major events can be purchased at the tourist office and from agencies, including **Bern Billett**, **Ticket Corner** and **Starticket**.

**THEATER VIS-A-VIS**
Tel.: 031 / 311 72 55
Gerechtigkeitsgasse 44

Signboard for a theatre on Gerechtigkeitsgasse

## Theatre and Cinema

The focal point of theatrical entertainment in Bern is the Stadttheater, which puts on classic and contemporary productions (in German or in French). The Stadttheater has joined forces with the Bern Symphony Orchestra to form the **Konzert Theater Bern**. The **Theater Remise** is an intimate setting for both dance performances and drama. Two other major theatrical venues in Bern are the **DAS Theater an der Effingerstrasse**, which specializes in modern drama, and the **Theater am Käfigturm**, which is often used by visiting drama companies.

Bern also has an unusually large number of fringe theatres, many of them tucked away in the cellars of houses along the streets of the Old Town.

Bern's 23 cinemas screen a regular programme of international films, many in their original language. Arthouse films are shown at the Kunstmuseum *(see pp60–61)*.

BERNER SYMPHONIE ORCHESTER

SAISON 02 - 03

Poster advertising a concert by the Bern Symphony Orchestra

## Festivals

From chamber music to jazz, Bern is alive to the sound of live music, with several music festivals taking place throughout the summer months. The city's largest and best-known annual musical event is the celebrated **International Jazz Festival Bern**, which takes place from March to May, with concerts staged at many venues throughout the town.

The **Gurtenfestival** is over the penultimate weekend in July. This large-scale rock-music event is staged in Gurtenpark, over the Aare to the south of the Old Town. Altstadtsommer is a series of summer concerts organized in the Old Town.

During the **Buskers Street Festival**, in early August, street artists invade the Old Town with mime and music.

The Stadttheater, on Kornhausplatz

The Kultur Casino Bern, on Herrengasse

## Cultural Centres

Bern's main cultural centre is the **Kornhaus**, a former granary. This large building is the venue for a wide range of events, including exhibitions of architecture, design and photography, and seminars, concerts and theatrical productions.

Another of the town's major cultural centres is the popular **Kulturhallen Dampfzentrale**, installed in a disused boiler house. The spacious auditorium here is used as a dance, film and jazz theatre, and the centre also has a restaurant, pub and bar.

The **Reitschule** (also known as the Reithalle) was established in the 1980s when protesters took over a former riding school. Fashionably alternative and politically controversial, the Reitschule is run as a cooperative and stages film shows and concerts. There is also a nightclub and a café bar.

## Music and Clubs

Most concerts given by the renowned Bern Symphony Orchestra take place in the **Kultur Casino Bern**. The orchestra also plays at other venues, including the Kornhaus, and occasionally in churches.

Bern boasts several music clubs, some devoted to a variety of musical styles. They include the famous **Marians Jazzroom**, where traditional jazz is played. Other clubs specialize in rock, funk and other types of popular music. Peculiar to Bern are music clubs occupying disused factories, a fact that is often reflected in their names. Very popular are Musig-Bistrot, **Gaskessel** and the **Wasserwerk Club**, where the sounds range from techno to South American dance music, often live.

Other venues include **Shakira**, a South American bar and disco, and Babalu, on Gurtengasse, which specializes in techno and house music.

## Gambling

Bern's main casino is the Grand Casino in the Allegro hotel at Kornhausstrasse 3. As well as gambling tables and slot machines, it has a restaurant and bars, open until 2am.

## Children

Bern offers several indoor and outdoor entertainments for the young. The **Berner Puppen Theater** puts on puppet shows that will amuse children even if they do not speak German.

With its European animals, **Dählhölzli Tierpark Zoo** offers a close-up experience of many kinds of wildlife.

A Bern bear at Dählhölzli Tierpark Zoo

# DIRECTORY

## Information & Tickets

**Bern Billett**
Nägligasse 1. **Tel** 031 329 52 52. 🔳 bernbillet.ch

**Bern Tourismus Internationales**
Bahnhofplatz & Amthausgasse 4. **Tel** 031 328 12 12. 🔳 bern.com

**Starticket**
**Tel** 0900 325 325.
🔳 starticket.ch

**Ticket Corner**
**Tel** 0900 800 800.
🔳 ticketcorner.ch

## Theatres

**DAS Theater an der Effingerstrasse**
Effingerstrasse 14.
**Tel** 031 382 72 72.

🔳 dastheater-effingerstr.ch

**Konzert Theater Bern**
Kornhausplatz 20. **Tel** 031 329 51 11. 🔳 konzert theaterbern.ch

**Theater am Käfigturm**
Spitalgasse 4. **Tel** 031 311 61 00. 🔳 theater-am-kaefigturm.ch

**Theater Remise**
Laupenstrasse 51.
**Tel** 031 859 12 77.
🔳 theaterremise bern.ch

## Festivals

**Buskers Street Festival**
🔳 buskersbern.ch

**Gurtenfestival AG**
🔳 gurtenfestival.ch

**International Jazz Festival Bern**
🔳 jazzfestivalbern.ch

## Cultural Centres

**Kornhaus**
Kornhausplatz 18.
**Tel** 031 312 91 10.

**Kulturhallen Dampfzentrale**
Marzilistrasse 47.
**Tel** 031 310 05 40.

**Reitschule**
Neubrückstrasse 8.
**Tel** 031 306 69 69.

## Music & Clubs

**Gaskessel**
Sandrainstrasse 25.
**Tel** 031 372 49 00.

**Kultur Casino Bern**
Herrengasse 25.
**Tel** 031 328 02 28.
🔳 kulturcasino.ch

**Marians Jazzroom**
Engestrasse 54.
**Tel** 031 309 61 11.

**Shakira**
Hirschengraben 24.
**Tel** 031 552 15 15.

**Wasserwerk Club**
Wasserwerkgasse 5.
🔳 wasserwerkclub.ch

## Children

**Dählhölzli Tierpark Zoo**
Tierparkwege 1.
**Tel** 031 357 15 15.

**Puppen Theater**
Gerechtigkeitsgasse 31.
**Tel** 031 311 95 85.

# SHOPPING IN BERN

Bern's shopping district lies along Gerechtigkeitsgasse, Kramgasse, Marktgasse and Spitalgasse, streets that form a continuous east–west axis through the centre of the Old Town. Shops also line Postgasse, which runs parallel to Gerechtigkeitsgasse on its northern side.

Beneath arcades with vaulted roofs that cover the pavement below are shops selling an almost endless variety of goods. On offer here is a range of souvenirs, including bears in all imaginable guises, as well as Swiss-made shoes, high-quality clothes and leather goods, fine jewellery and watches, Swiss army knives and musical boxes, hand-woven textiles and woodcarvings, and, of course, the famous Swiss chocolate. On the squares at the Old Town's western extremity are several open-air markets, with colourful flower and produce stalls, and two large department stores on Spitalgasse.

Display of handcrafted goods at Heimatwerk, on Kramgasse

## Markets and Fairs

Twice a week several of the squares in Bern's Old Town are filled with lively open-air markets. On Tuesdays and Saturdays from April, and daily from May to October, a large fruit, vegetable and flower market is held on **Bärenplatz** and the adjoining **Bundesplatz**. There is also a meat and dairy produce market on **Münstergasse** on Tuesday and Saturday mornings, plus on Thursdays from April to October. A general market takes place on **Waisenhausplatz** all day Tuesday and Saturday. A flea market is held on **Mühleplatz**, in the Matte district, on the third Saturday of the month from May to October.

Bern's annual fairs are major attractions. The magnificent Geranienmarkt, or Geranium Fair, takes place on Bundesplatz, Bärenplatz and Waisenhausplatz in April or May. In late November a party atmosphere breaks out as Zibelemärit, the onion fair, gets under way *(see p36)*. A **Christmas market**, with gifts and handicrafts, is held on Waisenhausplatz and Münsterplatz daily through December.

## Art and Antiques

The best art galleries and antique shops in Bern are located on Kramgasse, Postgasse and Gerechtigkeitsgasse. Some art galleries also hold exhibitions of contemporary art. Antique dolls and toys, meanwhile, are the speciality of **Puppenklinik**, on Gerechtigkeitsgasse.

## Crafts and Souvenirs

The Swiss take pride in their traditional handicrafts, particularly those associated with Alpine culture and folklore. Handicrafts from all Switzerland, including wood carvings, ceramics, music boxes, jewellery and hand-woven textiles, linen and embroidery, are available at **Heimatwerk Bern**, on Kramgasse.

A wide selection of pocket knives, particularly the multifunctional Swiss Army knives, is available at **Klötzli Messerschmiede**, on Rathausgasse. **Kunsthandwerk Anderegg**, on Kramgasse, specializes in beautifully handmade toys from Switzerland and other countries.

Traditional Swiss cut-out

## Watches and Jewellery

Fine jewellery and the clocks and watches that have brought Swiss craftsmanship international renown have many retail outlets in Bern.

Fruit and vegetable stall in the market, Bärenplatz

Window display at Bucherer, a jeweller's on Marktgasse

Two of the city's best clock, watch and jewellery shops are **Bucherer**, on Marktgasse, and **Gübelin**, on Bahnhofplatz.

## Music and Books

Having close associations with music, Bern has several excellent music stores. **Musik Müller**, in Zeughausgasse, concentrates uniquely on musical instruments. **Musikhaus Krompholz**, on Spitalgasse, also stocks a good range of CDs, as well as sheet music, musical scores and all kinds of books on music. Bern also has the largest and reputedly the best bookshop in Switzerland. This is **Stauffacher English Books**, on Neuengasse with an excellent range of books in English on offer.

## Shoes and Leather Goods

Leather shoes and accessories made by the internationally known Swiss shoe manufacturer **Bally** are available from a large branch of its outlets on Spitalgasse. Another major outlet for high-quality leather goods is **Hummel Lederwaren**, on Marktgasse. Stock here includes luggage, briefcases, purses and wallets, and a range of accessories, made in Switzerland and elsewhere in Europe.

## Chocolate

Like every other Swiss city, Bern has several shops offering tempting arrays of Swiss chocolates and other confectionery. Just two of them are **Eichenberger Tea Room**, on Bahnhofplatz, famous for its hazelnut *Lebkuchen* (spicy honey biscuits), and **Tschirren**, on Kramgasse, which has been making and selling its own chocolates for over 90 years.

Doll in traditional Swiss costume

## Department Stores

Bern's two main department stores are **Loeb** and **Globus**, both located on Spitalgasse, on the western side of the Old Town. Their many departments stock an enormous variety of goods, and they are also known for their clothes, including designer labels, for both men and women.

# DIRECTORY

## Markets & Fairs

**Bundesplatz/ Bärenplatz**
(Fruit, vegetables, flowers). **Open** 8am–noon Tue & Sat.

**Mühleplatz**
(Handicrafts). **Open** May–Oct: 3rd Sat of the month.

**Münstergasse**
(Meat and dairy). **Open** 8am–noon Tue & Sat.

**Waisenhausplatz**
(General).
**Open** 8am–6pm Tue & Sat.

## Art & Antiques

**Mäder Wohnkunst**
Kramgasse 54.
**Tel** 031 311 62 35.

**Puppenklinik**
Gerechtigkeitsgasse 36.
**Tel** 031 312 07 71.

## Crafts & Souvenirs

**Heimatwerk Bern**
Kramgasse 61.
**Tel** 031 331 30 00.

**Klötzli Messerschmiede**
Rathausgasse 84.
**Tel** 031 311 00 80.

**Kunsthandwerk Anderegg**
Kramgasse 48.
**Tel** 031 311 02 01.

## Watches & Jewellery

**Bucherer**
Marktgasse 2.
**Tel** 031 328 90 90.

**Gübelin**
Bahnhofplatz 11.
**Tel** 031 310 50 30.

## Music & Books

**Musik Müller**
Zeughausgasse 22.
**Tel** 031 311 41 34.

**Musikhaus Krompholz**
Spitalgasse 28.
**Tel** 031 328 52 11.

**Stauffacher English Books**
Neuengasse 25–27.
**Tel** 031 313 63 63.

## Shoes & Leather Goods

**Bally**
Kramgasse 55.
**Tel** 031 311 54 81.

**Hummel Lederwaren**
Marktgasse 18.
**Tel** 031 311 20 66.

## Chocolate

**Eichenberger Tea Room**
Bahnhofplatz 5.
**Tel** 031 311 33 25.

**Tschirren**
Kramgasse 73.
**Tel** 031 311 17 17.

## Department Stores

**Globus**
Spitalgasse 17–21.
**Tel** 031 320 40 40.

**Loeb**
Spitalgasse 47–51.
**Tel** 031 320 71 11.

# MITTELLAND, BERNESE OBERLAND AND VALAIS

These three regions occupy the western central section of Switzerland. The Mittelland, or Swiss Heartland, is a fertile area of rolling hills. While the Bernese Oberland, a massif in the heart of Switzerland, contains some of the country's most spectacular peaks, the Valais, in the south, has Switzerland's highest mountains, including the Matterhorn and the Dom.

The Mittelland, the heart of the Swiss farming industry, is made up mostly of the small canton of Solothurn and the northern part of the large canton of Bern. Unlike Bern and Basel, Solothurn remained Catholic after the Reformation. By contrast, the predominantly German-speaking people of the canton of Bern embraced the Reformation and have been Protestant since the 16th century.

The southern part of the canton of Bern makes up the Bernese Oberland, a mountainous area that rises to the south of two lakes, the Thunersee and the Brienzersee. These lakes are bordered by the towns of Thun, Interlaken and Brienz. A land of natural wonders, the Bernese Oberland has some dramatically high peaks, with excellent skiing pistes, but also many gentler valleys that are ideal countryside for hiking.

The Valais, also known as Wallis, encompasses the Rhône valley and the Pennine Alps. It is divided into two regions: Lower Valais, a French-speaking and Catholic region to the west, and Upper Valais, which is German-speaking and Protestant, to the east. The lower-lying parts of the Valais are agricultural. By contrast, its more mountainous regions, with the large international resorts of Verbier, Crans-Montana, Zermatt and Saas Fee, support a thriving year-round tourist industry.

The dramatic landscape of the Lauterbrunnen valley, near Interlaken

◄ The Obere Schleuse, a distinctive wooden sluice gate on the River Aare, Thun

# Exploring the Mittelland, Bernese Oberland and Valais

Each of these regions is exceptionally scenic. While the area contains some of Switzerland's most historic towns, including Bern, Solothurn and Sion, it also has many natural wonders. The Thunersee and the Brienzersee, two beautiful lakes, lie at the foot of the Bernese Oberland, a paradise for skiers and hikers. The region also includes the Eiger, Monch and Jungfrau. To the south, in the Valais, lie the sunny Rhône valley and the rugged Pennine Alps, which include the Matterhorn.

## Getting Around

As Bern has only a small airport, with relatively infrequent flights, it is best reached by train or car. The A1 motorway runs from Zürich, via Olten and Solothurn, to Bern. Bern also has motorway links with Thun and Biel/Bienne. Two routes lead south to the Rhône valley: the A6 follows the Aare valley and the A11 skirts the mountains, running west. The motorway linking Martigny with Sion and Sierre runs along the Rhône valley. Interlaken is the hub of a network of Alpine train and cable-car lines, with destinations that include the Jungfraujoch, the Schilthorn and Schynige Platte.

Hillsides covered with vineyards in the Rhône valley

## Key

▬▬ Motorway

▪ ▪ Motorway under construction

▬ Main road

⋯⋯ Minor road

▬ Scenic route

—•— Main railway

— Minor railway

▬▬ International border

▬▬ Canton border

△ Summit

*For hotels and restaurants see pp248–55 and pp264–75*

The resort of Zermatt with the Matterhorn in the distance

A2
OLTEN
Zürich

A1
Zofingen
Langenthal
Luzern

Huttwil

Luzern
Langnau
Trubschachen
ENTAL
Emme

0 kilometres       20
0 miles            20

BRIENZ ⑩  ⑪  FREILICHTMUSEUM
BALLENBERG
BRIENZERSEE ⑨
Beatenberg    Axalp    ⑫ MEIRINGEN    ⑪
NTERLAKEN ⑧
Faulhorn
2681m
WENGEN ⑰    ⑯ GRINDELWALD    Andermatt
erbrunnen    Eiger
3970m    Gletsch
RREN ⑱    ⑬ JUNGFRAUJOCH
Jungfrau    Finsteraarborn
4158m    4274m    ⑲
Münster

Aletschhorn
4195m
ALETSCH GLACIER ㊳
bberg-    Blatten    Fiesch
el
BRIG ㊱    Simplon
Visp    Tunnel
bône
talden    ㊲ SIMPLON
PASS
Simplon
ALAIS    Fletschhorn
3995m
Dom    ㉟ SAAS FEE
4545m
Tasch
ZERMATT
Gornergrat
3089m
㉞ MONTE ROSA

Scenic alley in Sion

## Sights at a Glance

① Olten
② Weissenstein
③ *Solothurn pp76–7*
④ Biel/Bienne
⑤ The Emmental
⑥ Thun
⑧ Interlaken
⑨ Brienzersee
⑩ Brienz
⑪ *Swiss Open Air Museum
   Ballenberg pp84–5*
⑫ Meiringen
⑬ Jungfraujoch
⑭ Kandersteg
⑮ Adelboden
⑯ Grindelwald
⑰ Wengen
⑱ Mürren
⑲ The Simmental
⑳ Gstaad
㉑ Martigny

㉒ Grand St Bernard Pass
㉓ Verbier
㉔ St Pierre-de-Clages
㉕ *Sion pp90–91*
㉖ Barrage de la Grande
   Dixence
㉗ Val d'Hérens
㉘ Crans-Montana
㉙ Sierre
㉚ Val d'Anniviers
㉛ Leukerbad
㉜ Zermatt
㉝ Matterhorn
㉞ Monte Rosa
㉟ Saas Fee
㊱ Brig
㊲ Simplon Pass
㊳ Aletsch Glacier

## Tour

⑦ *Thunersee pp78–9*

**For keys to symbols** *see back flap*

## ❶ Olten

**Road map:** D2. 🏔 19,000. 🚐 🚌
ℹ️ Frohburgstrasse 1; 062 213 16 16.
🌐 oltentourismus.ch

The small town of Olten has a picturesque location on the banks of the River Aare. Pedestrian access to the old part of the town is provided by the Alte Brücke, a covered bridge dating from 1802.

The Old Town is dominated by the tall Gothic belfry of a church that was demolished in the 19th century. There are many fine historic houses, particularly on Hauptgasse and along the Old Town's riverbank. Also of interest are the 17th-century monastery church and the Neo-Classical Stadtkirche, dating from 1806–12 and decorated with paintings by Martin Disteli. Many works by this artist, together with 19th- and 20th-century paintings and sculpture, are exhibited in the **Kunstmuseum**.

🏛 **Kunstmuseum**
Kirchgasse 8. **Tel** 062 212 86 76. **Open** Tue–Fri 2–5pm, Sat & Sun 10am–5pm.
🌐 kunstmuseumolten.ch

Houses along the banks of the Aare, Olten

## ❷ Weissenstein

**Road map:** C2. ℹ️ Solothurn, Hauptgasse 69; 032 626 46 46.

Some of the most spectacular views of the Mittelland can be enjoyed from the summit of the Weissenstein, a ridge of the Jura that rises like a rampart 1,284 m (4,213 ft) high. It is situated 40 km (25 miles) southwest of Olten and 10 km (6 miles) north of Solothurn. It is accessible by road or rail to Oberdorf, from where you can either hike to the summit or take a chair lift (closed on Mondays).

On the ridge is the Kurhaus Weissenstein, a hotel with a restaurant. The hotel is a good base for hiking, rock-climbing and paragliding in summer, and for sledging in winter. Other attractions include a botanical garden with plants and flowers of the Jura, a small regional museum, the Nidleloch, a limestone cave, and the Planetenweg, or Planet Trail, a walk with a schematic layout of the Solar System.

## ❸ Solothurn

*See pp76–7.*

## ❹ Biel/Bienne

**Road map:** C3. 🏔 55,000. 🚐 🚌 🚢
ℹ️ In the train station; 032 329 84 84.
🎭 Bieler Lauftage (Jun), Bieler Seefest (Jul & Aug), Onion Market (Oct).
🌐 biel-seeland.ch

Biel, known as Bienne in French, is the second-largest town in the canton of Bern. It was founded in the 13th century, and from then until the 19th century it was ruled by the prince-bishops of Basel. Biel/Bienne's principal industry is watchmaking, its factories producing such leading brands as Omega and Rolex. It is Switzerland's largest bilingual town: two-fifths of its inhabitants speak German, and the rest French.

The town is set on the shores of the Bielersee (or Lac de Bienne) at the point where the River Schüss (or Suze) flows into it. The Old Town, which has narrow cobbled streets and decorative fountains, is set on a hill. Its nucleus is a square known as the **Ring**, which is surrounded by fine arcaded houses. One of them is the house of the guild of foresters. This beautiful building has a 16th-century circular corner turret topped by an onion dome. Also on the square is the 15th-century church of St Benedict, with impressive late Gothic stained-glass windows.

At the intersection of Burggasse and Rathausgasse, west of the Ring, stands the Rathaus, the Gothic town hall, which dates from the 1530s. It is fronted by a Fountain of Justice. The late 16th-century Zeughaus, or arsenal, nearby is now used as a theatre.

Biel/Bienne has several museums and galleries. The **Museum Neuhaus**, now integrated into the Neues Museum, re-creates 19th-century bourgeois life, with other sections devoted to industry and archaeology. The dynamic **Centre Pasquart** stages a programme of changing exhibitions of contemporary art and photography.

🏛 **Museum Neuhaus**
Seevorstadt 52. **Tel** 032 328 70 30.
**Open** 11am–5pm Tue–Sun. 🗢
🌐 nmbiel.ch

🏛 **Centre Pasquart**
Seevorstadt/Faubourg du Lac 71–73.
**Tel** 032 322 55 86. **Open** 2–6pm
Wed–Fri, 11am–6pm Sat & Sun. 🗢
🌐 pasquart.ch

**Environs**
**Twann**, a medieval town, **La Neuveville**, which has cobbled streets, **Erlach**, which has a castle, and **St Petersinsel** can all be visited by boat from Biel/Bienne. There are also boat trips on the lake, with views of vineyards on the surrounding hillsides. A riverboat service runs between Biel/Bienne and Solothurn.

Foresters' guildhouse, Biel/Bienne

Schloss Burgdorf, the castle of the Zähringers, in the Emmental

## ⑤ The Emmental

**Road map:** C3. 🚉 🚌 ℹ️ Langnau, Schlossstrasse 3; 034 402 42 52.
🅦 emmental.ch

The Emmental, the long, wide valley of the River Emme, has a beautiful landscape of green meadows, which provide grazing for cows. The valley, which has excellent cycling and hiking routes, is dotted with traditional wooden chalets with high roofs, eaves almost reaching to the ground and windows with decorative carvings.

The local culture of the Emmental is traditional and conservative, with a farming economy. This is also where the famous Emmental cheese is made, most of it by hand. At the **Schaukäserei** (show dairy) in Affoltern, visitors can see every stage in the process of producing this holey, nutty-tasting cheese. It is also on sale in the dairy's shop and on the menu in its restaurant. Many inns along the valley also serve this highly prized local speciality.

**Burgdorf** is a small town in the north of the Emmental. The old part of the town, on top of a hill, has arcaded houses, a Gothic church and a castle, founded by the Zähringers in the 7th century. **Trubschachen**, a village further up the valley, has pottery workshops where the colourful local ware is made and offered for sale.

The Emmental also has the longest arched wooden bridge in Europe. Built in 1839, the Holzbrücke spans the Emme just downstream of the villages of **Hasle-Rüegsau**.

**🏛 Schaukäserei**
Schaukäsereistrasse 6, Affoltern.
**Tel** 034 435 16 11. **Open** 9am–5pm daily. ♿

## ⑥ Thun

**Road map:** C3. 🏔 41,000. 🚉 🚌
ℹ️ Bahnhof; 033 225 90 00.
🅦 thuntourismus.ch

The historic market town of Thun is set on the River Aare, at the northern end of the Thunersee. The origins of Thun go back to 1191, when Berthold V, Duke of Zähringen, built a castle on a hill above the river here.

Thun's Old Town spreads out beneath the castle, on the right bank of the river. Obere Hauptgasse, the main street running parallel to the river, is split into two levels. The walkway is built on the roofs of the arcaded buildings lining the street, so that pedestrians step downstairs to enter the shops below. Stepped alleys off Obere Hauptgasse lead up to the castle, **Schloss Thun**, from which there are impressive views of the town and the Bernese Oberland. Inside the castle's massive turreted keep, which looms over Thun, is a museum documenting the town's history. Other rooms

Detail of a fountain in Thun

in the castle contain collections of clocks, dolls and household objects, weapons and uniforms, glass and ceramics, coins and toys. The huge Knights' Hall, with an imposing fireplace, is used as a concert hall. Also on the hill is the Stadtkirche, the town's church. A short walk east of the castle and down to the river leads to the **Kunstmuseum**, which contains a large collection of contemporary and modern Swiss art.

On the left bank of the river is Schadau Park. Near the lake here stand a Neo-Gothic folly and a cylindrical pavilion, whose interior walls are painted with the **Wocher Panorama**. This visual record of daily life in Thun was painted by Marquard Wocher in 1814, and is the oldest such panorama in the world.

**🏰 Schloss Thun**
Schlossberg 1. **Tel** 033 223 20 01.
**Open** Feb & Mar: 1–4pm daily; Apr–Oct: 10am–5pm daily; Nov–Jan: 1–4pm Sun. ♿ 🅦 schlossthun.ch

**🏛 Kunstmuseum**
Hofstettenstrasse 14. **Tel** 033 225 84 20. **Open** 10am–5pm Tue & Thu–Sun; 10am–7pm Wed. ♿
🅦 kunstmuseumthun.ch

**🏛 Wocher Panorama**
Seestrasse 45, Schadaupark.
**Tel** 033 225 84 20. **Open** Mar–Oct: 10am–5pm Tue–Sun; Jul & Aug: 10am–6pm daily. ♿
🅦 thun-panorama.ch

Buildings along the River Aare, in Thun

# ❸ Solothurn

Renowned as Switzerland's most beautiful Baroque city, Solothurn is the capital of the eponymous canton. It was founded by Celts and later became the second-largest Roman town north of the Alps after Trier. Having remained Catholic through the Reformation, Solothurn was chosen as the residence of French ambassadors to the Swiss Confederation. It was during this period, from 1530 to 1792, that the city's finest buildings were constructed. Today Solothurn is a vibrant city, with historical buildings, fascinating museums and good shopping opportunities.

### Exploring Solothurn

The historic nucleus of Solothurn, on the River Aare, occupies a small area on the north bank, a short walk from the railway station on the opposite side. The Kreuzackerbrücke, which spans the river, linking the old and new towns, leads to Klosterplatz. From here, Solothurn's main historic sights, including vestiges of fortifications on the northeastern side of the town, are within easy reach.

From Solothurn boat trips depart for Biel/Bienne, and follow a particularly beautiful stretch of the Aare.

### 🏠 St Ursen Kathedrale

Hauptgasse. Treasury: **Open** 8am–noon & 2–6pm daily (to 7pm in summer).

Built from 1763 to 1773, Solothurn's monumental Neo-Classical cathedral takes the form of a three-aisle basilica with a transept and a dome over the crossing. A bell tower rises next to the presbytery at the eastern end.

Set on a hill, the cathedral is reached by steps flanked by ornamental fountains. The two-tier façade, which shows the influence of the Italian Baroque, is faced by Corinthian columns divided by a frieze. The frieze contains figures, among which are those of the city's patron saints, Ursus and Victor, who were martyred by the Romans in Solothurn.

Baroque pulpit in St Ursen Kathedrale

The cathedral's interior features elaborate stucco-work. The treasury, in the crypt, contains an interesting collection of liturgical vestments dating from the 10th century.

### 🏛 Altes Zeughaus

Zeughausplatz 1. **Tel** 032 627 60 70. **Open** 1–5pm Tue–Sat, 10am–5pm Sun. 🅿

The former arsenal is a large four-storey Baroque building dating from 1609–14. Above the upper storey is a crane that was used to lift heavy armoury from the ground level to the upper floors.

The arsenal now serves as a museum of militaria. It contains a large collection of swords, suits of armour and cannons, and a tank used in World War II. Of particular interest is the collection of arms and uniforms used by Swiss mercenaries who served as bodyguards to French kings. Many of these mercenaries

came from Solothurn. The third floor houses special exhibitions.

### 🏛 Riedholzschanze

Solothurn was fortified several times in the course of its history. The oldest walls surrounded a Roman camp, and their remains can be seen on Friedhofplatz and at Löwengasse. A later ring of walls, with gates and towers, was built in the Middle Ages. In the early 16th century the city's defences were modernized with the addition of two gates, Bieltor and Baseltor, and three towers, Buristurm, Krummturm and Riedholzturm, all of which still stand. In 1667 work on new fortifications, with bastions, began. Although these were later levelled out to make way for streets and parks, Riedholz-schanze, a bastion at the northeastern corner of the old town, survives.

### 🏛 Kunstmuseum

Werkhofstrasse 30. **Tel** 032 624 40 00. **Open** 11am–5pm Tue–Fri, 10am–5pm Sat & Sun. 🅿 🆆 **kunstmuseum-so.ch**

This small art gallery contains some very fine works. Among its Old Master paintings are the exquisite *Madonna of Solothurn* (1522) by Hans Holbein the Younger, and *The Madonna in the Strawberries* (1425) by an anonymous artist. Most of the exhibition space is devoted to Swiss and French painting of the 19th and 20th centuries. There are landscapes by Caspar Wolf, Alexandre Calame and Giovanni Giacometti, and a dramatic depiction of William Tell emerging from the clouds by Ferdinand Hodler (*see p58*),

Part of the façade of the Altes Zeughaus, once the city's arsenal

The imposing entrance of the Rathaus

and many paintings by Van Gogh, Degas, Cézanne, Matisse, and Picasso. A section is devoted to contemporary Swiss artists, including Deiter Roth, Markus Raëtz and Meret Oppenheim.

### 🏛 Rathaus

Rathausplatz.

Solothurn's town hall, on the east side of Rathausplatz, is in an ornate Mannerist style. The building's complex appearance is the result of work on the building having occurred in successive stages over many years.

The Gothic building that was begun in 1476 was not completed until 1711, when the town hall acquired its

narrow three-part façade, with a central tower and onion domes crowning the lateral sections. The interior has a spiral staircase known as the Schnecke (Snail), which curves upwards, leading to the grand hall.

### 🏛 Jesuitenkirche

Hauptgasse.

Dating from 1680–89, Solothurn's Jesuit church is a magnificent example of High Baroque architecture. While the exterior is sparsely decorated, the interior glistens with frescoes and is encrusted with stucco-work by masters from Ticino.

The Baroque nave and high altar of the Jesuitenkirche

On the high altar, which dates from the early 18th century, is a huge altarpiece by Franz Carl Stauder depicting the Assumption of the Virgin. Stones, some with Roman inscriptions, are also displayed in the church.

### 🏛 Zytglogge

Marktplatz.

Its lower part dating from the 12th century and its upper from the 15th, the clock tower is Solothurn's oldest surviving building. The astronomical clock was made in 1545. It contains mechanical figures, including a knight, a figure of Death and the King of Jesters, which form a procession on the hour.

## Solothurn City Centre

① St Ursen Kathedrale
② Altes Zeughaus
③ Riedholzschanze
④ Kunstmuseum
⑤ Rathaus
⑥ Jesuitenkirche
⑦ Zytglogge

For keys to symbols *see back flap*

# ❼ Thunersee

A beautiful lake in a spectacular mountain setting, the Thunersee forms a slender arc between Thun and Interlaken in the valley of the River Aare. Some 18 km (11 miles) long and almost 4 km (3 miles) wide, the lake offers many kinds of water sports, including sailing, windsurfing, water-skiing and diving. The surrounding areas are ideal for hiking and cycling. A ferry service links the towns, villages and other places of interest on the lakeshore, and vintage steamships take visitors on tours of the lake.

### ① Thun
The historic centre of Thun, still dominated by a medieval castle, was built mostly in the 12th century. The raised pavements of the upper Hauptgasse are worth a visit of their own.

### ② Hilterfingen
As well as a sailing school, Hilterfingen has a mid-19th-century castle, Schloss Hünegg. It is in the Neo-Renaissance style, with Art Nouveau interiors.

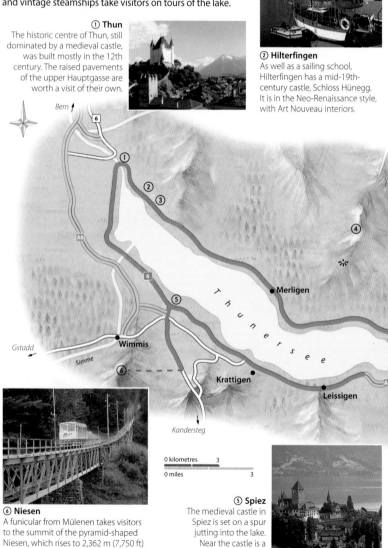

### ⑥ Niesen
A funicular from Mülenen takes visitors to the summit of the pyramid-shaped Niesen, which rises to 2,362 m (7,750 ft) and offers a fine view of the Thunersee and its surroundings.

### ⑤ Spiez
The medieval castle in Spiez is set on a spur jutting into the lake. Near the castle is a Romanesque church with a fine Baroque interior.

0 kilometres 3
0 miles 3

## Tips for Visitors

**Tour length:** about 50 km (30 miles).
**Stopping-off points:** There are restaurants in every village around the lake.
**Boat tours of the lake:** BLS Schiffahrt, Lachenweg 19, Thun. **Tel** 058 327 48 11.
**W** bls.ch/schiff

### ③ Oberhofen
The lakeside castle here dates from the 12th century. It is now an outpost of the Bernisches Historisches Museum (see p65).

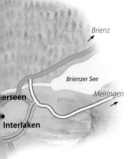

Brienz

Brienzer See

Meiringen

erseen

Interlaken

### ④ Niederhorn
Accessed by a mountain railway, Niederhorn offers breathtaking views of the Bernese Alps.

### Key

🟰 Motorway
🟰 Suggested route
🟰 Scenic route
═ Other roads
- - Funicular

The Hôtel du Lac at Interlaken and the jetty on the Brienzersee

## ❽ Interlaken

**Road map:** D4. 🏔 13,500. 🚌
🚉 🛈 Höheweg 37; 033 826 53 00. **W** interlaken.ch 🏛
Musikfestwochen (Aug).

Interlaken lies on a narrow strip of land between the Thunersee and the Brienzersee. In prehistory the isthmus between the lakes, known as the Bödeli, was inhabited by Celts. The present town owes its name to the monastery that was founded here in the 12th century. It was named Inter Lacus, meaning "between lakes" in Latin.

Today Interlaken is a popular resort that makes an excellent base for mountaineers and hikers in summer and for skiers in winter. Interlaken is also a rail junction on the route by rack railway up to the Jungfrau region (see p83), to Wengen (see p87) and beyond. A funicular also takes visitors up to the summit of the Heimwehfluh (669 m/2,195 ft).

Interlaken's popular attraction is the **Jungfrau Park**, a theme park that introduces visitors to the great unsolved mysteries of the world. It consists of several pavilions, in which elaborate displays focus on the meaning of mysterious ancient monuments, such as the pyramids of Egypt, question how the ancient Maya devised their complex calendar, and investigate the origins of religion in ancient cultures. A further section is devoted to outer space and the search for extraterrestrial intelligence.

Rugen Forest, on the south side of Interlaken, is the bucolic setting for open-air productions of Schiller's play Wilhelm Tell. On the opposite side of the Aare is Unterseen. The **Touristikmuseum** here documents the evolution of tourism in the Jungfrau region since the 19th century.

### Environs

Alpine fauna can be seen at the zoo at **Harder**, accessible by cable car from Interlaken. **Schynige Platte**, which can be reached by rack-railway from Wilderswil, south of Interlaken, is a 2,000-m- (6,564-ft-) high plateau offering magnificent views of the two lakes. There is also a botanical garden here, with Alpine plants and flowers.

🏛 **Jungfrau Park**
Obere Bönigstrasse 100, Interlaken. **Tel** 033 827 57 57. **Open** May–Oct: 10am–6pm daily. 🅿 **W** jungfraupark.ch

🎭 **Wilhelm Tell**
Performances: late Jun–mid-Sep: Thu & Sat. Tickets via **W** tellspiele.ch; 033 822 37 22, and tourist offices in the region.

🏛 **Touristikmuseum**
Obere Gasse 28, Unterseen. **Tel** 033 822 98 39. **Open** May–Oct: 2–5pm Tue–Sun. 🅿 **W** touristik museum.ch

Flower clock in front of the Kursaal in Interlaken

For hotels and restaurants see pp248–55 and pp264–75

The small town of Brienz, at the eastern tip of the Brienzersee, with the Brienzer Rothorn in the background

## ❾ Brienzersee

**Road map:** D4. 🚂 🚌 ℹ Haupt-strasse 143, Brienz; 033 952 80 80. Boat trips on the lake: **Tel** 033 951 24 16. 🆆 **steamchen.com** Grandhotel Giessbach: **Tel** 033 952 25 25. **Open** Apr–Oct.

Lying east of Interlaken and the Thunersee *(see pp78–9)*, the clear waters of the Brienzersee stretch out in a setting of forested slopes and waterfalls, with majestic mountains rising in the background. Some 14 km (9 miles) long and almost 3 km (2 miles) wide at its broadest point, the Brienzersee is slightly smaller than the Thunersee and much less developed, with fewer sports centres and less boating activity. As such, it is much more appealing to anglers.

From Interlaken, places of interest around the shore can be visited by bicycle or by taking a boat trip on the lake. On the north side of the lake are the ruins of **Goldswil** castle and the village of **Ringgenberg**, where there is a small Baroque church. The small town of **Brienz** lies at the eastern tip of the lake. On the south side is Axalp, good for skiing in winter and walking in summer, and the magnificent **Giessbachfälle**, waterfalls that can be viewed from the terrace of the Grand Hotel Giessbach, reachable by a funicular.

## ❿ Brienz

**Road map:** D3. 🏔 3,000. 🚂 🚌 ℹ Hauptstrasse 143; 033 952 80 80. 🆆 **brienz-tourismus.ch**

Located at the eastern end of the Brienzersee, Brienz is the main town on the lakeshore. It is a good base not only for mountain hikers but also for anglers and water-sports enthusiasts. Axalp, nearby, has a small ski and snowboarding centre.

Being the centre of Swiss woodcarving, Brienz is full of shops selling all kinds of wooden objects. The workshops of its renowned woodcarving school, the **Schule für Holzbildhauerei**, are open to visitors during term-time. Students can be seen at work, and there is also an exhibition of their finished pieces.

Alley in Brienz, lined with traditional houses

Another speciality of Brienz is violin-making. The **Geigenbauschule**, where future violin-makers learn their craft, also welcomes visitors, and there is an exhibition of instruments.

**Environs**
The summit of the **Brienzer Rothorn**, which rises to 2,350 m (7,710 ft) about 5 km (3 miles) north of Brienz, can almost be reached by steam-driven rack railway, which runs to 2,244 m (7,383 ft). It is one of the few still in use, though the carriages are sometimes pulled by a diesel locomotive. The 7.6-km (4.75-mile) route up the mountain passes through six tunnels. The short walk from the summit station is rewarded by breathtaking views of the Brienzersee and the Bernese Alps.

🏛 **Schule für Holzbildhauerei**
Schleegasse 1. **Tel** 033 952 17 51. Exhibition: **Open** 8–11:30am & 2–5pm Mon–Fri.

🏛 **Geigenbauschule**
Oberdorfstrasse 94. **Tel** 033 951 18 61. **Open** by prior arrangement.

## ⓫ Swiss Open Air Museum, Ballenberg

*See pp84–5.*

◀ The characteristic Swiss Alpine landscape around Wengen

## ⑫ Meiringen

**Road map:** D4. 🏔 4,500. 🚉 🚌
ℹ️ Bahnhofplatz 12; 033 972 50 50.

This small town lies in the heart of the Hasli valley, the Upper Aare valley east of the Brienzersee. It is a snow sports resort in winter, and a base for hiking and mountain biking in summer.

Meiringen lies near the **Reichenbachfälle**, the waterfalls chosen by the writer Arthur Conan Doyle as the scene of Sherlock Holmes' "death" after a struggle with Professor Moriarty. The **Sherlock Holmes Museum**, in the basement of a church, features a representation of Holmes' drawing room at 221B Baker Street, London. A statue of the fictional detective graces Conan Doyle Place.

Also of interest in Meiringen is the small church at the top of the town. It was built in 1684 over the crypt of an early Romanesque church. The town has two regional museums, one of which is open only in summer.

🏛 **Sherlock Holmes Museum**
Bahnhofstrasse 26. **Tel** 033 971 41 41.
**Open** May–Sep: 1:30–6pm Tue–Sun; Oct–Apr: 4:30–6pm Wed & Sun. 🏷
ⓦ sherlockholmes.ch

### Environs
From Meiringen a funicular takes visitors to the top of the **Reichenbachfälle**. From here there is a stupendous view of the cascading waters. Equally impressive is the **Aareschlucht**, a deep gorge cut by the Aare between Meiringen and Innertkirchen.

Statue of Sherlock Holmes in Meiringen

🎿 **Reichenbachfälle**
**Tel** 033 972 9010. **Open** early May–Jun, Sep & Oct: 9–11:45am & 1:15–5:45pm; Jul & Aug: 9am–6pm.

🎿 **Aareschlucht**
**Tel** 033 971 40 48. **Open** Apr–Oct: 8:30am–5:30pm. Floodlit illumination, mid-Jun–mid-Oct: 8:30am–10pm Wed–Sun.

The Eiger, Mönch and Jungfrau, the highest peaks in the Jungfrau massif

## ⑬ Jungfraujoch

**Road map:** D4. ℹ️ Höheweg 37, Interlaken; 033 826 53 00.
ⓦ jungfrau.com

South of Interlaken lies the Bernese Oberland's most impressive mountain scenery, centred on a giant triple-peaked ridge: the Eiger (3,970 m/ 13,025 ft), the Mönch (4,099 m/ 13,448 ft) and the Jungfrau (4,158 m/13,642 ft). A network of rail and cable-car routes from Interlaken (see p79) makes it easy to travel around this area.

The best-known rail excursion (not inexpensive but a unique experience) is to the Jungfraujoch. This icy saddle, which lies just below the summit of the Jungfrau, has been dubbed the "Top of Europe", and at 3,454 m (11,333 ft) above sea level, the train station here is the highest in Europe.

As there are two different routes up to the Jungfraujoch, this excursion can easily be done as a circular journey. Trains head from Inter-laken to Lauter-brunnen, where you change to the rack railway that climbs up through Wengen (see p87) and on further up to the dramatic station at Kleine-Scheidegg, which nestles directly beneath the famous North Face of the Eiger. Different trains head from Interlaken to Grindelwald (see p86), where you again change to the rack railway, which from the other direction climbs up to Kleine-Scheidegg. From Kleine-Scheidegg, a separate line heads up to the Jungfraujoch itself. Seat reservations are recommended from April to September.

The engineering on the lower sections of the rail route, around Wengen, is impressive enough but the topmost line, above Kleine Scheidegg, is extraordinary. It runs through steep tunnels blasted out of the heart of the Eiger. At the top, which can be quite crowded, there are cafeteria-style restaurants, a post office (where mail is stamped with a unique "Top of Europe" postmark), a set of ice sculptures, and other attractions. It is, however, far more rewarding to focus on the spectacular views, eastward out to the Black Forest, in Germany, westward to the Vosges, in France, and south into Italy.

There are also opportunities for walking and skiing, including routes down the massive Alestsch glacier. The famous Concordia mountain refuge is a short walk from here and offers overnight accommodation. A mountain guide and suitable gear are required.

A passenger train to Jungfraujoch approaching the Kleine-Scheidegg station

*For hotels and restaurants see pp248–55 and pp264–75*

# ⑪ Swiss Open Air Museum Ballenberg

From simple Alpine chalets to entire farmsteads, about 100 historic rural buildings and 250 farmyard animals fill this 66-hectare (160-acre) open-air museum. The buildings, some of wood, others of stone or brick, come from several regions of Switzerland. Carefully dismantled, they were transported and reconstructed here, most being saved from demolition. The buildings are grouped according to their area of origin, and each group is linked by paths. The museum grounds also have gardens and fields with crops and farm animals. All the buildings are authentically furnished.

**★ Richterswil House**
Built in 1780 at Richterswil, near Zürich, this two-family house is an example of the half-timbered buildings typical of northeastern Switzerland, particularly the Zürich area. The house was once inhabited by a vineyard owner.

**Villnachern Family House**
Built of limestone in 1630, this was probably the home of a wealthy family.

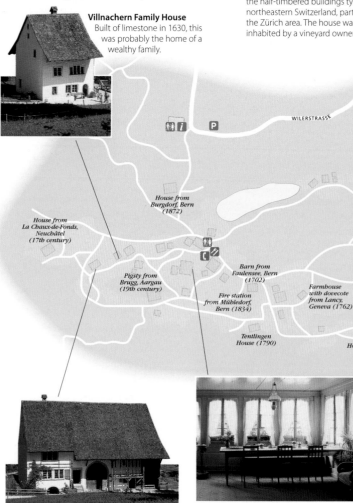

WILERSTRASSE

House from
Burgdorf, Bern
(1872)

House from
La Chaux-de-Fonds,
Neuchâtel
(17th century)

Winery from
Schaffhausen
(17th century)

Pigsty from
Brugg, Aargau
(19th century)

Barn from
Faulensee, Bern
(1702)

Fire station
from Mühledorf,
Bern (1834)

Farmhouse
with dovecote
from Lancy,
Geneva (1762)

Tentlingen
House (1790)

House from Malvaglia,
Ticino (1515–64)

**Therwil House**
Built in stone, with a wooden outbuilding, this house is typical of the architecture of the Jura. It dates from 1675.

**★ Ostermundigen House**
This large house was built in 1797. Although it is made of wood, the façade was painted grey to resemble stone. In the work areas of the house, the rooms are set up as exhibition galleries.

*For hotels and restaurants see pp248–55 and pp264–75*

## Workshops

Some of the houses at the museum have workshops where craftsmen using authentic tools and original machinery demonstrate some of the crafts and trades of Switzerland's regions. Among these crafts are weaving, spinning, pottery, wickerwork, lace-making and cheese-making. The museum also stages fairs and festivals in which folk traditions are revived.

### VISITORS' CHECKLIST

**Practical Information**
Road map: D4. Brienzwiler.
Swiss Open Air Museum
Ballenberg: 3 km (2 miles) east
of Brienz. Tel 033 952 10 30.
W ballenberg.ch.
Interiors: Open early Apr–Oct:
10am–5pm daily. Ticket office
& park: Open mid-Apr–Oct:
9am–5pm daily.

**Transport**

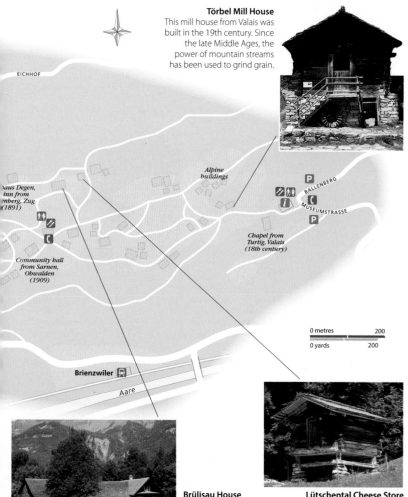

### Törbel Mill House
This mill house from Valais was built in the 19th century. Since the late Middle Ages, the power of mountain streams has been used to grind grain.

EICHHOF

Alpine buildings

Haus Degen, inn from ...enberg, Zug (1891)

BALLENBERG

MUSEUMSTRASSE

Chapel from Turtig, Valais (18th century)

Community hall from Sarnen, Obwalden (1909)

0 metres 200
0 yards 200

Brienzwiler

Aare

### Brülisau House
This wooden house, typical of the architecture of eastern Switzerland, was built in 1754.

### Lütschental Cheese Store
Like other houses and outbuildings of the Bernese Oberland, this storehouse for cheese has a ridge roof with protruding eaves and gable ends.

**For keys to symbols** see back flap

The parish church in Kandersteg

# ⑭ Kandersteg

**Road map:** C4. 🏔 800. 🚉
ℹ️ Hauptstrasse; 033 675 80 80.
🌐 kandersteg.ch

The village of Kandersteg
stretches out along the valley
of the River Kander, west of the
Jungfrau massif. The village is
located near the north entrance
to the old Lötschberg Tunnel,
through which trains run for
15 km (9 miles) under the
Lötschberg to emerge at
Goppenstein, in eastern Valais. In
2008, a 35-km (22-mile) tunnel
opened beneath the old line,
dramatically cutting travel times.

Apart from its interesting
16th-century parish church,
Kandersteg's main interest to
visitors is as a resort. In winter, the
gentle slopes around the village
make ideal skiing pistes for
beginners. In summer the village
is a popular base for hiking and
paragliding or simply for exploring
the stunningly beautiful lakes and
mountains in the vicinity.

The **Oeschinensee**, a small
lake surrounded by towering
cliffs, can be reached by a
chairlift from the eastern edge
of the village. Fit hikers can
walk back down to Kandersteg.
The **Blausee**, a small boating
lake surrounded by a pine
forest, is a ten-minute drive
north of Kandersteg.

The **Blümlisalphorn** (3,671 m/
12,044 ft) and Hockenhorn
(3,297 m/10,820 ft), two nearby
peaks, offer mountaineers a
more demanding challenge.

# ⑮ Adelboden

**Road map:** C4. 🚉 🏔 3,650.
Dorfstrasse 23; 033 673 80 80.
🌐 adelboden.ch

Located at the head of
Engstligental, a wide valley,
Adelboden is an attractive
village with chalets, pleasant
streets and well-kept gardens.
The small parish church here
was built in 1433 and is of
interest for its frescoes and
stained-glass windows by
Augusto Giacometti. The village
also has an interesting museum
documenting local history and
daily life in the Engstligental.

Adelboden is, however,
primarily a resort. With 72
ski lifts and some 210 km
(130 miles) of pistes in the
Adelboden-Lenk region ski pass,
the area is popular with
families. Adelboden also offers
facilities for extreme
sports as well as ice
rinks for skating and
curling. In summer
it is a base for
mountain biking
and hiking.

The **Engstligen-
fälle**, spectacular
waterfalls tumbling
from Engstligenalp,
4 km (3 miles) above
Adelboden, are
accessible by cable
car. There are several
hiking trails, which
lead up to higher altitudes,
including Ammertenspitz
(2,613 m/8,573 ft) and also
down past the falls, that can
be started from here.

Epitaph in Adelboden's
parish church

# ⑯ Grindelwald

**Road map:** D4. 🚉 ℹ️ Dorfstrasse 110;
033 854 12 12. 🌐 grindelwald.ch

The road and railway line
into the mountains diverge
just south of Interlaken. One
branch continues into the
Lauterbrunnen valley, with
access to Lauterbrunnen,
Wengen and Mürren, and the
other heads east along the
Lütschen valley to Grindelwald.

Nestled beneath the giant
Wetterhorn, Mettenberg and
Eiger, this lively resort village
has long been one of the most
popular destinations in the Alps.
In winter it offers good skiing,
and in summer excellent hiking.
A one-hour walk east of the
village leads to the trailhead
for a scenic stroll through
woodland to the awe-inspiring
Oberer Gletscher, a glacier
inching its way down
the Wetterhorn.

Some of the
region's best hiking
trails lie in the area
around **First**, which
is served by its own
gondola. A classic
half-day route
from First gives a
superb ridge-top
walk along to the
glittering Bachalp-
see tarn and on to
the summit of the
**Faulhorn** (2,681 m/
8,795 ft), where refreshment
can be found at a restaurant
and an inn. From here the
views of the sunrise and
sunset are breathtaking.

Snow-covered chalets at the resort of Wengen

Schloss Wimis, the 16th-century castle in the Nieder Simmental

## ⑰ Wengen

**Road map:** C4. 🏔 1,405. 🚆
ℹ️ Dorfstrasse; 033 856 85 85.
🆆 wengen.ch

The road and rail line from Interlaken terminate in Lauterbrunnen, a quiet village on the floor of the stunning Lauterbrunnen valley, the world's deepest U-shaped valley. This is classic Swiss Alpine scenery, with the sheer cliffs, waterfalls, green meadows where cows graze, and snowy peaks.

Mountain trains climb from Lauterbrunnen towards the Jungfraujoch (see p83), stopping midway at Wengen, a village of chalets and large hotels tucked on a shelf of southwest-facing pasture. Just like its neighbours Grindelwald and Mürren, car-free Wengen has been a magnet for summer and winter visitors for a century or more.

Skiing terrain is extensive, and in summer the country-side around Wengen offers superb hiking. Trails lead down to the flowery meadows around Wengwald, and up to Männlichen (which can also be reached by cable car). From here visitors can enjoy spectacular views down over Grindelwald on one side and the Lauterbrunnen valley on the other.

## ⑱ Mürren

**Road map:** C4. 🏔 350. 🚆 ℹ️ 033 856 86 86. 🆆 muerren.ch

From Lauterbrunnen there are two ways of reaching the small car-free village of Mürren, on the opposite side of the valley from Wengen. Both routes are spectacular. A cable car rises to Grütschalp, from where a tram takes a scenic route along the cliff-edge to reach Mürren. Alternatively, buses head along the valley-floor road from Lauterbrunnen (past a magnificent set of waterfalls at Trümmelbach) to Stechelberg, from where a cable car climbs to Mürren, perched 800m (2,625 ft) above the valley floor. The views, down the valley and up to a dazzling panorama of snowy crags, are astounding. A cable car heads further up, to the ice-bound summit of the Schilthorn (2,970 m/9,744 ft), where there is a famous revolving restaurant.

## ⑲ The Simmental

**Road map:** C4. 🚆 🚌 ℹ️
Rawilstrasse 3, Lenk; 033 736 35 35.
🆆 lenk-simmental.ch

The Simmental, the long valley of the River Simme, is divided into two sections. Nieder Simmental, the lower section, runs from Spiez, where the Simme enters the Thunersee, westwards to Boltigen. Here the valley veers southwards, becoming Obere Simmental, the upper section. This part stretches up to the resort and spa town of **Lenk**, near the source of the Simme.

Several villages lie along the Simmental. **Erlenbach** is the starting point for white-water rafting down the Simme. **Zweisimmen**, at the confluence of the Kleine Simme and Grosse Simme, is the trailhead of roads that run along the valley floor up towards Lenk and Gstaad. From Lenk, ski lifts take hikers and skiers up to Metschberg, Betelberg and Mülkerblatten.

The Saane River near Gstaad, excellent for white-water rafting

## ⑳ Gstaad

**Road map:** C4. 🏔 2,500. 🚆 🚌
ℹ️ Haus des Gastes; 033 748 81 81.
🎈 Hot Air Balloon Week (Jan), Swiss Open Tennis Tournament (Jul), Menuhin Festival (Jul–Sep).
🆆 gstaad.ch

For one of Switzerland's smartest resorts, Gstaad is a surprisingly small village, its size out of proportion to its international prestige. Lying at the junction of four valleys, Gstaad connects into a larger regional skipass network, including the Diablerets glacier.

In summer Gstaad attracts numerous visitors who come to enjoy rock climbing, hiking, cycling, tennis and fun sports, such as rafting on the turbulent waters of the Saane.

By avoiding high-rise developments and remaining faithful to traditional Swiss-style architecture, Gstaad has maintained its romantic character. Its main street, the Promenade, is lined with shops, cafés, restaurants and art galleries. Craftsmen can be seen at work on woodcarvings and decorative paper cut-outs.

Luxuriously furnished interior of a chalet in Gstaad

# ㉑ Martigny

**Road map:** B5. ☒ 13,000. ⊞ ⊟
ⓘ Ave de la Gare 6; 027 720 49 49.
ⓦ martigny.com

Located at the confluence of the
Drance and the Rhône, at the
point where the latter curves
northward, Martigny (Octodorus)
was established by the Romans
in about 15 BC. Excavations have
revealed a complex of Roman
buildings, including a temple
dedicated to Minerva, baths
and an amphitheatre.

The town is dominated by the
**Tour de la Bâtiaz**, a 13th-century
fortress set on a promontory. Other
buildings of interest in Martigny's
old district are the 15th-century
**Maison Supersaxo** and the
**Chapelle Notre-Dame-de-
Compassion**, built in the 1620s.

Martigny's main attraction is
the **Fondation Pierre Gianadda**,
a museum built on the ruins of a
Gallo-Roman temple. It consists
of several collections. While the
main gallery stages important
temporary exhibitions, the
Musée Archéologique Gallo-
Romain contains statues,
coins, pottery and
bronzes uncovered
during excavations.
The Musée de l'Auto,
in the basement, has
about 50 vintage cars,
including Swiss-
made models. A
small number of
paintings, by Van
Gogh, Cézanne, Toulouse-
Lautrec and other important
artists, are shown in the more
intimate Salle Franck. Modern
sculpture fills the Parc des
Sculptures, an open area
around the museum.

**▥ Fondation Pierre Gianadda**
59 Rue du Forum. **Tel** 027 722 39 78.
**Open** Jun–Nov: 9am–7pm daily;
Dec–May: 10am–6pm daily. ◪
ⓦ gianadda.ch

### Environs

The small town of **St-Maurice**, 15
km (9 miles) north of Martigny,
has an Augustinian abbey
founded in 515. The church is
part of the oldest surviving abbey
north of the Alps. Northwest of
Martigny lies the extensive

The mountain refuge at the Col du Grand-St-Bernard

Franco-Swiss skiing area known
as the **Portes du Soleil**, which
can be reached via the town of
Monthey. The area comprises
12 resorts and has about
650 km (400 miles) of pistes.

# ㉒ Grand St Bernard Pass

**Road map:** B5. ⊟ ⓘ Grand-
St-Bernard; 027 775 23 81.
ⓦ st-bernard.ch

Situated on the
border with Italy at
an altitude of 2,469 m
(8,103 ft), the St Bernard
Pass, or Col du Grand-St-
Bernard, is the oldest of all
Alpine pass routes.
An isolated nexus
between western
Europe and Italy,

Roman head of a bull in
Martigny

it has been used since at least
800 BC. Julius Caesar came over
the pass in the 1st century BC,
followed by Charlemagne in

800, on the return from his
coronation in Milan, and
Napoleon in 1800.

The pass is named after
Bernard of Menthon, Bishop
of Aosta, who built a hospice
for travellers here in 1049. In
recognition of his missionary
work, St Bernard was beatified
after his death, in the 1080s,
and was later made patron
saint of the Alps.

The hospice on the pass has
been inhabited by monks ever
since. It is open to travellers all
year round, though access in
winter is only by skis or
snowshoes. The present
building, which dates from the
18th century, incorporates a
17th-century church, in which a
casket containing the remains
of St Bernard is displayed. The
treasury has a collection of
liturgical vessels. There is also a
museum, **Musée et Chiens du
Saint-Bernard**, with exhibits
documenting the history of

### St Bernard Dogs

Named after the hospice at the Grand
St Bernard Pass where they were kept
by monks, these sturdy dogs, with a
body weight of up to 100 kg (220 lb),
are synonymous with mountain
rescue. Athough the monks probably
began to breed them in the Middle
Ages, training them to sniff out
travellers lost in snow or swallowed
by avalanches, the earliest mention
of St Bernards dates from the late
17th to early 18th centuries. However,
most rescue work is now done
with helicopters.

St Bernard with a handler

the pass since pre-Roman times and kennels for the famous rescue dogs. The dogs can be watched training, and walking excursions where each child is given a dog can be arranged.

Because of its elevation and heavy snowfalls in winter, the pass itself can be used only between mid-June and October. However, the St Bernard Tunnel, running 6 km (4 miles) under the pass, provides a year-round route between Switzerland and Italy.

**Musée et Chiens du Saint-Bernard**
Route du Levant 34, CP 245, Martigny. **Tel** 027 720 49 20. **Open** 10am–6pm.
 **museesaintbernard.ch**

## ㉓ Verbier

**Road map:** C5. 2,600.
Place Centrale; 027 775 38 88.
**verbier.ch** Xtreme Verbier (Mar); Verbier Festival (late Jul).

Few Swiss resorts match Verbier in terms of its beautiful location and the range of winter activities that it offers. At an altitude of 1,500 m (4,921 ft), the resort lies on a wide plateau that opens to the south onto views of peaks in Italy, France and Switzerland alike. Just below Verbier lies a picturesque valley, the Val de Bagnes.

Verbier is renowned for its extreme skiing events and challenging runs. Summer sports here include golf, tennis, horse riding and mountain biking. The town is also a good starting point for hikes along the Val de Bagnes, at the head of which is a dam, the Barrage de Mauvoisin, and for climbing the mountains in the vicinity, including Pierre Avoi (2,472 m/8,113 ft), which offers a breathtaking view of Mont Blanc.

Xtreme Verbier is a winter event in which skiers and snowboarders descend steep faces studded with cliffs. In summer the town hosts the Verbier Festival, an international festival of classical music with free workshops open to everyone.

The Romanesque church at St Pierre-de-Clages

## ㉔ St Pierre-de-Clages

**Road map:** B5. 600.
Fête du Livre (late Aug).

The tiny village of St Pierre-de-Clages is set on the southern, vineyard-covered slopes of the Rhône valley. Apart from an annual literary festival, the village's main attraction is its beautiful Romanesque church. Dating from the late 11th to the early 12th century, it originally formed part of a Benedictine priory. The rib-vaulted interior is almost entirely devoid of decoration, and this pleasing austerity is accentuated by the bare stonework of the walls and columns. The stained glass dates from 1948.

## ㉕ Sion

*See pp90–91.*

## ㉖ Barrage de la Grande Dixence

**Road map:** C5. late Jun–mid-Oct. mid-Jun–Sep: 11:30am, 1:30pm, 3pm & 4:30pm. **grande-dixence.ch**

The world's highest gravity wall dam and the greatest feat of modern engineering in Switzerland, the Barrage de la Grande Dixence is a hydro-electric dam 285 m (935 ft) high across the River Dixence, at the head of the Val d'Hérémence.

The Lac des Dix, a stretch of water filling the valley above the dam, is surrounded by mountains. Rising to the west is Rosablanche (3,336 m/10,945 ft); to the east Les Aiguilles Rouges (3,646 m/ 11,962 ft); and to the south Mont Blanc de Cheilon (3,870m/12,697 ft) and Pigne d'Arolla (3,796m/ 12,454 ft). A cable car runs from the foot of the dam, where there is a restaurant, up to the lake. From here you can take a boat to the Cabane des Dix, a mountain refuge, walk around the lake or go on a hike – for example, to the small resort of Arolla.

Val d'Hérémence joins Val d'Hérens *(see p92)* at the level of Hérémence. This small town is a good base for skiing on the eastern slopes of Mont Rouge and for hiking in the mountains.

Interior of the Romanesque church at St Pierre-de-Clages

# ㉕ Sion

The capital of the canton of Valais, Sion (Sitten in German) is a pleasant town with a rich heritage. It lies on a plain on the north bank of the Rhône, at the foot of two hills, each of which is crowned by a medieval castle. A Roman settlement named Sedunum was established here in the 1st century. The two castles that tower above the town are vestiges of its powerful bishopric, which ruled over Valais for centuries. In the Middle Ages Sion was also an important producer of wine and fruit, for which the fertile Rhône Valley is still renowned. Sion's Fendant wines are also highly prized.

Sion, seen from Valère, one of two hills overlooking the town

## Exploring Sion

Sion's old town, with quiet cobbled streets and fine houses, is easily explored on foot. The castles can also be reached on foot, or by the tourist train (summer only) from Rue des Châteaux to an area of level ground between the two hills. From here steep paths lead left to Tourbillon and right to Valère. Both hills offer panoramic views of the town and of the vineyard-covered hillsides all around.

## 🏰 Château de Tourbillon

**Tel** 027 606 47 45. **Open** mid-Mar–Apr & Oct–mid-Nov: 11am–5pm daily; May–Sep: 10am–6pm daily.

Standing on the higher of the two hills, this great medieval fortress is surrounded by crenel-lated walls set with tall square towers. The castle was built in the late 13th century as the fortified residence of Bishop Boniface de Challant. It was besieged and rebuilt on several occasions and in 1788 it was destroyed by fire. The castle itself is now in ruins, but much of the ramparts remain. The chapel, with ribbed vaulting and carved capitals, contains medieval wall paintings.

## 🏰 Château de Valère

Church: **Tel** 027 606 47 15. **Open** Jun–Sep: 10am–6pm daily; Oct–May: 10am–5pm Tue–Sun. 🎧 or guided tours of choir; free entry to nave but no access during services. Musée d'Histoire du Valais: **Tel** 027 606 47 15. **Open** Jun–Sep: 11am–6pm daily; Oct–May: 11am–5pm Tue–Sun. 🎧

Built in the 12th to 13th centuries, with a square tower, curtain wall and rampart walk, the Château de Valère is in fact a fortified church, Notre-Dame-de-Valère. It stands on the site of an 11th-century fortress and a Roman building. The impressive heights of Valeria overlooking Sion are a National Heritage Site.

Romanesque capitals and Gothic frescoes grace the interior of the church. Other notable features are the stunning 15th-century murals, 17th-century stalls and a remarkable organ. Dating from about 1430–40, it is the oldest playable organ in the world.

Next to the church stands a 12th-century building that was originally the canon's residence. It now houses the Musée d'Histoire du Valais. The museum's collection includes more than 1,000 objects, scale models and inter-active displays detailing the history of Valais, from the first traces of human occupation to the present day. Sections on the prehistoric hunter-gatherers, medieval pageants of the court of the Bishop-Prince, Swiss mercenaries and the industrial 19th century trace the developments that have shaped Valais.

## 🏛 Musée d'Art du Valais

15 Place de la Majorie. **Tel** 027 606 46 90. **Open** Jun–Sep: 11am–6pm Tue–Sun; Oct–May: 11am–5pm Tue–Sun. 🎧 **W** musees-valais.ch

This art gallery occupies two 15th-century houses that were once the residence of episcopal officers. Ranging from the 17th century to the present, the collection

Notre-Dame-de-Valère, the fortified church on a hill overlooking Sion

Rue du Grand-Pont, with the white-fronted Hôtel de Ville

concentrates mainly on paintings by Valais artists, including some folk art.

### 🏛 Hôtel de Ville
12 Rue du Grand-Pont. **Open** only for those on the Tourist Office walking tour.

With its clock tower crowned by a cupola and lantern, Sion's 17th-century town hall stands out among other fine buildings on Rue du Grand-Pont.

The town hall, which dates from 1657–65, has finely carved wooden doors at the entrance. Stones with Roman inscriptions are embedded in the walls of the hall within. Among them is a stone with

a Christian inscription dating from 377, the earliest of its kind in Switzerland. The council chamber on the upper floor of the town hall has rich furnishings and decorative woodwork.

### 🏛 Maison Supersaxo
Rue de Conthey. **Open** 2–5pm Mon–Fri.

This ornate late Gothic mansion was built in about 1505 for Georges Supersaxo, the local governor. A wooden spiral staircase leads up to the grand hall, which has a wooden ceiling lavishly painted in the late Gothic style. The centrepiece of the ceiling is a painted medallion by Jacobinus de Malacridis depicting the Nativity. Busts of the Prophets and the Magi fill alcoves lining the walls.

### 🏛 Cathédrale Notre-Dame du Glarier
Rue de la Cathédrale 13. **Tel** 027 322 80 66. **Open** 7am–7pm daily; access only via the tourist office guided tour.

Although the main part of the cathedral dates from the 15th century, it contains earlier elements, including a 12th-century Romanesque belfry

Nativity medallion in Maison Supersaxo

crowned by an octagonal steeple. Interesting features of the interior include tombs of the bishops of Sion, early Baroque stalls and a wooden triptych depicting the Tree of Jesse. The Église St Théodule, the late Gothic church just to the south of the cathedral, dates from 1514–16. The 19th-century building opposite the cathedral is the Bishop's Palace.

### 🏛 Tour des Sorciers
Avenue de la Gare 42. **Open** for private functions.

The Witches' Tower, so named because of its conical roof, is the only remaining part of Sion's medieval fortifications. Located just north of the old town, the tower once defended the town's northwestern aspect.

## Sion Town Centre
① Château de Tourbillon
② Château de Valère
③ Musée d'Art du Valais
④ Hôtel de Ville
⑤ Maison Supersaxo
⑥ Cathédrale Notre-Dame du Glarier
⑦ Tour des Sorciers

The unusual rock formation known as Pyramides d'Euseigne, in the Val d'Hérens

## ㉗ Val d'Hérens

**Road map:** C5. ㊀ 🅘 Rue Principale 13, Euseigne; 027 281 28 15. 🆆 **valdherens-tourisme.ch**

Stretching southeast from Sion, the Val d'Hérens (Eringertal in German) reaches into the Pennine Alps. This tranquil valley has enchanting scenery and villages with wooden chalets. Women wearing traditional dress can be seen working in the fields.

A striking geological feature of the Val d'Hérens is a group of rock formations known as the **Pyramides d'Euseigne**. These jagged outcrops of rock, which are visible from the valley road, jut out of the hillside like fangs. They were formed during the Ice Age by the erosive action of wind, rain and ice. Each point is capped by a rock, which protected the softer rock beneath from erosion, so producing these formations.

The village of Evolène, 15 km (9 miles) south of the village of Euseigne, is a good base for hiking. At the head of the valley is the hamlet of Les Haudères, where there is a Geology and Glacier Centre, with an interesting museum. Beyond Les Haudères the Val d'Hérens extends into the Val d'Arolla. The road ends at the small resort of Arolla.

## ㉘ Crans-Montana

**Road map:** C4. ㊀ 4,500. ㊀ 🅘 027 485 04 04. 🆆 **crans-montana.ch**
🏌 European Masters Golf Tournament (Sep).

The fashionable ski and golf resort of Crans-Montana lies on a plateau north of the Rhône valley, with a clear view of the Valais Alps to the south. In the late 19th century, as the fashion for mountain holidays grew, Crans and Montana expanded but they remain two separate villages.

Crans-Montana can be reached by road from Sion. From Sierre it is accessible either by a road that winds up through vineyards and pasture, or by funicular. This extremely sunny resort has a network of cable cars and ski lifts, accessing over 140 km (87 miles) of pistes and the glacier of Plaine Morte, popular for cross-country skiing.

 *(Window with flowers image placement)*

Window with flowers, a typical sight in Valais

Summer activities include golf, paragliding and hot-air ballooning. A plateau lying at an altitude of 2,927 m (9,603 ft), Plaine Morte offers stunning views of the Valais Alps and of Mont Blanc to the south-west. From here mountain trails lead to Bella Lui and Bisse du Roh.

## ㉙ Sierre

**Road map:** C4. ㊀ 11,000. 🚉 🚌
🅘 Place de la Gare 10; 027 455 85 35.
🆆 **sierretourisme.ch**

Located in the Rhône valley, Sierre (Siders in German) lies on the linguistic border separating French speakers from German speakers. Enjoying an exceptionally sunny climate, it is surrounded by vineyards, and contains several historic buildings, including a 16th-century castle, the **Château des Vidomnes**. The Baroque town hall contains a small museum of pewter objects.

The local winemaking tradition is documented by the **Musée Valaisan de la Vigne et du Vin**, a wine museum whose collections are displayed in two places. One part occupies a wing of the 16th-century Château de Villa in Sierre, and the other the 16th-century Zumofenhaus in Salgesch (Salquenen in French), a village east of Sierre. The two locations are linked by a Sentier Viticole, or wine route, running for 6 km (4 miles) through villages and vineyards, with wine-tasting stops along the way.

🏛 **Musée Valaisan de la Vigne et du Vin**
Château de Villa, 4 Rue Ste-Catherine. **Tel** 027 456 35 25. **Open** Mar–Nov: 2–5pm Tue–Sun. 🅿
🆆 **museevalaisanduvin.ch**

The 16th-century Château des Vidomnes in Sierre

Characteristic wooden houses in Grimentz, Val d'Anniviers

## ⑳ Val d'Anniviers

**Road map:** C4. 🚌 027 476 17 15.
W valdanniviers.ch

Surrounded by the high peaks of the Pennine Alps and washed by the River La Navisence, the rugged Val d'Anniviers begins opposite Sierre and runs southwards up to the glaciers of Zinal. The valley is dotted with villages, which offer visitors winter skiing and summer hiking and cycling.

From Soussillon you can make a trip to the medieval village of **Chandolin**, which has wooden chalets and spectacular views. From Vissoie it is worth going to sun-drenched **Saint-Luc** at 1,650 m (5,413 ft) for a breathtaking view of the Val d'Anniviers. From Saint-Luc you can proceed further up, to the top of Bella Tola (3,025 m/9,924 ft).

**Grimentz** is a fascinating village, full of traditional tall wooden chalets built on the underlying bedrock. From here hiking trails lead up to the Moiry dam, and the **Glacier de Moiry**. The highest village in the valley is **Zinal** at 1,670 m (5,479 ft). This resort is a ski centre in winter and a good base for hiking in summer. From Zinal it is possible to hire a guide for the climb to the summit of the Zinal-Rothorn (4,221 m/13,848 ft), the Pyramide des Besso, Oberes Gabelhorn and Pointe de Zinal. There are many easier peaks for less ambitious climbers, and several highly scenic rambling routes.

## ㉛ Leukerbad

**Road map:** C4. 🚠 1,600. 🚌
ℹ️ Rathausstrasse 8; 027 472 71 71.
W leukerbad.ch

Lying at the head of the Dala valley, at an altitude of 1,400 m (4,595 ft), Leukerbad (Loèche-les-Bains in French) is one of the highest spa resorts in Europe. The therapeutic properties of its hot springs, which are rich in calcium, sulphur and gypsum, have been appreciated since Roman times.

Leukerbad has several public spa complexes, with indoor and outdoor pools and many other facilities, including various treatments and rehabilitation programmes.

Leukerbad also has skiing pistes. Above the resort, and accessible by cable car, lies the Gemmi Pass, on the hiking trail to Kandersteg *(see p86)* and the Bernese Oberland.

## ㉜ Zermatt

**Road map:** C5. 🚠 4,200. 🚗 🚌
ℹ️ Bahnhofplatz 5; 027 966 81 00.
W zermatt.ch

Nestling at the foot of the Matterhorn *(see p94)* and surrounded by mountains over 4,000 m (13,000 ft), Zermatt is Switzerland's best-known resort. Closed to motorized tourist traffic, Zermatt is reached by train from Brig, Visp or Täsch.

A ski paradise in winter, Zermatt is a centre of hiking and mountaineering in summer. Glacier skiing and snowboarding are popular all through the summer.

The **Matterhorn Museum** in Zermatt documents the history of mountaineering in the region, with a display devoted to Edward Whymper, who led the first ascent of the Matterhorn in 1865. The small Anglican church here was built in the 19th century for English climbers scaling the neighbouring peaks. The town square, surrounded by historic houses, features a fountain with marmot statues.

From Zermatt a series of lifts runs to the summit of the Klein Matterhorn (3,883 m/12,739 ft), and a rack railway climbs to the Gornergrat (3,089 m/10,134 ft) from where there are breathtaking views of the Matterhorn and the Gornergletscher.

Marmot on a fountain in Zermatt

Municipal baths in Leukerbad

The Matterhorn, for daring climbers only

## ⓷ Matterhorn

**Road map:** C6. **ℹ️** Zermatt,
Bahnhofplatz; 027 966 81 00.
**W** **zermatt.ch**

Although the Matterhorn is
not the highest mountain in
Switzerland, it is certainly the
most awesome. It straddles
the Swiss-Italian border, and
with its distinct pyramidal
peak, which reaches 4,478 m
(14,692 ft), it has become one
of Switzerland's national
symbols. Shrouded in legend,
it continues to claim the lives
of several of the 2,000 people
brave enough to climb it each
summer. The best views of the
mountain are from the centre
of Zermatt *(see p93)*.

The Matterhorn (Cervino in
Italian) was first conquered on
14 July 1865 by a team led by
the British explorer Edward
Whymper. The expedition
ended in tragedy when three
of the English mountaineers
and a Swiss guide were killed
during the descent. Their
tombs lie in Zermatt along
with those of others who lost
their lives on the mountain.

The Matterhorn is still a
challenge to recreational
climbers. The most difficult
ascent route is on the east face,
which was not conquered
until 1932.

## ⓸ Monte Rosa

**Road map:** C5.

Right on the international
border, Monte Rosa is divided
into Swiss and Italian territory.
Although it is not as famous
as the Matterhorn, the Monte

Rosa massif boasts the highest
peak in Switzerland and the
second highest in the Alps
after Mont Blanc. This is the
Dufourspitze, which culminates
at 4,634 m (15,203 ft).

Because of its shape, Monte
Rosa does not present as much
of a challenge to climbers as the
Matterhorn. Situated on its
Italian side, near the summit
at 4,556 m (14,947 ft), is the
Capanna Regina Margherita, the
highest mountain shelter in
Europe, built in 1893. The Monte
Rosa massif is encircled by the
Gornergletscher, a vast glacier;
stretching lower down are the
slopes of Stockhorn and
Gornergrat, with long pistes
and many ski lifts.

## ⓹ Saas Fee

**Road map:** D5. **🚠** 1,700. **🚌**
**Tel** 027 958 18 58. **W** **saas-fee.ch**
**🎭** Alpaufzug (Jun), Älplerfest
(mid-Aug).

A village with a history
going back to the 13th
century, Saas Fee, in the
Pennine Alps, has been
a resort since the early
19th century. It is the
main town in the Saas
Valley, through which
flows the River Saaser
Vispa. Saas Fee has a
magnificent setting at
the foot of the Dom
(4,545 m/14,908 ft)
and is surrounded
by several other
tall peaks.

The resort is closed to
motorized traffic. It has many
traditional wooden chalets,
which are built on high stone

foundation walls. Saas Fee,
more than many resorts,
cherishes its traditional rural
culture and several local
traditions are enacted for the
benefit of visitors. These include
processions marking Corpus
Christi, cow fights and yodelling
contests, folk festivals
celebrating Swiss National Day,
and the Alpaufzug festival in
late spring, which marks the
time when cows are taken
up to their summer pastures.
The Saaser Museum, which
is devoted to regional folk
traditions and culture, includes
the reconstruction of a typical
local house, and a large
collection of crafts and
costumes.

The view up from the
village, winter or summer,
is of snowy glaciers and
glistening crevasses. Skiing is
possible year-round on the
Feegletscher (Fairy Glacier)
in the Mischabel massif.

In summer visitors have a
choice of hiking trails, ranging
from easy to demanding,
leading to the surrounding
peaks or to other sites, such as
the Mattmarksee, an artificial
lake. A cable car also runs up to
Felskinn. From here the Alpine
Metro runs to Mittelallalin,
where there is a revolving
restaurant at 3,500 m (11,480 ft).

## ⓺ Brig

Monument to a guide in
Saas Fee

**Road map:** D4. **🚠** 10,000. **🚌**
**ℹ️** Bahnhofplatz 1; 027 921
60 30. **W** **brig-belalp.ch**

Brig is the major town
in the Upper Valais. It
lies at the crossroads
of the main Alpine
routes leading over the
Simplon, Furka, Grimsel
and Nufenen passes
and through the
Lötschberg Tunnel.
Located on the Rhône,
the town takes its
name from the
bridges that span
the river at this spot,
where a Roman settlement
once stood. During the 17th
century, the trade route to
Italy, leading over the Simplon

The towers of the Stockalper Palace in Brig

## Customs of the Lötschental

The Lötschental is a remote valley just east of Leukerbad *(see p93)*. For centuries the valley's inhabitants were isolated from the outside world during winter, and they have retained many ancient rituals, customs and traditions. Now studied by ethnographers and cultural anthropologists, they have also become a visitor attraction. One such ancient custom is Tschäggätta, a festival that lasts from Candlemas until Shrovetide. During this time young bachelors don sheepskin coats, with the fleece on the outside, and wear grotesque masks. Masked processions are held on the last Thursday and Saturday of the carnival.

Tschäggätta mask

Pass, was controlled by the Stockalper family of merchants. Kaspar Jodok Stockalper von Thurm gave Brig its finest monument, a Renaissance-Baroque palace built in 1658–78. The building is set with three tall square towers crowned by cupolas known as Caspar, Melchior and Balthazar. The palace has an attractive arcaded courtyard and a chapel dedicated to the Three Kings, with an exquisite silver altarpiece made by Samuel Hornung of Augsburg. The palace houses various offices and a history museum.

Brig also has other historic buildings, town houses and churches, including the pilgrimage church in Glis, built in 1642–59.

## ③ Simplon Pass

**Road map:** D5. *i* Simplon Dorf; 027 979 10 10. **w** simplon.ch

At 2,005 m (6,580 ft), the Simplon Pass is one of the most important routes between Switzerland and Italy, and between western and southern Europe. It also marks the border between the Pennine and Lepontine Alps. The route, once used by the Romans, has played an important role in trade since the Middle Ages.

The strategic importance of the pass was recognized by Napoleon, on whose orders a

new road was built here in 1800–06. It is about 64 km (40 miles) long and runs from Brig, over the pass and through the village of Simplon, to the Italian town of Domodossola.

## ③ Aletsch Glacier

**Road map:** D4. *i* Bahnhofstrasse 7, Riederalp; 027 928 60 50. **w** aletsch.ch

The longest glacier in the Alps, the Aletsch Glacier (or Grosser Aletschgletscher) stretches for about 23 km (14 miles) from the Jungfrau *(see p83)* to a plateau above the Rhône valley. At its widest point the glacier is 2 km (1 mile) across. Together with the Jungfrau and Bietschhorn mountain ranges, the Aletsch

Glacier has been declared a UNESCO Natural Heritage Site.

The best starting point for a hike to the Aletsch Glacier is the small mountain resort of **Riederalp**, just above the Rhône valley. It is closed to motor traffic but can be reached by cable car from Mörel.

The tourist information centre in Riederalp contains a small Alpine museum with a traditional cheese dairy. Within walking distance is the secluded Villa Cassel at **Riederfurka**. The Pro Natura Zentrum Aletsch here is a scientific centre that provides information and permanent exhibitions on Alpine glaciers and the environmental protection of this region.

Skiers above the Aletsch Glacier

# GENEVA

With its beautiful lakeside setting, Geneva is a cosmopolitan city whose modest size belies its wealth and importance on the world stage. French-speaking yet Calvinistic, it is a dynamic centre of business with an outward-looking character tempered by a certain reserve. It is also the European headquarters of the United Nations and the birthplace of the International Red Cross.

A city with a population of just 185,000, Geneva is the capital of the canton of the same name. Sharing 95 per cent of its border with France, the canton is joined to the rest of Switzerland only by a narrow strip of land on its north side.

Loosely bound to the Holy Roman Empire from the 9th century, Geneva was later controlled by Savoy, from which it won independence in 1536. In 1602, when the Savoyards attempted to retake the city, they were repulsed. This event is commemorated to this day by a festival known as L'Escalade (Scaling the Walls).

By the 16th century, the city of Geneva was established as a prosperous centre of trade. When Jean Calvin began to preach here, Geneva also became a stronghold of the Reformation. Known as the Protestant Rome, it attracted Protestant refugees from all over Europe, who further increased the city's wealth and boosted its cosmopolitan character. Briefly an independent republic, Geneva was annexed by France from 1798 to 1813. In 1815, the city and its canton joined the Swiss Confederation.

The seat of over 250 international organizations, mostly NGOs, Geneva is today a centre of international diplomacy. It is also the home of the European Laboratory for Particle Physics (CERN), one of the world's most advanced scientific laboratories.

International flags on the approach to the Palais des Nations, in Geneva's International Area

◄ The impressive Jet d'Eau, Geneva's iconic fountain

# Exploring Geneva

Set at the western extremity of Lake Geneva at the point where the Rhône flows away towards France, Geneva is divided by water. On the South Bank (Rive Gauche) is the 16th-century Old Town (Vieille Ville), once surrounded by walls. Plainpalais, southwest of the Old Town, is the university district, while further south is Carouge, a picturesque suburb with a population of artists. The North Bank (Rive Droite), dominated by grand quayside hotels, is Geneva's main commercial area. Further north lies the Cité Internationale, base of international organizations. Both riverbanks have pleasant green areas. From La Rade, the harbour, rises the Jet d'Eau, Geneva's famous fountain.

## Sights at a Glance

1. Jet d'Eau
2. Jardin Anglais
3. Île Rousseau
4. *Cathédrale St-Pierre pp102–3*
5. Place du Bourg-de-Four
6. Musée Barbier-Mueller
7. Maison Tavel
8. Parc des Bastions
9. *Musée d'Art et d'Histoire pp106–7*
10. Cathédrale Orthodoxe Russe
11. International Red Cross and Red Crescent Museum
12. Palais des Nations

Monument to the conquest of space in the Parc des Nations

*For hotels and restaurants see pp248–55 and pp264–75*

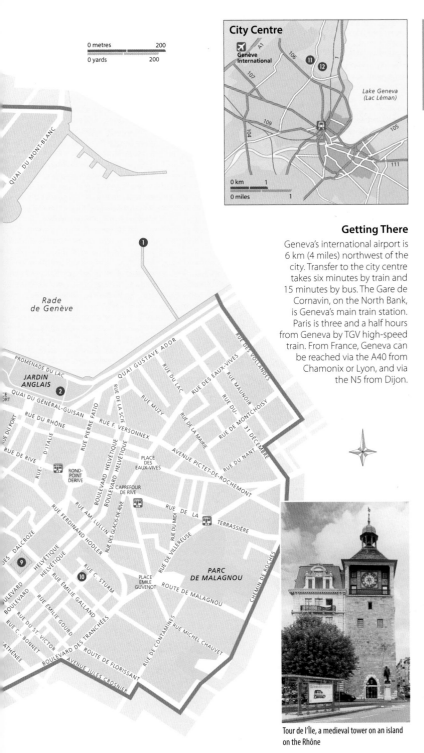

## City Centre

Genève International

Lake Geneva
(Lac Léman)

0 km 1
0 miles 1

0 metres 200
0 yards 200

*Rade de Genève*

PROMENADE DU LAC

**JARDIN ANGLAIS**

QUAI DU GÉNÉRAL-GUISAN

QUAI GUSTAVE ADOR

RUE DU LAC

RUE DES EAUX-VIVES

RUE DES VOLLANDES

RUE MAUNOIR

RUE DU RHÔNE

RUE DE RIVE

RUE D'ITALIE

RUE DE LA SCIE

RUE PIERRE FATIO

RUE F. VERSONNEX

RUE MUZY

RUE DE LA MARIE

RUE DU 31 DÉCEMBRE

RUE DE MONTCHOISY

AVENUE PICTET-DE-ROCHEMONT

RUE DU NANT

ROND-POINT DERIVE

BOULEVARD HELVÉTIQUE

BOULEVARD HELVÉTIQUE

PLACE DES EAUX-VIVES

CARREFOUR DE RIVE

RUE AMI LULLIN

RUE DES GLACIS-DE-RIVE

RUE DE LA TERRASSIÈRE

RUE DU MIDI

RUE DE VILLEREUSE

RUE FERDINAND HODLER

RUES DALCROZE

HELVÉTIQUE

HELVÉTIQUE

RUE C. STURM

RUE ÉMILE GALLAND

RUE ÉMILE GOURD

PLACE ÉMILE GUVENOT

ROUTE DE MALAGNOU

**PARC DE MALAGNOU**

CHEMIN DE ROCHES

BOULEVARD

BOULEVARD

RUE DU ST. VICTOR

RUE C. BONNET

ATHÉNÉE

BOULEVARD DES TRANCHÉES

ROUTE DE FLORISSANT

AVENUE JULES CROSNIER

RUE DE CONTAMINES

RUE MICHEL CHAUVET

QUAI DU MONT-BLANC

### Getting There

Geneva's international airport is 6 km (4 miles) northwest of the city. Transfer to the city centre takes six minutes by train and 15 minutes by bus. The Gare de Cornavin, on the North Bank, is Geneva's main train station. Paris is three and a half hours from Geneva by TGV high-speed train. From France, Geneva can be reached via the A40 from Chamonix or Lyon, and via the N5 from Dijon.

Tour de l'Île, a medieval tower on an island on the Rhône

**For keys to symbols** *see back flap*

# Street-by-Street: Old Town

Set on elevated ground on the south bank of the Rhône, the Old Town (Vieille Ville) clusters around the cathedral and Place du Bourg-de-Four. This atmospheric district, whose main thoroughfare is the pedestrianized Grand' Rue, has narrow cobbled streets lined with historic limestone houses. While the southern limit of the Old Town is marked by the Promenade des Bastions, laid out along the course of the old city walls, its northern side slopes down to the quay, which is lined with wide boulevards and the attractive Jardin Anglais.

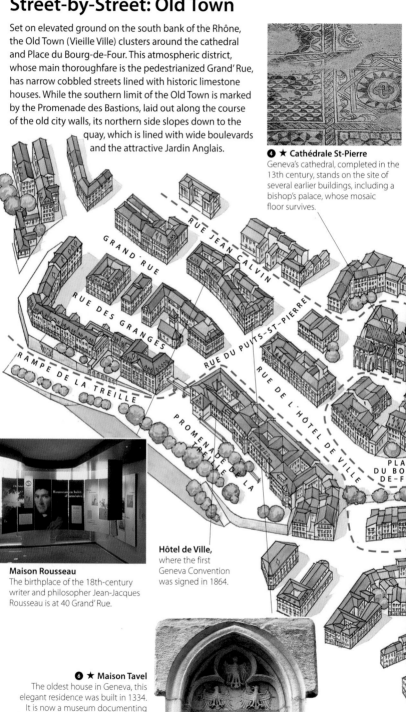

**❹ ★ Cathédrale St-Pierre**
Geneva's cathedral, completed in the 13th century, stands on the site of several earlier buildings, including a bishop's palace, whose mosaic floor survives.

GRAND-RUE
RUE JEAN CALVIN
RUE DES GRANGES
RAMPE DE LA TREILLE
RUE DU PUITS-ST-PIERRE
RUE DE L'HÔTEL DE VILLE
PROMENADE DE LA TREILLE
PLACE DU BOU DE-FO

**Maison Rousseau**
The birthplace of the 18th-century writer and philosopher Jean-Jacques Rousseau is at 40 Grand' Rue.

**Hôtel de Ville,**
where the first Geneva Convention was signed in 1864.

**❻ ★ Maison Tavel**
The oldest house in Geneva, this elegant residence was built in 1334. It is now a museum documenting daily life in Geneva through the ages.

**Locator Map**

**⑤ ★ Place du Bourg-de-Four**
This central square was used as a marketplace in the Middle Ages. It is still lined with old inns, as well as modern cafés and restaurants.

**Key**

— Suggested route

0 metres 50
0 yards 50

# ❶ Jet d'Eau

Off Quai Gustave-Ador.

Standing in isolation on a jetty on the south bank of Lake Geneva, the Jet d'Eau is the world's highest fountain, shooting a plume of water 140 m (460 ft) into the air, at a rate of 500 litres (113 gallons) per second and a speed of 200 km per hour (125 mph). It came into existence almost by accident.

In the late 19th century a purely functional fountain was set up to relieve excess water pressure while a reservoir system was being installed. Such was the fountain's popularity that the authorities decided to construct a permanent fountain, which became more spectacular as increasingly powerful pumps were installed. Visible from afar and floodlit after dark, the Jet d'Eau is the pride of Geneva and has been adopted as the city's emblem.

# ❷ Jardin Anglais

Quai du Général-Guisan.

Laid out on the lakeside at the foot of the Old Town, the Jardin Anglais (English Garden) offers a view of the harbour, and of the buildings along the quay on the north bank. The entrance to the garden is marked by a large floral clock, the **Horloge Fleurie**. Created in 1955 as a tribute to

**Statue of Jean-Jacques Rousseau**

Switzerland's clockmaking tradition, it consists of eight intersecting wheels with 6,500 flowering plants. The **Monument National** nearby commemorates Geneva's accession to the Swiss Confederation in 1814.

Protruding from the lake at a point just north of the Jardin Anglais are two stones brought down by glaciers during the Ice Age. They are known as the **Pierres du Niton** (Neptune's Stones), and the larger of the two was once used as the reference point from which altitude was measured in Switzerland.

# ❸ Île Rousseau

Pont des Bergues.

A walkway jutting out at a right angle from the centre of the Pont des Bergues leads to a medieval bastion in the Rhône. Now known as the Île Rousseau, it is named after Jean-Jacques Rousseau (1712–78), the writer and philosopher of the Enlightenment who was one of Geneva's most distinguished citizens.

Rousseau, the son of a clockmaker, left Geneva at the age of 16. Although he praised the city in his writings, his views elicited the disapproval of the authorities and his books were burned. However, in 1834, 56 years after his death, a statue was installed on the bastion that now bears his name.

Floral clock at the entrance to the Jardin Anglais

# ❹ Cathédrale St-Pierre

Built over a span of some 70 years from 1160 to 1230, with later additions, Geneva's vast cathedral is in a mixture of styles. Basically Gothic, it incorporates earlier Romanesque elements and has an incongruous Neo-Classical portal, which was added in the 18th century. In 1536 it became a Protestant church, losing most of its lavish Catholic decoration. Only the stalls and the stained glass in the chancel escaped the purge. The result, however, is a plain interior of awesome austerity. The cathedral stands on the site of an episcopal cluster – comprising places of worship as well as residential and administrative buildings – that was erected around AD 380.

**Calvin's Chair**
Calling for a radical reform of the Church, Jean Calvin preached many sermons in the cathedral, reputedly seated in this chair.

**The Nave**
The groin-vaulted nave combines Romanesque and early Gothic elements. The arches are surmounted by a triforium.

**Chapelle des Macchabées**
This side chapel in the flamboyant Gothic style was added in the early 15th century. With later frescoes and stained glass, it is a contrast to the austere nave.

Main entrance

### VISITORS' CHECKLIST

**Practical Information**
Cour St-Pierre 6–8. **Tel** 022 310 29
29. Archaeological site: **Open**
10am–5pm daily. **W** site-archeo
**logique.ch** Church: **Open** 9am–
7pm daily (Oct–Mar: 5:30pm). 🅿️

**Stained Glass of St Andrew**
The stained-glass windows in
the presbytery are copies of the
original 15th-century windows.
These are on display in Geneva's
Musée d'Art et d'Histoire.

**Tomb of Henri de Rohan**
Henri, Duc de Rohan, head of
the Reformed Church in
France in the 16th
and 17th centuries,
is buried here.

★ **Capitals**
Masterpieces of
Romanesque and Gothic
stonework, these capitals are
among the few decorative
features to have survived
the Reformation.

★ **Stalls**
The stalls, with intricately
carved back panels and
canopy, originally stood
near the choir.

Place du Bourg-de-Four, filled with
café tables

## ❺ Place du Bourg-de-Four

Probably overlying Geneva's
Roman forum, the Place du
Bourg-de-Four was the city's
marketplace in the Middle Ages.
Today, graced by an 18th-
century fountain and lined with
16th-century houses, art
galleries and antique shops, and
with busy cafés and restaurants,
the square is still the hub of
Geneva's Old Town.

The imposing **Palais de
Justice** on the southeastern
side of the square was built in
1707–12 and has been used as
the city's law courts since 1860.
Nearby, on Rue de l'Hôtel-de-
Ville on the southwestern side of
the square, stands the **Hôtel de
Ville**, with a Renaissance façade.
Built in the 15th century with
additions in the 16th, 17th and
18th centuries, it was originally
the city hall and now serves as
the seat of the cantonal
authorities. The ramp in the
courtyard allowed cannons to
be pulled up into the building
and enabled dignitaries to ride
their horses to the upper floors.
The Tour Baudet, a tower dating
from 1455 and the oldest part
of the city hall, once housed
the cantonal archives. On the
ground floor of the Hôtel de
Ville is the Alabama Room,
where the Geneva Convention
was signed in 1864 and where
the International Red Cross
was recognized as a
humanitarian organization.
It was also here that the League
of Nations assembled for the
first time, in 1920.

Opposite the Hôtel de Ville
stands the **Ancien Arsenal**, a
granary that became a weapons
store in the 18th century.

Sculpture of a human head on the façade of Maison Tavel

## ❻ Musée Barbier-Mueller

Rue Jean-Calvin 10. **Tel** 022 312 02 70. **Open** 11am–5pm daily. 🅿️
🆆 barbier-mueller.ch

Almost hidden away in a back street near the Cathédrale St-Pierre is this art museum with stunning works from tribal and classical antiquity. It was founded in 1977 to preserve a collection begun in 1907 by Josef Mueller and continued by his daughter Monique and her husband Jean Paul Barbier-Mueller. The beautifully displayed collection includes masks, sculptures and other artifacts from Africa, Asia and Oceania, as well as items from Greece, Italy and other parts of the ancient world.

## ❼ Maison Tavel

6 Rue du Puits-St-Pierre. Musée du Vieux Genève: **Tel** 022 418 37 00. **Open** 10am–6pm Tue–Sun.
🆆 institutions.ville-geneve.ch

This fine limestone building is the oldest house in Geneva. The Gothic façade, with three tiers

of windows and a turret at one corner, is decorated with the arms of the Tavel family, who built the house, and with curious stone sculptures of animal and human heads. Although it was rebuilt after the fire of 1334, which destroyed a large part of Geneva, the earliest record of the house goes back to 1303.

The Maison Tavel now houses the **Musée du Vieux Genève**, a museum devoted to daily life in Geneva from the 14th to the 19th centuries. While the basement is reserved for temporary exhibitions, the rest of the house is filled with exhibits ranging from coins and ironwork to tiles, wooden doors and other elements of ancient houses. Twelve rooms on the second floor illustrate urban life in the 17th century. In the attic is a huge model of Geneva, made in 1850, before the city's medieval fortifications were demolished. A son-et-lumière presentation highlights points of interest on the model.

A separate section is devoted to Général Dufour (1787–1875), the son of a Genevese clockmaker who created a 1:100,000-scale topographic map of Switzerland. As commander of the Federal forces during the civil war of 1847, he managed to defeat the separatists. He was also a founder of the International Red Cross.

## ❽ Parc des Bastions

Created in the 18th century, the Parc des Bastions was laid out just outside the ramparts on the south side of the city. A vast and slightly forbidding monument looms up on the eastern edge of the park. This is the **Mur de la Réformation** (or Reformation Wall), erected in 1909 to mark the 400th anniversary of the birth of Jean Calvin and the 350th anniversary of the foundation of Geneva's Academy, a famous Protestant school. The monument takes the form of a wall 100 m (330 ft) long on which stand 5-m (16-ft) statues of the four leaders of the Reformation in Geneva: Guillaume Farel; Jean Calvin; Théodore de Bèze, first rector of the Academy; and John Knox. On the pavement in front of the monument the arms of Geneva are shown between the Bear of Bern and the Lion of Scotland, symbolizing the religious alliance between these Swiss cities and Scotland. The monument is

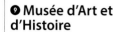

Equestrian statue of Général Dufour

flanked by memorials to Martin Luther and Ulrich Zwingli, two other leaders of the Reformation.

## ❾ Musée d'Art et d'Histoire

*See pp106–7.*

## ❿ Cathédrale Orthodoxe Russe

Rue Lefort. **Tel** 022 346 47 09. **Open** 9am–noon Tue–Fri, 9am–noon & 2–8pm Sat.

Set on a hilltop in the smart residential district of Les Tranchées, the Russian Orthodox church is visible from afar, its gilt onion domes glittering in the sun.

In the 19th century, Geneva was a popular place of residence and recreation for wealthy Russians. Among them was Grand Duchess Anna

Four leaders of the Reformation, on a monument in the Parc des Bastions

The Cathédrale Orthodoxe Russe, with distinctive gilt onion domes

Feodorovna, who funded the construction of a Russian church. Completed in 1869, it is built on the plan of a Greek cross. The interior is richly decorated in the Byzantine style, with a marble iconostasis and a gilt wooden doorway.

## ⓫ International Red Cross and Red Crescent Museum

17 Avenue de la Paix. **Tel** 022 748 95 11. **Open** 10am–5pm Wed–Mon. ♿ 🅦 **micr.org**

Moving and harrowing yet inspiring hope, this museum within the headquarters of the International Committee of the Red Cross is devoted to documenting human kindness and compassion, as well as the cruelty and suffering that the Red Cross has sought to alleviate since its foundation in 1863. The building itself takes the form of a glass and concrete bunker designed in such a way that natural light illuminates the rooms. At the entrance is a group of stone figures, blindfolded and with their hands tied, symbolizing the violation of human rights.

The museum initiates visitors into contemporary humanitarian action with an exhibition organized around three zones designed by internationally renowned architects from different cultural backgrounds:

*Defending Human Dignity* (Gringo Cardia, Brazil), *Reconstructing the Family Link* (Diébédo Francis Kéré, Burkina Faso) and *Refusing Fatality* (Shigeru Ban, Japan). Within each zone, visitors firstly come to an interactive phase where they "live through" an intense emotional experience, with the aim of raising awareness of an issue. Historical and background information is then provided. The "On the Spot" area shows the latest news from the field on an interactive globe.

Monument, International Red Cross and Red Crescent Museum

## ⓬ Palais des Nations

Public entrance: 14 Avenue de la Paix. **Tel** 022 917 48 96. **Open** Apr–June: 10am–noon & 2–4pm daily; Jul & Aug: 10am–4pm daily; Sep–Mar: 10am–noon & 2–4pm Mon–Fri. Identification necessary. 🎧 for guided tour. 📷 🅦 **unog.ch**

The world's largest conference centre for international peace and security, the Palais des Nations is the focal point of Geneva's international area. It was built in 1929–36 as the headquarters of the League of Nations, founded in 1920 to preserve world peace in the aftermath of World War I. In 1946, when the League of Nations was dissolved, the complex became the European

headquarters of the United Nations Organization (Organisation des Nations Unies, or ONU, in French). Some 3,000 people from all over the world work here, and the whole building is international territory.

Parts of it are open to the public, with guided tours available in 15 languages. Winding through long corridors, the tours take in the **Salle du Conseil** (Council Chamber), whose walls and ceiling are decorated with allegorical paintings by the Catalan artist José Maria Sert depicting technical, social and medical advances and a vision of a future free of conflict. Visitors will also step into the **Salles des Assemblées** (Assembly Hall). With seating for 2,000, it is the largest of the UNO's 30-odd conference rooms.

The **Parc des Nations**, which surrounds the UNO, is planted with trees and decorated with sculptures, including a bronze astrolabe donated by the United States, and a tall, tapering monument that rears up into the sky. Clad in high heat-resistant titanium, it is a tribute to the conquest of space and was donated by the former USSR (*see illustration on p98*).

Bronze astrolabe in the Parc des Nations

# ⑨ Musée d'Art et d'Histoire

The huge collection of paintings, sculpture and artifacts on display at Geneva's museum of art and history covers a timespan ranging from prehistory to the end of the 20th century. The large archaeological section contains pieces from Egypt, Greece, Rome and other ancient cultures. The displays of applied arts feature furniture, stained glass and other fine objects. Most of the collection will be on display at alternative Geneva museums, including Maison Tavel and Musée Rath, during the museum's five-year renovation due to start in January 2016.

**★ Miraculous Draught of Fishes**
This painting is part of the altarpiece that Konrad Witz made for the Cathédrale St-Pierre *(see pp102–3)* in 1444. In the background is a view of Geneva.

**Hodler's Furniture**
Side chairs, armchairs, a table and a bookcase come from the set of oak furniture that Josef Hoffmann, of the Vienna Workshops, designed for the 19th-century Swiss painter Ferdinand Hodler *(see p58)*.

Ground floor

**★ Statuette of Nemtynakht**
This serene sculpture in hard yellow quartzite depicts a dignitary of the Middle Kingdom, dating from c.1750 BC.

Main entrance

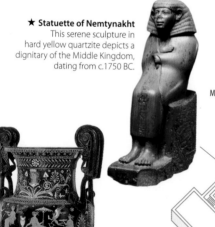

**Greek Vase**
Decorated by the Master of Bari, this beautiful vase from Taranto dates from c.350 BC. It is a fine example of Greek red-figure vase-painting.

Lower ground floor

First floor

**VISITORS' CHECKLIST**

**Practical Information**
2 Rue Charles-Galland. **Tel** 022 418
26 00. **Open** 11am–6pm Tue–Sun.
**Closed** from 2016. 🎨 temporary
exhibitions. 🅦 **mah-geneve.ch**

**Le Quai des Pâquis à Genève**
The French painter Camille
Corot was a regular visitor
to Geneva. He completed
this view of the lake in 1863.

**Ferme à Monfoucault**
Rural scenes such as
this one, painted in
1874, were frequently
chosen as subjects by
the French Impressionist
painter Camille Pissarro
(1830–1903).

Mezzanine

**Gallery Guide**

*The lower ground floor houses
the museum's collection of
antiquities. The ground floor
is devoted to temporary
exhibitions and the applied
arts, while the mezzanine
contains reconstructions of
palatial rooms. The first floor
contains the museum's galleries
of painting and sculpture.*

**Le Bain Turc**
Félix Vallotton (1865–1925), a Swiss artist who worked in
Paris, pays homage in this 1907 painting to Neo-Classical
painter Jean-Auguste-Dominique Ingres' masterpiece
*The Turkish Bath.*

**Key**

▢ Antiquities
▢ Applied arts
▢ Regional archaeology
▢ Reconstructed palace rooms
▢ Painting and sculpture gallery
▢ Temporary exhibitions

**★ Lower Castle Zizers**
Rooms from the 17th-century Lower
Castle Zizers, in Grisons, have been
painstakingly reconstructed and
furnished in elaborate period detail.

**For keys to symbols** *see back flap*

# ENTERTAINMENT IN GENEVA

Geneva enjoys a lively and wide-ranging cultural life. Sharing the Orchestre de la Suisse Romande with Lausanne, the city is a leading centre of classical music, and a world-class programme of concerts is staged here throughout the year. Opera and ballet, performed at several venues in the city centre, occupy an equally important place in Geneva's cultural calendar. Geneva also has an English-speaking theatre company and a renowned amateur operatic society. Film is another aspect of the city's culture, and on summer evenings open-air showings take place around the lake.

The Fêtes de Genève is the city's most popular festival. It takes place from late July to early August, when the lakeshore comes alive with concerts, colourful parades and spectacular firework displays. Other international events include the annual regatta on Lake Geneva.

Yachts at a regatta on Lake Geneva

## Information and Tickets

Geneva's daily newspaper *Le Temps* carries listings of all major entertainments in the city. Other sources of information are *Genève Agenda* and *Genève: Le Guide*, both published in French and English, and both available at the city's tourist office.

Tickets for most mainstream events can be purchased from the agencies **Ticket Corner** or **FNAC**. Tickets for plays and operas performed in English are obtainable from the **Theatre in English**. The larger department stores and supermarkets *(see p111)* such as Manor, Migros, Globus and Bon Génie also sell tickets for most of the mainstream events taking place in the city.

## Classical Music, Theatre and Dance

Geneva is one of Europe's leading centres of classical music. The prestigious Orchestre de la Suisse Romande, which is based in Geneva and Lausanne, gives regular concerts in the Victoria Hall. Another major venue for classical music is the **Grand-Théâtre de Genève**, where opera productions are staged, and where solo recitals and chamber concerts are given. The **Geneva Amateur Operatic Society** offers a programme of entertainments in English. These range from light opera and musicals to cabaret and pantomime. Opera, jazz and classical music, as well as modern dance, are also staged at the **Bâtiment des Forces-Motrices**, a former power station on the Rhône. Free concerts take place in several of Geneva's churches throughout the year, as well as in the city's parks during the summer months.

The theatrical scene in Geneva ranges from the classic to the avant-garde. While the **Comédie de Genève** concentrates on classical productions, the **Théâtre du Grütli** specializes in experimental theatre, producing contemporary Swiss drama as well as foreign plays. Modern drama is also staged at the **Théâtre de Carouge**.

The **Théâtre des Marionnettes de Genève** is a dynamic puppet theatre that puts on magical shows aimed at audiences ranging from young children to adults. Geneva also has a children's theatre, the **Théâtre Am Stram Gram**. Although its productions are in French,

A band performing at the Fêtes de Genève

Scene from *Romeo and Juliet* at a theatre in Geneva

English-speaking audiences can enjoy certain plays and other entertainments that are staged here. Most theatrical productions are in French, however, the **Geneva English Drama Society** stages plays in English. Each season features four productions and a series of play readings. The society also organizes workshops and other activities.

The **Fêtes de Genève**, which is held from late July to the beginning of August, is the city's principal and most popular festival. The festival's programme of indoor and outdoor events includes concerts of classical, techno and rock music, theatrical performances and children's shows, as well as street parades.

There are firework displays on the lakeshore too.

## Nightclubs

Geneva's nightclub scene encompasses more than 40 cabaret venues, bars, discos and clubs. Between them they offer the full range of musical styles, from 1960s music at **La Coupole Avenue** to house and techno music at other venues. Conveniently located in the Grand Kempinski Hotel, the **Jazzclub** has a sophisticated clientele and a beat that continues until dawn.

While many nightclubs are closed on Mondays, at weekends they stay open into the early hours of the morning, or until the last guest leaves.

## Cinema

As well as many small cinemas both in the city centre and in outlying districts, Geneva has a large central cinema complex, the **Pathé Balexert**. Some screenings are dubbed, but most films are shown in their original language, with French and German subtitles. In newspaper listings this is indicated by the letters (for *version originale*). French films are usually shown with English, and sometimes also with German, subtitles.

A particular pleasure for visitors to Geneva in summer are the open-air film screenings on the lakeshore. Taking place from late June to mid-August, the series is organized by **Cinélac**, and a different film is shown each night at three outdoor venues.

Fireworks around the lake at the Fêtes de Genève

## DIRECTORY

### Information & Tickets

**FNAC**
16 Rue de Rive.
**Tel** 022 816 12 30.

**Office du Tourisme**
18 Rue du Mont-Blanc.
**Tel** 022 909 70 00.
W genevatourism.ch

**Theatre in English**
22 Chemin des Batailles,
1214 Vernier.
**Tel** 022 341 51 92.

**Ticket Corner**
**Tel** 0900 800 800.
W ticketcorner.ch

### Classical Music, Theatre & Dance

**Bâtiment des Forces-Motrices**
2 Place des Volontaires.
**Tel** 022 322 12 20.

**Comédie de Genève**
6 Blvd des Philosophes.
**Tel** 022 320 50 01.

**Fêtes de Genève**
**Tel** 022 909 70 70

**Geneva Amateur Operatic Society**
W gaos.ch

**Geneva English Drama Society**
W geds.ch

**Grand-Théâtre de Genève**
11 Boulevard du Théâtre.
**Tel** 022 322 50 50.

**Théâtre Am Stram Gram**
56 Route de Frontenex.
**Tel** 022 735 79 24.

**Théâtre de Carouge**
39 Rue Ancienne,
Carouge. **Tel** 022 343 43 43.

**Théâtre du Grütli**
16 Rue du Général-Dufour.
**Tel** 022 328 98 68.

**Théâtre des Marionnettes de Genève**
3 Rue Rodo.
**Tel** 022 807 31 07.

**Victoria Hall**
14 Rue du Général-Dufour.
**Tel** 022 418 35 00.

### Nightclubs

**La Coupole Avenue**
116 Rue du Rhône.
**Tel** 022 787 50 10.

**Jazzclub**
19 Quai du Mont-Blanc.
**Tel** 022 908 90 88.

### Cinema

**Pathé Balexert**
27 Avenue Louis-Casaï.
W pathe.ch

**Cinélac**
W cine.ch

# SHOPPING IN GENEVA

Geneva has been described as a shopper's paradise. Catering for a wealthy clientele, the city's smartest shops glitter with trays of diamond-studded watches and opulent jewellery, and attract attention with seductive displays of clothes by international designers. A leading centre of the art market, the city also has many art galleries and antique shops.

Away from the city's smartest streets, however, are shops that offer more affordable goods, from watches at more modest prices to high-quality craft items and a variety of handmade souvenirs. Swiss specialities such as chocolate, cheese and the locally produced wines are also available. Beyond the city centre are colourful street markets selling everything from books to collectables.

A display of painted cow bells in a souvenir shop in Geneva

## Opening Hours

Most shops in Geneva are open from 8am to 6:30pm Monday to Friday, and from 8am to 4pm or 5pm on Saturday. Late opening for shops in the city centre is until 8pm on Thursdays. The only shops open on Sunday are those selling souvenirs, and supermarkets and general stores at petrol stations, at the airport and the train station.

## Department Stores

The **Migros**, Coop, **Globus** and **Manor** supermarket chains and department stores all have large branches in Geneva. **Bon Génie** specializes in designer clothing and high-class cosmetics. One of the city's largest shopping centres is Balexert. Another large shopping centre is La Praille, near the football stadium.

## Markets

Geneva's largest outdoor markets are held at **Plaine de Plainpalais**, southwest of the Old Town. A fruit and vegetable market takes place here on Tuesday and Friday mornings, and there are interesting flea markets all day Wednesday and Saturday, where you may be able to discover some real finds, such as old watches, furniture ranging from antique to modern, ornaments and clothes from all over the world. Lively markets are also held on Wednesday and Saturday mornings in Place du Marché, near Carouge, and in Boulevard Helvétique, in the city centre. **Place de la Fusterie** hosts a variety of markets – crafts, local produce and books – throughout the week.

## Watches and Jewellery

With its Geneva branch on Place du Molard, the **Gübelin** chain of shops offers a choice of clocks and watches by leading Swiss makers, and a range of gemstones, jewellery and pens. **Bucherer** and **Cartier**, both on Rue du Rhône, one of Geneva's smartest shopping streets, are two other upmarket watch and jewellery shops selling renowned brands.

Swiss watch

## Souvenirs

Geneva abounds in shops selling high-quality goods associated with Switzerland, from penknives and cuckoo clocks to fine linen, leather goods and a wealth of high-quality craft items, as well as a more affordable range of watches and jewellery. **Swiss Corner, Cadhor** and **Molard Souvenirs** are three of the best.

Bookstore and antique shop at 20 Grand' Rue, in the Old Town

Logo of Rolex, a leading Swiss watchmaker

## Art and Antiques

The greatest concentration of antique shops and art galleries in Geneva is along Grand'Rue, in the Old Town. While many galleries along this street are filled with expensive Old Master paintings, others specialize in more affordable types of art, such as modern paintings and graphics, and a variety of attractive prints.

The Carouge district, to the south of the Old Town, has many small specialist studios and craft shops where craftsmen can be seen at work.

## Books

A good range of books in English is stocked by **OffTheShelf**, on Boulevard Georges-Favon. **Payot**, on Rue Chantepoulet, is well-known for stocking the largest selection of English books in French-speaking Switzerland. **Les Recyclables** on Rue de Carouge is a secondhand bookshop with a café.

## Confectionery

The local chocolate manufacturer is Favarger. Its brand products may be bought in factory outlets, as well as in Mercury chain stores and the food halls of department stores. Several traditional manufacturers have their own factory outlets in various parts of the city. There are also many chocolate shops in Geneva's Old Town. Two of the best are the **Chocolaterie du Rhône** and the **Chocolaterie Stettler**, which sells such specialities as *pavés de Genève* (Genevese chocolate squares).

Chocolate rabbit

## Cheese and Wine

A great variety of Swiss cheeses *(see pp260–61)* can be purchased in many specialist shops all over the city. Among them are **Ursula Antonietti**, on Rue de Cornavin, and **Fromagerie Bruand**, on Boulevard Helvétique. The area around Geneva is a prime wine-growing region *(see pp262–63)*. Bottled wine of an excellent quality can be bought directly from winegrowers in several villages around the city. Many outlets allow customers to sample the wines before they buy.

Colourful flower stall in a street in Geneva

## DIRECTORY

### Department Stores

**Bon Génie**
34 Rue du Marché.
**Tel** 022 818 11 11.

**Globus Grand Passage**
48 Rue du Rhône.
**Tel** 058 578 50 50.

**Manor**
6 Rue Cornavin.
**Tel** 022 909 46 99.

**Migros Plainpalais-Centre**
64 Rue de Carouge.
**Tel** 022 807 09 60.

### Markets

**Plaine de Plainpalais**
(fruit, vegetables, souvenirs)

Tue & Fri, 8am–1pm.
(flea market) Wed &
Sat 8am–6pm.

**Place de la Fusterie**
(handicrafts) Thu 9am–8pm.
(books) Tue & Fri
8am–6:45pm.
(local produce) Wed & Sat
6:30am–6:45pm.

### Watches & Jewellery

**Bucherer**
45 Rue du Rhône.
**Tel** 022 319 62 66.

**Cartier**
35 Rue du Rhône.
**Tel** 022 818 54 54.

**Gübelin**
1 Place du Molard.
**Tel** 022 310 86 55.

### Souvenirs

**Cadhors**
Rue du Mont-Blanc 11.
**Tel** 022 732 28 25.

**Molard Souvenirs**
Rue de la Croix d'Or 1.
**Tel** 022 311 47 40.

**Swiss Corner**
Rue des Alpes 7.
**Tel** 022 731 06 84.

### Books

**OffTheShelf**
15 Blvd Georges-Favon.
**Tel** 022 311 10 90.
**w** offtheshelf.ch

**Payot**
5 Rue Chantepoulet.
**Tel** 022 731 89 50.

**Les Recyclables**
53 Rue de Carouge.
**Tel** 022 328 23 73.

### Confectionery

**Chocolaterie du Rhône**
3 Rue de la Confédération.
**Tel** 022 311 56 14.

**Chocolaterie Stettler**
10 Rue de Berne.
**Tel** 022 732 44 67.

### Cheese

**Fromagerie Bruand**
29 Boulevard Helvétique.
**Tel** 022 736 93 50.

**Ursula Antonietti**
1 Rue de Cornavin.
**Tel** 022 731 25 05.

# WESTERN SWITZERLAND

A predominantly French-speaking region, western Switzerland consists of three distinct geographical areas: the mountainous terrain of the Swiss Jura in the north, the western extremity of the Mittelland plateau in the east, and the Alpine region in the southeast. Western Switzerland's geographical hub is Lake Geneva (Lac Léman), on whose banks lie Geneva, Lausanne, Vevey and Montreux.

Western Switzerland is a region of lakes and rolling hills, great cities and atmospheric medieval towns, and small villages with beautiful ancient churches. It consists of the cantons of Geneva, Vaud, Jura, Fribourg and Neuchâtel. Western Switzerland is bordered by France, but the canton of Geneva is surrounded on three sides by French territory. Western Switzerland is known as Suisse Romande, or Romandie, and it has a strong French-Swiss cultural identity.

While Geneva's high profile in global events and its role as a centre of world banking give it an international character, Lausanne, with its great cathedral and its university, is a centre of culture and intellectual life. Fribourg, straddling the River Sarine, is a bilingual town, French being spoken on the west side of the river and German on the east. The purest French in Suisse Romande is supposed to be spoken in Neuchâtel.

It was in western Switzerland, particularly in the Jura, that the country's world-famous watchmaking industry was born and where it continues to flourish today. The region is also renowned for its wines, most especially from the vineyards that border Lake Geneva. Western Switzerland also has one of the country's most memorable sights, the beautiful Château de Chillon, set serenely beside the sparkling blue waters of Lake Geneva.

Vineyard overlooking the placid Lake Geneva

◄ The medieval Château de Chillon, on an islet on the eastern shore of Lake Geneva

# Exploring Western Switzerland

A region with a diverse landscape, western Switzerland has many atmospheric towns and internationally famous cities. The Jura mountains in the west have much to offer hikers and cross-country skiers, and the southeastern part of the region has many ski resorts. With Lake Geneva as its focal point, the centre of the region is a land of great lakes, with vineyards covering sunny hillsides. The cities of Geneva, Lausanne, Fribourg and Neuchâtel are bustling centres of industry and culture with a wealth of museums and historic buildings. By contrast, the sophisticated towns of Vevey and Montreux, situated on the shores of Lake Geneva, offer relaxation in an unequalled setting.

Escaliers du Marché, leading off Place de la Palud, in Lausanne

## Getting There

The main gateways to western Switzerland are Geneva's and Zürich's international airports. From Geneva, the A1 motorway gives access to the whole region. Western Switzerland is also served by a rail network. Trains depart both from Geneva's airport and from the city itself. While the main rail route runs from Geneva north to Neuchâtel and Biel/Bienne, fast trains also run along the shores of Lake Geneva to Fribourg and beyond, both northwards to Bern and southwards via Lausanne and Montreux to Valais. Most of the rail route is extremely scenic.

Rooftops in Murten/Morat, from the town walls

## Key

━━━ Motorway
━━━ Main road
┄┄┄ Minor road
━━━ Scenic route
┈┈┈ Main railway
─── Minor railway
▬▬▬ International border
▬▬▬ Canton border
△ Summit

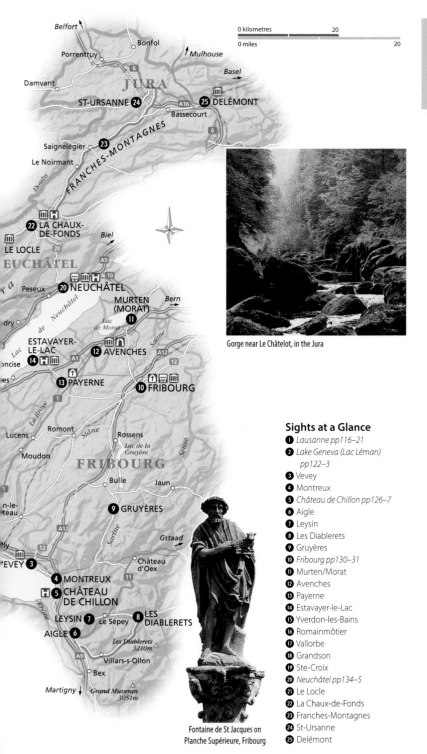

0 kilometres        20

0 miles        20

Belfort

Bonfol

Porrentruy

Mulhouse

Damvant

Basel

JURA

St-Ursanne **24**

**25** DELÉMONT

Bassecourt

Saignelégier **23**

FRANCHES-MONTAGNES

Le Noirmant

Doubs

**22** LA CHAUX-DE-FONDS

Biel

LE LOCLE

EUCHÂTEL

Peseux

**20** NEUCHÂTEL

Lac de Neuchâtel

Bern

ESTAVAYER-LE-LAC

**14**

MURTEN (MORAT) **11**

Lac de Morat

Saâne

**12** AVENCHES

**13** PAYERNE

**10** FRIBOURG

La Broye

Lucens

Romont

Slâne

Rossens

Lac de la Gruyère

Moudon

FRIBOURG

Sense

Bulle

Jaun

**9** GRUYÈRES

Sarine

Gstaad

Château d'Oex

EVEY **3**

**4** MONTREUX

**5** CHÂTEAU DE CHILLON

LEYSIN **7**

Le Sépey

**8** LES DIABLERETS

AIGLE **6**

Les Diablerets 3210m

Villars-s-Ollon

Bex

Martigny

Grand Muveran 3051m

Gorge near Le Châtelot, in the Jura

Fontaine de St Jacques on Planche Supérieure, Fribourg

## Sights at a Glance

**For keys to symbols** *see back flap*

# ❶ Lausanne

With an outstandingly beautiful setting on the north shore of Lake Geneva, Lausanne is one of Switzerland's finest cities. It was founded in the 1st century as a Roman lakeshore settlement, but for greater safety its inhabitants later moved to higher ground on the hills above the lake. This area is now Lausanne's Old Town (Vieille Ville). It became a bishopric in the late 6th century, and its Fondation Académie was founded in 1537. Lausanne is a centre of the cultural and economic life of French-speaking Switzerland. It is also the seat of the Federal Supreme Court and the location of the International Olympic Committee's headquarters.

Detail of the 18th-century Église St-Laurent

## Exploring Lausanne

A city of steep gradients, Lausanne's city centre is set on three hills that rise in tiers from the lakeshore. The hub of the city is Place St-François. To the north is the city's shopping district, centred on Rue de Bourg. Further north lies the Old Town (Vieille Ville), dominated by Lausanne's great cathedral *(see pp118–19)*. The district of Bel Air, to the west, overlooks a valley where the Flon stream once flowed. The Grand-Pont, a bridge across the valley, offers fine views of Bel-Air and of the Old Town, which rises behind it.

## 🏛 Tour Bel-Air and Salle Métropole

1 Place Bel-Air. **Tel** 021 345 00 29. Set on a steep slope, at the foot of the Old Town, the Tour Bel-Air was the first high-rise structure to be built in Switzerland. Standing 50 m (165 ft) high, the Tour Bel-Air contains offices, residential apartments and the Salle

Métropole. Completed in 1931, the building gives Lausanne's townscape a touch of metropolitan verve, while the theatre has become a cultural hub.

## 🏛 Église St-Laurent

Rue St-Laurent.
Less than a hundred paces from Bel-Air, amid the well-preserved houses of the Old Town, stands the Protestant Église St-Laurent. It was built in 1716–19, on the ruins of a 10th-century church. Its façade, designed by Rodolphe de Crousaz in the second half of the 18th century, is one of the few examples of Neo-Classical architecture in Lausanne.

## 🏛 Place de la Palud

The south side of this market square is dominated by Lausanne's town hall, a two-storey arcaded building fronted by the arms of the city. Built in the Renaissance style, it dates from the 17th century. On 10 April 1915, the official documents ratifying the establishment of the International Olympic Committee and the archives of the modern Olympic era were signed here.

Place de la Palud is a popular meeting area. A street market takes place here on Wednesdays and Saturdays, and once a month the square is filled with a crafts fair.

At the centre of the square is the 16th-century Fontaine de la Justice, with an allegorical

figure of Justice. The covered wooden stairs beyond the fountain are known as the Escaliers du Marché. They lead up to Rue Viret, from where further steps lead up to the cathedral.

The bare Gothic interior of the Église St-François

## 🏛 Place St-François

At the centre of this square stands the Église St-François, built in the 13th and 14th centuries as the church of the Franciscan monastery. The monastery was dissolved during the Reformation and the church stripped of its decoration. Although the façade was restored in the 1990s, the interior is disappointingly bland.

The streets leading off Place St-François are among the city's smartest. Rue du Bourg, which is lined with old houses, contains upmarket jewellers' shops and boutiques, as well as bars and jazz clubs.

## 🏛 Musée Historique

4 Place de la Cathédrale. **Tel** 021 315 41 01. **Open** 11am–6pm Tue–Thu, 11am–5pm Fri–Sun (Jul & Aug: also 11am–6pm Mon). 🛈

Figure on the Fountain of Justice

Lausanne's museum of history fills the restored rooms of the former bishop's palace, which dates from the 11th century. The museum's collections constitute a detailed account of the city's

history from prehistory to the present day. A particularly interesting exhibit is the model of Lausanne as it was in 1638.

### 🏛 Cathédrale Notre-Dame
*See pp118–19.*

### 🏛 Palais de Rumine
6 Place de la Riponne. Musée Cantonal des Beaux-Arts: **Tel** 021 316 34 45. **Open** 11am–6pm Tue & Wed, 11am–8pm Thu, 11am–5pm Fri–Sun. Musée Cantonal d'Archéologie et d'Histoire: **Tel** 021 316 34 30. **Open** 11am–6pm Tue–Thu, 11am–5pm Fri–Sun.

**Wall decoration, Palais de Rumine**

The imposing Neo-Renaissance Palais de Rumine, built in 1896–1906, housed Lausanne's university until the latter moved to new premises on the outskirts of the city. The building now contains the university library and five museums.

The Musée Cantonal des Beaux-Arts, on the ground floor, has a fine collection of Swiss paintings from the 18th to the 20th centuries.

Of particular interest here are 19th-century landscapes of the Vaud countryside and works by François Bocion and Giovanni Giacometti, father of the more famous Alberto Giacometti. The museum of archaeology and history, on the sixth floor, is devoted to finds made during local excavations. The exhibits range from the Bronze Age to the medieval period, and one of the finest is the gold bust of Marcus Aurelius, discovered at Avenches in 1939.

The other three museums are devoted to geology, numismatics and zoology.

### 🏛 Château St-Maire
Place du Château. **Closed** to visitors.
This massive brick and sandstone edifice was built in 1397–1427 as the palace of the bishops of Lausanne, who ruled the city. When they were overthrown, the château became the residence of new overlords, the bailiffs of Bern. The fight for the independence

of Lausanne and canton of Vaud was led by Jean Davel, who was beheaded in 1723 on the orders of the Bernese authorities. A monument to his memory stands in front of the château. The building is now the seat of the cantonal authorities of Vaud.

**Château St-Maire, fronted by a statue of Jean Davel**

## Lausanne City Centre

① Bel-Air Métropole
② Église St-Laurent
③ Place de la Palud
④ Place St-François
⑤ Musée Historique
⑥ Cathédrale Notre-Dame
⑦ Palais de Rumine
⑧ Château St-Maire

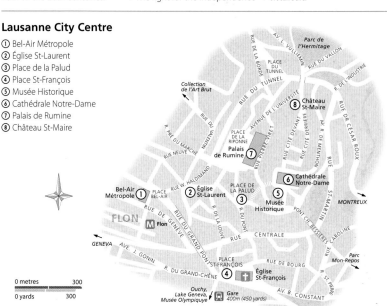

```
0 metres    300
0 yards     300
```

For keys to symbols *see back flap*

# Cathédrale Notre-Dame

Begun in the mid-12th century and completed in the 13th, the Cathédrale Notre-Dame in Lausanne is the finest Gothic building in Switzerland. It is built on the site of a Roman camp and overlies the foundations of Carolingian and Romanesque basilicas. With a central nave flanked by aisles, a transept over which rises a tower, an apse and an ambulatory, the cathedral's design and decoration show the influence of the French Gothic style. Consecrated by Pope Gregory X in 1275, Notre-Dame has been a Protestant cathedral since the Reformation. The top of the southwest tower commands a spectacular view of the city and Lake Geneva.

**Nave**
Alternating thick and slender columns line the nave. The thick columns support the central vaulting.

**Stalls**
Decorated with expressive figures of saints, the stalls in the Chapelle St-Maurice are masterpieces of late Gothic woodcarving.

**★ Chapelle St-Maurice**
Located under the unfinished north tower, the chapel is filled with exquisitely carved late Gothic stalls dating from the early 16th century.

① 

**Montfalcon Portal**
The entrance at the west end, known as the Montfalcon Portal, is decorated with replicas of Gothic carvings dating from 1515 to 1536.

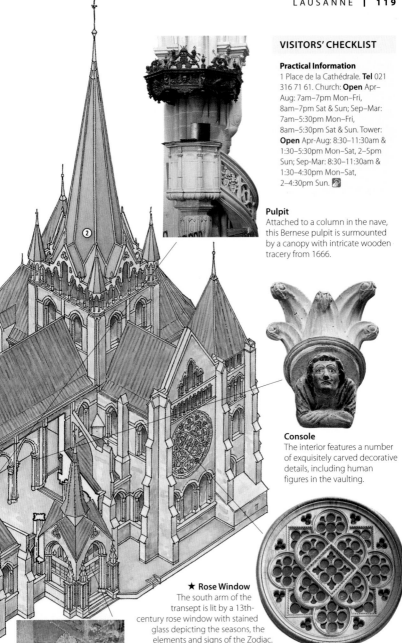

**Pulpit**
Attached to a column in the nave,
this Bernese pulpit is surmounted
by a canopy with intricate wooden
tracery from 1666.

**Console**
The interior features a number
of exquisitely carved decorative
details, including human
figures in the vaulting.

**★ Rose Window**
The south arm of the
transept is lit by a 13th-
century rose window with stained
glass depicting the seasons, the
elements and signs of the Zodiac.

**KEY**

① **North tower**, containing the
Chapelle St-Maurice

② **The tower** over the crossing
was completed in the 19th century.
The spire surmounting it is 75 m
(246 ft) high.

**Wall Paintings**
The vestibule is decorated
with late Gothic murals dating
from the early 16th century.

### Beyond the city centre

West of Place St-François is the offbeat district of Flon, which is filled with art galleries, restaurants and bars. North of the Old Town stretches the extensive Parc de l'Hermitage. To the south of the city centre lies the old fishing village of Ouchy, now a popular lakeside resort and the location of the Musée Olympique.

### ▥ Collection de l'Art Brut

11 Avenue des Bergières. **Tel** 021 315 25 70. 🚌 2 from Place St-François. **Open** Jul & Aug: 11am–6pm daily; Sep–Jun: 11am–6pm Tue–Sun. ♿ (free adm 1st Sat of the month). 🌐 artbrut.ch

Art Brut is the name that the French painter Jean Dubuffet (1901–85) gave to art created by people living on the fringe of society, including criminals, psychotics, patients at psychiatric hospitals or other institutions, and spiritualist mediums, who had no artistic training. The ideas for art came from their own imaginations, free from established cultural influences and the history of a fine arts tradition. The originality, freshness and often indecency of Art Brut inspired Dubuffet in his search for creative expression, and in 1945 he began to amass a private collection. In 1971 he presented it to the city of Lausanne, and the Collection de l'Art Brut opened in 1976.

Only about 1,000 pieces from the present holding of about 30,000 are on display at any one time. The exhibits are laid out on four floors in converted stables at the 18th-century Château de Beaulieu, northwest of the city centre. Ranging from paintings, drawings and painted fabrics to woodcarvings, sculptures and even an illustrated novel, these extraordinary works of art have a striking force and spontaneity. Alongside each exhibit is a short biography of the artist, giving the visitor some insight into the mental attitude and personal circumstances in which these works were created.

### ▥ Fondation de l'Hermitage

2 Route du Signal. **Tel** 021 320 50 01. 🚌 3 from the main train station or 🚌 16 from Place St-François. **Open** 10am–6pm Tue–Sun (10am–9pm Thu). ♿ 🌐 fondation-hermitage.ch

The imposing Neo-Gothic villa set in magnificent parkland north of Lausanne was built in 1842–50 by Charles-Juste Bugnion, a wealthy banker, and donated to the city by his descendants. Now known as the Fondation de l'Hermitage, it is a gallery with a permanent collection of nearly 800 French paintings. Of particular note are the Impressionist and Post-Impressionist paintings, as well as the works of 20th-century Vaudois artists. Every year the Fondation also stages two or three large-scale temporary exhibitions of the work of world-class artists.

The Parc de l'Hermitage, the extensive grounds in which the villa is set, is landscaped with exotic trees. At its northern extremity is the Signal de Sauvabelin, a hill which rises to a height of 647 m (2,120 ft) and offers views of Lausanne and Lake Geneva, with the Alps in the background. Beyond the hill are woods and the Lac de Sauvabelin, where there is a reserve for ibexes and other Alpine animals.

### ⬛ Parc Mon-Repos

Avenue Mon-Repos.
This landscaped park, laid out in the 19th century to the southeast of the city centre, is the most elegant of all Lausanne's gardens. It contains a Neo-Gothic tower, a Neo-Classical temple, a conservatory and a rockery with a cave and a waterfall. At the centre of the park stands an 18th-century villa, which at the time that it was built was surrounded by vineyards. The 18th-century French writer Voltaire lived in the villa during his stay in Lausanne.

**Statue in Parc Mon-Repos**

The villa also has associations with the Olympic Games. The Olympic spirit was resurrected by the French aristocrat Baron Pierre de Coubertin (1863–1937), who believed that sport plays an essential role in the development of citizens and nations. De Coubertin set up the International Olympic Committee (IOC) in Paris in 1894, with himself as president, and two years later the first modern Olympic Games were held in Athens. During World War I De Coubertin moved the IOC's head office to Switzerland. From 1922 until his death, the villa at Mon Repos was his residence and until the 1970s it was also the headquarters of the IOC, and the location of the first Olympics museum to be set up.

At the north end of Parc Mon-Repos stands the building of the Federal Tribunal, Switzerland's supreme court.

*Le Cinema* (c.1950) by Collectif d'Enfants at the Collection de l'Art Brut

Hôtel du Château d'Ouchy, one of many lakeside hotels in Ouchy, on the outskirts of Lausanne

## Ouchy

On Lake Geneva, 2 km (1 mile) south of central Lausanne, accessible by metro (M2 line).

Once a fishing village, Ouchy, on the outskirts of Lausanne, is now a popular lakeside resort. It has a beautiful setting on Lake Geneva, with views of the surrounding mountains, and a tree-lined promenade along the lakeshore. Cruises on the lake depart from here.

All that remains of the 12th-century castle that once defended the harbour is a tower, which now forms part of the Neo-Gothic Château d'Ouchy, built in the 1890s. The château is now a hotel and restaurant.

Several other late 19th- to early 20th-century hotels line the lakeshore. They include the Beau-Rivage Palace, a fine example of Art Nouveau architecture, and the Hôtel d'Angleterre, the house where Lord Byron stayed when he came to Lausanne and where he wrote *The Prisoner of Chillon (see pp126–7).*

### 🏛 Olympic Museum

1 Quai d'Ouchy. **Tel** 021 621 65 11. **Open** May–Oct: 9am–6pm daily; Nov–Apr: 10am–6pm Tue–Sun. 🅿 W **olympic.org/museum**

The Olympic Museum illustrates the history of the Olympic movement, from the athletes of Ancient Greece to the modern Olympic Games. With its facilities for school groups, the museum draws over 200,000 visitors a year. Multimedia presentations, archive film footage, interactive equipment, photographs and postage stamps show the development of individual sport disciplines and the achievements of Olympic champions, many of whom have donated their Olympic medals to the museum.

Figures of cyclists in the Olympic Park

The museum is set in parkland planted with Mediterranean trees and shrubs. A restaurant offers fine views of Lake Geneva and the surrounding mountains.

### 🏛 Musée Romain

24 Chemin du-Bois-de-Vaux. **Tel** 021 315 41 85. **Open** 11am–6pm Tue–Sun (Jul & Aug: 11am–6pm daily). 🅿 🄿 W **lausanne.ch/mrv**

About ten minutes' walk west of Ouchy are the remains of Lousonna and Vidy, two Roman towns that flourished from 15 BC to the 4th century AD. The ruins have been excavated, and the finds that were uncovered are on display in the Musée Romain nearby. The objects are laid out in the reconstruction of a Roman house. They include glassware and pottery, jewellery, coins and votive figures and some fine examples of classic Roman mosaics.

Entrance to the Olympic Museum in the Olympic Park

# ② Lake Geneva (Lac Léman)

Lying in an arc bordered by the Jura mountains to the west, the French Alps to the south and the Mittelland to the northeast, Lake Geneva, known as Lac Léman in French, is the largest lake in the Alps. While most of the southern shore is French territory, the greater part of the lake lies within Switzerland. Its shores are dotted with towns and villages, many of which are the departure points of boat trips on the lake. An important stop on the Grand Tour of Europe in the 19th century, Lake Geneva attracted and inspired many Romantic writers. With the mountains reflected in its still blue waters, it is one of Switzerland's most spellbinding sights.

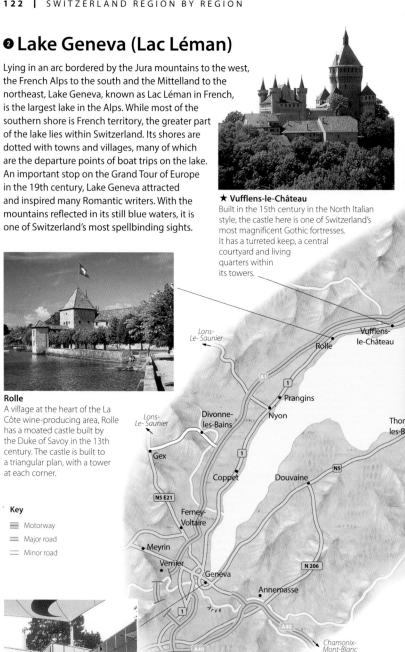

**★ Vufflens-le-Château**
Built in the 15th century in the North Italian style, the castle here is one of Switzerland's most magnificent Gothic fortresses. It has a turreted keep, a central courtyard and living quarters within its towers.

**Rolle**
A village at the heart of the La Côte wine-producing area, Rolle has a moated castle built by the Duke of Savoy in the 13th century. The castle is built to a triangular plan, with a tower at each corner.

**Key**

▬▬ Motorway

▬▬ Major road

▬▬ Minor road

**Geneva**
This is the largest city on the lakeshore. The headquarters of more than 250 international organizations, Geneva has a prominent place on the world stage.

0 kilometres    5

0 miles    5

### Cully

One of many scenic villages around Lake Geneva, Cully is a centre of the local wine trade. The sun-drenched hillsides above it are covered with vineyards.

### St-Saphorin

This romantic winemaking village has steep cobbled streets and a 7th-century church that was remodelled in the 16th century, in the flamboyant Gothic style.

### Montreux

Stretching along the lakeshore, Montreux is a cosmopolitan resort. Renowned for its music festivals, it is also an important cultural centre.

### ★ Vevey

This stately and traditional resort offers a choice of cultural events. It is renowned for the Fête des Vignerons, a grape-harvest festival held here every 25 years.

### Aigle

At the intersection of the Ormonts and Rhône valleys, Aigle is the capital of the Chablais winemaking region. Its 12th-century castle, which contains the Musée de la Vigne et du Vin, is surrounded by vineyards.

**For keys to symbols** see back flap

The lakeside resort of Vevey, with mountains in the background

## ❸ Vevey

**Road map:** B4. 🏔 16,000. 🚉 🚌
ℹ️ Montreux, 5 Rue du Théâtre; 0848
86 84 84. 🅦 **montreuxriviera.com**
🎭 Street Artists Festival (Aug).

With Montreux, Vevey is one of
the two best-known holiday
resorts of the Swiss Riviera, the
stretch of land bordering the
northwestern shores of Lake
Geneva between Lausanne and
Villeneuve. The region began to
develop as a centre of tourism
in the 19th century. Known for
its sophisticated ambience,
Vevey soon attracted an
international clientele, which
included the Austrian painter
and playwright Oskar
Kokoschka, the writer Ernest
Hemingway and the comedian
Charlie Chaplin, who spent
the last 25 years of his life in
Vevey and who was buried
here in 1977.

Known in Roman times
as Viviscus, Vevey was once
Lake Geneva's main port. It
continued to flourish through
the Middle Ages and by the
19th century was the first
industrial town in the canton of
Vaud. It was here, in 1867, that
Henri Nestlé established the
powdered milk factory that
revolutionized baby foods.
Now one of the world's largest
food and beverage companies,
Nestlé still has its international
headquarters in Vevey.

The most attractive part of
Vevey is its Grande Place (also
known as Place du Marché).
On Tuesday and Saturday
mornings this huge square
is filled with a market, and
in summer regional growers
offer wine tastings. A folk arts

market is also held here on
Saturday mornings in July and
August. La Grenette (1808), a
handsome building on the
north side of the square, was
once the town's granary.

The narrow alleys of
Vevey's historic quarter
continue to the east of
Grande Place. On Quai
Perdonnet stands a
statue of Charlot, the
French name by which
Charlie Chaplin is known
here. Le Manoir-de-Ban,
Chaplin's former home, is
due to open to the public
as the **Charlie Chaplin
Museum** in spring
2016. To the east of the
train station is the
**Musée Jenisch**.
The museum
houses paintings
and sculpture
by 19th- and
20th-century Swiss
artists, as well as the Fondation
Oskar Kokoschka, which
contains 800 Expressionist
paintings by this Austrian artist.
The Musée Jenisch also houses
an outstanding collection of
prints, which includes not only
the largest assemblage of
lithographs of Rembrandt in
Europe but also works by such
major artists as Albrecht Dürer
and Jean-Baptiste Corot.

🏛 **Charlie Chaplin Museum**
2 Route de Fenil, Le Manoir-de-Ban.
**Open** check the website for the
latest information. 🅦 **chaplin
museum.com**

🏛 **Musée Jenisch**
2 Avenue de la Gare. **Tel** 021 925 35
20. **Open** 10am–6pm Tue–Sun (to
9pm Thu). 🎭 🅦 **museejenisch.ch**

## ❹ Montreux

**Road map:** B4. 🏔 20,000. 🚉 🚌
ℹ️ 5 Rue du Théâtre; 0848 86 84 84.
🅦 **montreuxriviera.com** 🎭
Narcissus Festival (spring); Montreux
Jazz Festival (Jul).

Often described as the jewel
of the Swiss Riviera, Montreux
is an upmarket resort that is
renowned for its annual jazz
festival. The town began to
develop as an international
tourist resort in about 1815,
and its golden age lasted until
the outbreak of World War I in
1914. In the 19th century the
charm of the area captivated
artists, writers and musicians,
including Lord Byron and Mary
Shelley, Leo Tolstoy and Hans
Christian Andersen.

Montreux has many *belle
époque* hotels. The most
famous of them is the
Montreux Palace on
Grand'Rue, west of the
town centre. Opposite
this hotel is the
Centre des Congrès, a
modern conference
centre. It contains the
Auditorium Stravinsky,
a concert hall built in
1990 and dedicated to
Igor Stravinsky (1882–
1971), who com-
posed *The Rite
of Spring* in
Montreux.
The metal-
framed market hall

Statue of Freddie Mercury in
Montreux

in Place du Marché was built in
1890 with funds donated by
Henri Nestlé, founder of the
multinational food company. At
the end of the square, on the
lakeshore, is a statue of Freddie
Mercury, vocalist in the band
Queen. Montreux was his
second home and it was here
that he recorded his last songs.

East of the statue, on the
lakeshore promenade, is a
casino rebuilt after a fire that
has entered into rock legend.
On 4 December 1971, during a
concert given by Frank Zappa
and the Mothers of Invention, a
rocket-flare was fired into the
ceiling and the building was
suddenly engulfed by flames. As
clouds of smoke soared above
the waters of the lake, Ian Gillan,

Château d'Aigle, once a bailiff's castle and now the home of a museum of wine and winemaking

of the band Deep Purple, who was watching from his hotel room, was inspired by the sight to write "Smoke on the Water".

## ❺ Château de Chillon

*See pp126–7.*

## ❻ Aigle

**Road map:** B4. 🚹 6,500. 🚉 🚌
ℹ️ 5 Rue Colomb; 024 466 30 00.
🌐 aigle-tourisme.ch

Aigle is the capital of the Chablais, a wine-growing region and a major cycling centre, that lies southeast of Lake Geneva and produces some of

Wooden chalets along a street in the ski resort of Leysin

Switzerland's best wines *(see pp262–63)*. Set among vineyards covering the foothills of the Alpes Vaudoises, the town is dominated by a turreted castle, the Château d'Aigle. Built in the 12th century by the Savoyards, it was severely damaged in the 15th century but was later rebuilt to serve as the residence of the region's Bernese bailiffs.

The castle now houses the **Musée de la Vigne et du Vin**, whose exhibits illustrate the age-old methods of vine cultivation and wine-making. The 16th-century Maison de la Dîme opposite the castle contains the **Musée International de l'Etiquette**, which documents the history of wine labels over 200 years.

**🏛️ Musée de la Vigne et du Vin and Musée International de l'Étiquette**
Château d'Aigle, Place du Château 1.
**Tel** 024 466 21 30. **Open** Apr–Oct:
11am–6pm Tue–Sun; Jul–Aug:
11am–6pm daily. 🎫
🌐 museeduvin.ch

## ❼ Leysin

**Road map:** B4. 🚹 2,700. 🚉
🚌 ℹ️ Place Large; 024 493 33 00.
🌐 leysin.ch

The small village of Leysin, now a popular winter and summer resort, occupies a sun-drenched

mountain terrace with views across to the Dents du Midi and down onto the Rhône valley. Lying at an altitude of 1,260 m (4,135 ft), Leysin enjoys an unusually dry and sunny climate. Once a centre for the treatment of tuberculosis, the village later evolved into a ski resort. Cable cars carry visitors up to the Tour de Mayen (2,326 m/7,631 ft) and to Berneuse (2,037 m/6,683 ft), where there is a revolving restaurant that enables diners to admire a panoramic view of the Alps.

## ❽ Les Diablerets

**Road map** B4. 🚹 1,300. 🚉 🚌
ℹ️ Rue de la Gare; 024 492 00 10.
🌐 diablerets.ch

Set among Alpine meadows in the Ormonts valley, the small ski resort of Les Diablerets lies at an altitude of 1,150 m (3,775 ft) in the Alpes Vaudoises. Above it rise the peaks of Les Diablerets, 3,210 m (10,531 ft) high and among which lies the glacier of the same name.

There is no downhill skiing in summer, but the glacier is open and offers cross-country skiing, dog sleigh rides and the world's highest bobsleigh on rails – the Alpine Coaster. The Monster Snowpark, for freestyle skiers and boarders, opens as early as October.

# ❺ Château de Chillon

This enchanting medieval castle, set on a rocky spur on the eastern shore of Lake Geneva, is one of Switzerland's most evocative sights. Built for the Dukes of Savoy, its origins probably go back to the 11th century but its present appearance dates from the 13th century. In 1536, the castle was captured by the Bernese, and from then until 1798 it was the seat of the region's Bernese bailiffs. The centre of court life, the castle was also used as a prison. Its most famous captive was François de Bonivard, imprisoned there from 1530 to 1536 for political incitement.

**Defences**
Surrounded by thick walls, the castle is also defended by three semicircular turrets.

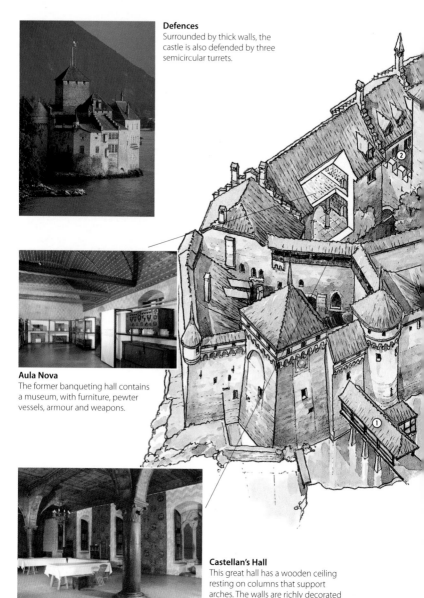

**Aula Nova**
The former banqueting hall contains a museum, with furniture, pewter vessels, armour and weapons.

**Castellan's Hall**
This great hall has a wooden ceiling resting on columns that support arches. The walls are richly decorated with paintings.

**★ Grand Ducal Hall**
This large room, also known as the Aula Magna, has chequered walls and its original 15th-century wooden ceiling, which is supported by black marble columns.

## VISITORS' CHECKLIST

### Practical Information
**Road map:** B4. Ave de Chillon 21.
**Tel** 021 966 89 10.
**Open** Mar: 9:30am–5pm daily; Apr–Sep: 9am–6pm daily; Oct: 9:30am–5pm; Nov–Feb: 10am–4pm daily.
🖥 **w** chillon.ch

### Transport

**Ducal Chamber**
This chamber, also known as the Camera Domini, has a wooden beamed ceiling and contains Gothic furniture.

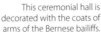

**Heraldic Hall**
This ceremonial hall is decorated with the coats of arms of the Bernese bailiffs.

## KEY

① **The covered bridge** leading to the gatehouse was originally a drawbridge.

② **A guest room**, the Camera Paramenti, and another bedchamber are located here.

③ **Bergfrieg**, the tower that was the castle's final defence, is one of its oldest elements.

④ **The chapel**, dedicated to St George, is in the early Gothic style, with a rib-vaulted ceiling. The walls and ceiling are covered with frescoes.

**★ Bonivard's Prison**
The castle's vaulted underground chambers were once used as a prison. François de Bonivard, who spent six years in captivity here, was immortalized by Lord Byron in *The Prisoner of Chillon*, a poem that he wrote in Ouchy in 1816.

## Gruyères

**Road map:** B4. 🏔 1,200. 🚉 to
Pringy. 🚌 ℹ️ 26 Place des Alpes,
Bulle; 0848 424 424. 🌐 **la-gruyere.ch**

Visible from afar against the
backdrop of Alpine scenery,
the well-preserved medieval
village of Gruyères is a popular
destination for visitors, and is
often crowded during the
summer. As its only street is
restricted to pedestrians,
vehicles must be left in the
parking areas below.

The village has houses dating
from the 15th to the 17th
centuries and is crowned
by a castle, the **Château de
Gruyères**. Built in the 11th
century, the castle was
continuously inhabited by the
counts of Gruyères until the
mid-16th century, when the
bankrupted 19th count fled and
his lands were divided between
the lords of Bern and Fribourg.

In 1848, the castle was acquired
by the Bovys, a wealthy
Genevese family who carried out
extensive and much-needed
restoration. In 1939 the castle
passed into the ownership of the
cantonal authorities of Fribourg.
It now contains a museum.
Displayed in rooms with
frescoes and grand fireplaces, the
exhibits include 16th-century
Flemish tapestries and booty taken
after the Battle of Murten (1476).
Delicate landscapes by the French
Impressionist painter Jean-Baptiste
Corot (1796–1875), who stayed
at the castle, are also on view.

At **La Maison du Gruyère**, a
working dairy in Pringy, at the
foot of the village, visitors can
watch the famous local cheese

being made. The dairy also has
a restaurant and a shop selling
local produce.

🏛 **Château de Gruyeres**
8 Rue du Château. **Tel** 026 921 21 02.
**Open** Apr–Oct: 9am–6pm daily;
Nov–Mar: 10am–4:30pm daily. 📷
🌐 **chateau-gruyeres.ch**

🏛 **La Maison du Gruyere**
3 Place de la Gare, Pringy. **Tel** 026 921
84 00. **Open** Jun–Sep: 9am–7pm
daily; Oct–May: 9am–6pm daily.
🌐 **lamaisondugruyere.ch**

## Fribourg

*See pp130–31.*

## Murten/Morat

**Road map** B3. 🏔 5,000. 🚉 🚌
ℹ️ Französische Kirchgasse 6; 026
670 51 12. 🌐 **murtentourismus.ch**

The resort town of Murten
(Morat in French) lies on the
eastern shore of the Murtensee
(Lac de Morat). It has strong
historical associations. It was
at Murten, on 22 June 1476,
that the forces of the Swiss
Confederation crushed the
army of Charles the Bold, Duke
of Burgundy, killing 12,000 of his
soldiers, while losing only 410 of
their own. According to legend,
a messenger ran 17 km (10 miles)
from Murten to Fribourg with
news of the victory, dropping
dead with exhaustion on his
arrival. His sacrifice is
commemorated by an annual
run between Murten and
Fribourg that takes place on
the first Sunday in October.

The town was founded by the
Zähringer dynasty in the 12th

View from Murten's fortified walls

century, and is still encircled by
walls dating from the 12th to
the 15th centuries. Hauptgasse,
the main street through the old
town, is lined with 16th-century
arcaded houses with
overhanging eaves. The rampart
walk, reached from several
points along Deutsche
Kirchgasse, offers views of the
Murtensee, the castle and the
old town's brown-tiled houses.
At the western end of the town
is a 13th-century castle, with a
courtyard that provides a fine
view over the lake. At the
eastern end stands Berntor (or
Porte de Berne), a Baroque
gatehouse with a clock dating
from 1712. The **Musée
Historique**, in a disused mill
on the lakeshore, has prehistoric finds from local
excavations and items relating
to the Burgundian Wars.

🏛 **Musée Historique**
Ryf 4, Murten. **Tel** 026 670 31 00.
**Open** Apr–Oct: 2–5pm Tue–Sat,
10am–5pm Sun. 📷

## Avenches

**Road map:** B3. 🏔 2,000. 🚌 ℹ️ 3
Place de l'Église; 026 676 99 22.
🌐 **avenches.ch** 🎭 Opera Festival
(Jul); Rock Oz'Arènes (Aug); Musical
Parade (military bands; Sep).

Originally the capital of the
Helveti, the Celtic tribe that
once ruled western Switzerland,
Avenches was conquered by
the Romans in the 1st century
BC. Named Aventicum, it
became the capital of the

The Château de Gruyères, seat of the counts of Gruyères for 500 years

Roman province of Helvetia. At its peak in the 2nd century AD, Aventicum was larger than the present town of Avenches. Encircled by 6 km (4 miles) of walls set with watchtowers, it supported a population of 20,000. By 260, however, much of it had been razed by the Alemani, a Germanic tribe, and by 450 it had lost its importance.

Vestiges of the Roman city can still be seen to the east of the medieval town centre. The most complete of these remains is the amphitheatre, with seating for 6,000. Other features include the Tornallaz, a tower that is the only surviving part of the old city walls, the forum, the baths and a 12 m (40 ft) Corinthian column known as the Tour du Cigognier.

The **Musée Romain**, in a medieval square tower within the amphitheatre, contains an impressive display of Roman artifacts discovered during excavations at Aventicum. The exhibits range from items of daily life, such as pottery, tools and coins, to bronze and marble statues of Roman deities, mosaics and wall paintings, and a replica of a gold bust of Marcus Aurelius.

**🏛 Musée Romain**

Tour de l'Amphitheatre. **Tel** 026 557 33 15. **Open** Apr–Sep: 10am–5pm Tue–Sun; Oct: 2–5pm Tue–Sun; Nov–Jan: 2–5pm Wed–Sun; Feb–Mar: 2–5pm Tue–Sun. 🖼

Nave of the Romanesque abbey church in Payerne

**⓭ Payerne**

**Road map:** B3. 🔼 7,000. 🚌 ℹ 10 Place du Marché; 026 660 61 61. 🌐 **payerne.ch**

The small market town of Payerne, in the canton of Vaud, is distinguished by its remarkable church, one of the most beautiful Romanesque buildings in Switzerland.

The **Église Abbatiale** was built in the 11th century as the abbey church of a Benedictine monastery, of which little remains. Stripped of its decoration during the Reformation, the church's interior is bare, but this only serves to accentuate its

Knocker on the abbey church in Payerne

impressive grandeur and the contrasting colours of its soaring limestone and sandstone columns. The portico features 12th-century frescoes and one of the chapels in the apse has 15th-century Gothic paintings. There are monthly organ recitals.

**⛪ Église Abbatiale**

**Tel** 026 662 67 04. **Open** May–Sep: 10am–noon & 2–6pm Tue–Sun; Oct–Apr: 10am–noon & 2–5pm Tue–Sun. 🖼

**⓮ Estavayer-le-Lac**

**Road map:** B3. 🔼 4,000. 🚌 ℹ 16 Rue de l'Hôtel de Ville; 026 663 12 37. 🌐 **estavayer-payerne.ch**

Surrounded on three sides by the canton of Vaud, this small town on the southern shore of Lake Neuchâtel lies within an enclave of the canton of Fribourg. A popular yachting centre, Estavayer-le-Lac is also a pleasant medieval town with arcaded streets. Its focal point is the Château de Cheneaux, a fine Gothic castle that is now the seat of local government.

The **Musée des Grenouilles**, housed in a 15th-century mansion, contains an eclectic assemblage of exhibits, including kitchen implements. It also boasts an unusual curiosity, namely a collection of 108 stuffed frogs and other creatures arranged in poses that parody the social life of the mid-19th century. The scenes were created by François Perrier, an eccentric resident of Estavayer who served in the Vatican's Swiss Guard and who produced this bizarre display in the 1860s.

**🏛 Musée des Grenouilles**

Rue du Musée 13. **Tel** 026 664 80 65. **Open** Mar–June: 10am–noon & 2–5pm Tue–Sun; Jul & Aug: 10am–noon & 2–5pm daily; Sep & Oct: 10am–noon & 2–5pm Tue–Sun; Nov–Feb: 2–5pm Sat & Sun. 🖼

The Roman amphitheatre in Avenches

# ⑩ Street-by-Street: Fribourg

With steep cobbled streets, immaculately preserved Gothic houses and numerous fountains, Fribourg (Freiburg in German) is one of Switzerland's most attractive towns. Set on a rocky peninsula within a bend of the River Sarine (Saane in German), it was founded in 1157 by Berthold IV of Zähringen, and joined the Swiss Confederation in 1481. Despite the Reformation, Fribourg remained Catholic, and a Catholic university was founded here in 1889.

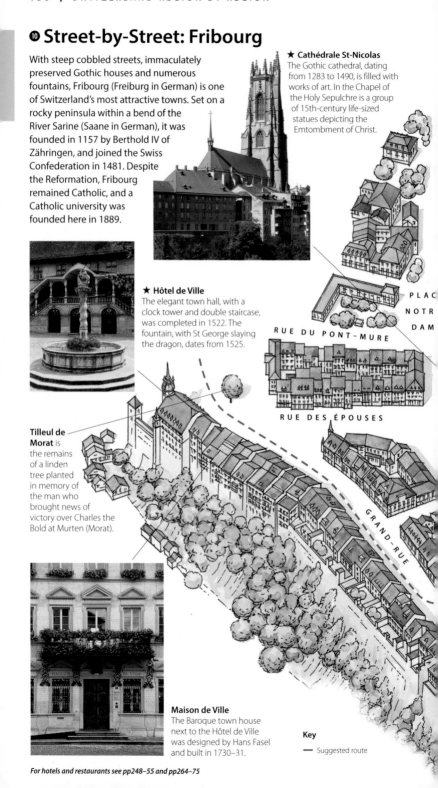

**★ Cathédrale St-Nicolas**
The Gothic cathedral, dating from 1283 to 1490, is filled with works of art. In the Chapel of the Holy Sepulchre is a group of 15th-century life-sized statues depicting the Emtombment of Christ.

**★ Hôtel de Ville**
The elegant town hall, with a clock tower and double staircase, was completed in 1522. The fountain, with St George slaying the dragon, dates from 1525.

PLAC
NOTR
DAM

RUE DU PONT–MURE

RUE DES ÉPOUSES

GRAND–RUE

**Tilleul de Morat** is the remains of a linden tree planted in memory of the man who brought news of victory over Charles the Bold at Murten (Morat).

**Maison de Ville**
The Baroque town house next to the Hôtel de Ville was designed by Hans Fasel and built in 1730–31.

**Key**
— Suggested route

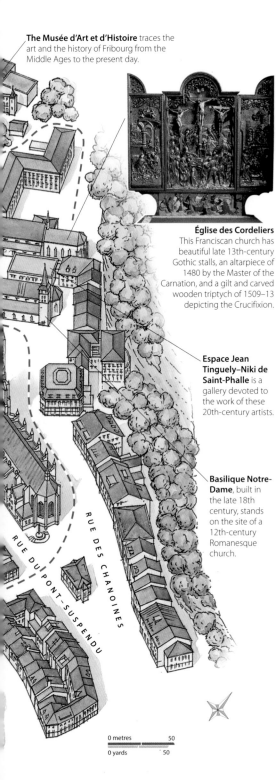

**The Musée d'Art et d'Histoire** traces the art and the history of Fribourg from the Middle Ages to the present day.

**Église des Cordeliers**
This Franciscan church has beautiful late 13th-century Gothic stalls, an altarpiece of 1480 by the Master of the Carnation, and a gilt and carved wooden triptych of 1509–13 depicting the Crucifixion.

**Espace Jean Tinguely–Niki de Saint-Phalle** is a gallery devoted to the work of these 20th-century artists.

**Basilique Notre-Dame**, built in the late 18th century, stands on the site of a 12th-century Romanesque church.

RUE DES CHANOINES

RUE DU PONT-SUSPENDU

0 metres    50
0 yards      50

**VISITORS' CHECKLIST**

**Road map:** B3. 36,500. 1 Place Jean-Tinguely; 026 350 11 11. fribourgtourism.ch Carnival (late Feb); International Folklore Festival (mid-Aug); Celebration of St Nicholas (Dec).

### Exploring Fribourg

While Fribourg's major sights are clustered around the cathedral, there is much else of interest in this ancient district of the town.

On Rue de Morat, north of the cathedral, is the **Éspace Jean Tinguely–Niki de Saint-Phalle**. This vast gallery contains kinetic sculptures by Jean Tinguely, who was born in Fribourg, and installations by his wife, Niki de Saint-Phalle. South of the cathedral, streets lead down to Place du Petit St-Jean, on the peninsula. **Rue d'Or**, just north of the square, is lined with Gothic houses. The peninsula is connected to the south bank of the river by the **Pont de Berne**. This wooden bridge leads to Place des Forgerons, where there is a Renaissance fountain and vestiges of fortifications.

Around Planche Supérieure, a square to the east of the peninsula, are the Église St-Jean and a museum of archaeology. From here, the Pont de St-Jean leads across the river to Neuveville, a low-lying area above which stands the town hall.

Pont de Berne, a wooden bridge across the Sarine in Fribourg

### 🏛 Gutenberg Museum
Place de Notre Dame 16. **Tel** 026 347 38 28. **Open** 11am–6pm Wed, Fri & Sat, 11am–8pm Thu, 10am–5pm Sun. gutenbergmuseum.ch

This museum shows the history of printing and communication through language, images and text. It is housed in a restored granary dating from 1527.

The 13th-century Château d'Yverdon, focal point of Yverdon-les-Bains

## ⑮ Yverdon-les-Bains

**Road map:** B3. 🗺 22,000. 🚌 💬 ℹ
1 Avenue de la Gare; 024 423 61 01.
ⓦ **yverdonlesbainsregion.ch**

Situated at the southwestern extremity of Lake Neuchâtel, Yverdon-les-Bains is Vaud's second town after Lausanne. The Celtic settlement that was originally established here later became a Gallo-Roman camp, Eburodunum, and the Romans built thermal baths here so as to use the hot sulphurous springs. Yverdon's town centre overlies the Roman settlement. The focal point is the **Château d'Yverdon**, a massive castle built by Peter II of Savoy in the 13th century.

Part of the castle now houses a museum of local history, with a collection of Gallo-Roman finds and other exhibits. A section of the museum is devoted to the life and work of Johann Heinrich Pestalozzi (1746–1827), the Swiss educational reformer who set up a school for deprived children in the castle in 1805. Influenced by the writings of Jean-Jacques Rousseau, his revolutionary teaching methods were based on a flexible school curriculum suited to the character of each child.

Place Pestalozzi, opposite the castle, is dominated by the Hôtel de Ville, the town hall built in 1768–73 on the site of a former market hall. The collegiate church on the west side of the square dates from 1757. The arched pediment of its Baroque façade features an allegory of Faith. Of particular interest to fans of science fiction is the **Maison d'Ailleurs** (House of Elsewhere). This museum presents temporary exhibits related to science fiction, utopian worlds and fantasy. The library of 60,000 volumes is open only to researchers.

Yverdon's thermal baths lie on Avenue des Bains, about 1 km (half a mile) southeast of the town centre. The **Centre Thermal** is one of Switzerland's largest and most modern spa centres. With indoor and outdoor pools, saunas and physiotherapy, the centre is used by some 1,300 people every day. Rich in minerals, the water here is particularly effective in curing respiratory ailments and rheumatism.

**🏰 Château d'Yverdon**
**Open** Jun–Sep:11am–5pm Tue–Sun;
Oct–May: 2–5pm Tue–Sun. 🐾

**🏛 Maison d'Ailleurs**
14 Place Pestalozzi. **Tel** 024 425 64 38.
**Open** 2–6pm Tue–Fri, 11am–6pm Sat
& Sun. 🐾 ⓦ **ailleurs.ch**

**♨ Centre Thermal**
22 Avenue les Bains. **Tel** 024 423 02
32. **Open** 8am–10pm Mon–Sat,
8am–8pm Sun & public holidays.
ⓦ **cty.ch**

### Environs
Beyond Clendy, the northern suburb of Yverdon-les-Bains, is a Neolithic stone circle. It stands near the shore of Lake Neuchâtel and is one of several similar ancient monuments around the lake.

## ⑯ Romainmôtier

**Road map:** A4. 🗺 400. 🚌 💬 La
Porterie. ℹ 024 453 38 28.
ⓦ **romainmotier-tourisme.ch**

The small village of Romainmôtier, set in beautiful wooded hills, is worth a detour for its remarkable abbey church. One of Switzerland's most beautiful Romanesque religious buildings, the **Église Abbatiale de Romainmôtier** was built between the late 10th and early 11th centuries by monks from the Abbaye de Cluny, in France. The interior contains fine 13th- and 14th-century frescoes and a medieval statue of the Virgin. Although the 15th-century monastery was dissolved in 1536, in the wake of the Reformation, the abbey church and part of the cloister have survived.

**⛪ Église Abbatiale de Romainmôtier**
**Tel** 024 453 14 65. **Open**
7am–8pm daily.

The nave of the Romanesque Église Abbatiale de Romainmôtier

## ⑰ Vallorbe

**Road map:** A3. 🗺 3,000. 🚌 💬 ℹ
11 Rue des Grandes-Forges; 021 843
25 83. ⓦ **vallorbe-tourisme.ch**

This small industrial town lies near the Franco-Swiss border. From the Middle Ages up to recent times, the town was an iron-smelting centre. It was also at Vallorbe that the tunnel beneath the Jura was built, thus creating the Paris–Istanbul rail route.

World War II tank at the Fort de Pré-Giroud, near Vallorbe

This is reflected in the **Musée du Fer et du Chemin de Fer** (Iron and Railway Museum), which traces the history of the Swiss iron industry, with a section that is devoted to the Swiss railways.

About 3 km (2 miles) southwest of Vallorbe are the **Grottes de Vallorbe**. These are caves with stalactites and stalagmites. The caves form a tunnel over the River Orbe, which surges through a gorge. A short distance west of Vallorbe is the **Fort de Pré-Giroud**, which was built as a surveillance post on the eve of World War II to observe the French border. Disguised as a chalet, it is a large underground bunker with space for over 100 people.

🏛 **Musée du Fer et du Chemin de Fer**
11 Rue des Grandes-Forges. **Tel** 021 843 25 83. **Open** Apr–Oct: 2–6pm Mon, 10am–6pm Tue–Sun; Nov–Mar: 2–6pm daily. 🚫 🅿

🏛 **Grottes de Vallorbe**
**Tel** 021 843 22 74. **Open** Apr, May, Sep & Oct: 9:30am–4:30pm daily; Jun–Aug: 9:30am–5:30pm daily. 🅿

## ⓲ Grandson

**Road map:** B3. 🅰 2,000. 🚌 🚏 ℹ Maison de Terroirs, Rue Haute 13, 024 445 60 60. 🅦 grandson-tourisme.ch

Dominated by its great medieval castle, the town of Grandson is associated with a momentous event in the history of the Swiss Confederation. This was the defeat of Charles the Bold, Duke of Burgundy, at the Battle of Grandson on 2 March 1476.

In February 1476, the duke's army laid siege to Grandson and its castle, eventually securing the surrender of the garrison, which was put to death. However, after raising an army of 18,000, the Confederates marched on Grandson to wreak revenge on the duke and his army. Fleeing in panic, the Burgundians abandoned their arms, horses and tents, as well as the ducal treasury. The booty is now displayed in the Historisches Museum in Bern (*see p65*).

Built between the 11th and 14th centuries, the **Château de Grandson** rises proudly from the shore of Lake Neuchâtel. It contains a model of the battlefield and a diorama illustrating the town's history from the Middle Ages to the present day. In the basement is an automobile museum with exhibits including a white Rolls Royce that belonged to Greta Garbo and Winston Churchill's Austin Cambridge car.

🏛 **Château de Grandson**
Place du Château. **Tel** 024 445 29 26. **Open** Apr–Oct: 8:15am–6pm daily; Nov–Mar: 8:15am–5pm daily. 🅿

Capital in the Église St-Jean-Baptiste in Grandson

## ⓳ Ste-Croix

**Road map:** B3. 🅰 4,500. 🚌 🚏 ℹ 10 Rue Neuve; 024 445 41 42. 🅦 sainte-croix-les-rasses-tourisme.ch

Appropriately known as the Balcony of the Jura, the town of Ste-Croix lies at an altitude of 1,092 m (3,584 ft) and commands a wide view of the Alps, the Swiss Upland and the Jura mountains.

Since the early 19th century Ste-Croix has been the world capital of musical-box manufacture. Two local museums are devoted to this art. In the course of a guided tour of the **Musée du CIMA** (Centre International de la Méchanique d'Art), the guide sets in motion an assortment of musical boxes with performing acrobats, drummers and accordionists.

🏛 **Musée du CIMA**
2 Rue de l'Industrie. **Tel** 024 454 44 77. **Open** for guided tours only; call for times. 🚫 (free last Sun of month). 🅿 🅦 musees.ch

### Environs
The **Musée Baud**, in the village of L'Auberson, 6 km (4 miles) west of Ste-Croix, has similar exhibits. The collection was created by the Baud family of musical-box makers.

🏛 **Musée Baud**
23 Grand-Rue, L'Auberson. **Tel** 024 454 24 84. **Open** 2–5pm Sat, 10am–noon & 2–6pm Sun (Jul–mid-Sep: 2–5pm daily). 🚫 obligatory. 🅿 🅦 museebaud.ch

One of the musical boxes in the Musée du CIMA in Ste-Croix

# ⑳ Neuchâtel

Lying on the northwestern shore of Lake Neuchâtel, no more than about 20 km (12 miles) from the French border, Neuchâtel is a graceful town with a strikingly Gallic atmosphere. It is also notable for its pale yellow limestone buildings, which famously led the writer Alexandre Dumas to describe the town as looking as if it were carved out of butter. Neuchâtel, a university town, owes its wealth to its watchmaking and precision-engineering industries, which go back to the 18th century. The region is also renowned for its wines, which are celebrated each September at the Fête des Vendanges wine festival.

*Église Collégiale, fronted by a statue of Guillaume Farel unveiled in 1876*

## Exploring Neuchâtel

Neuchâtel's graceful Old Town (Ville Ancienne) is filled with houses built of soft, yellow sandstone, and its streets have numerous fountains. While Place des Halles, the old market square, has many busy cafés, the town's smartest district lies on the lakeshore northeast of the harbour. The rampart walk around the castle walls gives a panoramic view of the town.

### 🏛 Château de Neuchâtel

Rue de la Collégiale. **Tel** 032 889 60 00, 🕐 Apr–Sep: 10am, 11am, noon, 2pm, 3pm, 4pm Mon–Fri, 2pm, 3pm, 4pm Sat, 2pm, 3pm, 4pm Sun.

*Coat of arms in the Château de Neuchâtel*

For over 1,000 years, the castle of the lords of Neuchâtel has been the seat of authority. Today it houses the law courts and the cantonal government. While the west wing dates from the 12th century, the rest of the castle was built in the 15th and 17th centuries. The interior has been altered many times. Of particular interest, however, is the castle's Salle des États, the state room decorated with the coats of arms of the families who married into Neuchâtel's ruling dynasty.

### 🏛 Église Collégiale

Rue de la Collégiale. **Open** undergoing renovations until 2020, but remains open to the public.

The early Gothic collegiate church, in a combination of Romanesque and Burgundian Gothic styles, was consecrated in 1276.

The Reformation was introduced to Neuchâtel by Guillaume Farel (1489–1565), who led the religious movement in western Switzerland, and in 1530 the church became a centre of Protestant worship.

It houses a Gothic tomb known as Le Cénotaphe. This memorial, dating from 1372, consists of life-sized figures of the counts of Neuchâtel arranged in pious poses. It is an outstanding example of medieval sculpture. The other elements of the tomb were added in the 15th century, some being taken from other churches.

During the Reformation the tomb, along with the church's other furnishings and decoration, narrowly escaped destruction at the hands of iconoclastic zealots. The commemorative plaque in the choir proclaims that the cult of images was abolished here in 1530. In accordance with the strictures of the Reformation, Farel's tomb has no monument of any kind. Neuchâtel's great reformer is, however, commemorated by a plaque in the south aisle, and by a 19th-century statue in front of the church.

### 🏛 Maison des Halles

Place des Halles.

The elegant turreted Renaissance market hall dates from the 16th century. Here grain was sold on the ground floor, and cloth on the upper floor. The richly ornamented eastern wall bears the coat of arms of the Orléans-Longueville family.

The influence of French culture brought to Neuchâtel

*Place des Halles, with the turreted Maison des Halles in the background*

by this dynasty can be seen in the Louis XIII and Louis XIV style of many of the houses in Place des Halles and in the streets around this central square.

### 🏛 Hôtel de Ville
Rue de l'Hôtel de Ville.
The large Neo-Classical town hall stands in the eastern part of the Old Town, near the harbour. Completed in 1790, it was designed by Pierre-Adrien Paris, court architect to Louis XVI.

### 🏛 Musée d'Art et d'Histoire
Esplanade Léopold-Robert.
**Tel** 032 717 79 25. **Open** 11am–6pm Tue–Sun. 🐾 free on Wed.
**W** mahn.ch

Neuchâtel's unusual and fascinating art and history museum is divided into three main sections. Devoted to art, the upper floor is crammed with paintings by 19th- and 20th-century Swiss artists, including Ferdinand Hodler and Albert Anker. There is also a collection of French Impressionist paintings.

The ground floor and the mezzanine are devoted to the history of the canton of Neuchâtel and to local decorative arts. The star attractions here are three automata that demonstrate the ingenuity and sophistication of 18th-century Swiss watchmakers.

The figures were made by Pierre Jaquet-Droz, a watchmaker of La Chaux-de-Fonds, and his son Henri-Louis, between 1768 and 1774. Le Dessinateur (The Draughtsman) produces six different drawings, including a profile of Louis XV and a picture of a butterfly. La Musicienne (The Musician) is a young woman playing an organ. Her bosom heaves as she breathes, and she bends forward, sits up and plays several melodies, striking the keyboard with her fingers. The most sophisticated automaton is L'Écrivain (The Writer), who composes a text consisting of 40 letters, dipping his quill pen in an inkpot as he writes. He can also be made to write any phrase.

*La Musicienne, in the Musée d'Art et d'Histoire*

The automata are on permanent display; visitors can request a demonstration to see each of them performing.

## VISITORS' CHECKLIST

**Practical Information**
**Road map:** B3. 🚗 33,000.
🛈 Hôtel des Postes;
032 889 68 90.
**W** neuchateltourisme.ch
🍇 Fête des Vendanges (Grape Harvest Festival; last weekend in Sep).

**Transport**
🚌 🚆

### 🏛 Laténium, Parc et Musée d'Archéologie de Neuchâtel
Espace Paul Vouga, Hauterive, 3 km (2 miles) northeast of the town centre.
🚌 1. **Tel** 032 889 69 17. **Open** 10am–5pm Tue–Sat. **W** latenium.ch

Covering 3 hectares (7 acres), the Laténium is a large and modern museum complex.

Its primary purpose is to illustrate the history of human activity and settlement in the region of Lake Neuchâtel from the end of the Ice Age to the Middle Ages. Among many fine displays, the centrepiece is the section devoted to the lakeside settlement of La Tène, which was founded by Celts in the 5th century BC. Stunning examples of Celtic metalwork and other fine objects paint a vivid picture of their lives.

## Neuchâtel Town Centre

① Château de Neuchâtel
② Église Collégiale
③ Maison des Halles
④ Hôtel de Ville
⑤ Musée d'Art et d'Histoire

0 metres 200
0 yards 200

Château des Monts, home of the Musée d'Horlogerie in Le Locle

# ㉑ Le Locle

**Road map:** B3. 🚗 🚌 🌐 **lelocle.ch**

The town of Le Locle has the distinction of being the birthplace of Swiss watchmaking, and has been awarded World Heritage status by UNESCO. In 1705 the young watchmaker Daniel Jeanrichard arrived from Neuchâtel to settle in Le Locle, where he set up a workshop. The apprentices that he trained then established workshops of their own in La Chaux-de-Fonds, so launching the Swiss watchmaking industry.

The **Musée d'Horlogerie**, which is in a stately 18th-century mansion (the elegant Château des Monts) with beautiful interiors, presents a large collection of timepieces from around the world, as well as several elaborate automata.

### Environs
About 2 km (1 mile) west of Le Locle are the **Moulins Souterrains du Col-des-Roches**. In use from the 16th to the 19th centuries, these underground mills were built to harness the waters of the River Biel, whose energy was used to work machinery. Having fallen into disuse, they have now been restored and their wells, waterwheels and galleries – with both permanent and temporary exhibitions – are open to visitors.

🏛 **Moulins Souterrains du Col-des-Roches**

Le Col 23. **Tel** 032 889 68 92. **Open** May–Oct: 10am–5pm; Nov–Apr: 2–5pm. 🚗 🎫 🌐 lesmoulins.ch

# ㉒ La Chaux-de-Fonds

**Road map:** B3. 🚟 37,800. 🚗 🚌
ℹ 1 Rue Espacité; 032 889 68 95.

If Le Locle is the birthplace of the Swiss watchmaking industry, La Chaux-de-Fonds may be regarded as its cradle. The largest town in the canton of Neuchâtel, La Chaux-de-Fonds lies in the Jura at an altitude of 1,000 m (3,280 ft). Introduced to the town in the early 18th century, watchmaking was initially a cottage industry. In time it was industrialized and La Chaux-de-Fonds became the leading centre of Swiss watchmaking. The industry reached its peak in the late 18th and 19th centuries.

After it was destroyed by a fire in 1794, the town was rebuilt to a grid pattern, with long, wide avenues. It is now dotted with several modernist buildings.

La Chaux-de-Fonds' illustrious past is celebrated in the magnificent **Musée International d'Horlogerie**. The museum's collection of some 3,000 pieces from around the world illustrates the history of timekeeping from its beginnings in antiquity to state-of-the-art instruments able to record time lapses of infinitesimal fractions of a second. In purely visual terms, many of the finest pieces on display were made in La Chaud-de-Fonds during the town's apogee. Musical, astrononomical, atomic and quartz clocks are also on display.

Carillon at the Musée International d'Horlogerie, La Chaux-de-Fonds

## A World-famous Industry

The earliest watchmaking workshops in Switzerland were established in the 17th century by Huguenot refugees who had settled in Geneva. Soon after, many other workshops were set up in the Jura, most notably at La Chaux-de-Fonds. In the 19th century, innovations in precision mechanics introduced by Abraham-Louis Breguet enabled watchmaking to be industrialized, and the canton of Neuchâtel then became its leading centre. In 1967, the Centre Horloger Neuchâtelois produced the first quartz watch. This nearly led to the collapse of the Swiss watchmaking industry. Now able to mass-produce cheap watches, other countries quickly gained the largest market share. However, thanks to the inexpensive and fashionable Swatch and renewed interest in prestige watches, Switzerland has regained a share of the market and is now the third country in the world (after China and Hong Kong) in terms of watch production.

Giant pocket watch as a shop sign

The museum has audiovisual facilities, a library and a restoration workshop for antique clocks and watches. At the entrance is a tubular steel carillon that sounds every 15 minutes.

La Chaux-de-Fonds is also the birthplace of the modernist architect Charles-Édouard Jeanneret, known as Le Corbusier (1887–1965). Before he moved to Paris in 1917, Le Corbusier built several houses here, and an itinerary taking in buildings that he designed and places associated with him is available from the town's tourist office. Only one, however, is open to visitors. This is the Villa Schwob, better known as the **Villa Turque** (Turkish Villa) because of its Islamic-style features. The villa, which launched Le Corbusier's career, is now an office building and not open to the public.

**▥ Musée International d'Horlogerie**
29 Rue des Musées. **Tel** 032 967 68 61. **Open** 10am–5pm Tue–Sun. 🖼
**W** mih.ch

**▥ Villa Turque**
167 Rue du Doubs.

## ㉓ Franches-Montagnes

**Road map:** B2. 🚆 🚌 ℹ
Saignelégier, 6 Place du 23 Juin; 032 420 47 74. 🏇 Marché-Concours (2nd weekend in Aug).
**W** juratourisme.ch

The part of the Jura mountains that lies within the canton of Jura itself are known as the Franches-Montagnes. The area received its name in the 14th century, when the prince-bishop of Basel, who owned the territory that now constitutes the canton of Jura, granted its inhabitants a *franchise*, or exemption from taxation, so as to encourage migration to this sparsely populated region.

The Franches-Montagnes lie at an altitude of 1,000–1,100 m (3,300–3,600 ft) in the southwest of the canton of Jura. With forests, pastures and

Portal of the church at St-Ursanne

picturesque low houses, this outstandingly beautiful plateau has extensive hiking trails, and cycling and cross-country skiing routes. It is also famous for its sturdy breed of horses.

The region's principal town is **Saignelégier**. Every year, in the second week in August, it hosts the Marché Concours National des Chevaux, a showpiece for the area's unique breed of Franches-Montagnes horses.

## ㉔ St-Ursanne

**Road map:** C2. 🚆 1,100. 🚌
ℹ Place Roger Schaffter; 032 420 47 73. **W** juratourisme.ch

A charming medieval walled town with fortified gates, St-Ursanne is set in a deep canyon washed by the River Doubs. The town grew up around the hermitage that Ursicinus, a disciple of St

Columba, established here in the early 7th century.

The focal point of the town is its beautiful Romanesque and Gothic **church**. It has a fine Romanesque portal, with statues of the Virgin and St Ursicinus. There is an old stone bridge across the River Doubs, on the south side of St-Ursanne, which provides a good view of the town and its setting. The bridge features a statue of St John Nepomucene, who is often considered the patron saint of bridges.

## ㉕ Delémont

**Road map:** C2. 🚆 11,500. 🚆 🚌
ℹ 9 Place de la Gare; 032 420 47 71.
**W** juratourisme.ch

The capital of the canton of Jura, Delémont is a quiet town with a well-preserved medieval centre. From 1212 until 1792 it served as the summer residence of the prince-bishops of Basel.

Historic buildings in the old town, which has cobbled streets and fountains, include the Château de Delémont, the prince-bishops' 18th-century mansion; the Hôtel de Ville, built in 1745 in the Baroque style; and the 18th-century Église St-Marcel, in a Rococo and Neo-Classical style. The **Musée Jurassien d'Art et d'Histoire** contains artifacts relating to local history from prehistoric times to the 18th century.

**▥ Musée Jurassien d'Art et d'Histoire**
52 Rue du 23-Juin. **Tel** 032 422 80 77. **Open** 2–5pm Tue–Sun. 🖼
**W** mjah.ch

Façade of the prince-bishops' palace in Delémont

# NORTHERN SWITZERLAND

Bordered by the Rhine to the north and the Jura to the southwest, northern Switzerland is a largely Protestant, German-speaking region with a strongly industrial economy. It consists of the half-cantons of Basel-Stadt and Basel-Landschaft in the west, Aargau in the centre, and part of the canton of Zürich in the east.

Being the most industrialized and densely populated region of Switzerland, this northern, relatively flat area is less scenic than other parts of the country. With Zürich, Switzerland's richest and most populous city, and Basel, its most industrial, northern Switzerland is noticeably less oriented towards tourism than other areas further south. However, as well as several fine historic towns, the region has a large number of world-class museums and art galleries. It is here, in Switzerland's industrial heartland, that privately acquired wealth has been translated into some of the world's most exquisite art collections.

The Rhine marks part of Switzerland's northern border and also connects this landlocked country to the sea. Set on the Rhine, Basel is Switzerland's only port, with a direct shipping link to Rotterdam and out to the North Sea.

Besides being a large industrial port, Basel is a major centre of the pharmaceuticals and chemicals industries. With the oldest university in Switzerland and the Kunstmuseum, an art gallery of international standing, Basel is also one of the country's cultural capitals.

Winterthur, another of Switzerland's major industrial centres, also has a wealth of art galleries and museums. The bustling city of Zürich, in the east of the region, is Switzerland's financial capital and burgeoning centre of popular culture.

Looking over Basel and the Rhine from the top of the Münster

◄ The clock on the façade of Basel's brightly painted Rathaus

# Exploring Northern Switzerland

Flanked by Basel in the west and Winterthur and Zürich in the east, this region is bordered by the Rhine to the north, while to the south lies the Mittelland. Just outside the great city and port of Basel lie the extensive remains of the Roman town of Augusta Raurica. Other focal points here include the spa resort of Baden, and the attractive towns of Zofingen and Aarau, capital of Aargau. While small towns and villages dot the landscape of vineyards in the east of the region, the industrial town of Winterthur has several exceptional art galleries. The lakeside city of Zürich is the Swiss capital of finance as well as a vibrant centre of culture.

A side altar in the monastery church at Wettingen

## Sights at a Glance

1. Basel *pp142–51*
2. Riehen
3. Augusta Raurica
4. Dornach
5. Zofingen
6. Aarau
7. Muri
8. Kloster Königsfelden
9. Baden *pp158–9*
10. Wettingen
11. Regensberg
12. Kaiserstuhl
13. Eglisau
14. Winterthur *pp160–61*

Painting in Eglisau's Reformed Church

## Getting There

With international airports and rail links to the country's major towns, Basel and Zürich are the two main hubs of northern Switzerland's transport network. Motorway links from Zürich include the A1 north to Winterthur and west to Baden, and the A51 to Eglisau. From Baden, the A3 runs west as far as Basel, which is also connected to Bern and western Switzerland via the A2. The more scenic A7 follows the Rhine as far as Kaiserstuhl then turns south to Winterthur.

**Key**

━━━ Motorway
= = Motorway under construction
━━ Main road
···· Minor road
━━ Scenic route
┈┈ Main railway
── Minor railway
▓▓ International border
▒▒ Canton border

The Benedictine monastery in Muri

Houses in Basel's northern district, Kleinbasel

**For keys to symbols** see back flap

# ① Basel

The origins of the city of Basel (Bâle in French) lie in a Roman settlement, Basilia, that was established in 44 BC. Under Frankish control from the 7th century, it became part of the German empire in the early 11th century. Located at a point where the Rhine becomes navigable, it is Switzerland's only port. Basel is a major centre of commerce and industry, specializing in pharmaceuticals. The city also hosts Art Basel, the world's largest contemporary art fair, and is famous for its festivals, the largest of which are Vogel Gryff and Fasnacht, an exuberant masked carnival.

The Spalentor seen from Spalenvorstadt

## Exploring Basel

Straddling the Rhine, Basel is divided into two districts. Grossbasel (Greater Basel), on the south bank, is the oldest part of the city. On the north bank lies Kleinbasel (Lesser Basel), a largely residential area, and the Messe, the city's great conference centre.

## 🏛 Spalentor

This monumental Gothic gate stands on the west side of the Old Town (Altstadt), at the entrance to Spalenvorstadt, a narrow alley lined with picturesque shuttered houses. Built in 1370, the Spalentor formed part of the defensive walls that once encircled Basel. The tower consists of a pair of crenellated turrets framing a square central section, which has a pointed roof laid with glazed tiles. The gate, which has wooden doors and a portcullis, is embellished with sculptures and on its west side it bears the arms of the city.

## 🏛 Jüdisches Museum der Schweiz

Kornhausgasse 8. **Tel** 061 261 95 14. **Open** 2–5pm Mon & Wed, 11am–5pm Sun. 🚻 🖥 juedisches-museum.ch

Through a variety of artifacts dating back to the 13th century, including liturgical objects and items used at religious feasts, the museum illustrates Jewish religion and customs, and the history and daily life of Jewish people. It is the only Jewish museum in Switzerland.

Basel's Jewish community of 2,000 is the second largest in the country after Geneva's. It was in Basel that the first Zionist Congress took place, in 1897.

## 🏛 University

Petersplatz 1.

Founded in 1460, Basel's university is the oldest in Switzerland. Among the illustrious figures with whom it is associated are the humanist Erasmus of Rotterdam (1466–1536), the physician Paracelsus

(1493–1541), the mathematician Jakob Bernoulli (1654–1705), and the philosophers Friedrich Nietzsche (1844–1900) and Karl Jaspers (1883–1969).

The present university building is the Kollegienhaus, a great Modernist edifice on the east side of Petersplatz. It was completed in 1946. The entrance to the building is embellished with mosaics depicting the university's founders and the main hall has stained-glass windows.

Additional university buildings are located in Petersgraben and in other parts of the city. The university's botanical garden lies east of Petersplatz, beyond which is the university library.

## 🏛 Spielzeug Welten Museum Basel

Steinenvorstadt 1. **Tel** 061 225 95 95. **Open** 10am–6pm daily. 🚻 🖥 🖥

With more than 6,000 items laid out on four floors, the Toy Worlds Museum in Basel is the largest of its kind in Europe.

Bust of Basel poet J P Hebel outside the Peterskirche

Most of the exhibits date from the late 19th to the early 20th centuries, although there are also some contemporary pieces. All the doll's houses and miniature shops on display are meticulously decorated and furnished.

The collection also includes mechanical toys, teddy bears and other stuffed toys made by leading toymakers of today and yesterday.

Shuttered houses along Spalenvorstadt in the Old Town

### ⬚ Pharmaziehistorisches Museum Basel

Totengässlein 3. **Tel** 061 264 91 11.
**Open** 10am–6pm Tue–Fri, 10am–5pm
Sat. ⬚ ⬚

Appropriately for a world centre of the pharmaceuticals industry, Basel has a museum devoted to the history of medicinal chemistry. Its collection includes instruments and medicines used by apothecaries through the ages and is located in the house where Erasmus and Paracelsus once lived. There are also reconstructions of a pharmacy and a laboratory.

### ⬚ Marktplatz

Every weekday morning Marktplatz is filled with the stalls of a produce market, and on public holidays it becomes the hub of Basel's great seasonal festivals. The square is lined with fine buildings, particularly those dating from late 19th to early 20th centuries. At its northern end is Fischmarkt, where a fountain with statues of the Virgin and saints stands.

Just to the northeast of Marktplatz is Mittlere Rheinbrücke. Near the bridge is a curious figure of a bearded man, the Lällekönig (Tongue King), which has become the symbol of Basel. It is a static replica of an amusing 19th-century mechanical figure that rolled its eyes and stuck out its tongue at the inhabitants of Kleinbasel, on the north bank. The original figure is in the Historisches Museum.

### ⬚ Rathaus

Marktplatz 9. ⬚ available in English through the tourist office.

Figure of Justice, a painting on the façade of the Rathaus

## VISITORS' CHECKLIST

**Practical Information**
**Road map:** C2. ⬚ 190,000.
⬚ Stadtcasino, Barfüsserplatz, Steinenberg 4 and in the train station; 061 268 68 68. ⬚
Fasnacht (late Feb); Blues Festival (Apr); Art Basel (mid-Jun); Tattoo Festival (Jul); Jazz Festival (late Aug). ⬚ **basel.com**

**Transport**
⬚ ⬚

The main feature of Basel's Marktplatz is the eyecatching Rathaus, the Gothic town hall whose bright red façade is decorated with allegorical figures. The central arcaded section of the building dates from 1504–21. The present façade *(see illustration on p138)* has been restored so as to recreate its appearance as it was in about 1600. The tower and annexe date from the 19th century.

The inner courtyard is painted with 16th-century (though heavily restored) frescoes.

---

## Basel City Centre

① Spalentor
② Jüdisches Museum Basel
③ University
④ Spielzeug Welten Museum Basel
⑤ Pharmaziehistorisches Museum Basel
⑥ Marktplatz
⑦ Rathaus
⑧ Leonhardskirche
⑨ Historisches Museum
⑩ Kunsthalle and Architekturmuseum
⑪ Haus zum Kirschgarten
⑫ Kunstmuseum
⑬ Antikenmuseum
⑭ Münster
⑮ Augustinergasse

0 metres 1000
0 yards 1000

**Key**

Street-by-street map pp144–5

# Street-by-Street: Old Town

The nucleus of Basel's medieval Old Town, or Altstadt, lines the escarpment of the south bank of the Rhine. The hub of the Old Town is Barfüsserplatz, a buzzing square lined with cafés and crossed by trams, and its major landmarks are the Münster, Basel's great Romanesque-Gothic cathedral, and the unmistakable Rathaus, the brightly painted town hall on Marktplatz. With smart shopping streets, several churches, steep alleyways and leafy courtyards, this is Basel's busiest district. However, as many streets in the Old Town are closed to motor traffic, it is a pleasant area to explore on foot.

**Mittlere Rheinbrücke**, a stone bridge spanning the Rhine, links Grossbasel, on the south bank, to Kleinbasel, a district on the north bank.

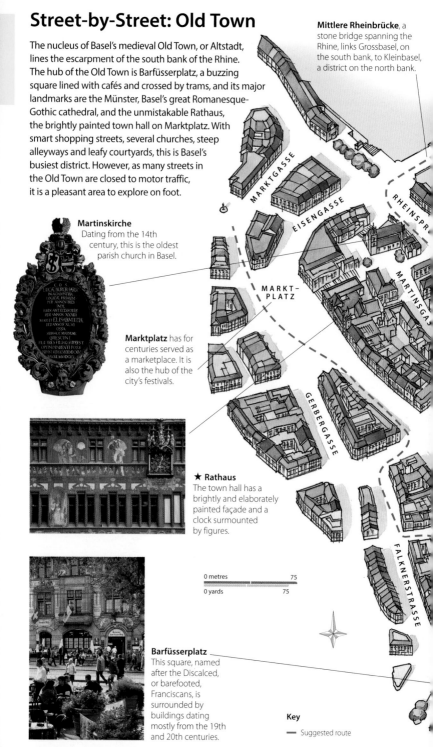

**Martinskirche**
Dating from the 14th century, this is the oldest parish church in Basel.

**Marktplatz** has for centuries served as a marketplace. It is also the hub of the city's festivals.

**★ Rathaus**
The town hall has a brightly and elaborately painted façade and a clock surmounted by figures.

MARKTGASSE

EISENGASSE

RHEINSPR

MARTINSGA

MARKT–PLATZ

GERBERGASSE

FALKNERSTRASSE

| 0 metres | 75 |
| 0 yards | 75 |

**Barfüsserplatz**
This square, named after the Discalced, or barefooted, Franciscans, is surrounded by buildings dating mostly from the 19th and 20th centuries.

**Key**
— Suggested route

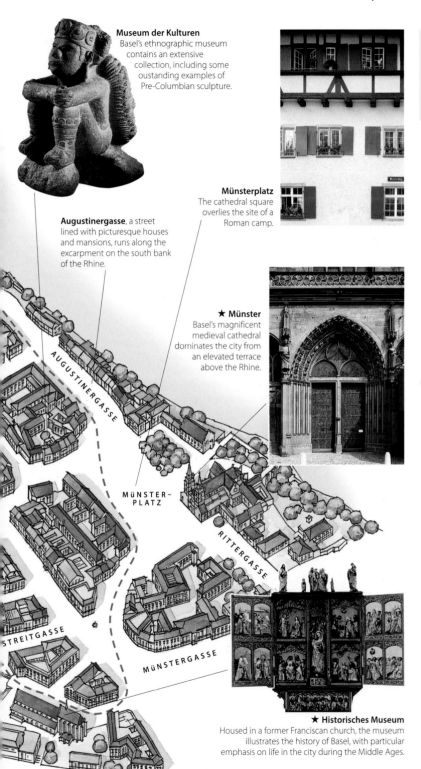

**Museum der Kulturen**
Basel's ethnographic museum contains an extensive collection, including some oustanding examples of Pre-Columbian sculpture.

**Münsterplatz**
The cathedral square overlies the site of a Roman camp.

**Augustinergasse**, a street lined with picturesque houses and mansions, runs along the excarpment on the south bank of the Rhine.

★ **Münster**
Basel's magnificent medieval cathedral dominates the city from an elevated terrace above the Rhine.

AUGUSTINERGASSE

MÜNSTER–PLATZ

RITTERGASSE

STREITGASSE

MÜNSTERGASSE

★ **Historisches Museum**
Housed in a former Franciscan church, the museum illustrates the history of Basel, with particular emphasis on life in the city during the Middle Ages.

# Exploring Basel

With over 60 museums and art galleries, ranging from the cutting-edge Kunsthalle to the venerable Kunstmuseum, Basel is one of Switzerland's most cultured cities. East of the Old Town lies St Alban-Vorstadt, a quiet district of medieval streets where it is pleasant to stroll. Opposite the Old Town, on the north bank of the Rhine, lies Kleinbasel, a prosperous suburb. At Basel's port (Hafen), downstream from the Old Town, an obelisk marks the point at which the Swiss, German and French borders meet.

The Tinguely Fountain, outside the Kunsthalle

### ⬆ Leonhardskirche

Kohlenberg. **Open** 9am–5pm Tue–Sat.
The church of St Leonard overlooks the city from its hilltop location. It stands on the site of an 11th-century church, whose Romanesque crypt survives. After the 1356 earthquake that destroyed much of Basel, the church was rebuilt in the Gothic style. The interior features 15th- and 16th-century Gothic paintings and an exquisite rood screen of 1455. The musical instruments on display in a wing of the adjoining monastery are part of the Historisches Museum collection.

Emblem of Basel in the Leonhardskirche

### 🏛 Historisches Museum

Barfüsserplatz. **Tel** 061 205 86 00.
**Open** 10am–5pm Mon & Wed.
🐾 🗂 🚻 🖥 🌐 hmb.ch
Occupying the Barfüsserkirche, a former Franciscan church, this museum traces Basel's history

from Celtic times. Exhibits include wooden chests, pottery, silver-mounted vessels, Gothic, Renaissance and Baroque liturgical vessels and other items from the cathedral treasury, plus tapestries, altarpieces and weapons.

### 🏛 Kunsthalle

Klostergasse 5. **Tel** 061 206 99 00. **Open** 11am–6pm Tue, Wed & Fri, 11am–8:30pm Thu, 11am–5pm Sat & Sun. 🐾 🗂 🚻 🖊
🌐 kunsthallebasel.ch

Thanks to the Kunsthalle, Basel's position at the forefront of trends in modern art is well established. One of the city's most prominent cultural institutions, the Kunsthalle hosts a continuous programme of exhibitions of the work of leading contemporary artists.

The Kunsthalle is located opposite the Theater Basel, another institution at Basel's cultural hub. On the square between the two buildings

stands a fountain that incorporates several of Jean Tinguely's kinetic sculptures, with moving elements.

### 🏛 Architekturmuseum

Steinenberg 7. **Tel** 061 261 14 13.
**Open** 11am–6pm Tue, Wed & Fri, 11am–8:30pm Thu, 11am–5pm Sat & Sun. 🐾 🗂 🚻 🌐 sam-basel.org
The Kunsthalle also houses Switzerland's museum of architecture. Concentrating on the early 20th century onwards, the museum hosts temporary exhibitions of the work of Swiss architects, and of international architecture, as well as related subjects such as architectural photography and the links between art and architecture.

### 🏛 Haus zum Kirschgarten

Elisabethenstrasse 27–29. **Tel** 061 205 86 78. **Open** 10am–5pm Tue–Fri & Sun, 1–5pm Sat. 🐾 🌐 hmb.ch
This Rococo mansion was built in 1775–80 as the residence of J R Burckhardt, the owner of a silk mill. Furnished in period style, it now houses a museum illustrating patrician life in the 18th and 19th centuries. On the first and second floors there are elegantly furnished drawing rooms, a dining room, a music room and a kitchen.

The topmost floor contains a display of dolls, rocking horses and other toys. The ground floor and basement are filled with a fine collection of clocks and ceramics, including Italian faience, and of porcelain made at Meissen and other major European factories.

### 🏛 Kunstmuseum

See pp150–51.

The wide nave of the Leonhardskirche

*For hotels and restaurants see pp248–55 and pp264–75*

### 🏛 Antikenmuseum

St-Alban-Graben 5. **Tel** 061 201 12 12.
**Open** 10am–5pm Tue–Sun. 🐾 🔲
♿ 🔲

Basel's museum of antiquities is
devoted to the four great early
civilizations of the Mediterranean
basin, namely those of ancient
Greece, Etruria, Rome and
Egypt. The display of Greek
pieces includes a fine collection
of vases from the Archaic to
the Classical periods, marble
sculpture, bronze figurines,
pottery, coins and jewellery. The
collections of Etruscan pottery
and of Roman and Egyptian art
are equally impressive.

### 🏛 Münster

*See pp148–9.*

### 🏛 Augustinergasse

Naturhistorisches Museum:
Augustinergasse 2. **Tel** 061 266 55 00.
**Open** 10am–5pm Tue–Sun. 🐾 ♿
Museum der Kulturen: Münsterplatz
20. **Tel** 061 266 56 00. **Open**
10am–5pm Tue–Sun. 🐾 ♿ 🔲

Augustinergasse is a
picturesque alley that runs
north from Münsterplatz, along
the escarpment on the south
side of the Rhine. As well as a
Renaissance fountain with a
figure of a basilisk, the street
contains several fine 14th-
and 15th-century houses.

The Neo-Classical building
at no. 2 houses the **Naturhistorisches Museum**, which
contains an extensive collection
of minerals, and sections
devoted to palaeontology and
zoology. Around the corner is
the **Museum der Kulturen**,
housed in a building designed
by Basel architects Herzog and
de Meuron. This anthropology
museum presents a collection
of items from various cultures
around the world. Among the
finest pieces are wooden reliefs
from Tikal, the ancient Mayan
site in Guatemala.

### 🏛 St Alban

Basler Papiermühle: St Alban-Tal 37.
**Tel** 061 225 90 90. **Open** 11am–5pm
Tue–Fri & Sun, 1–5pm Sat. 🐾 ♿
🔲 **papiermuseum.ch**
Museum für Gegenwartskunst: St
Alban-Rheinweg 60. **Tel** 061 206 62
62. **Open** 11am–5pm Tue–Sun. 🐾

The St Alban-Tor, a 13th-century gate, in
the district of St Alban

The district of St Alban takes its
name from the church of a
former Benedictine monastery
founded on the outskirts of Basel
in the 11th century. It is an
attractive district, with a
mix of old and modern
buildings. The canal that
runs through St Alban
was used to power the
monastery's mills.
One of these, the
**Basler Papier-
mühle**, now houses
a museum of paper,
writing and printing.
Visitors can watch
paper being made
by hand. The **Museum für
Gegenwartskunst** (Museum of
Contemporary Art), in a modern
building a short distance from
the mill, showcases art from the
1960s to the present day.

**Statue in Kleinbasel**

### Kleinbasel

The first permanent bridge over
the Rhine at Basel was built in
1226. A small fortress was then
established on the north bank,
and the settlement that grew
up around it became part of the
city in the late 14th century. For
many centuries, Kleinbasel, as
the district was known, was
inhabited mainly by the poorer
sector of the city's population.

### 🏛 Museum Tinguely

Paul-Sacher Anlage 2. **Tel** 061 681 93
20. **Open** 11am–6pm Tue–Sun. 🐾
🔲 ♿ 🔲 **tinguely.ch**

This pale pink sandstone
building, designed by the Swiss
architect Mario Botta, stands in
Solitude Park, on the banks of
the Rhine. The museum is
devoted to the work of Jean
Tinguely, famous for his kinetic
sculptures. Born in Fribourg in
1925, he was educated in Basel.
He settled in New York in 1960,
but in 1968 returned to
Switzerland, where he stayed
until his death in 1991.

The nucleus of the
collection consists of
works by Tinguely,
donated by his wife,
the artist Niki de
St-Phalle. These,
with many later
gifts, bequests and
purchases, trace
Tinguely's artistic
development.

While the mezzanine contains
engine-driven contraptions that
visitors can set in motion, the
upper floor contains various
items associated with Tinguely.
The central exhibit on the ground
floor is a huge sculpture, *Grosse
Méta Maxi-Maxi Utopia* (1987).
The museum also stages exhibitions concentrating on individual
aspects of Tinguely's work.

The Museum Tinguely, fronted by one of the artist's sculptures

# Münster

With dark red sandstone walls and a patterned roof, Basel's monumental cathedral is a conspicuous and majestic presence. The church that originally stood on the site was built in the 8th century. The present cathedral was begun in the 12th century. Partly damaged by an earthquake in 1356, it was rebuilt in the Gothic style, although elements of the earlier building were incorporated into the structure. In the 16th century, as a result of the Reformation, the cathedral was stripped of almost all its furnishings and decoration. However, some fine Romanesque and Gothic sculpture, and 14th-century frescoes in the crypt, survive. All the stained glass dates from the 19th century.

**★ Crypt Paintings**
The ceiling of the crypt is covered with frescoes of the life of the Virgin and the childhood of Christ. One of the finest is this Nativity scene.

**Stained-Glass Window**
The ambulatory is lit by 19th-century stained-glass windows with medallions depicting the Nativity, the Crucifixion and the Resurrection of Christ.

**Tomb of Queen Anna**
Queen Anna of Habsburg, consort of Rudolf of Habsburg, died in 1281 and was entombed with her infant son, Karl. Their portraits appear on the lid of the sarcophagus.

## KEY

① **Carved elephants** adorn the windows of the choir.

② **The Georgsturm** features a figure of St George. The whiter stonework at its lower levels formed part of the 11th-century church.

③ **The Martinsturm** terminates in a decorative fleuron that was completed in 1500.

**★ Galluspforte**
The magnificent Romanesque portal closing the north arm of the transept dates from about 1180. The carvings depict judgment day and works of mercy.

**Font**
Intricately carved with figured reliefs, the font dates from 1486. It is an outstanding example of late Gothic sculpture.

**★ Panel of the Apostles**
This late Romanesque panel in the north aisle shows six of the apostles, arranged in pairs within three arches. The panel dates from the late 11th century.

**Main Portal**
The sculptures on the main portal include figures of Emperor Heinrich II and his wife Kunigunde, patron saints of Basel. The emperor is shown holding a model of the cathedral.

**Cloisters**
The peaceful Gothic cloisters on the south side of the cathedral are filled with tombs. The walls are covered with epitaphs.

# Kunstmuseum

The prestigious Kunstmuseum in Basel is said to be the world's oldest public art museum. It is the largest in Switzerland. Its collections fall into four main categories: 15th- and 16th-century paintings and drawings, including an extensive collection of German art and the largest assemblage in the world of works by Hans Holbein the Younger; 17th-century Dutch and Flemish paintings; 19th-century Swiss, German and French paintings, with works by Delacroix and Pissarro; and 20th-century art, including works by Rousseau, Picasso, Dalí and Giacometti. The courtyard is filled with sculptures, among which is Rodin's *Burghers of Calais*. In 2016, a new extension will open for large and temporary exhibitions.

**Senecio**
This lyrical portrait of a boy by Paul Klee dates from 1922, and is one of several works by this artist in the gallery's collection.

## Gallery Guide
*While the ground floor is mainly reserved for temporary exhibitions, the galleries on the first floor are hung with works of art from the 15th- to 19th-centuries. The second floor is devoted to 20th-century art.*

**Key**
- ▨ Sculpture
- ▨ 17th- and 18th-century paintings
- ▨ 15th- and 16th-century paintings
- ▨ 19th-century paintings
- ▨ 20th-century paintings

**★ Ta Matete**
The gestures of the figures in *Ta Matete* (The Fair), as well as the colours used in the composition, make this a powerful example of Paul Gauguin's Symbolist style. The work dates from 1892.

**★ Burning Giraffe**
Salvador Dalí painted this poignant Surrealist painting in 1936–7. It shows skeletal figures and a flaming giraffe set against an eerily empty landscape. It is located on the ground floor.

Main entrance

## VISITORS' CHECKLIST

**Practical Information**
St Alban-Graben 16. **Tel** 061
206 62 62. **Open** 10am–6pm
Tue–Sun. 🖼 📷 🖉 🖵 🏛
W **kunstmuseumbasel.ch**

### The Jungle
Henri Rousseau, known as Le Douanier, painted this picture in 1910, the year of his death. In the setting of a luminously painted and dreamlike forest, a man is attacked by a leopard.

Second floor

### ★ Christ in the Tomb
Painted in 1521, this unusual picture, one of the most striking by Hans Holbein the Younger, carries a strong visual and emotional charge. Dostoyevsky refers to it in his novel *The Idiot*.

First floor

### Mermaids at Play
Arnold Böcklin, who was born in Basel, was one of the most important Swiss artists of the late 19th century. This work of Romantic fantasy is typical of his atmospheric yet rather sentimental style.

Ground floor

### David Presenting Saul with the Head of Goliath
Dating from 1627, this small-scale painting of the well-known biblical story is one of Rembrandt's earlier works.

**For keys to symbols** *see back flap*

## ❷ Riehen

**Road map:** C2. 🏔 20,600. 🚌 🚊
🌐 riehen.ch

Now almost engulfed by the encroaching outskirts of Basel, the small town of Riehen is linked to the city by a tram line. This charming area, northeast of Basel's city centre, is filled with smart villas and old country houses and has much to interest visitors.

Wettsteinhaus, the residence of a 17th-century mayor, houses the **Spielzeugmuseum**. This superb toy museum contains exhibits ranging from toy trains to board games. Also in the house are the **Dorfmuseum**, which documents daily life in Riehen in 1900, and the **Rebbaumuseum**, devoted to the local winemaking industry.

Riehen's largest museum is the exceptional **Fondation Beyeler**. It was set up by Hilda and Ernst Beyeler, art collectors who assembled some 200 pieces. These were put on public display in 1997, in a building designed by the Italian architect Renzo Piano. Most of the paintings in the collection date from the late 19th and 20th centuries. Among them are Impressionist paintings by Monet, works by Cézanne, Van Gogh, Picasso and Matisse, and canvases by Miró, Mondrian, Bacon, Rothko, Warhol and other major artists of the 20th century. A selection of artifacts from other parts of the world, including Africa and Oceania, complements the paintings. The foundation also stages temporary exhibitions of modern art.

🏛 **Spielzeugmuseum, Dorfmuseum & Rebbaumuseum**
Baselstrasse 34. **Tel** 061 641 28 29.
**Open** 11am–5pm Mon & Wed–Sun. 📷

🏛 **Fondation Beyeler**
Baselstrasse 101. **Tel** 061 645 97 00.
**Open** 10am–6pm Thu–Tue,
10am–8pm Wed. 📷 ♿ 🖥 📷
🌐 fondationbeyeler.ch

The Goetheanum in Dornach, the world centre of anthroposophy

## ❸ Augusta Raurica

**Road map:** C2. 🚌 🚊 🚌

The Roman town of Augusta Raurica lies 11 km (7 miles) east of Basel, at the confluence of the Ergolz and the Rhine. It was founded in 27 BC and at its height in about AD 200 it had a population of 20,000. By about AD 350, the town had been largely destroyed by the Alemani, a northern tribe.

Carefully excavated, Augusta Raurica is now a large and fascinating open-air museum. The site includes restored temples, amphitheatres, baths and sewers, as well as a forum and numerous houses.

Some of the many objects unearthed during excavations are displayed in the **Römermuseum**, next to the open-air excavation site. They include a hoard of silver discovered at the foot of the town's fortress. The reconstruction of a Roman house furnished with pieces found at the site illustrates daily life in the town. In the animal park, visitors can see some of the domestic animals that were kept in Roman times.

Tombstone of Dannicus in Augusta Raurica

🏛 **Römermuseum**
Giebenacherstrasse 17, Augst.
**Tel** 061 816 22 22. **Open** Mar–Oct:
1–5pm Mon, 10am–5pm Tue–Sun;
Nov–Feb: 1–5pm Mon, 11am–5pm
Tue–Sun. 📷

## ❹ Dornach

**Road map:** C2. 🏔 6,300. 🚌 🚌
ℹ 🌐 dornach-tourismus.ch

The small town of Dornach, on the southern outskirts of Basel, is the location of the world centre of anthroposophy. Founded in about 1912 by the Austrian-born social philosopher Rudolf Steiner (1861–1925), anthroposophy holds that spiritual development, nourished by myth-making and other creative activities, is of prime importance to humanity. In the development of this philosophy, Steiner was strongly influenced by the writing of the German poet Goethe.

The **Goetheanum**, a huge concrete building overlooking Dornach, is the seat of the Anthroposophical Society. Replacing the original building, which was destroyed by fire in 1922, the present Goetheanum was completed in 1928. According to the principles of anthroposophy, it has no right angles, and is regarded as being a prime example of Expressionist architecture. The interiors, completed in 1998, are decorated so as to depict anthroposophy's themes.

The centre of the building contains an auditorium with seating for 1,000 people. It is used for concerts and operas and for plays produced according to the movement's principles. The auditorium is also used for conferences on anthroposophy and for other gatherings. The School of Spiritual Science is also here.

◀ Baden's Old Town, with its wooden bridge over the River Limmat

**▥ Goetheanum**
Rüttiweg 45. **Tel** 061 706 42 42. **Open**
8am–10pm daily. ⏰ Apr–Sep: 2pm
Sat (in English). ♿

## ❺ Zofingen

**Road map:** D2. ▦ 11,000.
🛈 Kirchplatz 26. **Tel** 062 745 71 72.
Ⓦ **zofingen.ch**

Zofingen, in the canton of
Aargau, is a charming town
whose history goes back to the
12th century. Its well-preserved
old town is surrounded by a
green belt laid out along the
course of the former fortifications. Almost all the town's
sights are clustered around
three neighbouring squares,
Alter Postplatz, Kirchplatz and
Niklaus-Thut-Platz.

On one side of Alter Postplatz
stands Alte Kanzlei, a notable
Baroque building. In the centre
of the square is an historic
arcaded market hall that is still
used for a weekly market today.
Kirchplatz (Church Square) takes
its name from the Stadtkirche, a
parish church built in the
Romanesque style and enlarged
in the 15th century, when it
acquired Gothic elements, and
again in the mid-17th century,
when the west tower, in the
Renaissance style, was added.
Notable features of the church's
interior are its Gothic stalls and
stained-glass windows.

The centre of Niklaus-Thut-
Platz is marked by a fountain
with a statue of Niklaus Thut,
hero of the Battle of Sempach

Fountain with the figure of a knight, in
Niklaus-Thut-Platz, Zofingen

fought in 1386, when the
Confederates routed the
Austrians. Among the fine
buildings surrounding the
square are the Metzgern-
Zunfthaus (butchers' guild
house), dating from 1602, and
the Baroque town hall, whose
council chamber is furnished
in the Neo-Classical style.

## ❻ Aarau

**Road map:** D2. ▦ 20,000.
🛈 Schlossplatz 1; 062 834 10 34.
Ⓦ **aarauinfo.ch**

The capital of the canton of
Aargau, Aarau has a scenic
location on the River Aare.
The old part of the town is
built on terraces that rise
steeply from the riverbank.

Aarau was granted the
privileges of township in the
13th century. Part of Habsburg

territory for many years, it
passed to Bernese control
in 1415. Briefly the capital
of the Helvetic Republic
(see p43), Aarau became the
capital of Aargau in 1803.
Its wealth is derived from
the textiles industry.

The town's highest point
is marked by Schlössli, an
11th-century castle that now
houses a museum of history.
Other notable buildings are the
16th-century town hall with a
Romanesque tower and the
Stadtkirche, a Gothic church built
in the 15th century. Some of the
houses that line the
narrow streets of
Aarau's old districts
have stepped
gables and are
decorated with
floral motifs.

The town also
has an art gallery,
the **Aargauer
Kunsthaus**, with
a fine collection of
modern paintings,
and Naturama, a
museum of natural
history.

Decoration on a
house in Aarau

**▥ Aargauer Kunsthaus**
Aargauerplatz. **Tel** 062 835 23 30.
**Open** 10am–5pm Tue, Wed & Fri–Sun,
10am–8pm Thu. ♿ 🚻 ♿ 🖥 📷

**Environs**
The small town of Lenzburg,
about 10 km (6 miles) east of
Aarau, has an interesting castle.
A museum of local history fills
some of its rooms.

The castle at Lenzburg, near Aarau

## ❼ Muri

**Road map:** D2. 🚆 7,200.
ℹ️ Marktstrasse 10; 056 664 70 11.
🌐 muri.ch

The splendidly restored Benedictine monastery in Muri constitutes this town's main attraction. **Kloster Muri** was founded by Ita von Lothringen and Count Redebot von Habsburg in 1027 and was inhabited by a community of monks until 1841. It then fell into disrepair and was gutted by fire in 1889. In 1960, after it had been meticulously restored, a small group of Benedictine monks returned to the monastery, where they ran a hospice.

The oldest surviving parts of the monastery's church include its Romanesque presbytery, crypt and transept. Some Gothic elements also survive. The main body of the church, however, is in the Baroque style. Built to an octagonal plan and crowned by a dome, it dates from the 17th century. Most of the church furnishings were made in the late 17th and 18th centuries.

The peaceful cloisters adjoining the church are the burial place of the hearts of Emperor Karl I and his wife Zita. An exhibition of paintings by the Swiss artist Caspar Wolf and items from the monastery's treasury are also on display here.

The twin-towered church of Kloster Muri

---

🔲 **Kloster Muri**
Church: **Open** until 7:30pm daily.
Museum: **Open** Mar–Oct: Tue–Sun.

## ❽ Kloster Königsfelden

**Road map:** D2. 🚉 Klosterkirche, Windisch: ℹ️ 056 441 88 33.
**Open** Apr–Oct: 10am–5pm Tue–Sun; Nov–Mar: by request. 🅿️
🌐 klosterkoenigsfelden.ch

The Franciscan Abbey of Königsfelden lies between the quaint villages of Brugg and Windisch. It was founded in 1308 by Elizabeth von Habsburg to mark the spot where her husband Albrecht I was murdered by Duke Johann of Swabia. The monastery was later given to a community of Franciscan monks and nuns of the Order of St Clare. After Elizabeth's death, building work on the abbey was continued by her daughter, Agnes of Hungary.

During the Reformation both of these religious communities were dissolved and in 1804 the monastery buildings were converted into a psychiatric hospital. When the hospital moved to new premises later in the 19th century, most of the monastery buildings were dismantled.

The church, however, survives. Built in 1310–30, it takes the form of a monumental Gothic basilica with a wooden ceiling. In the aisles are wooden panels with depictions of knights and coats of arms. The 11 large stained-glass windows in the presbytery are some of the finest in Switzerland. Made between 1325 and 1330 and restored in the 1980s, the windows show scenes from the lives of Christ, the Virgin, the Apostles and the saints.

---

## ❾ Baden

*See pp158–9.*

## ❿ Wettingen

**Road map:** D2. 🚆 20,200.
ℹ️ Seminarstrasse 54; 056 426 22 11.
🌐 wettingen.ch

Set among hills bordering the scenic Limmat valley, Wettingen is a small town with a magnificent Cistercian abbey, **Zisterzienserkloster**. The monastery was dissolved in 1841, and the complex now serves as a school. Its church and the adjoining cloisters are open to visitors.

The abbey church was founded in 1227 and was remodelled several times. Although the Renaissance stalls survive, the church's interior is furnished and decorated in an extravagant Baroque style, with an ornate gilt pulpit, altars and statuary.

The Gothic cloisters, whose arcades were glazed in modern times, now contain a display of stained glass ranging

Baroque pulpit in the church at Wettingen

from the 13th to the 17th centuries.

🔲 **Zisterzienserkloster**
Klosterstrasse 11. **Tel** 056 437 24 10.
Church: **Open** Mar–Oct: 9am–5pm Mon–Sat. 🅿️ Cloisters: **Open** Mar–Oct: 9am–5pm Sat & Sun.

## ⓫ Regensberg

**Road map:** D2. 🚆 500.

The attractive winegrowing village of Regensberg lies on a minor road off the highway running between Zürich and Waldshut, via Dielsdorf. Set on a hillside amid vineyards, it is one of the best-preserved medieval villages in Switzerland. Its main square and oldest streets are lined with half-timbered houses.

Half-timbered houses in the village of Regensberg

The history of Regensberg goes back to 1245. The oldest building in the town is the castle's circular crenellated keep, from the top of which there is a fine view of the vineyards and countryside around. The castle itself dates from the 16th and 17th centuries and now serves as a school for children with learning difficulties. Also of interest is the early 16th-century parish church, which overlies the foundations of a medieval building.

Linde. Kaiserstuhl's historic centre also contains many beautiful old houses, most of them having shuttered windows and steeply pitched roofs. Also of interest is Mayenfisch, a Baroque mansion, and a former Augustinian monastery, whose 16th-century building now accommodates the offices of the local authorities. The parish church of St Catherine has a fine pulpit and notable stalls. From Kaiserstuhl, visitors can cross the bridge over the Rhine, arriving at Hohentengen, on the north bank, where there is a castle, Schloss Rötelen.

Oberer Turm, the medieval tower in Kaiserstuhl

## ⑫ Kaiserstuhl

**Road map:** D2. **i** 056 265 00 30. **w** kaiserstuhl.ch

Lying on a gently sloping hillside on the left bank of the Rhine, on the border with Germany, Kaiserstuhl is a beautiful small medieval town. Its historic centre, which is contained within an irregular triangle, is a listed conservation area.

The upper corner of the triangle is marked by Oberer Turm (Upper Tower), a medieval bastion that once formed part of the town's fortifications. Nearby stands the Baroque Landhaus, Zur

### Environs

The spa town of Zurzach lies about 12 km (7 miles) west of Kaiserstuhl. Of interest to visitors here is the town's historic centre, as well as museums and a castle, Schloss Zurzach, which contains a display of paintings by August Deusser. Zurzach also has two churches: the Obere Kirche, in the Gothic style, and the Verenamünster, with Romanesque and Gothic elements incorporated into later rebuilding in the Baroque style.

## ⑬ Eglisau

**Road map:** E2. ⛰ 4,500. 🚐
**i** Untergass 7, 044 867 36 12.
**w** eglisau.ch

Eglisau straddles the River Rhine and is close to the German border. The town is surrounded by gentle hills covered in vineyards. Its origins go back to medieval times, when it was established at what was then a ford across the river, on an ancient route south to Zürich.

When a hydroelectric dam was built across the Rhine, the picturesque houses that once stood on the riverbank were engulfed by water. Eglisau's historic covered bridge was also lost. The higher part of the old town, with its 18th-century domed church, now stands just above water level. This historic centre is filled with half-timbered houses with steeply pitched roofs. Some of the houses are decorated with colourful murals.

The belvedere behind the church offers a view of the river. Nearby, a high viaduct reminiscent of an ancient aqueduct carries a railway line past the town.

### Environs

Some 10 km (6 miles) northeast of Eglisau is the small town of Rheinau. Its early 11th-century Benedictine monastery, with a fine Baroque church, is set on a sheltered bend of the Rhine.

Polychrome wall painting on a house in Eglisau

# ❾ Baden

One of Switzerland's oldest health resorts, Baden (meaning "Baths") is a peaceful, stately town. The therapeutic properties of its hot sulphur springs, which the Romans knew as Aquae Helveticae, have been exploited since ancient times. From the Middle Ages, Baden's location on the River Limmat contributed to its becoming an important centre of trade, and its beautiful Old Town (Altstadt) is the legacy of this historical status. Still a popular health resort with facilities for large numbers of visitors, Baden today is also a thriving industrial town, specializing in electromechanical engineering.

### Exploring Baden

A good starting point for a stroll around Baden's Old Town is the Landvogteischloss, the castle on the east bank of the Limmat. From here, the rest of the Old Town, on the hillside to the west, is reached by crossing a wooden bridge. A short walk north along the river leads to the spa area.

### 🏛 Schweizer Kindermuseum

Ländliweg 7. **Tel** 056 222 14 44.
**Open** 2–5pm Tue–Sat,
10am–5pm Sun. 🅦
🆆 kindermuseum.ch

Housed in an old mansion, this museum contains a collection of toys and everyday objects that illustrate various aspects of childhood, including children's mental development and education. Young visitors are encouraged to play with many of the exhibits.

### 🏚 Ruine Stein

The ruins of a castle overlook the Old Town from the top of a hill, beneath which runs a road tunnel. Originating in the 10th century, the castle was rebuilt in the 13th century as an arsenal and fortress for Austrian forces, when Baden and the surrounding area were under Habsburg rule. The castle was destroyed in 1712, during conflicts between Protestant and Catholic cantons. Now surrounded by greenery, these ruins make a pleasant place for a stroll. The hilltop offers a splendid view over the River Limmat and the Old Town.

### 🏚 Stadtturm

This tall four-sided tower, built in the 15th century, originally guarded the entrance to the Old Town. It is set with four corner turrets and is crowned by a belfry. The tower also features a clock, which is framed by a fresco and sundial on the southern façade.

### 🏛 Pfarrkirche Mariä Himmelfahrt

Kirchplatz. **Tel** 056 222 57 15.
The Church of the Assumption, Baden's parish church, was built between 1457 and 1460. Although it was remodelled on several occasions, acquiring Baroque features in the 17th century and Neo-Classical elements in the early 19th, it retains its original Gothic outline, and is crowned by a pointed spire. The church treasury, with a collection of liturgical objects, is open to visitors by appointment only.

**Coat of arms on the Stadtturm**

The Stadthaus (town hall), north of the church, contains a beautifully restored council chamber, the Tagsatzungssaal, where an early version of Switzerland's parliament sat from 1426 to 1712. The chamber is lined with fine wood panelling and stained-glass windows featuring the emblems of each of the Swiss cantons.

### 🏚 Holzbrücke

This picturesque wooden bridge spans the Limmat from the base of the Landvogteischloss. Built in 1810 to replace an earlier bridge, the Holzbrücke is a single-span structure covered by a ridge roof (see illustration on pp152–3).

Landvogteischloss, the Gothic bailiff's castle

### 🏛 Landvogteischloss

**Tel** 056 222 75 74. **Open** 1–5pm
Tue–Fri, 10am–5pm Sat & Sun. 🅦
🆆 museum.baden.ch

The massive Gothic castle on the east bank of the Limmat was built in the 15th century, and from 1415 to 1798 was the residence of Baden's bailiffs. The castle keep now houses a museum of local history.

The Baroque interior of the Pfarrkirche Mariä Himmelfahrt

NORTHERN SWITZERLAND | **159**

Rooftops of Baden's Old Town

Its archaeological section includes Roman pottery, coins and other objects found in and around Baden. There are also displays of weapons, religious items, traditional costumes of the Aargau region, and a set of interiors furnished and decorated in the style of successive historical periods.

A modern wing, which extends along the riverbank, contains displays of objects relating to Baden's more recent history, focusing mainly on the town's industrial development from the 19th century onwards.

### 🛢 Spa area

Baden's 18 thermal springs spout warm sulphur-rich waters that are especially effective in curing rheumatism and respiratory ailments.

The spa centre consists of several hotels with their own pools and wellness areas. Construction of a new public complex is being planned. Designed by renowned architect Mario Botta, it is set to open in 2017. The new facility will feature thermal pools, whirlpools, saunas and solariums, as well as massage and other treatment areas.

### 🏛 Museum Langmatt

Römerstrasse 30. **Tel** 056 200 86 70. **Open** Mar–Nov: 2–5pm Tue–Fri, 11am–5pm Sat & Sun.
Ⓦ **langmatt.ch**

On Römerstrasse, a short walk westwards from the spa area, stands a charming villa that once belonged to the art connoisseur Sidney Brown (1865–1941). The villa was built in 1900–1901; a few years later a wing was added, which, like the house itself, contains an exquisite art collection.

The nucleus of the collection consists of French Impressionist paintings, with works by Corot, Monet,

**VISITORS' CHECKLIST**

**Practical Information**
**Road map:** D2. 🚗 18,400.
ℹ Bahnhofplatz 1; 056 200 87 87. Ⓦ **baden.ch**

**Transport**
🚌 🚍

Pissarro, Renoir, Sisley, Degas and Cézanne. The collection also includes 18th-century Venetian townscapes, several works by Fragonard and Watteau, and paintings by Van Gogh and Gauguin. Some of the rooms contain 17th- and 18th-century French furniture.

Fountain in the gardens around the Museum Langmatt

---

## Baden Town Centre

① Schweizer Kindermuseum
② Ruine Stein
③ Stadtturm
④ Pfarrkirche Mariä Himmelfahrt
⑤ Holzbrücke
⑥ Landvogteischloss

0 metres 200
0 yards 200

**For keys to symbols** *see back flap*

# ⑭ Winterthur

A thriving industrial centre now associated chiefly with textiles and mechanical engineering, Winterthur is the second-largest city in the canton of Zürich. Despite its industrial character, Winterthur is a pleasant town, with many leafy streets and open green spaces. It also has several outstanding art galleries, the most celebrated of which contains paintings donated by Oskar Reinhart (1885–1965), a native of Winterthur who became a wealthy industrialist and one of Europe's greatest art collectors.

Marktgasse, the main street in Winterthur's Old Town

## Exploring Winterthur

Free of motorized traffic, Winterthur's old town centre is pleasant to explore on foot. A Museumbus circles the town every hour, stopping at each of Winterthur's principal museums and art galleries.

### 🏛 Stadtkirche

**Open** 10am–4pm Mon–Sat.

This Gothic parish church, which was built on the site of an 8th-century shrine, dates from the mid-13th century and was extended several times until the 1500s. It takes the form of a vaulted basilica with a square apse flanked by Baroque towers. Decorative features of the interior include an organ screen, a font, which dates from 1656, wall paintings and fine 19th-century stained-glass windows.

Stained-glass window in the Stadtkirche

### 🖼 Kunsthalle Winterthur

Marktgasse 25. **Tel** 052 267 51 32. **Open** noon–6pm Wed–Fri, noon–4pm Sat & Sun. 🅆 **kunsthalle winterthur.ch**

The former Waaghaus (Weigh House) has been converted into a spacious exhibition hall, the Kunsthalle Winterthur, which organizes temporary shows of modern art. Marktgasse, the Old Town's pedestrianized main artery and its principal shopping street, is lined with several other fine historic buildings. Among the oldest and most attractive is Zur Geduld (Patience House), which dates from 1717.

### 🏛 Rathaus

Marktgasse 20. **Tel** 052 267 51 26. **Open** 2–5pm Tue–Sat, 10am–noon & 2–5pm Sun. 🎨 🅒 🅑

Winterthur's Neo-Renaissance town hall was built in 1872–4 on the site of a former Gothic structure. In 1878, the ground floor was converted into a shopping arcade. The upper floors, however, have remained intact.

The rooms here include a stucco-decorated Festsaal, and former residential quarters and offices that now contain two museums. On the first floor is the private collection of paintings amassed by Jakob Briner and consisting mainly of 17th-century Dutch Old Masters. On the floor above is a collection of miniatures donated by E S Kern.

### 🏛 Museum Oskar Reinhart am Stadtgarten

Stadthausstrasse 6. **Tel** 052 267 51 72. **Open** 10am–8pm Tue, 10am–5pm Wed–Sun. 🎨 🅒 🅑

Oskar Reinhart amassed one of the greatest private art collections of the 20th century. He donated part of his collection to the town in 1951, and the rest was bequeathed to Winterthur after his death.

The collection on display in the Stadtgarten includes works by German, Austrian and Swiss artists of the late 18th to the early 20th centuries. These range from German Romantic painting to portraits of children. The Swiss artists Albert Anker, Ferdinand Hodler and Giovanni Giacometti are well represented. The best-known works from Reinhart's collection hang at Römerholz, his villa on the edge of the town.

### 🏛 Sammlung Oskar Reinhart am Römerholz

Haldenstrasse 95. **Tel** 052 269 27 40. **Open** 10am–5pm Tue & Thu–Sun, 10am–8pm Wed. 🎨 🅒 🅑 🅔 🖼

The villa where Oskar Reinhart lived from 1926 until his death contains about 200 works of art from his collection. Most of these are French Impressionist paintings, with stunning canvases by Manet, Degas, Renoir and Monet, but there are also works by artists such as Holbein, Grünewald, Cranach, Poussin, El Greco and Goya.

The main entrance to the Kunstmuseum

### 🏛 Kunstmuseum

Museumstrasse 52. **Tel** 052 267 51 62. **Open** 10am–8pm Tue, 10am–5pm Wed–Sun. 🎨 🅒 🅑 🅔 🖼 🅆 **kmw.ch**

An excellent collection of 19th- and 20th-century

paintings by an international span of artists fills the rooms of the Kunstmuseum.

Exhibits include paintings by Monet and Van Gogh, and Cubist works, including paintings by Picasso, as well as Surrealist works. Important painters and sculptors, such as Rodin, Hodler, Miró, Brancusi, Mondrian, Kandinsky and Alberto Giacometti, are also well represented.

The building also houses a natural history museum and a museum that is designed specifically for children.

### 🏛 Stadthaus
Stadthausstrasse 4a.
The imposing Neo-Renaissance Stadthaus houses the town's main

concert hall. Built in 1865–9, it was designed by Gottfried Semper, a professor of architecture at Zürich's Technical University. Semper also designed Dresden's opera house. The Stadthaus in Winterthur is considered to be one of Gottfried Semper's finest buildings.

### 🏛 Fotomuseum
Grüzenstrasse 44. **Tel** 052 234 10 60.
**Open** 11am–6pm Tue & Thu–Sun; 11am–8pm Wed. 🅿 📷 ♿ 🖥

This oustanding museum is one of the finest of its kind in Europe. It occupies a spacious and well restored warehouse about ten minutes' walk from the town centre. On view here is a

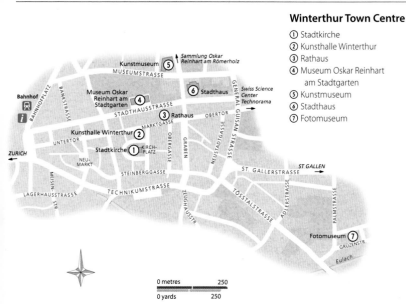

The Neo-Renaissance Stadthaus, designed by Gottfried Semper

comprehensive range of photographs, from the early beginnings of photography to the most recent examples of the art, by an international span of photographers. The museum also stages a programme of world-class exhibitions.

### 🏛 Swiss Science Center Technorama
Technoramastrasse 1. **Tel** 052 244 08 44. **Open** 10am–5pm Tue–Sun.
🅿 🆆 technorama.ch

Designed to entertain and educate, and featuring more than 500 fascinating interactive exhibits, Switzerland's only science museum is a family-friendly affair, with indoor picnic rooms and barbecue facilities in the leafy park.

## Winterthur Town Centre

① Stadtkirche
② Kunsthalle Winterthur
③ Rathaus
④ Museum Oskar Reinhart am Stadtgarten
⑤ Kunstmuseum
⑥ Stadthaus
⑦ Fotomuseum

Kunstmuseum ⑤
Sammlung Oskar Reinhart am Römerholz
MUSEUMSTRASSE
Bahnhof
BANKSTRASSE
BAHNHOFPLATZ
Museum Oskar Reinhart am Stadtgarten ④
⑥ Stadthaus
Swiss Science Center Technorama
STADTHAUSSTRASSE
GENERAL GUISAN STRASSE
③ Rathaus
OBERTOR
MARKTGASSE
Kunsthalle Winterthur ②
UNTERTOR
OBERGASSE
Stadtkirche ①
KIRCH-PLATZ
GRABEN
NEUSTADTGASSE
ZURICH
NEU-MARKT
ST. GALLERSTRASSE
ST GALLEN
STEINBERGGASSE
MEISENSTR
LAGERHAUSSTRASSE
TECHNIKUMSTRASSE
ZEUGHAUSSTR
TÖSSTALSTRASSE
ADLERSTRASSE
PALMSTRASSE
Fotomuseum ⑦
GRÜZENSTR
Eulach

0 metres 250
0 yards 250

**For keys to symbols** see back flap

# ZÜRICH

An international centre of banking and industry, Zürich is Switzerland's capital of finance and its richest city. Zürich's exuberant popular culture and vibrant arts scene also make it one of the liveliest cities in Europe. With a lakeshore setting and elegant quays, Zürich is a beautiful city, and the cobbled streets and squares of its historic centre are lined with many fine buildings.

Capital of the densely populated canton of the same name, the city of Zürich lies on the north shore of the Zürichsee at the point where the River Limmat flows north out of the lake. By the 1st century BC, a Celtic settlement, Turicum, had been established on the Lindenhof. This hill, now in the heart of the old city, was later the site of a Roman fortress. In the 9th century, a Carolingian palace was built on the Lindenhof, and a trading settlement developed at its base. Briefly under the control of the Zähringen dynasty, Zürich passed to the Holy Roman Empire in 1218 and joined the Swiss Confederation in 1351.

By the early Middle Ages, the silk, wool, linen and leather trade had already brought Zürich's merchants great wealth. However, having become too powerful, this merchant class was overthrown and replaced by guilds, who in turn held power until the late 18th century.

In the 16th century, mainly because of the activities of Ulrich Zwingli, who preached from the Grossmünster, the city's great cathedral, Zürich embraced the Reformation. Becoming rich and influential, the city then reached its apogee, only to fall into relative obscurity in the 17th and 18th centuries. In the 19th century, Zürich underwent rapid industrial growth and, thanks to Switzerland's stability and neutrality, emerged from the aftermath of both world wars as a major centre of finance. Zürich enjoys a prestigious position in international banking. It is one of the world's largest gold-trading markets and its stock exchange is one of the most important in the world.

Detail of Richard Kissling's fountain on Bahnhofplatz, in front of the main railway station

◄ Zürich's Old Town, dominated by the tower of St Peters Kirche

# Exploring Zürich

Spanned by elegant low bridges, the Limmat bisects the city as it flows north out of the Zürichsee. On the west bank is the Old Town (Altstadt), Zürich's medieval heart, dominated by the Fraumünster and St Peters Kirche. While the Old Town is now the city's commercial centre, Bahnhofstrasse, which follows the western course of the former city walls, is its smartest shopping street. On the east bank, where the Grossmünster is the principal landmark, lie the historic districts of Niederdorf and, south of Marktgasse, Oberdorf. A pleasant walk south along Utoquai leads to Zürichhorn Park, the city's largest green space.

Relief depicting a Bacchic procession, at the Johann Jacobs Museum in Zürichhorn Park

## Sights at a Glance

1. Schweizerisches Landesmuseum pp166–7
2. Museum für Gestaltung
3. Migros Museum für Gegenwartskunst
4. Hauptbahnhof
5. Bahnhofstrasse
6. Lindenhof
7. Augustinerkirche
8. St Peters Kirche
9. Zunfthaus zur Meisen
10. Fraumünster
11. Wasserkirche
12. Grossmünster
13. Rathaus
14. Limmatquai
15. Niederdorf
16. Predigerkirche
17. Eidgenössische Technische Hochschule
18. Zürich University
19. Kunsthaus pp174–5
20. Opernhaus
21. Zürichhorn Park
22. Museum Bellerive
23. Sammlung E G Bührle
24. Zürichsee
25. Museum Rietberg
26. Städtische Sukkulentensammlung

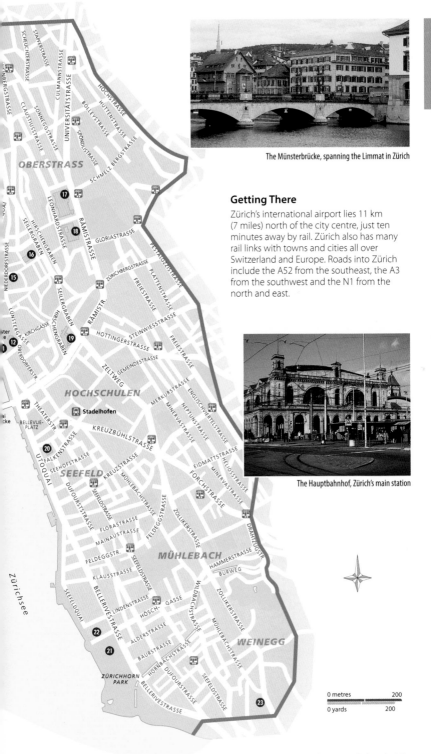

The Münsterbrücke, spanning the Limmat in Zürich

### Getting There

Zürich's international airport lies 11 km (7 miles) north of the city centre, just ten minutes away by rail. Zürich also has many rail links with towns and cities all over Switzerland and Europe. Roads into Zürich include the A52 from the southeast, the A3 from the southwest and the N1 from the north and east.

The Hauptbahnhof, Zürich's main station

| 0 metres | 200 |
| 0 yards | 200 |

For keys to symbols *see back flap*

# ❶ Schweizerisches Landesmuseum

The collections of the Swiss National Museum illustrate the country's history and culture from prehistoric times to the present day. The museum has outposts at locations around the country but its headquarters are in Zürich, which contains the largest collection of objects illustrating the cultural history of Switzerland. Highlights here include artifacts from Switzerland's rich archaeological past and a medieval treasury. There are also reconstructions of period interiors, as well as displays of costume and Swiss handicrafts. Currently undergoing renovation, the museum now features extensive sections showcasing its History of Switzerland, Swiss Homes and Furnishings, and Collections galleries.

**"Feather" Dress**
Among the fashion exhibits here, including traditional costumes, uniforms from the 17th to the 21st century and designer clothes, is this modern catwalk dress.

**Collections Gallery**
This gallery contains a large selection of exhibits covering Switzerland's cultural history, with displays of many Swiss handicrafts.

**Splendid Sleigh**
This hand-carved and exquisitely painted miniature sleigh from 1680 shows outstanding artistry.

Grour floor

Main entrance

## Gallery Guide

*While some exhibitions have moved due to the renovations, the ground floor contains early historical artifacts, the Collections gallery and historic rooms. The first floor houses the History of Switzerland gallery and more period rooms, while the second and third floors display the arms collections.*

**Key**

- ☐ Collections gallery
- ☐ Tower of Arms
- ☐ History of Switzerland
- ☐ Temporary exhibitions
- ☐ Swiss Homes and Furnishings

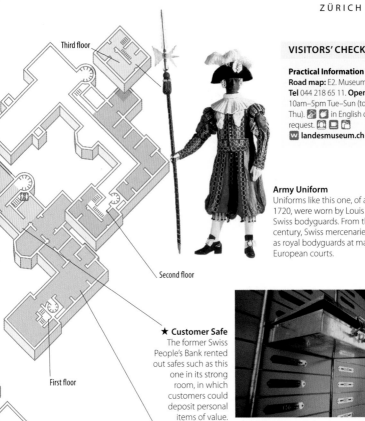

Third floor

Second floor

First floor

## VISITORS' CHECKLIST

**Practical Information**
**Road map:** E2. Museumstrasse 2.
**Tel** 044 218 65 11. **Open**
10am–5pm Tue–Sun (to 7pm
Thu). 🚌 🚗 in English on
request. 🏠 📷 📱
Ⓦ **landesmuseum.ch**

### Army Uniform
Uniforms like this one, of about
1720, were worn by Louis XIV's
Swiss bodyguards. From the 15th
century, Swiss mercenaries served
as royal bodyguards at many
European courts.

### ★ Customer Safe
The former Swiss
People's Bank rented
out safes such as this
one in its strong
room, in which
customers could
deposit personal
items of value.

### Family at Johann Caspar Lavater's Deathbed
Antonio Orazio Moretto's painting of the 18th-century Swiss
poet and physiognomist in 1801 is representative of works
of art portraying Switzerland's historical and cultural figures.

### ★ Globe
Among the scientific instruments on
display, this globe by Jost Bürgi (1552–1632)
demonstrates an outstanding combination
of scientific knowledge and artistic skills.

**For keys to symbols** *see back flap*

The Museum für Gestaltung, a museum of design and the applied arts

## ❷ Museum für Gestaltung

Ausstellungsstrasse 60. **Tel** 043 446 67 67. **Open** 10am–5pm Tue–Sun (to 8pm Wed). 🅿 🖪 🖭 📷 **W** museum-gestaltung.ch

Architecture, graphic art, industrial design and the applied arts are the main focus of the exhibitions mounted by the Museum of Design. Although it is devoted mostly to temporary exhibitions, the museum also has its own permanent collection of posters, with examples by Henri de Toulouse-Lautrec, as well as a collection of drawings dating from the 16th century.

## ❸ Migros Museum für Gegenwartskunst

Limmatstrasse 270. **Tel** 044 277 20 50. **Open** noon–6pm Tue, Wed & Fri, noon–8pm Thu, 11am–5pm Sat & Sun. 🅿 🖪 in English on request. **W** migrosmuseum.ch

Several galleries with a dynamic programme of art exhibitions have made Zürich a leading international centre of contemporary art. One such gallery is the Migros Museum für Gegenwartskunst, which is located in the former Löwenbräu brewery. It specializes in organizing exhibitions of current art by Swiss and foreign artists. The museum provides an interactive space for reflection and viewing the works on display.

## ❹ Hauptbahnhof

Bahnhofplatz.

Zürich's monumental Neo-Renaissance train station is one of the city's greatest icons. Completed in 1871, it is well preserved and the original structure of the main hall is unaltered. The clean, well-kept concourse is lined with the stylish signboards of shops. Throughout the year, this space is filled with stalls, and it is also used for seasonal fairs and markets. Beneath the concourse is a modern shopping centre.

From the concourse ceiling hangs an eye-catching statue, its vibrant, almost garish colours contrasting with the sobriety of the surroundings. This is *Guardian Angel*, by Niki de St-Phalle (1930–2002), the French sculptor and wife of the Swiss installation artist Jean Tinguely.

## ❺ Bahnhofstrasse

Uhrenmuseum Beyer: Bahnhofstrasse 31. **Tel** 043 344 63 63. **Open** 2–6pm Mon–Fri. 🅿 🖪 **W** beyer-ch.com

Running north to south from Bahnhofplatz to the edge of the Zürichsee, Bahnhofstrasse is a long avenue that lies on the course of the medieval city's moat. Mostly pedestrianized, and with tramlines running along it, Bahnhofstrasse is Zürich's principal shopping street and the centre of its commercial activity. It is lined with upmarket shops and chic restaurants, as well as the headquarters of several major Swiss banks.

Between Bahnhofstrasse and Löwenstrasse (to the east and west) and Schweizergasse and Sihlstrasse (to the north and south) are Zürich's foremost department stores, Globus and Jelmoli. Both offer exclusive brands and upmarket cafeteria-style dining.

Beneath Beyer, a watch and jewellery shop at Bahnhofstrasse 31, is the **Uhrenmuseum Beyer**. This clock museum contains a collection of timepieces ranging from the simplest timekeeping devices, such as sundials, to elegant modern watches.

Level with Fraumünster, Bahnhofstrasse opens onto Paradeplatz on its western side. Once a military parade ground, the square is now lined with large buildings, including the headquarters of Sprüngli, the Swiss chocolatier, and of the bank Credit Suisse.

Bahnhofstrasse, Zürich's most upmarket shopping street

*For hotels and restaurants see pp248–55 and pp264–75*

Bahnhofstrasse ends at Bürkliplatz. Facing onto the Zürichsee, this square is the departure point for boat trips on the lake.

## ❻ Lindenhof

A tree-covered hill rises on the west bank of the Limmat. This is the Lindenhof, whose strategic position made it an ideal location for a Celtic settlement and later for a Roman fort. In the 10th century, an imperial palace stood here. Although no buildings survive, an observation platform offers a view of the surrounding rooftops and of the university buildings to the east. The hilltop also has a giant chessboard for open-air games.

The ascetically bare interior of the Augustinerkirche

## ❼ Augustinerkirche

Augustinerhof 8. **Tel** 044 211 12 75. **Open** 10am–5pm Mon–Fri, noon–5pm Sat.

This beautiful, unpretentious early Gothic church was built in the late 13th century for a community of Augustinian monks. When the monastery was dissolved during the Reformation, the church was deconsecrated and stood unused for almost 300 years. The interior was restored in the 1840s and in 1847 the church was reconsecrated and taken over by Roman Catholics.

The church's present appearance is the result of remodelling carried out in 1958–9. The building takes the form of a vaulted basilica, with a small presbytery enclosed on three sides. None of the church's historic furnishings have survived.

Augustinergasse leads to the heart of the Old Town, its winding alleys densely packed with fine old houses with oriel windows. It is full of small restaurants and cafés, as well as art galleries, antique shops and boutiques.

## ❽ St Peters Kirche

St-Peter-Hofstatt 6. **Tel** 044 211 25 88. **Open** 8am–6pm Mon–Fri, 10am–4pm Sat, 11am–5pm Sun.

The most distinctive feature of the Church of St Peter is its clockface. With a diameter of 8.7 m (28 ft), it is the largest church clockface in Europe.

The church stands on the site of a pre-Romanesque structure dating from the 9th century and of an early Romanesque church dating from about 1000. The oldest surviving vestiges are those of a late Romanesque church erected in the early 13th century. They include the simple rectangular presbytery, which is lit by a semicircular window with an intricate frame. The presbytery is crowned by a tower, the upper section of which dates from the mid-15th century.

The main body of the church dates from 1705–16. It takes the form of a galleried basilica with a striking Baroque interior. The dark panelling contrasts with the red columns of the nave and the brilliant whiteness of the stucco decoration.

St Peters Kirche, distinguished by the large clockface on its tower

## ❾ Zunfthaus zur Meisen

Münsterhof 20. **Tel** 044 221 28 07. **Open** 10am–5pm Thu–Sun.

This elegant late Baroque house was built in the 18th century as the guild house of wine merchants. It has fine proportions, with pedimented columns dividing the façade into three sections.

The house now contains a collection of 18th-century faience and porcelain from the Schweizerisches Landesmuseum (see pp166–7). While the collection features some exquisite pieces by leading European porcelain manufacturers, including Meissen and Sèvres, some of the most interesting exhibits are locally made items produced by Schooren and other Swiss manufacturers.

Zunfthaus zur Meisen, once the wine merchants' guild house

## ⑩ Fraumünster

Am Münsterhofplatz. **Tel** 044 211 41 00. **Open** Nov–Mar: 10am–4pm daily; Apr–Oct: 10am–6pm daily.

The history of the Fraumünster, or Women's Minster, goes back to 853, when King Ludwig the German made his daughter Hildegard the abbess of a convent here. The convent was dissolved during the Reformation, and the site is occupied by the Stadthaus, a Neo-Gothic building that is now used for exhibitions.

The church, however, survives. It has a mid-13th century presbytery in the late Romanesque style, an early Gothic transept and a nave that has been remodelled several times. The Neo-Gothic façade was added in 1911.

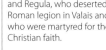
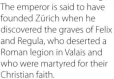
*Window by Chagall in the Fraumünster*

The presbytery is lit by stained-glass windows designed by Marc Chagall (1887–1985) and made in 1970. They depict biblical themes, and a different colour predominates in each. The central window, where green is the dominant colour, depicts scenes from the life of Christ. It is flanked by a blue window with a design inspired by the visions of Jacob, and by a yellow window, known as the Zion Window, featuring King David and the New Jerusalem. The orange window in the north

wall depicts the Prophets and that in the south wall, in red and navy blue, depicts the Law. Chagall also designed the rosette in the south transept, illustrating the Creation. The north transept has a window with a giant vision of Paradise created by Augusto Giacometti and installed in 1940.

The Romanesque cloisters on the south side of the church are decorated with frescoes executed by Paul Bodmer in 1923–32. They tell the story of the convent's foundation and illustrate the lives of Felix and Regula, patron saints of Zürich, and of the city's legendary links with Charlemagne. The emperor is said to have founded Zürich when he discovered the graves of Felix and Regula, who deserted a Roman legion in Valais and who were martyred for their Christian faith.

## ⑪ Wasserkirche

Limmatquai 31. **Tel** 044 261 66 19. **Open** 2–5pm Mon & Wed–Fri, 9am–noon Tue.

This late Gothic church marks the spot where Felix and Regula were martyred in Roman times *(see above)*. The Wasserkirche, meaning "Water Church", owes its name to its location on an islet that is now joined to the

*The Wasserkirche with the adjoining Helmhaus on the left*

mainland. Built in 1479–84, the church has an austere interior. Alongside the Wasserkirche stands the Helmhaus, a former guildhall that is now used for exhibitions of modern art.

## ⑫ Grossmünster

Grossmünsterplatz. **Tel** 044 252 59 49. Cloister & Church: **Open** Mar–Oct: 10am–6pm daily; Nov–Feb:10am–5pm Mon–Sat, noon–5pm Sun. Tower: **Open** Mar–Oct: 10am–5pm Mon–Sat, 12:30–5:30pm Sun; Nov–Feb: 10am–4:30pm Mon–Sat, 12:30–4:30pm Sun. ⓦ **grossmuenster.ch**

The tall twin towers of the Grossmünster, or Great Minster, dominate Zürich's skyline from the east bank of the Limmat. According to legend, Charlemagne founded a church here in the late 8th to early 9th century, on the graves of Felix and Regula. After they were killed at the site of the Wasserkirche, these martyrs are said to have carried their heads up the hill to the spot now marked by the Grossmünster.

Construction on the present Romanesque-Gothic basilica began in about 1100, and the west towers were eventually completed in the late 15th century.

Boats moored along the east bank of the River Limmat, with the Grossmünster in the background

*For hotels and restaurants see pp248–55 and pp264–75*

It was from the pulpit of the Grossmünster that the humanist Ulrich Zwingli preached the Reformation, which then spread to other cities, such as Bern and Basel. In line with reformist ideals, the minster was stripped of its furnishings and decoration, so that the interior is now almost completely bare. However, vestiges of Gothic frescoes as well as the fine Romanesque capitals of the nave survive.

The Grossmünster's large crypt contains a 15th-century statue of Charlemagne, which originally graced the south tower. (The present statue on the tower is a replica.) Other notable features of the Grossmünster are its Romanesque portal, with a bronze door (1935), and stained-glass windows by Augusto Giacometti (1932).

The Grossmünster's bronze doors, within a fine Romanesque portal

## ⑬ Rathaus

Limmatquai 55. **Tel** 043 259 68 11. **Open** 10–11:30am Tue & Thu.
🎫 book one month in advance.
🔲 kantonsrat.zh.ch

Zürich's town hall was built on piles driven into the riverbed, and the waters of the Limmat flow beneath the platform on which it stands. Replacing a medieval town hall, the present two-storey building, in the Baroque style, dates from 1694–8.

The façade is ornamented with friezes featuring masks and the windows are crowned with broken pediments filled with busts. The marble doorway has

### Dada

An avant-garde artistic movement, Dada came to prominence in Zürich in about 1916, as an anarchic reaction against the senseless carnage of World War I. The focus of the movement was the Cabaret Voltaire in Zürich and among its main exponents were Tristan Tzara, Hans Arp and Francis Picabia. Dada's essential aim was to flout convention and the traditional values of the artistic establishment, and to produce art by haphazard or absurd methods. Dada later spread to France, Germany and the United States.

A Dadaist work by Hans Arp

gilt decoration. One of the most impressive rooms within is the grand Baroque council chamber.

## ⑭ Limmatquai

This attractive riverside boulevard runs along the east bank of the Limmat, from Bellevueplatz in the south to the Bahnhofbrücke in the north. The most interesting stretch of Limmatquai is its southern section, in the vicinity of the Grossmünster and Rathaus. Here the boulevard is lined with guild houses, which have been converted into shops or restaurants.

Among the finest of these houses are Haus zur Saffran at no. 54, dating from c. 1720; Haus zur Rüden at no. 42, dating from the 17th century; and the adjoining Haus zur Zimmerleuten, an 18th-century building with a colourful oriel window. Most of these houses are half-timbered.

Haus zur Rüden, a 17th-century guild house on Limmatquai

## ⑮ Niederdorf

Consisting of a dense network of cobbled alleys leading towards Limmatquai, the district of Niederdorf constitutes the heart of the Old Town's eastern section. The main artery through this historic district is Niederdorfstrasse, a pedestrianized thoroughfare that is continued by Münstergasse to the south.

Niederdorf's narrow alleys are lined with antique shops and art galleries, as well as small hotels, cafés, restaurants, beer halls and fast-food outlets.

Detail on house on Niederdorfstrasse

## ⑯ Predigerkirche

Predigerplatz. **Tel** 044 261 09 89.
**Open** 10am–6pm Mon–Sat, noon–6pm Sun.

Set amid the worldly bustle of Niederdorf, this church is a haven of peace. Its origins go back to the 13th century, when it formed part of a monastery. During the Reformation, the monastery was dissolved and Predigerkirche became a Protestant church. It is now the university's main church. The building underwent much alteration. In the 17th century the nave was rebuilt in the Baroque style. The spire on the west tower, added in 1900, is the tallest in Zürich.

## ⓱ Eidgenössische Technische Hochschule

Rämistrasse 101. Graphische Sammlung der ETH: **Tel** 044 632 40 46. **Open** 10am–5pm Mon, Tue, Thu & Fri, 10am–7pm Wed. Thomas-Mann-Archiv: Schönberggasse 15. **Tel** 044 632 40 45. **Open** 2–4pm Wed & Sat.

The Federal Institute of Technology, or ETH, was founded in 1855 and is now one of the most highly regarded universities in the world. It occupies a Neo-Renaissance building designed by Gottfried Semper, a prominent German architect who was also the institute's first professor of architecture.

The building is of architectural interest in its own right, as is the collection of drawings and graphic art (**Graphische Sammlung**), and for the temporary exhibitions that often fill its corridors. The ETH also owns the **Thomas-Mann-Archiv**, in a building nearby. The archive is the entire literary legacy of this great German writer, who died in Zürich in 1955.

The terrace of the ETH building commands a magnificent view of the city. Just to the north of the ETH is the upper station of the Polybahn, a funicular that runs down to Central, a large square on the east side of the Bahnhofbrücke.

## ⓲ Universität

Rämistrasse 71. Archäologische Sammlung: Rämistrasse 73. **Tel** 044 634 28 11. **Open** 1–6pm Tue–Fri, 11am–5pm Sat & Sun.

Set on a hillside east of Niederdorf, Zürich's university buildings overlook the city. Athough the present complex dates from 1911–14, the university was founded in 1833. It is now the largest in Switzerland, and is a prominent centre of research and higher education.

The university's collection of archaeological artifacts (**Archäologische Sammlung**) is displayed in the

The Heidi Weber Museum, near Zürichhorn Park

adjoining building. It contains some fine Egyptian, Etruscan and Mesopotamian pieces.

## ⓳ Kunsthaus

*See pp174–5.*

## ⓴ Opernhaus

Falkenstrasse 1. **Tel** 044 268 64 00. Ⓦ opernhaus.ch

Zürich's Neo-Baroque opera house was designed by the Viennese architects Hermann Helmer and Ferdinand Fellner and completed in 1891 *(see illustration on p176)*. The elegant façade is fronted by two tiers of columns and a balcony framed by porticoes. Allegorical statues crown the roof. One of the city's most prestigious cultural venues, the Opernhaus stages a world-class programme of operas and ballets.

Statues on the façade of the Opernhaus

## ㉑ Zürichhorn Park

Chinagarten: **Open** mid-Mar–mid-Oct: 11am–7pm daily. Atelier Hermann Haller: Höschgasse 6. **Tel** 044 383 42 47. **Open** Jul–Sep: noon–6pm Fri–Sun. Heidi Weber Museum: Höschgasse 8. **Tel** 044 383 64 70. **Open** Jul–Oct: noon–6pm Wed–Sun.

This pleasant park to the south of the city centre stretches out beyond Utoquai, along the east shore of the Zürichsee and around the Zürichhorn, a promontory. The park contains sculptures by well-known modern artists. At the northern end stands a bronze sculpture by Henry Moore, and at the southern end a large kinetic sculpture that Jean Tinguely created for Expo 64 in Lausanne. The piece is entitled *Heureka*, and from April to October at 11.15am and 5.15pm every day its mechanism is set in motion.

In the eastern part of the park high walls enclose the **Chinagarten**. This Chinese garden, laid out in 1994, was a gift from Kunming, the Chinese city that is twinned with Zürich. It is filled with plants, buildings and objects typical of the Chinese art of creating a formal garden *(see illustration on p177)*.

The park is bordered by several interesting buildings. On Höschgasse is the **Atelier Hermann Haller**, the studio of this Swiss sculptor. Designed by Haller (1880–1950), it is a rare example of wooden Bauhaus architecture. The colourful pavilion next to it is the **Heidi Weber**

**Museum**, formerly known as Le Corbusier Haus. Designed by Le Corbusier, it is one of the last projects that this Swiss-born architect worked on before his death in 1965.

## ㉒ Museum Bellerive

Höschgasse 3. **Tel** 043 446 44 69. **Open** Apr–Nov: 10am–5pm Tue–Sun (to 8pm Thu); Dec–Mar: 10am–5pm Tue–Sun. 🖼 📷
**W** museum-bellerive.ch

Sculpture by Henry Moore in Zürichhorn Park

Specializing in the applied arts, as well as in design, decoration and crafts, the Museum Bellerive displays its permanent collection in the form of a continuous programme of temporary exhibitions. The museum's extensive holdings include furniture, tapestry, jewellery, stained glass and other pieces produced by the English Arts and Crafts Movement in the late 19th century, and Art Nouveau glass, jewellery and ceramics. The work of Swiss craftsmen and designers also figures prominently in the collections. The shop sells a great range of design objects.

## ㉓ Sammlung E G Bührle

Zollikerstrasse 172. **Tel** 044 422 00 86. **Open** first Sun of the month, by appointment only. 🖼 **W** buehrle.ch

A small but exquisite collection of Impressionist and Post-Impressionist paintings and other works of art is housed in a mansion south of Zürichhorn Park. The collection was formed by the Swiss industrialist Emil G Bührle between 1934 and 1956 and was opened to the public after his death in 1965. Besides paintings by Delacroix, Courbet and Corot, the collection includes little-known works by Monet, Degas, Van Gogh and Gauguin, as well as Dutch and Italian Baroque painting and fine Gothic woodcarving.

Pending an as-yet-undetermined move to the Kunsthaus (see pp174–5), the collection is open to the public by appointment only on the first Sunday of the month.

## ㉔ Zürichsee

Zürichsee Schifffahrtsgesellschaft: Mythenquai 333. **Tel** 044 487 13 33.

This beautiful glacial lake stretches in a 40-km (25-mile) arc from Zürich to the foot of the Glarner Alps. The many boat trips departing from Zürich range from short trips to half- and full-day cruises, taking in several lakeshore towns and villages. The main landing stage in Zürich is at Bürkliplatz. The lake's clear waters are unpolluted and safe for swimming.

## ㉕ Museum Rietberg

Gablerstrasse 15. **Tel** 044 206 31 31. Villa Wesendonck & Park-Villa Rieter: **Open** 10am–5pm Tue & Fri–Sun, 10am–8pm Wed & Thu. 🖼 single charge for both villas. 🖼 ♿ 📷
**W** rietberg.ch

The vast assemblage of ethnographic pieces and Oriental artifacts that make up the collections of this museum is displayed in two villas linked by extensive underground exhibition areas. **Villa Wesendonck**, a Neo-Classical mansion in which the composer Richard Wagner once stayed, houses the main collection. This consists of wooden, bronze and ceramic objects from Africa, India, Tibet, China, Japan and other Southeast Asian countries. The neighbouring **Park-Villa Rieter** is devoted to Asian art. Two floors of the house are filled with changing selections of Indian, Chinese and Japanese prints and paintings.

## ㉖ Städtische Sukku-lentensammlung

Mythenquai 88. **Tel** 044 412 12 80. **Open** 9am–4:30pm daily.

With more than 8,000 species of cacti, spurges, agaves, aloes and other succulents, this collection is one of the largest of its kind in Europe. Amazing succulents from every arid region of the world, from giant agaves to the tiniest cacti, are presented here in a fascinating display.

The Zürichsee, with Bürkliplatz in the left foreground and the Grössmunster in the right background

# ⑲ Kunsthaus

Switzerland's greatest art gallery, the Kunsthaus contains important works of art ranging from medieval religious paintings and Dutch Old Masters to Impressionist and Post-Impressionist paintings. The gallery's holdings also exemplify the major art movements of the 20th century. Highlights of this superb collection include paintings by the 19th-century Swiss artists Ferdinand Hodler and Albert Anker, the largest assemblage of the work of Edvard Munch outside Scandinavia, paintings by Marc Chagall, and paintings and sculpture by Alberto Giacometti. The Kunsthaus also stages large-scale temporary exhibitions.

**War**
In this dramatic painting dating from 1896, Arnold Böcklin depicted war as one of the terrifying Horsemen of the Apocalypse.

### Gallery Guide
*On the first floor, Swiss, European, American and contemporary works are exhibited. The second floor displays modern art and photography.*

Second floor

First floor

Ground floor

Main entrance

**Key**

- Swiss art
- Early 18th-century European art
- 19th-century French art
- Photography/Sculpture
- 19th and early 20th-century European art
- American art
- Contemporary art
- Temporary exhibitions

**Falstaff in the Laundry Basket**
Many paintings by the Swiss artist Henri Füssli were inspired by literature. This one, dating from 1792, illustrates a scene from Shakespeare's play *The Merry Wives of Windsor*.

Mezzanine

### Bird in Space
This elegant sculpture, created by Constantin Brancusi in 1925, is an abstract synthesis of the movement and apparent weightlessness of a bird in flight. Ovoid shapes typify Brancusi's mature work.

### VISITORS' CHECKLIST

**Practical Information**
Heimplatz 1. **Tel** 044 253 84 84.
**Open** 10am–6pm Tue, Sat & Sun,
10am–8pm Wed–Fri.
**w** kunsthaus.ch

### Guitar on a Pedestal Table
Like this painting of 1915, many works from Pablo Picasso's Cubist period feature a guitar.

### Au-dessus de Paris
The poetic imagery of Marc Chagall's paintings was inspired by his Russian Jewish origins. Floating figures, like those in this 1968 painting, are a recurring theme in his work.

### ★ Cabanes Blanches
Some of Vincent van Gogh's most powerful and richly expressive paintings are the views of the Provençal countryside that he painted in the final years of his tortured life.

### ★ The Holy Family
This tender painting by Peter Paul Rubens, dating from c.1630, is one of the most important pieces in the museum's collection of Flemish Baroque works.

**For keys to symbols** *see back flap*

# ENTERTAINMENT IN ZÜRICH

The most vibrant of all Swiss cities, Zürich enjoys an extremely active, innovative and multifaceted cultural life. The Schauspielhaus offers some of the best productions in German theatre. Zürich has its own symphony and chamber orchestras. Prestigious programmes of opera, ballet and classical music take place in the Opernhaus and Tonhalle, the main concert hall. Zürich's club scene, which is concentrated in the district of Zürich West and the Industrie-Quartier, has also burgeoned, and its nightclubs are among the liveliest of any European city. With art-house cinemas, small theatres, cutting-edge art galleries and a population of artists and musicians, Zürich West has become the hub of a lively underground culture. Boisterous street festivals with parades and music are also part of Zürich's cultural life.

The Opernhaus, Zürich's main venue for ballet and opera

## Information and Tickets

Cultural events taking place in Zürich are listed in several publications. *City Guide Zürich*, published quarterly by **Zürich Tourism**, is available free from the tourist office and can also be picked up at various points around the city. The bi-monthly *Zürich in Your Pocket* can be downloaded online or found at the airport, train stations and tourist offices. German-language *Züritipp* appears as a supplement to the Friday edition of *Tages Anzeiger*, the daily newspaper, and is also available from the tourist office. The Zürich Tourism website also offers podcasts (as MP3 downloads) with nightlife information.

Tickets for any type of event can be bought at tourist offices, train stations and supermarkets, as well as online from **Ticketcorner** or **Startticket**. Tickets can also be purchased from the box offices of individual venues.

## Theatre, Opera and Classical Music

Having no fewer than a dozen theatres, Zürich is a leading centre of the dramatic arts. Almost all productions are in German. Zürich's main theatre is the **Schauspielhaus**, which is renowned for its innovative productions. This theatre has two stages: the Schauspielhaus Pfauen, which is used for mainstream plays, and the Keller, where more experimental productions are staged. Other productions are staged in the main auditorium (Halle) of the **Schauspielhaus Schiffbau**, in the trendy district of Zürich West. The Schiffbau also has a studio stage.

The **Opernhaus** is one of Europe's leading opera and ballet theatres. As tickets for its highly regarded productions sell out rapidly, booking well in advance is usually necessary. Returns are, however, sometimes available.

The Tonhalle Orchestra and Zürich Chamber Orchestra both perform regularly at the **Tonhalle**. This grand Baroque building, completed in 1895, is renowned for its excellent acoustics. Its inaugural concert, in 1895, was given in the presence of the composer Johannes Brahms. The best way to ensure you obtain tickets for concerts at the Tonhalle is to book well in advance. This is not necessary, however, for organ recitals and concerts of choral and chamber music given in many of Zürich's churches.

Participants in the August Street Parade

Music festival in the courtyard of the Schweizerisches Landesmuseum

The Chinagarten in Zürichhorn Park

## Cinemas

Most films screened in Zürich's many cinemas are shown in their original language. The initials E/D/F in listings and on posters indicate that a film is shown in English with German and French subtitles; the letter D alone indicates that a film has been dubbed into German.

Large multiscreen complexes such as the **Abaton** and **Kino Corso** screen international blockbusters and the latest releases. **Kino Arthouse Alba** and **Kino Xenix**, by contrast, specialize in non-commercial productions. **RiffRaff**, in Zürich West, is a four-screeen cinema complex with a bistro and bar.

Most cinemas offer cheaper tickets on Mondays.

## Nightclubs

Zürich's nightclubs range from upmarket venues in the city centre to the more relaxed and innovative establishments concentrated in Zürich West. Among the smartest clubs are **Adagio**, with a medieval-style decor and jazz and rock music; **Icon Club**, with themes such as Ibiza and Russian Ladies; and **Kaufleuten**, with house and

hip-hop music. While **Mascotte** employs internationally known DJs and hosts concerts and English-language stand-up comedy, **Labor Bar** offers the full range of musical styles. **Rage Cruise Club**, meanwhile, is a focal point of Zürich's gay scene, filling a huge industrial space with theme rooms.

## Live Music

The top live music venue in Zürich is **Rote Fabrik**, an arts complex near the lakeshore in the city's southwestern suburbs. As well as staging concerts by international bands, Rote Fabrik is also an arts complex with facilities for film and theatre, and it has a bar and restaurant.

**Moods**, which shares the Schiffbau building with Schauspielhaus Schiffbau, is the city's foremost jazz venue, with international and local performers providing a continuous programme of all styles of jazz.

Gun in a courtyard of the Schweizerisches Landesmusem

# DIRECTORY

## Info & Tickets

**Event Guides**
🆆 cityguide.com
🆆 inyourpocket.com
🆆 zueritipp.ch

**Starticket**
**Tel** 0900 325 325.
🆆 starticket.ch

**Ticketcorner**
**Tel** 0900 800 800.
🆆 ticketcorner.ch

**Zürich Tourism**
Hauptbahnhof. **Tel** 044 215 40 00. 🆆 zuerich.com

## Theatre, Opera & Classical Music

**Opernhaus**
Theaterplatz 1. **Tel** 044 268 66 66. 🆆 opernhaus.ch

**Schauspielhaus Pfauen**
Rämistrasse 34.
**Tel** 044 258 77 77.
🆆 schauspielhaus.ch

**Schauspielhaus Schiffbau**
Schiffbaustrasse 4.
**Tel** 044 258 77 77.
🆆 schauspielhaus.ch

**Tonhalle**
Claridenstrasse 7. **Tel** 044 206 34 34. 🆆 tonhalle-orchester.ch

## Cinemas

**Abaton**
Heinrichstrasse 269.
**Tel** 0900 55 67 89.

**Kino Arthouse Alba**
Zähringerstrasse 44.
**Tel** 044 250 55 40.

**Kino Corso**
Theaterstrasse 10.
**Tel** 0900 55 67 89.

**Kino Xenix**
Kanzleistrasse 56.
**Tel** 044 242 04 11.

**RiffRaff**
Neugasse 57.
**Tel** 044 444 22 00.

## Nightclubs

**Adagio**
Gotthardstrasse 5.
**Tel** 044 206 36 66.

**Icon Club**
Augustinerhof.
**Tel** 044 448 11 33.

**Kaufleuten**
Pelikanstrasse 18.
**Tel** 044 225 33 00.

**Labor Bar**
Schiffbaustrasse 3.
**Tel** 044 272 44 02.

**Mascotte**
Theaterstrasse 10.
**Tel** 044 260 15 80.
🆆 mascotte.ch

**Rage Cruise Club**
Wagistrasse 13.
🆆 rage.ch

## Live Music

**Moods**
Schiffbaustrasse 6.
**Tel** 044 276 80 00.

**Rote Fabrik**
Seestrasse 395.
**Tel** 044 485 58 58.
🆆 rotefabrik.ch

# SHOPPING IN ZÜRICH

Bahnhofstrasse, which runs north to south from Zürich's train station, is reputed to be one of the most expensive shopping streets in the world. It is lined with smart boutiques, the windows of which are filled with glittering displays of the best watches and jewellery, as well as furs, porcelain, leather goods and other luxury items. However, Zürich also has an abundance of shops offering a great variety of high-quality items that are at more affordable prices. This city is one of the best places to buy souvenirs such as excellent handcrafted work, as well as delicacies including Swiss cheeses and chocolates. Along the narrow streets in the Old Town, on the west bank of the Limmat, and the cobbled alleys of Niederdorf, on the east bank, interesting antique and souvenir shops can be found.

Souvenir stall with a range of handcrafted items

## Opening Hours

Most shops in central Zürich are open from 9am to 8pm Monday to Saturday, although many shops close between 4pm and 6pm on Saturday. Some small shops and boutiques may close on Monday, but many stores on Bahnhofstrasse are open on Sunday.

## Watches and Jewellery

Expensive watches by prestigious makers such as Patek Philippe and Rolex and fine jewellery by such internationally renowned designers as Cartier can be found in the upmarket shops that line Bahnhofstrasse. **Gübelin** and **Bucherer** both have branches here, as does **Swatch Store**, which offers a good range of Swiss-made timepieces that are less expensive but renowned for their fashion and flair.

## Handcrafted Items and Souvenirs

One of the best outlets for high-quality handmade Swiss craft items, such as decorative glass, jewellery and ceramics, as well as Swiss designer clothing, is **Schweizer Heimatwerk**, which has several branches in the city and another at Zürich airport. **Dolmetsch**, on Limmatquai, stocks a large selection of penknives, watches and other Swiss-made items. The Schipfe district, along the River Limmat, has many handicraft shops.

A souvenir shop, with Swiss specialities

Other specialist handicraft shops can be found in the Niederdorf district and along Langstrasse.

## Leather Goods

Most of Zürich's high-class leather-goods shops are on Bahnhofstrasse. Among them is **Navyboot**, which offers shoes, belts, briefcases, handbags and wallets. Another excellent leather shop is **Lederladen**, on Schipfe, which has a fine stock of handmade items.

## Bookshops

An extensive range of books in English is stocked by the **English Bookshop**, part of the Orell Füssli chain, on Bahnhofstrasse. The **Travel Bookshop**, on Rindermarkt, also stocks travel books in English, as well as maps and Alpine trekking and mountaineering guides.

The upper area of the Niederdorf district contains many antiquarian bookshops, several specializing in particular subjects and many carrying selections of books in English.

## Art and Antiques

The streets of Zürich's Old Town contain many interesting art and antique shops. Once a locksmith's shop, **Limited Stock**, on Spiegelgasse, has an eclectic selection of objets d'art. **Greenwich**, on Rämistrasse, stocks antique watches.

Jelmoli, one of Zürich's leading department stores, on Seidengasse

## Chocolate

Shops offering Switzerland's famous brands of chocolate abound in Zürich. A particularly pleasant place to sample and buy Swiss chocolate is the branch of **Confiserie Sprüngli** on Paradeplatz. Its signature chocolate is the Luxemburgerli – macaroons in a great variety of flavours sandwiched together with chocolate. The shop also has a famous café. Other high-quality chocolatiers can be found on Bahnhofstrasse and at Zürich airport.

**Café Schober**, on Napfgasse, in the heart of Niederdorf, is a confectioner's with a café that is renowned for its excellent mugs of hot chocolate. Café Schober also sells cakes.

## Wine

Because they are rarely exported, Swiss wines are one of the country's best-kept secrets *(see pp262–3)*. Zürich has several vintners featuring wines from the cantons of Zürich, Valais, Vaud, Geneva and Neuchâtel.

Two of Zürich's leading vintners are **Baur au Lac Vins**, on Börsenstrasse, and **HoferWeine**, in Zeltweg. The latter stocks over 1,500 different wines and spirits from all over the world, including a good selection of Swiss wines. Some vintners invite customers to sample certain of the wines before they buy.

Signboard of an antique shop

## Department Stores

Zürich's two major department stores are **Jelmoli**, on Seidengasse, just west of Bahnhofstrasse, and **Globus**, on Löwenplatz, also west of Bahnhofstrasse. Both stock the full range of items associated with large department stores, including designer clothes for both men and women.

Both Jelmoli and Globus also have food halls selling high-quality foods from around the world. On offer here are many Swiss delicacies and specialities, including the finest cheeses *(see pp260–61)* and luxury chocolates.

A popular addition to Zürich West is **Im Viadukt**, a 500-metre-long shopping area that begins at Limmatstrasse 231. It features more than 30 stores, each located beneath an arch in the railway line. Built in 1894, the railway viaduct is now a bustling urban meeting place with bars, boutiques and a market hall. Here artisans sell local specialities, such as cheeses, cured meats and baked goods, as well as international foods.

## DIRECTORY

### Information

w zuerich.com

### Watches & Jewellery

**Bucherer**
Bahnhofstrasse 50.
**Tel** 044 211 26 35.

**Gübelin**
Bahnhofstrasse 36.
**Tel** 044 387 52 20.

**Swatch Store**
Bahnhofstrasse 94.
**Tel** 044 221 28 66.

### Handcrafted Items & Souvenirs

**Dolmetsch**
Limmatquai 126.
**Tel** 044 251 55 44.

**Schweizer Heimatwerk**
Bahnhofstrasse 2.
**Tel** 044 221 08 37.
Uraniastrasse 1.
**Tel** 044 222 19 55.

### Leather Goods

**Lederladen**
Schipfe 29.
**Tel** 044 221 19 54.

**Navyboot**
Bahnhofstrasse 69.
**Tel** 044 211 87 57.

### Bookshops

**English Bookshop**
Bahnhofstrasse 70.
**Tel** 044 211 04 44.

**Travel Bookshop**
Rindermarkt 20.
**Tel** 044 252 38 83.

### Antiques

**Greenwich**
Rämistrasse 2.
**Tel** 044 262 10 38.

**Limited Stock**
Spiegelgasse 22.
**Tel** 043 268 56 20.

### Chocolate

**Café Schober**
Napfgasse 4.
**Tel** 044 251 51 50.

**Confiserie Sprüngli**
Bahnhofstrasse 21.
**Tel** 044 224 47 11.

### Wine

**Baur au Lac Vins**
Börsenstrasse 27.
**Tel** 044 220 50 55.

**HoferWeine**
Zeltweg 26.
**Tel** 044 280 22 88.

### Department Stores

**Globus**
Schweizergasse 11.
**Tel** 058 578 11 11.

**Im Viadukt**
Viaduktstrasse.
**Tel** 044 201 00 60.

**Jelmoli**
Seidengasse 1.
**Tel** 044 220 44 11.

# EASTERN SWITZERLAND AND GRAUBÜNDEN

Traversed by the Rhine, which flows through the Bodensee, eastern Switzerland is a relatively low-lying region. As well as several large towns, it has extensive rural areas with the lush pastures that help produce its famous cheeses. The high Alpine region of Graubünden, to the south, is a magnet for mountaineers and winter-sports enthusiasts.

Eastern Switzerland consists of the cantons of Thurgau, Schaffhausen, St Gallen, Appenzell-Ausserrhoden and Appenzell-Innerrhoden, and Glarus. The region is bordered by Germany to the north and by Liechtenstein and Austria to the east. With a majority of German- and Italian-speakers, and a small minority who speak Romansh (a language related to Latin), eastern Switzerland is officially trilingual, and religion is divided between Protestant and Catholic. The prosperity of this less populated region is based on the service industries, fruit-growing and dairy products.

East of Glarus lies the tiny principality of Liechtenstein, a vestige of the Holy Roman Empire. An independent country, it is a member of the United Nations.

Graubünden, bordered by Austria, Italy and Liechtenstein, occupies the southeastern corner of the country. This mountainous region corresponds to the Roman province of Rhaetia Prima. While German predominates in and around urban centres in the north of the canton, Romansh survives among the rural population. With some of the country's best ski slopes and greatest resorts, Graubünden is a major centre for winter sports, and half of its population is involved in the tourist industry. South of the Rhaetian Alps are the sunny valleys of Graubünden's Italian-speaking region.

A mountain stream and pine forest in the Swiss National Park, southeastern Graubünden

◀ Beautiful ceiling frescoes in the St Gallen Cathedral

# Exploring Eastern Switzerland and Graubünden

Besides several thriving towns, such as Schaffhausen and St Gallen, and the attractive medieval village of Stein am Rhein, eastern Switzerland has vast expanses of unspoiled countryside, where ancient rural traditions and ways of life continue. Further south is the peaceful Engadine valley, where the façades of historic houses have sgraffito decoration. The resorts of St Moritz, Klosters and Davos, in Graubünden, attract visitors with superb skiing, snowboarding and tobogganing, as well as hiking and mountaineering. The Swiss National Park, in the far southeastern corner of Graubünden, is a pristine wilderness with a network of hiking trails.

Barrels at a wine-harvest festival in Graubünden

## Sights at a Glance

0 kilometres 20

0 miles 20

Bridge on the route from the Julier Pass to the Engadine

## Getting There

The easiest way to reach eastern Switzerland is by road or rail from Zürich. Intercity rail services operate from Zürich to Schaffhausen, and to St Gallen and Liechtenstein. Rail links also connect all major towns in eastern Switzerland and Graubünden. Motorway links from Zürich include the A7 to Frauenfeld and the A1 to St Gallen. From the Bodensee (Lake Constance) the A13 runs south along the Rhine valley, passing through Liechtenstein, Bad Ragaz and Chur, where it is joined by the A3 from Zürich. Continuing southward, the A13 runs beneath the San Bernardino Pass and on towards Italy.

**Key**

| | |
|---|---|
| ▬▬ | Motorway |
| ▬ | Main road |
| ⋯ | Minor road |
| ▬ | Scenic route |
| ▬▬ | Main railway |
| — | Minor railway |
| ▬ | International border |
| ▬ | Canton border |
| △ | Summit |
| ✕ | Pass |

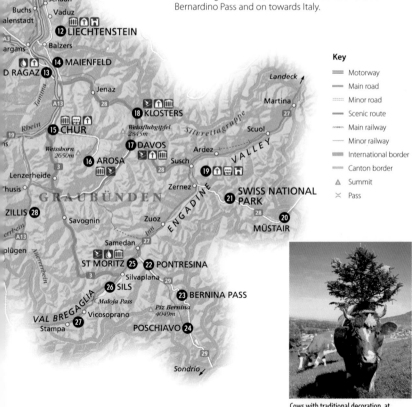

Cows with traditional decoration, at pasture in Appenzell

**For keys to symbols** *see back flap*

# ➊ Street-by-Street: Schaffhausen

Capital of the canton of the same name, Schaffhausen is set on the north bank of the Rhine, 4 km (3 miles) above waterfalls known as the Rheinfall. Lying at the point where boatmen unloaded their cargoes, the town was an important centre of trade from the early Middle Ages. The cobbled streets of Schaffhausen's Old Town (Altstadt) are lined with Gothic, Renaissance, Baroque and Rococo buildings, some with frescoed façades and others with graceful oriel windows. The Munot, a circular keep set on a hill to the east of the town, was built in the late 16th century, during the unrest caused by the Reformation. From the keep there is a fine view of the town and the river.

**Fronwagplatz**
This square, once a site of medieval markets, has two 16th-century fountains, the Metzgerbrunnen, with a statue of a mercenary, and the Mohrenbrunnen, with a statue of a Moorish king.

★ **Rathaus**
The town hall, completed in 1412 and decorated in Renaissance style, contains a beautiful council chamber.

**Altes Zeughaus**
The Old Armoury, in an imposing Renaissance style, is fronted by a doorway richly decorated with relief carvings.

★ **Haus zum Ritter**
The façade of the Knight's House is decorated with intricate Renaissance frescoes depicting aspects of knightly valour. They date from 1568–70.

**Hallen für Neue Kunst** is a gallery with an international collection of works of the 1960s and 1970s.

**Key**

— Suggested route

**Kirche St Johann**
This parish church was founded in the 11th century and completed in the early 16th. Some of its ancient wall paintings survive.

**VISITORS' CHECKLIST**

**Practical Information**
Road map: E2. 🏔 34,000.
ℹ Herrenacker 15; 052 632 40 20. 🅦 schaffhauserland.ch

**Transport**
🚊 🚉 🚌

**Schmiedstube**
This ornate Baroque doorway, with depictions of the tools of the blacksmith's trade, fronts the Smiths' Guild House.

**Museum zu Allerheiligen**, in a former monastery, has prehistoric and medieval artefacts and a collection of Swiss paintings and sculpture.

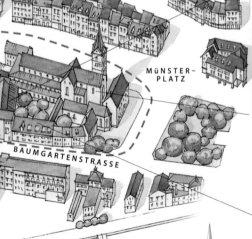

★ **Münster zu Allerheiligen**
The beautiful Romanesque minster, originally part of a Benedictine abbey founded in the 11th century, was completed in the mid-12th century.

**Schillerglocke**
The Schiller Bell in the monastery cloisters was cast in 1486. Its sound inspired the German poet Friedrich Schiller to write *Song of the Clock*.

0 metres      50
0 yards      50

The medieval town of Stein am Rhein, with Kloster St Georgen in the foreground

## ❷ Rheinfall

**Road map:** E2. 🚌 *i* Neuhausen,
Rheinfallquai 3; 052 670 02 37.
🆆 **schaffhauserland.ch**

Creating an awe-inspiring
spectacle of rainbow-tinted
spray, the waters of the Rhine
tumble off a cataract at
Neuhausen, 4 km (3 miles)
downriver from Schaffhausen.
These waterfalls, known as the
Rheinfall, are the largest in
Europe. Although they are only
23 m (75 ft) high, they are
remarkable for their width (about
150 m/492 ft) and their setting
between tree-covered banks.

The best view of the falls is
from **Schloss Laufen**, a turreted
Renaissance castle overlooking
the river from the south. From
the castle, steps lead down to
viewing platforms near the edge
of the falls. Boat trips around
the lake beneath the falls are
also offered. A spectacular
fireworks display is staged
at the Rheinfall on National
Day (1 August) each year.

## ❸ Stein am Rhein

**Road map:** E2. 🚊 3,000. 🚊 🚌 ⛴
*i* Oberstadt 3; 052 742 20 90.
🆆 **steinamrhein.ch.**

With many medieval half-
timbered buildings and
16th-century houses whose
façades are painted with
frescoes, Stein am Rhein is one
of the most beautiful sights in
Switzerland. Founded in Roman
times, this small town began to
prosper and expand in the late
11th century, when the German
emperor Heinrich II founded a
Benedictine monastery here.
The outline of the town walls

can be made out, and two of
the town gates, Obertor and
Untertor, still stand. Rathausplatz, the main square, is lined
with houses painted with motifs
reflecting their names, such as
House of the Sun or House of
the Red Ox, the town's oldest
tavern (*see illustration on pp8–9*).
The **Lindwurm Museum**
re-creates 19th-century middle-
class life over four floors of a
beautifully restored house in
the old town.

Overlooking the Rhine
stands Kloster St Georgen, a
Benedictine monastery, and its
12th-century church. The well-
preserved monastery rooms,
decorated in the early 16th
century, now house the
**Klostermuseum St Georgen**,
devoted to local history.

🏛 **Lindwurm Museum**
Understadt 18. **Tel** 052 741 25 12.
**Open** Mar–Oct: 10am–5pm daily. 🗺
🆆 **museum-lindwurm.ch**

🏛 **Klostermuseum St Georgen**
Fischmarkt. **Tel** 052 741 21 42. **Open**
Apr–Oct: 10am–5pm Tue–Sun. 🗺
🆆 **klostersanktgeorgen.ch**

## ❹ Frauenfeld

**Road map:** E2. 🚊 19,000. 🚊 🚌
*i* Bahnhofplatz 75; 052 721 31 28.
🆆 **frauenfeld.ch**

Located on the River Murg, west
of Lake Constance, Frauenfeld is
the capital of the canton of
Thurgau. It is a picturesque
town with many attractive
burgher houses in its historic
centre. They include the Baliere
in Kreuzplatz, a half-timbered
building that is now an art
gallery, and the Luzernhaus, a
Baroque building that houses a
museum of natural history. The
origins of Frauenfeld's castle
go back to the 13th century.
Its restored rooms house a
museum of local history.

### Environs
At **Ittingen**, about 4 km (3
miles) north of Frauenfeld, is the
Kartause Ittingen, a Carthusian
monastery founded in the 15th
century. No longer inhabited
by monks, the monastery is
open to visitors. As well as a
hotel, a restaurant and a farm
shop, the monastery also has a
museum illustrating monastic
life and a gallery of 20th-century
Swiss painting.

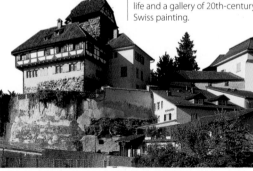
The riverside town of Frauenfeld, with a 13th-century castle keep

# ❺ Bodensee (Lake Constance)

Bordered by Germany and Austria, the Bodensee (Lake Constance) marks Switzerland's northeastern frontier. The lake, which is both fed and drained by the Rhine, is 64 km (40 miles) long and 12 km (7 miles) wide. Its western and southern shores, which belong to Switzerland, are lined with small resorts that have excellent fishing and watersports facilities. Boat trips depart from several points around the lakeshore.

④ **Kreuzlingen**
The Baroque Kirche St Ulrich is Kreuzlingen's finest building. This Swiss town is now a suburb of Konstanz (Constance), over the border in Germany.

② **Schloss Arenenberg**
In 1817, this 16th-century castle became the property of Queen Hortense, mother of Napoleon III. Empress Eugenie, his wife, bequeathed it to Thurgau in 1906, and it is now open to visitors.

③ **Gottlieben**
In 1415 the Czech reformer Jan Hus was held prisoner in the castle here.

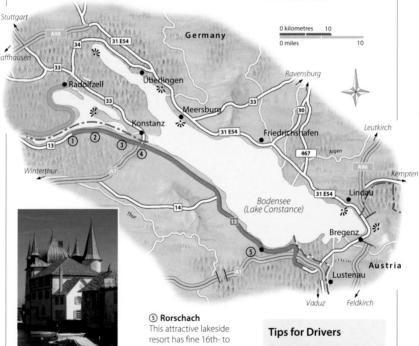

⑤ **Rorschach**
This attractive lakeside resort has fine 16th- to 18th-century houses.

① **Steckborn**
This small town has many fine historic houses. The 14th-century waterfront castle, or Turmhof, once belonged to the abbots of Reichenau. It now contains a museum of local history.

**Key**

▬ Suggested route
═ Motorway
▬ Scenic route
═ Other roads
--- National border

## Tips for Drivers

**Tour length:** 50 km (30 miles).
**Stopping-off points:** The resorts around Lake Constance offer a wide choice of hotels and restaurants.
**Additional attractions:** Arbon, close to the Austrian border, has many fine houses from the medieval period.

# ⑥ St Gallen

Capital of the canton of the same name, St Gallen is eastern Switzerland's largest town and home to a UNESCO World Heritage Site. Its origins go back to 612, when Gallus, an Irish monk, chose the spot for his hermitage. A Benedictine abbey was founded here in 747 and, with the establishment of a library in the 9th century, the abbey became a centre of learning and culture. By the Middle Ages, St Gallen was already an important producer of linen, exporting fine cloth all over Europe. In the 19th century, embroidery was St Gallen's major export, and the town is still renowned for this cottage industry.

Shoppers on Marktplatz, formerly St Gallen's main market square

### Exploring St Gallen

While the city's focal point is its magnificent cathedral (see pp190–91), its beautiful medieval centre contains many half-timbered houses and mansions with oriel windows. Most of St Gallen's museums are concentrated to the east of the Old Town (Altstadt).

### 🏛 Textilmuseum

Vadianstrasse 2. **Tel** 071 222 17 44. **Open** 10am–5pm daily (to 7pm Thu). 🎨

Reflecting St Gallen's importance as a centre of the textiles industry, this museum is filled with a comprehensive array of pieces from Switzerland and abroad, illustrating the art of weaving, as well as intricate embroidery and exquisite handmade lace. Local patterns and products, and the implements that were devised to produce them, are also shown.

Statue on a fountain in St Gallen

### 🏛 Stiftsbibliothek

Klosterhof 6d. **Tel** 071 227 34 15. **Open** 10am–5pm Mon–Sat, 10am–4pm Sun. **Closed** last two weeks in Aug. 🎨 📷 book via the tourist office. ☑ stibi.ch

Although most of the abbey was destroyed during the Reformation, its important library, the Stiftsbibliothek, was spared. The main room, designed by Peter Thumb in 1758–67, is a stunning Baroque masterpiece, with elaborate Rococo decoration. The wooden floor is intricately inlaid and the ceiling decorated with stuccowork by the Gigl brothers and with trompe-l'oeil paintings by Josef Wannenmacher.

The library contains more than 150,000 books and manuscripts, including an important collection of Irish manuscripts dating from the 8th to the 11th centuries, and rare works dating from the 8th century.

### ⛪ St Laurenzenkirche

Marktgasse. **Tel** 071 222 67 92. **Open** 9:30–11:30am & 2–4pm Mon, 9:30am–4pm Tue–Sat; in summer: until 6pm Tue–Fri.

This church was originally part of the abbey complex. During the 16th century it became the main centre of the Reformation in St Gallen. The building's present Neo-Gothic appearance is the result of remodelling carried out in the mid-19th century.

### 🏛 Marktplatz

Once the town's main market square, Marktplatz lies on the northern side of the Old Town. The square is surrounded by fine houses dating mainly from the 17th and 18th centuries. While most of them are built of brick and have intricately painted façades, others are half-timbered and decorated with relief carving. Many also have attractive oriel windows, a feature typical of St Gallen's architecture.

On Marktgasse, the street leading off the southern side of Marktplatz, Labhart is a watch-maker's shop with a collection of musical boxes. These include some fascinating examples of Swiss ingenuity.

### 🏛 Waaghaus

The elongated Bohl esplanade, leading off the eastern side of Marktplatz, is dominated by the dazzlingly white façade of the Waaghaus, a weighhouse built

The late 16th-century Waaghaus, on Bohl

in 1583. The building is now the seat of the city authorities, and is also used for concerts and exhibitions.

### 🏛 Kunstmuseum

Museumstrasse 32. **Tel** 071 242 06 71.
**Open** 10am–5pm Tue & Thu–Sun, 10am–8pm Wed.

This late 19th-century museum building is divided into two parts. One is devoted to natural history, and contains displays relating to the region's plants and animals, as well as its minerals. The other is an art gallery, with works dating mainly from the 19th and 20th centuries.

The Natur- und Kunstmuseum

### 🏛 Historisches und Völkerkundemuseum

Museumstrasse 50. **Tel** 071 242 06 42.
**Open** 10am–5pm Tue–Sun.

The history of the town and region of St Gallen is the focus of the displays at this museum.

Besides many archaeological pieces, there are documents, mementos and reconstructed domestic rooms of various periods. Highlights include a scale reconstruction of St Gallen's abbey and a model of the city as it was in the 17th century. The museum also has an ethnographic collection, with Asian, African and South American artefacts.

### 🏛 Universität

Dufourstrasse 50. **Tel** 071 224 21 11.

The university of St Gallen is of interest for its modern architecture and its decoration. Created by innovative artists of the 20th century, the paintings and sculpture are closely integrated with the buildings' physical structure.

The main building, completed in 1963, features a ceramic frieze by Joan Miró, wall paintings by Antoni Tápies, a mosaic by Georges Braque and sculptures by Alberto Giacometti. A bronze sculpture by Jean Arp stands in the courtyard. A later building, completed in 1989, contains several works by the painters Gerhard Richter, Josef Felix Müller and Luciano Fabro.

### 🏛 Kunst Halle Sankt Gallen

Davidstrasse 40. **Tel** 071 222 10 14.
**Open** 2–6pm Tue–Fri, 11am–5pm Sat & Sun. 🅿 🌐 k9000.ch

This contemporary art hall sees itself as an experimental space for artists to express themselves freely. The exhibits change regularly, keeping pace with developments in the world of contemporary art.

### 🏛 Bierflaschen Museum

St Jacobstrasse 37. **Tel** 071 243 43 43.
**Open** 8am–6:30pm Mon–Fri, 8am–5pm Sat. 🌐 schuetzengarten.ch

Switzerland's first beer bottle museum features over 2,000 bottles from 260 breweries – all empty. The well-presented exhibits are arranged by region, forming an impressive display of Swiss beer history.

## St Gallen City Centre

① Textilmuseum
② Stiftsbibliothek
③ St Laurenzkirche
④ Marktplatz
⑤ Waaghaus
⑥ Bierflaschen Museum
⑦ Kunstmuseum
⑧ Historisches und Völkerkundemuseum

0 metres 200
0 yards 200

# St Gallen Cathedral

The Benedictine abbey was established in 747 and was at the height of its importance from the 9th to the 11th centuries. The Romanesque church and monastery, built during that period, have not survived, their only remains being the crypt containing the tombs of the abbots. The present Baroque cathedral and monastery were completed in 1767. The master architect was Johann Michael Beer von Bildstein. The interior decoration was executed by the foremost artists of the day. Such is the importance of the abbey district, with its works of art and its library *(see p188)*, that it was made a World Heritage Site.

★ **Ceiling Frescoes**
The ceiling is decorated with dramatic frescoes by Josef Wannenmacher.

**Main Altarpiece**
The painting on the high altar, depicting the Assumption of the Virgin, is by Francesco Romanelli. Dating from 1645, it was later heavily retouched.

High altar

**Thrones**
Two thrones, made by Franz Joseph Anton Feuchtmayer and decorated by the Dirr brothers, stand among the choir stalls.

**Confessional**
The 16 Baroque confessionals in the nave are crowned with medallions featuring reliefs by Franz Joseph Anton Feuchtmayer and Anton Dirr dating from 1761–3.

**Crypt**
Beneath the Baroque cathedral is the Romanesque crypt of the earlier church.

**Pulpit**
The late Baroque pulpit, decorated with figures of the Evangelists and of angels, was made by Anton Dirr.

Main entrance

**★ Stalls**
The Baroque stalls (1763–70), made of walnut and decorated with painting and gilding, are by Franz Joseph Anton Feuchtmayer and craftsmen from his studio.

# ⑦ Appenzell

**Road map:** F2. 🚉 🚌 ℹ️ Appenzell,
Hauptgasse 4; 071 788 96 41.
🌐 **appenzell.ch** 🎪 Landsgemeinde
(last Sun in Apr, Appenzell).

Interior of the Kirche St Mauritius in Appenzell

Surrounded on all sides by the
canton of St Gallen, the region
known as Appenzell consists of
two half-cantons, Appenzell-
Ausserrhoden in the north
and west, and Appenzell-
Innerrhoden in the south. From
the 10th to the 15th centuries,
Appenzell formed part of the
territory owned by the abbey
at St Gallen (see p188). Having
gained its independence,
Appenzell joined the Swiss
Confederation in 1513.

While Appenzell-
Ausserrhoden, the larger of the
two half-cantons, is Protestant
and largely industrialized,
Appenzell-Innerrhoden is
Catholic and markedly more
bucolic, with a farming
economy and a developed
tourist industry. It is renowned
for its cattle-breeding and
its dairy products, most
especially its cheeses. Along
with its rural character,
Appenzell-Innerrhoden has
strong folk traditions and a
pristine natural environment.

Like many other towns in
the region, **Appenzell**, capital
of Innerrhoden, has a
Landsgemeindeplatz, a square
on which regular voting
sessions are held (see p34). The
well-preserved historic centre
of this small town is filled with

colourfully painted wooden
houses. Other buildings of
interest here are the
16th-century town hall and
the parish church, Kirche St
Mauritius, built in the 16th
century in the Baroque
style and remodelled in
the 19th century.

The history and culture
of Appenzell is amply
documented by the varied and
extensive collections of the
**Museum Appenzell**. These
range from costumes
and headdresses
to embroidery and
cowbells. The
privately run
**Museum im
Blauen Haus**
contains a similar,
though much
smaller, collection.

To the south of
Appenzell lies the
Alpstein massif,
whose highest peak,
the Säntis, rises to 2,504 m
(8,218 ft). Popular with hikers
and mountaineers, the Säntis
can be reached by road or by
cable car from Schwägalp.
The summit commands an
extensive panorama that takes
in the Bodensee (see p187) and
the Black Forest to the north,
the Zürichsee to the southwest and the Glarner Alps to
the south.

The picturesque village of
**Urnäsch**, in Ausserrhoden and
located northwest of the Säntis,
also has a museum of local folk
traditions. This is the **Museum**

Hauptgasse, the main street in Appenzell's
historic district

**für Appenzeller Brauchtum**,
whose collection includes
reconstructed farmhouse
interiors, as well as costumes
and craft items. North of
Urnäsch is **Herisau**, capital of
Appenzell-Ausserrhoden. The
town has attractive wooden
houses and a church with
Rococo furnishings dating from
1520. A museum of local history
occupies part of the town hall.

**Stein**, a quiet village east of
Herisau, has an interesting folk
museum and show dairy.
While the displays at the
**Appenzell Folklore
Museum** illustrate the
lives, culture and
crafts of the local
people, visitors
to the **Appen-
zeller Showcase
(Schaukäserei)**
can watch cheese
being made by
local methods.

The market town of
**Gais**, at the centre of Appenzell,
is of interest for its colourfully
painted wooden houses, many
of which have ornate gables.
Gais is also an excellent base
for exploring the region.

The small hilltop town
of **Trogen**, north of Gais, is
worth a visit for its Baroque
church and traditional
wooden houses.

House in Gais, with an
ornate gable

🏛️ **Museum Appenzell**
Appenzell, Hauptgasse 4. **Tel** 071 788
96 31. **Open** Apr–Oct: 10am–noon
& 2–5pm daily; Nov–Mar: 2–5pm
Tue–Sun.

### 🏛 Museum in Blauem Haus
Stein. **Tel** 071 787 12 84. **Open** 9am–6pm Mon–Fri, 10am–4pm Sat.

### 🏛 Museum für Appenzeller Brauchtumsmuseum
Urnäsch. **Tel** 071 364 23 22. **Open** 9–11:30am & 1:30–5pm Mon–Sat, 1:30–5pm Sun (Nov–Mar: 9–11:30am Mon–Sat).

### 🏛 Appenzeller Folklore Museum
Stein. 071 368 50 56. **Open** 10am–5pm Tue–Sun. 🖼

### 🏛 Appenzeller Showcase (Schaukäserei)
Stein. **Tel** 071 368 50 72. **Open** Mar–Oct: 9am–7pm daily; Nov–Feb: 9am–6pm daily. 📷 on request.

## ❽ Toggenburg

**Road map:** E2. ℹ Wildhaus, Hauptstrasse; 071 999 99 11.
🌐 **toggenburg.org**

Washed by the River Thur, the Toggenburg is a long valley that lies on a north–south axis between Wil and Wattwil, then veers eastwards just above Alt St Johann, where it becomes Oberes Toggenburg. With the Alpstein massif to the north and Churfirsten to the south, Oberes Toggenburg then opens out onto the Rhine valley.

The Toggenburg has over 300 km (185 miles) of marked hiking trails and cycling routes, and its gentle slopes provide easy skiing pistes. The valley is dotted with attractive small towns and villages. Among them are **Wil**, the main town, and **Lichtensteig**, which is of interest for its historic houses.

A 17th-century house in Lichtensteig, in the Toggenburg

**Wildhaus**, a pleasant resort at the eastern extremity of Oberes Toggenburg, is the birthplace of Ulrich Zwingli, the leader of the Reformation in Switzerland. The farmhouse where he was born in 1484 is open to visitors. **Unterwasser** is worth a visit for its impressive waterfall, the Thurwasserfälle.

## ❾ Rapperswil

**Road map:** E3. 🚠 7,700.
ℹ Fischmarktplatz 1; 055 220 57 57.
🌐 **rapperswil.ch**

This small town, in the canton of St Gallen, is set on a promontory on the north side of the Zürichsee. Although the modern part of Rapperswil has nothing of great interest, the old district is a pleasant place to stroll.

Behind the lakeside promenade lie narrow streets lined with houses fronted by arcades, and small squares with cafés and restaurants that serve fresh locally caught fish. From

May to October the air is filled with the delicate perfume of more than 15,000 roses. Known as the City of Roses, Rapperswil has a handful of walled rose gardens, including one within a Capuchin monastery and another specially designed for the blind and the disabled.

Besides the 15th-century town hall and the parish church, Rapperswil's main feature is its Gothic castle, whose three forbidding towers rise above the town. From the castle there are views of Zürich to the north and of the Glarus Alps to the southwest.

## ❿ Glarus

**Road map:** E3. 🚠 5,500.
ℹ Glarus Bahnhofstr. 23, 055 650 23 23; Glarmerland Rätstätte A3, Niederurnen, 055 610 21 25. 🖼 Landsgemeinde (1st Sun in May).

Capital of the canton of Glarus, this small town is also the urban centre of Glarnerland, an isolated and mountainous region lying between the Walensee and the Klausen Pass. Largely rebuilt after it was destroyed by fire in 1861, Glarus is laid out on a grid pattern and as such is a classic example of 19th-century urban planning. Notable buildings here include the town hall, an art gallery with a collection of 19th- and 20th-century Swiss paintings, and the Neo-Romanesque parish church whose treasury contains a collection of liturgical vessels.

With beautiful lakes and valleys, the mountains around Glarus, particularly those of the Glärnisch massif, are popular with hikers. Many of the slopes have excellent pistes.

**Environs**
South of Glarus, the main road continues to **Linthal**, from where a funicular ascends to **Braunwald**. This tranquil car-free resort is located on a plateau that offers superb hiking. Beyond Linthal the road leads through spectacular scenery over the **Klausen Pass** (1,948 m/6,391 ft) and down to Altdorf and Lake Lucerne (see p228).

High-altitude ski touring in the Toggenburg

View over the Walensee, with snowy mountain peaks in the background

## ⓫ Walensee

**Road map:** E3–F3.

This slender lake marks the border between the cantons of St Gallen and Glarus. About 15 km (9 miles) long and just 2 km (1 mile) across at its widest point, it lies in a steep-sided valley, with the rugged Churfirsten massif on its northern side and the Glarner Alps to the southeast. The region is also known as Heidiland.

A railway line and the motorway linking Zürich and Chur run along the south side of the lake. Most of the towns and villages on the steep north shore are accessible only by boat or on foot. Cruises on the lake take in **Weesen**, a charming town on the western shore.

A short distance south is **Näfels**, which has a late Renaissance palace, the Freulerpalast. The building houses a museum of local history. The neighbouring town of **Mollis** contains well-preserved burgher houses and fine 18th-century mansions.

**Walenstadt**, on the lake's eastern shore, is a convenient base for exploring the surrounding mountains, taking in **Walenstadtberg**, about 8 km (5 miles) northwest of Walenstadt, and **Berschis**, 6 km (4 miles) to the southeast, where there is a 12th-century chapel decorated with frescoes.

## ⓬ Liechtenstein

*See pp196–7.*

## ⓭ Bad Ragaz

**Road map:** F3. 4,580. Am Platz 1; 081 300 40 20. heidiland.com Maibär (spring festival, first week in May).

Bad Ragaz, set on the River Tamina, is one of Switzerland's foremost spa resorts. Its thermal springs are used to treat rheumatism and respiratory disorders, and also to promote general health. The resort has several indoor and outdoor thermal pools. The best known are Tamina-Therme, which are in the centre of the resort.

Bad Ragaz also has an early 18th-century parish church with Baroque wall paintings. The town hall contains a display of paintings and other graphic works of art of Bad Ragaz and its environs.

As well as skiing on the slopes of Pizol, Bad Ragaz offers golf, tennis and other sporting activities. It is also an excellent base for hiking in the surrounding hills.

**Environs**

About 5 km (3 miles) south of Bad Ragaz is **Bad Pfäfers**, a spa town with a beautiful Baroque church and a former Benedictine monastery that houses a local history museum.

Southwest of Bad Ragaz is the **Taminaschlucht**, a deep gorge carved out by the rushing waters of the Tamina. Also of interest is **Sargans**, with beautiful Neo-Classical buildings and a Gothic castle.

## ⓮ Maienfeld

**Road map:** F3. 2,390. Bahnhofstrasse 1; 081 330 18 00. heidiland.com

The village of Maienfeld, across the Rhine from Bad Ragaz, is also part of the Heidiland tourism area. It was this region of the Swiss Alps that Johanna Spyri chose as the setting for *Heidi*, the story of an orphaned girl that has become a classic of children's literature.

Bad Ragaz, a spa resort on the River Tamina

An easy walking trail leads from Maienfeld up to the hamlet of Oberrofels. Here visitors can see Heidi's House, a wooden chalet in which the fictional surroundings of Heidi's life with her grandfather are re-created.

## ⓯ Chur

*See pp198–201.*

## ⓰ Arosa

**Road map:** F4. 🚌 🚪 🚟 2,300.
ℹ️ Poststrasse; 081 378 70 20.
🆆 arosa.ch

Set in a bowl in the narrow Schanfigg valley, Arosa is one of Switzerland's most beautiful resorts. Although it lies at an altitude of 1,800 m (5,900 ft), it enjoys a gentle climate, with many days of sunny weather.

The town is divided into two areas. Ausserarosa is the main resort and Innerarosa the original village. The crafts and folk art on display in the **Schanfigg Heimatmuseum** here reflect mountain life in the days before the fashion for winter sports led to its transformation.

In winter the neighbouring slopes of Weisshorn, for experienced skiers, and of Hörnli and Prätschli, for intermediate skiers, provide superb downhill pistes. There are also extensive cross-country trails, a sleigh run and an ice rink. In summer visitors can enjoy over 200 km (125 miles) of hiking trails and mountain

Winter sports on the slopes of the Schanfigg valley, near Arosa

Davos, overlooked by the peaks of Schatzalp and Parsenn

biking routes. There is also a golf course, and the resort's two lakes, the Obersee and Untersee, offer a variety of water sports.

🏛️ **Schanfigg Heimatmuseum**
Poststrasse, Innerarosa. **Tel** 081 377 33 13. **Open** Winter: 2:30–4:30pm Tue & Fri; summer: 2:30–4:30pm Mon, Wed & Fri. 🅿️ 🆆 arosa-museum.ch

## ⓱ Davos

**Road map:** F3. 🚟 10,900. 🚪 🚌
ℹ️ Promenade 67; 081 415 21 21.
🆆 davos.ch 🎿 Swiss Alpine Marathon (Jul); Spengler Cup Ice Hockey Tournament (Dec).

Originally a remote village, Davos developed into a health resort for tuberculosis sufferers in the 1860s, and was transformed into a winter sports resort in the 1930s. Today it is one of the largest of Swiss resorts, host to world leaders at the Davos World Economic Forum.

Davos has close associations with the German writer Thomas Mann, who came here in 1911 and was inspired to write *The Magic Mountain.* Davos is also associated with the German Expressionist painter Ernst Ludwig Kirchner, who settled here in 1917. The largest collection of his work in the world, including many of the Alpine landscapes that he painted during his years in Davos, are displayed in the **Kirchner Museum**.

Poster in the Kirchner Museum, Davos

Although a 15th-century church and 16th-century town hall survive in its old district, Davos is geared primarily to its role as a leading winter sports resort.

It has some famous "off-piste" powder snow runs. However, for beginners, there are several ski and snowboarding schools, and some less demanding slopes. Davos also has toboggan runs and a large natural ice rink, where ice hockey is played.

In summer visitors can enjoy golf and tennis, hiking along trails, rock climbing and trekking on horseback.

🏛️ **Kirchner Museum**
Promenade 82. **Tel** 081 410 63 00. **Open** late Jun–mid-Oct & early Dec–mid-Apr: 10am–6pm daily; late Oct–early Dec & mid-Apr–mid-Jun: 2–6pm daily. 🅿️ 🆆 kirchnermuseum.ch

## ⓲ Klosters

**Road map:** F3. 🚟 4,000. 🚪 🚌
ℹ️ Alte Bahnhofstrasse 6; 081 410 20 20. 🆆 klosters.ch

Quieter and smaller than Davos, its neighbour to the south, the discreetly chic ski resort of Klosters has an intimate atmosphere. Of the medieval monastery from which it takes its name, the only remaining trace is Kirche St Jacob, which has beautiful stained-glass windows by Augusto Giacometti. The history of the village and its development into a resort are documented by displays in the **Nutli-Hüschi**, a 16th-century chalet. Klosters shares a skipass region with Davos, encompassing 320 km (199 miles) of ski terrain. It is suitable for a range of abilities, from beginner to experienced.

🏛️ **Nutli-Hüschi**
Talstrasse. **Tel** 079 440 69 48. **Open** 3–5pm Wed & Fri. 🅿️ 🆆 museum-klosters.ch

# ⑫ Liechtenstein

Lying in the eastern Rhaetian Alps, Liechtenstein borders Switzerland to the west and Austria to the east. It consists of the estates of Schellenberg and Vaduz, which were bought by Johann "Adam Andreas" von Liechtenstein in 1699 and 1712, and it was established as a principality in 1719. This German-speaking country, with a population of 36,700, is a democratic monarchy. Liechtenstein has no army and is one of the most highly industrialized countries in the world. The national currency is the Swiss franc. The capital, Vaduz, has the air of a pleasant provincial town and is worth a visit for its impressive art gallery, the Kunstmuseum Liechtenstein.

Switzerland

① **Balzers**
Burg Gutenberg, a 13th-century castle, dominates Balzers, Liechtenstein's southernmost town. Although the castle is not open to visitors, its courtyard is used as a venue for cultural events.

② **Triesen**
The St Mamerten Kapelle, a Gothic chapel with a Romanesque apse, is one of Triesen's historic buildings.

0 kilometres 2

0 miles 2

③ **Triesenberg**
This mountain village above the Rhine valley was settled by immigrants from Valais in the 13th century. It is now a popular holiday resort.

**④ Malbun-Steg**
Liechtenstein's only winter sports resort, Malbun-Steg has good skiing facilities. Chairlifts take visitors up to 2,000 m (6,580 ft).

**Tips for Drivers**

**Tour length:** 25 km (15 miles).
**Stopping-off points:** Vaduz has several hotels and restaurants.
**Other attractions:**
Kunstmuseum Liechtenstein, Städtle 32, Vaduz; (00 423) 235 03 00. W **kunstmuseum.li**
**Open** 10am–5pm Tue, Wed & Fri–Sun, 10am–8pm Thu.
ℹ️ Städtle 37; (00 423) 239 63 00. W **tourismus.li**

**⑤ Schloss Vaduz**
Dating from the 13th century, Schloss Vaduz is an imposing Gothic-Renaissance fortress defended by sturdy towers and turrets. It is still the residence of Liechtenstein's princely family.

**⑥ Vaduz**
Liechtenstein's small and unassuming capital city has several museums. The most important is the Kunstmuseum Liechtenstein, which houses a fine collection of international modern and contemporary art.

**⑦ Schaan**
The beautiful 12th-century church of Maria zum Trost in Schaan is decorated with paintings executed by Joseph Waller in 1746.

**⑧ Planken**
From its lofty mountain setting, Planken offers fine views of the Rhine valley below. It is also the base for trips into the Drei Schwestern Massif to the south.

**Key**

▨ Suggested route
▤ Motorway
═ Other roads
═ River, lake
--- National border

# ⑮ Chur

Located at the head of the Rhine valley, Chur lies at the crossroads of ancient trade routes between the Alpine passes to the south and the Bodensee to the north. The Romans founded a settlement here in the 1st century BC, and today Chur calls itself "the oldest Swiss city". Around AD 450 it became a bishopric and prospered under the rule of prince-bishops from the 12th to the 16th centuries. With the start of the Reformation, Chur passed to the secular rule of its merchant class, becoming the capital of the canton of Graubünden in 1803.

The 8th-century crypt beneath the Kirche St Luzius

## Exploring Chur

With the Obertor, a city gate, on its western side, the Old Town clusters around Kirche St Martin. The bishop's palace and the cathedral *(see pp200–1)* stand to the east. The narrow streets and squares of the Old Town are quiet and pleasant to explore.

## ⬆ Kirche St Luzius

This massive church, which is dedicated to the missionary who is said to have brought Christianity to the region, crowns a vineyard-covered hill on the east side of the Old Town. The building overlies the crypt of an 8th-century structure, which can be visited. There is also a monastery attached to the church, which houses a seminary.

## ⬆ Chur Cathedral

*See pp200–201.*

## ⬆ Bischöflicher Hof

Hofplatz.

The complex of buildings set on the terrace that rises to the east of the Old Town make up the bishop's palace. Founded in the 6th century on the site of a Roman fort, the palace was extended on several occasions, and its thick walls reflect the ruling bishops' need for defence. The palace's present appearance is mainly the result of remodelling in the 18th and 19th centuries. Since it is still the residence of the bishops of Chur, it is not open to visitors.

## ▥ Rätisches Museum

Haus Buol, Hofstrasse 1. **Tel** 081 257 48 40. **Open** 10am–5pm Tue–Sun.
 **raetischesmuseum.gr.ch**

The displays at this museum illustrate the history of Chur and its environs from prehistoric times to the 19th century.

Exhibits include archaeological finds from the time of the Rhaetians, who colonized the region in prehistory, and from Graubünden's Roman period. Medieval reliquaries and other precious pieces from the cathedral treasury are also displayed. Later exhibits include 17th-century furnishings and other objects. The culture and folk arts of Graubünden are also documented.

Stained-glass window by Augusto Giacometti in Kirche St Martin

## ⬆ Kirche St Martin

St Martinsplatz **Tel** 081 252 22 92. **Open** 8:30–11:30am & 2–5pm Mon–Fri.

The late Gothic church of St Martin was completed in 1491, replacing an 8th-century church that was destroyed by fire. Among the most notable features of its interior are the carved stalls and the three stained-glass windows created by Augusto Giacometti in 1917–19.

## ▦ Obere Gasse

Chur's smartest shopping street, Obere Gasse runs from St Martinsplatz to Obertor, the Gothic city gate on the banks of the Plessur. The historic houses along the street have been converted into boutiques, restaurants and cafés. On Saturday

The Bischöflicher Hof, with the cathedral on the left

*For hotels and restaurants see pp248–55 and pp264–75*

The commemorative obelisk in the centre of Regierungsplatz

mornings in summer, a market is held in Obere Gasse and Untere Gasse.

### ⊞ Rathaus

Poststrasse. **Open** by prior arrangement; 081 252 18 18.

Built in 1465, the Gothic town hall stands on the site of an earlier building that was destroyed by fire. At ground level is an arcaded area that was once used as a market-place. The upper floors of the town hall contain two finely decorated council chambers, one with a wooden ceiling and the other with Renaissance panelling. Both chambers have 17th-century tiled stoves.

The house at No. 57 Reichsgasse, nearby, is the birthplace of the Swiss painter Angelica Kauffmann. Born in 1741, she later moved to London, where she became a well-known portraitist and painter of mythological themes.

### ⊞ Regierungsplatz

Several historic buildings, now serving as the seat of the cantonal authorities, line this square on the north side of the Old Town. One of the finest is Graues Haus (Grey House), a stately three-storey residence dating from 1752.

The Vazerol-Denkmal, an obelisk in the centre of the square, commemorates the free association formed by the communes of Graubünden in the 14th century, when the local population began to organize itself against foreign domination.

Postplatz, at the northern end of Chur's Old Town

## Chur City Centre

① Kirche St Luzius
② Cathedral
③ Bischöflicher Hof
④ Rätisches Museum
⑤ Kirche St Martin
⑥ Obere Gasse
⑦ Rathaus
⑧ Regierungsplatz
⑨ Bündner Kunstmuseum
⑩ Naturmuseum

0 metres 200
0 yards 200

### Bündner Kunstmuseum

Postplatz. **Tel** 081 257 28 68.
**Open** 10am–5pm Tue–Sun.
**W** buendner-kunstmuseum.ch

Chur's museum of fine arts occupies a large Neo-Renaissance villa dating from 1874–5. The villa was built for Jacques Ambrosius von Planta, a merchant who traded in Egypt. This accounts for the Oriental character of the building's interior decoration.

Most of the paintings and sculptures that fill the rooms of the villa are by artists who were either born or worked in Graubünden between the 18th and the 20th centuries. They include Angelica Kauffmann, Giovanni Segantini, Ferdinand Hodler, Giovanni and Alberto Giacometti and Ernst Ludwig Kirchner. The rooms at the back of the villa are used for temporary exhibitions.

### Bündner Naturmuseum

Masanserstrasse 31. **Tel** 081 257 28 41.
**Open** 10am–5pm Tue–Sun.
**W** naturmuseum.gr.ch

This modern museum showcases the natural environment of Graubünden. The well-presented displays include a large collection of minerals from the region's mountains, as well as plants and stuffed animals.

### Environs

A cable car departing from the station on Kasernenstrasse, about five minutes' walk to the south of Chur, carries visitors up to the **Brambrüesch**, at an altitude of 1,600 m (5,250 ft). This is part of the Dreibündenstein massif, which has many scenic hiking trails. Its terrain also makes it popular with paragliders. During the summer months, a chairlift goes from Brambrüesch up to **Dreibündenstein**, at 2,176 m (7,155 ft). Hiking trails from Chur lead to Pizokel and Calanda, at 2,806 m (9,200 ft).

The spa town of **Passugg**, 5 km (3 miles) southwest of Chur on the road leading to Lenzerheide, has iron-rich mineral springs. Beyond Bad Passugg, the road leads to the spa region of Tschiertschen.

# Chur Cathedral

Begun in 1151 and completed in the mid-13th century, Chur's cathedral is in a mixture of Romanesque and Gothic styles. The earliest part of the basilica is its eastern section. The nave, with Romanesque columns and Gothic vaulting, and the tower, topped by a lantern, are later elements. The exterior was remodelled in the early 19th century, after the building was damaged by fire. The cathedral is built to an irregular plan, the axis of the sanctuary and that of the nave being out of alignment. The cathedral's finest feature is the renovated 15th-century altar triptych.

**Crypt Figures**
The crypt is supported by columns with capitals in the form of animal figures.

**★ Capitals of the Nave**
The capitals of the columns flanking the nave are outstanding examples of Swiss Romanesque stone carving.

**★ Sanctuary**
The Gothic sanctuary is decorated with delicate tracery and figures of saints.

*For hotels and restaurants see pp248–55 and pp264–75*

**Stalls**
The intricate decorations on the 15th-century stalls are fine examples of late Gothic woodcarving.

**VISITORS' CHECKLIST**

**Practical Information**
Chur Cathedral (Kathedrale St Mariä Himmelfahrt): Hofplatz.
**Tel** 081 258 60 60.
**Open** 8am–7pm daily.

**Pulpit**
Figures of putti and relief carvings of biblical scenes adorn the Baroque pulpit.

**Frescoes**
Gothic frescoes cover the walls of the baptistry.

**Stained-Glass Window**
The large stained-glass window in the west wall features medallions with scenes from the life of the Virgin.

Main entrance

**Tomb of Ortileb von Brandis**
The Gothic tomb of this 15th-century bishop of Chur was made in 1491.

Sgraffito decoration on the façade of a house in Guarda, Lower Engadine

## ⓳ Engadine Valley

**Road map:** G4. 🛈 Via San Gian 30, St Moritz; 081 830 00 01. 🆆 engadin. stmoritz.ch

The Engadine Valley begins at the foot of the Rhaetian Alps, near St Moritz, and extends northeastwards as far as the Austrian border. It is named after the River Inn (En in Romansh), which runs along the valley and on into Austria, where it joins the Danube.

This deep-cut valley lies between high cliffs. It is divided into an upper, southwestern section and a lower, northeastern section. The Upper Engadine (Oberengadin in German, Engiadin' Ota in Romansh), lies between the Maloja Pass and Zernez. With glaciers and snowy peaks on either side, the valley floor of the Upper Engadine lies at an altitude averaging 1,800 m (5,900 ft) and is dotted with winter sports resorts, including Pontresina and St Moritz (see p208).

The Lower Engadine (Unterengadin in German, Engiadina Bassa in Romansh) lies between Zernez and Martina. Remote, unspoiled and very picturesque, this region is dotted with attractive villages set on either side of the River Inn. Many of these villages have houses with painted façades or sgraffito decoration, in which the upper layer of plaster is cut away to create a design. Particularly fine sgraffito decoration can be seen in **Guarda**, a village overlooking the River Inn. The village of

**Ardez** is also notable for its painted houses, one of which is covered with a beautiful depiction of Adam and Eve in the Garden of Eden.

The principal town of the Lower Engadine is **Scuol** (Schuls in German), with a spa and a regional museum. On the opposite bank of the Inn lie the villages of **Vulpera**, which has picturesque houses and an 11th-century castle, and **Tarasp**, with a spa. Chaste Tarasp, a castle, perches on a rocky spur above the village. At **S-charl**, nearby, is a lead and silver mine that is open to visitors.

Most of the towns and villages in the Lower Engadine are good bases for exploring the Silvretta mountain range to the north and the Swiss National Parl (see pp206–7) to the south.

## ⓴ Müstair

**Road map:** G4. 🚞 830. 🛈 081 861 88 40. 🆆 val-muestair.ch

Tucked away at the bottom of Val Müstair (Münstertal in German), and almost on the border with Italy, Romansh-speaking Müstair (Münster in German) takes its name from the Carolingian monastery founded here.

Founded in about AD 780, reputedly by Charlemagne, and still inhabited by a community of Benedictine nuns, the convent is one of the most ancient buildings in Switzerland.

The convent church, known in Romansh as the **Baselgia San Jon** and in German as Klosterkirche St Johann, is decorated with exceptionally well-preserved 12th- and 13th-century Romanesque frescoes. Because of these,

House in Ardez, in the Engadine Valley, with Adam and Eve decoration

◀ Flower meadow in the Appenzell region

the church has been declared a UNESCO World Heritage Site. While the frescoes on the side walls depict scenes from the life of Christ, those in the presbytery show scenes from the life of St John. A depiction of the Last Judgment covers the west wall. Some of the frescoes have been moved to the Schweizerisches Landesmuseum in Zürich (see pp166–7). The church also contains a 12th-century statue of Charlemagne and an 11th-century relief of the Baptism of Christ. The small **museum** near the church contains Carolingian statuary and reliefs and Baroque figures.

**Statue of Charlemagne in Müstair's church**

### ⬆ Baselgia San Jon

Church: **Open** Apr–Oct: 7am–8pm daily; Nov–Mar: 7:30am–6pm daily. Museum: **Tel** 081 851 62 28. **Open** May–Oct: 9am–noon & 1:30–5pm Mon–Sat, 1:30–5pm Sun; Nov–Apr: 10am–noon & 1:30–4:30pm Mon–Sat, 1:30–4:30pm Sun. 🅿 🆆 **muestair.ch**

## ㉑ Swiss National Park

See pp206–7.

## ㉒ Pontresina

**Road map:** G4. 🚠 1,900. 🛈 Via Maistra 133; 081 838 83 00. 🆆 **pontresina.ch**

The resort of Pontresina, in the Upper Engadine, lies at the foot of Val Bernina at an altitude of 1,800 m (5,900 ft). With several large hotels, it has a mountaineering tradition as a summer resort dating back to the 19th century.

Among Pontresina's historic buildings is the Spaniola Turm, a Romanesque tower, and the chapel of Santa Maria. It contains Romanesque frescoes, some of which depict scenes from the life of Mary Magdalene. Exhibits in the **Museum Alpin** illustrate the history of the town and its surroundings.

Pontresina is a year-round resort. In winter the slopes of Diavolezza and Lagalb are linked into the 350-km (217-mile) network of the Engadine ski region. In summer, Pontresina offers gentle walking along wooded paths in the vicinity as well as more demanding hiking and mountaineering up to the summits of Alp Ota and Munt della Bescha. The trail up Val Roseg leads to a glacier at the foot of Piz Roseg. Experienced climbers can tackle Piz Bernina, which at 4,049 m (13,289 ft) is the highest peak in the Rhaetian Alps.

### 🏛 Museum Alpin

Via Maistra 199. **Tel** 081 842 72 73. **Open** Mid-Jun–mid-Oct & end Dec–mid-Apr: 4–6pm Mon–Sat. 🅿

## ㉓ Bernina Pass

**Road map:** G4.

At an altitude of 2,328 m (7,638 ft), the Bernina Pass (Passo del Bernina in Italian) is the highest point on the ancient route from St Moritz to Tirano, over the border in Italy. The pass marks the boundary between Romansh- and Italian-speaking Graubünden.

A road, the Berninastrasse, climbs up Val Bernina on the north side of the pass and descends Val di Poschiavo on its southern side. The pass is also served by ordinary trains and by the Bernina Express (see p33).

The breathtaking view from the pass takes in the peaks of the Rhaetian Alps to the north and Lago Bianco, an artificial lake, to the south.

## ㉔ Poschiavo

**Road map:** G4. 🛈 Stazione; 081 844 05 71. 🆆 **valposchiavo.ch**

The descent down Val di Poschiavo, the valley on the south side of the Bernina Pass, reveals a very different aspect of Switzerland. Here the climate and vegetation, as well as the culture, are Mediterranean. Buildings show an Italian influence and cypress trees and palms grow in sheltered gardens.

Poschiavo (Puschlav in German) is the main town in the valley. At its heart is the Piazza Communale, a square lined with Italianate *palazzi* and two churches, a late 15th-century Catholic church and a 17th-century Protestant church. Other notable buildings include the Casa Torre, a Romanesque tower, and the Palazzo Albricci. The so-called Spaniolenviertel (Spanish Quarter) has houses painted in a colourful Moorish style.

### Environs

At nearby Cavaglia are remarkable geological features known as cauldrons. These are natural wells, up to 3 m (10 ft) in diameter, that were carved into the rock by the circular action of stones and water released by a melting glacier.

The Piazza Communale in Poschiavo, lined with Italianate *palazzi*

# ㉑ Swiss National Park

Established in 1914, the Swiss National Park, or Parc Naziunal Svizzer, was the first national park to be created in the Alps. This pristine nature reserve covers an area of 170 sq km (66 sq miles) and its topography ranges from sheltered valleys with forests of pine and larch to flower-covered meadows and rocky, snow-covered peaks. The park is populated by ibex, chamois and deer, eagles and vultures, and colonies of marmots. Many rare plants, including edelweiss and alpine poppy, grow here. The best way to appreciate the park is to follow its well-marked hiking trails. Many of these start from parking areas off Ofenpassstrasse, the only highway through the park.

**⑤ Hotel Il Fuorn**
Built before the national park was established, the Hotel Il Fuorn is one of two places to stay within the park. The other is the Chamanna Cluozza, a hostel with dormitory accommodation.

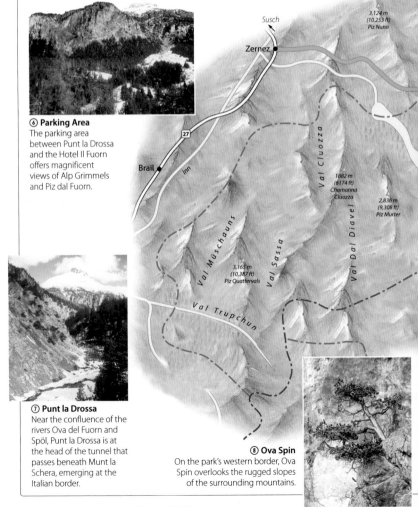

**⑥ Parking Area**
The parking area between Punt la Drossa and the Hotel Il Fuorn offers magnificent views of Alp Grimmels and Piz dal Fuorn.

Susch

Zernez

3,124 m
(10,253 ft)
Piz Nuna

27

Brail

Inn

Val Cluozza

1882 m
(6174 ft)
Chamanna
Cluozza

2,836 m
(9,308 ft)
Piz Murter

Val Müschauns

Val Sassa

Val Dal Diavel

3,165 m
(10,387 ft)
Piz Quattervals

Val Trupchun

**⑦ Punt la Drossa**
Near the confluence of the rivers Ova del Fuorn and Spöl, Punt la Drossa is at the head of the tunnel that passes beneath Munt la Schera, emerging at the Italian border.

**⑧ Ova Spin**
On the park's western border, Ova Spin overlooks the rugged slopes of the surrounding mountains.

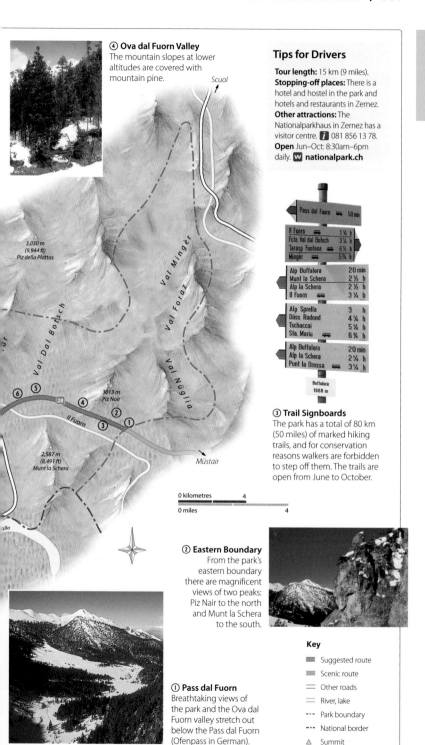

④ **Ova dal Fuorn Valley**
The mountain slopes at lower altitudes are covered with mountain pine.

*Scuol*

**Tips for Drivers**

**Tour length:** 15 km (9 miles).
**Stopping-off places:** There is a hotel and hostel in the park and hotels and restaurants in Zernez.
**Other attractions:** The Nationalparkhaus in Zernez has a visitor centre. 🛈 081 856 13 78.
**Open** Jun–Oct: 8:30am–6pm daily. 🅦 **nationalpark.ch**

| Pass dal Fuorn | | 50 min |
|---|---|---|

| Il Fuorn | | 1¾ h |
|---|---|---|
| Fcla. Val dal Botsch | | 3¼ h |
| Tarasp Fontana | | 6½ h |
| Minger | | 5¾ h |

| Alp Buffalora | 20 min |
|---|---|
| Munt la Schera | 2½ h |
| Alp la Schera | 2½ h |
| Il Fuorn | 3¼ h |

| Alp Sprella | 3 h |
|---|---|
| Döss Radond | 4¼ h |
| Tschuccai | 5¼ h |
| Sta. Maria | 6¾ h |

| Alp Buffalora | 20 min |
|---|---|
| Alp la Schera | 2¼ h |
| Punt la Drossa | 3¼ h |

| Buffalora |
| 1968 m |

③ **Trail Signboards**
The park has a total of 80 km (50 miles) of marked hiking trails, and for conservation reasons walkers are forbidden to step off them. The trails are open from June to October.

*3,030 m*
*(9,944 ft)*
*Piz della Plattas*

*Val Minger*

*Val Foraz*

*Val Dal Botsch*

*Val da Nüglia*

⑥ ⑤ ④ ② ①
**28**
*Il Fuorn* ③

*3013 m*
*Piz Nair*

*2,587 m*
*(8,491 ft)*
*Munt la Schera*

*Müstair*

0 kilometres  4
0 miles  4

② **Eastern Boundary**
From the park's eastern boundary there are magnificent views of two peaks: Piz Nair to the north and Munt la Schera to the south.

**Key**

▬▬ Suggested route
▬▬ Scenic route
═ Other roads
═ River, lake
--- Park boundary
▪▪▪ National border
△ Summit

① **Pass dal Fuorn**
Breathtaking views of the park and the Ova dal Fuorn valley stretch out below the Pass dal Fuorn (Ofenpass in German).

Cable car to Corviglia, above St Moritz

## ⑳ St Moritz

**Road map:** F4. 🚠 5,100.
ℹ️ Via Maistra 12; 081 837 33 33.
🌐 stmoritz.ch 🚗 British Classic
Car Rally (Jul).

The birthplace of winter tourism, still celebrated for its "champagne atmosphere" at 1,800 m (5,900 ft), St Moritz (San Murezzan in Romansh) lies on a sunny terrace on the north shore of the Moritzersee (Lej da San Murezzan). Surrounded by mountains, it offers superb skiing and snowboarding, and is a base for hiking and mountaineering in summer. It is also known for its curative springs, which have been exploited at least since the Middle Ages.

The town has two districts: St Moritz-Bad, the spa area on the southwestern side of the lake, and St Moritz-Dorf, on the northern side, with hotels, restaurants and boutiques.

Although little remains of the original village, St Moritz has two interesting museums. A domed building on Via Somplaz, ten minutes' walk west of St Moritz-Dorf, houses the **Giovanni-Segantini Museum**. This Symbolist painter, who spent the final years of his life in the Upper Engadine, is known for his sensitive Alpine scenes. Many are on display here, including his great triptych entitled *Birth, Life and Death*.

On Via dal Bagn, just below Via Somplaz, is the **Museum Engiadinais**, which is devoted to life in the Engadine and the history of the spa.

🏛️ **Giovanni-Segantini Museum**
Via Somplaz 30. **Tel** 081 833 44 54.
**Open** 10am–noon & 2–6pm. ♿

🏛️ **Museum Engiadinais**
Via dal Bagn 39. **Tel** 081 833 43 33.
**Open** 10am–noon & 2–5pm
Mon–Fri & Sun. ♿

## ㉖ Sils

**Road map:** F4. 🚠 600. ℹ️ 081 838
50 50. 🌐 sils.ch

With houses in the traditional style of the Engadine, the charming village of Sils (Segl in Romansh) has a picturesque setting on the north shore of the Silsersee (Lej da Segl).

The village consists of two parts: Sils Baselgia, on the lakeshore, and Sils Maria, to the south. Many writers, painters and musicians have been drawn to Sils. From 1881 to 1889, Sils Maria was the summer residence of the German philosopher Friedrich Nietzsche. The house where he lived, and where he wrote *Also Sprach Zarathustra*, has been converted into a small museum, the **Nietzsche Haus**. The exhibits include photographs of the philosopher and several of his manuscripts.

IN DIESEM HAUSE WOHNTE
FRIEDRICH NIETZSCHE
WÄHREND SCHAFFENSREICHER
SOMMERMONATE 1881–1888
Plaque commemorating Friedrich Nietzsche, in Sils

🏛️ **Nietzsche Haus**
Via Marias 67. **Tel** 081 826 53 69.
**Open** Jan–mid-Apr & mid-Jun–mid-Oct: 3–6pm Tue–Sun. ♿

## ㉗ Val Bregaglia

**Road map:** F4. ℹ️ Strada Principale
101, Stampa; 081 822 15 55.
🌐 bregaglia.ch

The western continuation of the Inn valley culminates at the Maloja Pass (1,815 m/5,955 ft), which marks the western boundary of the Engadine. On the western side of the pass a road winds down Val Bregaglia, one of Graubünden's Italian-speaking valleys.

Val Bregaglia, which has many scenic hiking trails and which contains extraordinary rock formations, is popular with mountaineers. It is also dotted with ruined castles and small churches.

The main village in Val Bregaglia is **Vicosoprano**, which has mansions and historic law courts. Further south lies **Stampa**, birthplace of the artists Augusto Giacometti and his son, Alberto. Buildings of interest in Stampa include the Casa Granda. This 16th-century palace contains a museum of local history and a display of works by Augusto and Alberto Giacometti.

The charming hamlet of **Soglio**, with narrow alleys, stone houses and *palazzi*, perches on the north side of the valley. The many hiking trails leading out of Soglio follow scenic routes both eastwards up Val Bregaglia and down towards the Italian border.

The hamlet of Soglio, on the north side of Val Bregaglia

One of the Romanesque panels in the Kirche St Martin, Zillis

## ❷❽ Zillis

**Road map:** F4. ℹ️ Poststelle Hauptstrasse; 081 661 13 83.
Ⓦ zillis-reischen.ch

In the village of Zillis (Ziràn in Romansh), on the east bank of the Hinterrhein, stands a small church that contains a remarkable cycle of Romanesque frescoes.

The wooden ceiling of **Kirche St Martin** (Baselgia Sontg Martegn) is covered with 153 square panels, painted between 1109 and 1114. While the exterior panels depict an ocean filled with sea monsters, those in the interior show scenes from the life of Christ and of St Martin. Figures of angels symbolizing the four winds fill the corners of the scheme. The history and subject matter of the frescoes, and the methods used to create them, are explained in an exhibition area within the church.

**Environs**
About 3 km (2 miles) south of Zillis is the **Via Mala Schlucht**, a 500-m (1,640-ft) canyon carved out by the waters of the Hinterrhein. Steps lead down to the bottom of the canyon.

🏛️ **Kirche St Martin**
Am Postplatz. **Tel** 081 661 22 55. **Open** 8am–6pm daily (Nov–Mar: from 9am).

## ❷❾ San Bernardino Pass

**Road map:** E4. ℹ️ Strada Cantonale; 091 832 12 14. Ⓦ sanbernardino.ch

On the great transalpine route running from the Bodensee, in the far northeast of Switzerland, down to Lake Como, in Italy, the San Bernardino is one of Europe's most important mountain passes. It lies at an altitude of 2,066 m (6,778 ft) between the Rheinwald forest to the north and the Valle Mesolcina, in the Italian-speaking region of Switzerland, to the south. Although snow usually blocks the pass from November through to May, the 7-km (4-mile) tunnel beneath it is permanently open.

The village resort of San Bernardino, on the south side of the pass, is a good base for exploring the surrounding mountains. Hiking trails lead up to the summit of Pizzo Uccello (2,724 m/8,937 ft), north of the village, and to Lago d'Osso, a lake 2 km (1 mile) to the south.

## ❸❿ Mesocco

**Road map:** F4. 🏔️ 1,200. **Tel** 091 822 91 40. Ⓦ mesocco.ch

The picturesque stone houses of Mesocco cluster on the banks of the River Moesa, which runs along the Valle Mesolcina. This valley stretches from the San Bernardino Pass southward to Bellinzona and, although it is in the canton of Graubünden, it has strong cultural links with Ticino.

The **Castello di Misox**, a ruined fortress set on a rocky outcrop above the town, commands a stunning view of the valley and the village of Soazza (*see below*). Built for the counts of Sax von Misox in the 12th century, the castle was significantly extended in the 15th century and in 1480 it passed into the ownership of the Trivulizio family, from Milan. The slender campanile is a remnant of the castle complex, which was almost completely destroyed in 1526.

At the foot of the castle stands the Romanesque church of **Santa Maria del Castello**. Built in the 12th century, the church was partly remodelled in the 17th. The nave has a coffered ceiling and the walls are decorated with 15th-century murals. These depict St George and the Dragon, St Bernard of Siena, patron saint of Valle Melsocina, and scenes symbolizing the months of the year.

**Environs**
About 4 km (3 miles) south of Mesocco is **Soazza**, a village with an attractive 17th-century church. About 15 km (9 miles) south of Soazza is **San Vittore**, where there is an 8th-century chapel. The **Val Calanca**, which runs into Valle Mesolcina, also merits exploration for its beautiful scenery.

Campanile of Santa Maria del Castello, in Mesocco

# CENTRAL SWITZERLAND AND TICINO

The cradle of the Swiss confederation and the birthplace of the legendary hero William Tell, central Switzerland is not only at the geographical hub but also the historical heart of the country. Beyond high mountains to the south lies Italian-speaking Ticino, a canton with its own distinctive culture and Mediterranean orientation.

Lake Lucerne and the four cantons bordering its eastern and southern shores have a unique place in Swiss history and culture. In 1291, the cantons of Schwyz, Uri and Unterwalden (now divided into the half-cantons of Obwalden and Nidwalden) swore the oath of eternal alliance that led to the formation of the Swiss Confederation. The region is suffused with historic resonance. Rütli Meadow, on the south shore of Lake Lucerne, is hallowed as the spot where the oath was sworn. The towns of Bürglen and Altdorf, in the canton of Uri, have vivid associations with William Tell. The two other cantons that make up central Switzerland are Luzern, on the west shore of the lake, and Zug.

Schwyz, Uri, Luzern and Unterwalden are known as the Waldstätte, or Forest Cantons. Central Switzerland is largely Catholic and German-speaking.

Hemmed in by the Alps to the north and bordered on almost all other sides by Italy, Ticino is a geographically, culturally and linguistically separate entity. Long ruled by the dukes of Milan, Ticino was conquered by the Swiss Confederates in the early 16th century but only joined the Confederation as a free canton in 1803. This large canton in the sunny foothills of the southern Alps is Italian-speaking and mostly Catholic, with a lifestyle that is markedly more relaxed than elsewhere in Switzerland.

The impressive crenellated walls of Castelgrande, Bellinzona

◀ The Santuario della Madonna del Sasso in Locarno, on the shore of Lake Maggiore

# Exploring Central Switzerland & Ticino

With excellent transport facilities and a landscape that matches the classic image of Swiss rural life, central Switzerland is easy to explore. While to the northwest of Lake Lucerne the land is relatively flat, the area to the east and south is more mountainous. Several of the high peaks here have excellent hiking trails, and their summits offer breathtaking views. Towards Andermatt, in the northern foothills of the Alps, the terrain becomes more rugged, culminating in several high mountain passes. The route over the St Gotthard Pass leads down to the idyllic wooded valleys of northern Ticino. Further south, beyond Bellinzona, are Lake Maggiore and Lake Lugano, two of southern Ticino's most beautiful natural features.

Costumed participants in Fasnacht, Luzern's carnival

## Sights at a Glance

Interior detail of the Jesuit church, Luzern

Höllgrotten in Baar, to the north of Zug

## Getting There

With its international airport, Zürich is the gateway to central Switzerland. The region itself has an excellent network of road and rail routes. The A14 motorway connects Zürich with Luzern. From here the A2 motorway continues southeast, passing through the St Gotthard Tunnel and on into Ticino. With an airport at Lugano, Ticino can also be reached by air. Postbuses, which serve even remote communities, follow some very scenic routes.

### Key

▬ Motorway

— Main road

┈┈ Minor road

▬ Scenic route

╌╌ Main railway

— Minor railway

▬▬ International border

▬ Canton border

△ Summit

≍ Pass

A scenic rail route across rugged terrain

**For keys to symbols** *see back flap*

# ❶ Lake Lugano

Nestling between steep Alpine slopes, this sheltered lake is one of Ticino's most beautiful natural features. Although most of it lies in Swiss territory, its southwestern shore and northeastern branch, and a small central enclave, belong to Italy. The road bridge that crosses the lake leads up to the St Gotthard Tunnel. The best way of exploring Lake Lugano (Lago di Lugano or Ceresio in Italian) is by boat, from Lugano and several other points along the lakeshore. Fine views of the lake can be enjoyed by taking the cable car from Lugano to the summit of mountains flanking the resort.

**Lugano**
The lakeside resort of Lugano lies in a sheltered bay, with Monte San Salvatore to the south and Monte Brè to the east.

**Monte Tamaro**
The chapel on the summit of this mountain, north of Lugano, was designed by Mario Botta and decorated by Enzo Cucchi. It was completed in 1996.

**★ Melide**
The main attraction of Melide is the Swissminiatur, a park with 1:25 scale models of Switzerland's most notable buildings and natural features.

**Morcote**
The small church of Santa Maria del Sasso overlooks Morcote, one of the most attractive hamlets in Ticino.

Lugano

Agno

Caslano

S 233

Ponte Tresa

Melide

Figino

Brusimpiano

Bis

Morcote

SP 61

Brusino Arsizio

Porto Ceresio

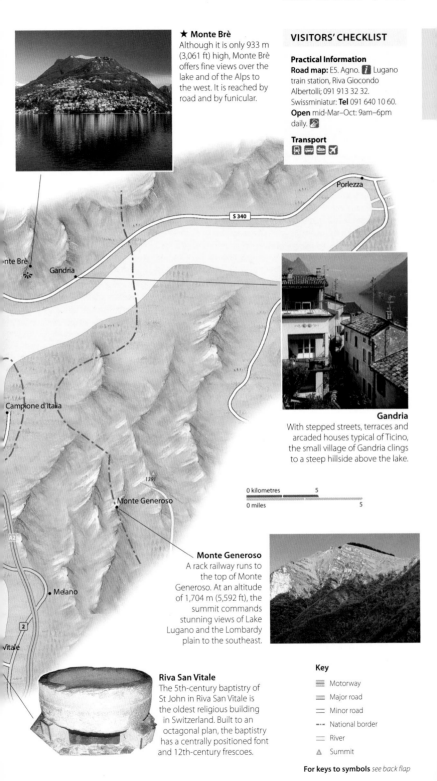

**★ Monte Brè**
Although it is only 933 m (3,061 ft) high, Monte Brè offers fine views over the lake and of the Alps to the west. It is reached by road and by funicular.

**Gandria**
With stepped streets, terraces and arcaded houses typical of Ticino, the small village of Gandria clings to a steep hillside above the lake.

0 kilometres 5
0 miles 5

**Monte Generoso**
A rack railway runs to the top of Monte Generoso. At an altitude of 1,704 m (5,592 ft), the summit commands stunning views of Lake Lugano and the Lombardy plain to the southeast.

**Riva San Vitale**
The 5th-century baptistry of St John in Riva San Vitale is the oldest religious building in Switzerland. Built to an octagonal plan, the baptistry has a centrally positioned font and 12th-century frescoes.

**Key**

▧ Motorway
═ Major road
─ Minor road
-∙-∙ National border
═ River
△ Summit

**For keys to symbols** *see back flap*

# ❷ Street-by-Street: Lugano

Lying in a shallow inlet on the north shore of Lake Lugano, this is the largest town in Ticino and one of the canton's great lakeside resorts. Lugano is also a centre of finance and banking. With piazzas, stepped streets and narrow, winding alleys, the Old Town (Centro Storico) has an Italianate character. Its hub is Piazza della Riforma, a square lined with tall shuttered buildings and filled with busy pavement cafés. Palm-fringed promenades line the quays, and the distinctive sugar-loaf outlines of Monte Brè and Monte San Salvatore rise to the east and south.

**Palazzo Riva**
This 18th-century palace has decorated windows with wrought-iron balconies.

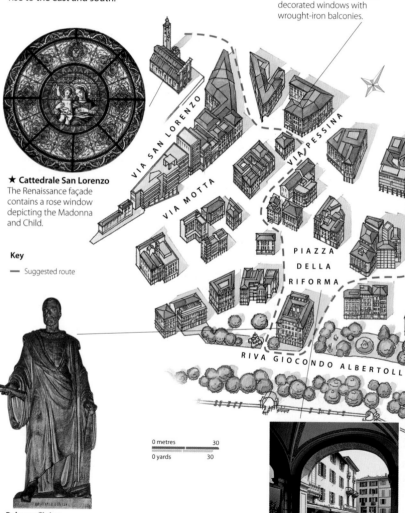

**★ Cattedrale San Lorenzo**
The Renaissance façade contains a rose window depicting the Madonna and Child.

**Key**

— Suggested route

**Palazzo Civico**
The Neo-Classical town hall was built in 1844–5 and features a statue of the architect Domenico Fontana from Melide.

**Piazza della Riforma**
Filled with pavement cafés, this spacious square is the social and geographical hub of Lugano's historic centre.

0 metres 30
0 yards 30

*For hotels and restaurants see pp248–55 and pp264–75*

**San Rocco**
Replacing an earlier Gothic church, San Rocco, with its Baroque high altar, was built after the plague that swept through the city in 1528.

**VISITORS' CHECKLIST**

**Practical Information**
Road map: F4. 52,000.
Palazzo Civico, Riva Albertolli, 091 913 32 32. Longlake Festival (Jul & Aug).
lugano-tourism.ch

**Transport**

**Palazzo dei Congressi**
This conference centre, built in 1975, is set in a park with fountains and modern statuary.

VEGEZZI

RIVA GIOCONDO ALBERTOLLI

VIA ELVEZIA

★ **Villa Ciani**
Built in the 17th century and remodelled in the mid-19th, this villa houses the Museo Civico di Belle Arti, which contains a collection of 15th- to 20th-century paintings.

Renaissance frescoes in Chiesa Santa Maria degli Angioli

**⌂ Santa Maria degli Angioli**
Piazza Luini 3. **Tel** 091 922 01 12.
This early 16th-century church, in a square southwest of the Piazza della Riforma, once belonged to a Franciscan monastery. The interior is decorated with Renaissance frescoes by Bernardino Luini and Giuseppe Antonio Petrini. Dating from the first half of the 16th century, they depict scenes from the life of Christ. The sacristy contains a small display of religious artifacts from the monastery's treasury.

**▥ Museo d'Arte**
Villa Malpensata, Riva Caccia 5. **Tel** 058 866 72 14. **Open** 9am–6pm Tue–Sun.
mdam.ch
Occupying an elegant 18th-century villa, this museum conserves the municipal art collection and focuses on art of the 20th and 21st centuries. Prominent artists whose work has been exhibited at the museum include Francis Bacon, Edvard Munch, Amedeo Modigliani and Egon Schiele.

**▥ Museo Cantonale d'Arte**
Via Canova 10. **Tel** 091 815 79 71.
**Open** 2–5pm Tue, 10am–5pm Wed–Sun.
museo-cantonale-arte.ch
With a section devoted to the work of Ticinese artists of the 19th and 20th centuries, this gallery contains an interesting display of paintings depicting local peasant life. The main focus is on the region as a defining influence on the exchange of artistic ideas between North and South. Also on view are paintings by Degas, Renoir, Turner and Klee, as well as avant-garde works by contemporary Swiss artists.

# ❸ Locarno

With an enchanting setting at the northern tip of Lake Maggiore, Locarno lies in a wide bay in the shelter of the Lepontine Alps. It is often said to be the sunniest of all Swiss towns, and date palm, fig, pomegranate and bougainvillea thrive in its mild climate. During the Middle Ages, Locarno was the centre of a dispute between the bishops of Como and the dukes of Milan, who finally gained control of the town in the 14th century but who lost it to the Swiss Confederates in 1512. The capital of Ticino from 1803 to 1878, Locarno is now a resort that attracts visitors from north of the Alps who come to enjoy its Mediterranean climate.

Promenade Lungolago Giuseppe Motta, fringed with palms

Wall paintings at Castello Visconteo

### Exploring Locarno

The old district of Locarno lies west of Piazza Grande, a short distance away from the lakeshore. It is roughly defined by Castello Visconteo, Chiesa San Francesco, Chiesa Sant'Antonio Abate and Chiesa Nuova. To the north of the old district rises the spur on which another church, the Santuario della Madonna del Sasso, is set.

### 🏛 Chiesa San Francesco

Via Cittadella 20.
Completed in 1572, the church of St Francis stands on the site of a 13th-century Franciscan monastery. The eagle, ox and lamb on its Renaissance façade represent Locarno's aristocrats, ordinary citizens and country-dwellers respectively. The decoration of the interior dates mainly from the 18th century.

### 🏛 Castello Visconteo

Piazza Castello 2. **Tel** 091 756 31 80. **Open** Apr–Oct: 10am–5pm Tue–Sun. 🗟
The origins of Castello Visconteo go back to the 12th century, when it was built for the Orelli family. In 1342 the castle came into the ownership of the Visconti, a Milanese family, who

enlarged it in the late 15th century. The dove-tailed crenellation of the walls and the towers dates from that period, as does the ravelin fortification, believed to be the work of Leonardo da Vinci. The castle was partly destroyed when the Swiss Confederates seized control of Locarno. The building's surviving wing now houses a museum of history and archaeology. The collection of Roman artifacts is particularly good.

### 🏛 Palazzo della Conferenza

Via della Pace.
It was in this *palazzo* that the Treaty of Locarno, drawn up between Germany and other European countries in the aftermath of World War I, was ratified in 1925.

### 🏛 Promenade Lungolago Giuseppe Motta

Lined with trees, plants and shrubs from around the world, this lakeshore promenade resembles the seafront boulevards of the French Riviera. The promenade leads north-wards to the end of the lake and southwards towards a beach and impressive public pool.

### 🏛 Chiesa di San Vittore

Via Collegiata, Muralto.
The 12th-century Romanesque basilica of San Vittore stands on the site of a 10th-century church in Muralto, east of the train station. The belfry, which was begun in the 16th century but not completed until 1932, has a Renaissance relief of St Victor. The austere interior bears traces of medieval frescoes, and the crypt beneath the presbytery contains columns with carved capitals.

### 🏛 Piazza Grande

This rectangular paved square is the focus of life in Locarno. Along its north side are 19th-century buildings with arcades of shops, cafés and restaurants. During the International Film Festival, held for ten days in early August, the square becomes an open-air cinema.

Piazza Grande, hub of Locarno's social life

### ⬆ Chiesa Nuova
Via Cittadella.

This church, also known as the new Chiesa Santa Maria Assunta, was completed in 1636, and its construction was funded by the architect Christoforo Orelli. It has a splendid Baroque interior, with sumptuous stuccowork and paintings depicting scenes from the life of the Virgin. A large statue of St Christopher graces the west front. The Palazzo Christoforo Orelli, next to the church, now serves as the canon's office.

### ⬛ Casa Rusca
Piazza Sant' Antonio. **Tel** 091 756 31 85. **Open** 10am–5pm Tue–Sun.

This elegant 18th-century residence, with an arcaded courtyard, houses Locarno's art gallery. With a permanent collection, as well as a progamme of temporary exhibitions, the gallery specializes in the work of modern and contemporary artists, many of whom have donated pieces of their work to the gallery. A highlight of the permanent collection is a display of work by Hans Arp (1886–1966), the Dadaist artist who spent the final years of his life in Locarno.

### ⬆ Chiesa Sant'Antonio Abate
Via Sant'Antonio.

The Baroque church of St Anthony was completed in 1692 and remodelled in 1863, when the façade and dome were renewed. The high altar, dating from 1740, features a depiction of Christ's deposition from the Cross by G A F Orelli.

### ⬆ Santuario della Madonna del Sasso
**Open** 6:30am–7pm daily.

The pilgrimage church of the Madonna of the Rock (Santa Maria Assunta) overlooks the town from the summit of a wooded spur. Dating from 1596, the church stands on the site of a chapel that was built

in 1487 to mark the spot where the Madonna appeared to Bartolomeo da Ivrea, a Franciscan monk. The present church is decorated with frescoes and oil paintings, notable among which is an altarpiece with the *Flight into Egypt* painted by Bramantino in 1522.

The Santuario della Madonna del Sasso

## Locarno Town Centre

① Chiesa San Francesco
② Castello Visconteo
③ Palazzo della Conferenza
④ Promenade Lungolago Giuseppe Motta
⑤ Chiesa di San Vittore
⑥ Piazza Grande
⑦ Chiesa Nuova
⑧ Casa Rusca
⑨ Chiesa Sant'Antonio Abate
⑩ Santuario della Madonna del Sasso

# ❹ Around Lake Maggiore

Only the northern tip of this long, slender lake lies in Switzerland, the remaining portion curving southwards into Italian territory. Some 60 km (40 miles) long and 6 km (4 miles) wide, Lake Maggiore is hemmed in by mountains to the north, south and west. Sheltered by these mountains, this beautiful lake basks in a Mediterranean climate. Boats and hydrofoils cross the lake from Ascona, Locarno and Brissago, taking passengers all the way down to the resorts in its Italian section.

**⑤ Ascona**
Renowned for its mild climate and beautiful setting, this fashionable resort once attracted many artists.

**③ Ronco**
Set on a steep mountainside, this small town has beautiful views of the lake and of the Isole di Brissago.

**④ Isole di Brissago**
One of these two islands can be reached by boat from Locarno, Ascona and Ronco.

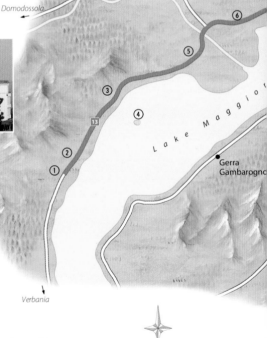

**② Brissago**
This lakeside town is well-known for its cigar factory. It is also the burial place of the Italian composer Ruggero Leoncavallo (1858–1919).

**① Madonna di Ponte**
This 16th-century Renaissance church is located in Brissago. On the high altar is a painting of the Assumption of the Virgin dating from 1569.

0 kilometres 5

0 miles 5

## Tips for Drivers

**Tour length:** 40 km (25 miles).
**Stopping-off places:** Ascona and Locarno have the widest choice of restaurants.
**Other attractions:** Tenero is a very popular lakeside beach resort at the northern tip of the lake. **Open** Apr–Oct: 9am–6pm daily. 🚗 ℹ️ 091 791 00 91; 🌐 **ascona-locarno.com**

### ⑥ Locarno
The Santuario della Madonna del Sasso (*see pp218–19*), which towers over Locarno, is accessible on foot or by funicular.

### ⑦ Magadino
In summer, organ recitals take place in Magadino's Neo-Classical parish church.

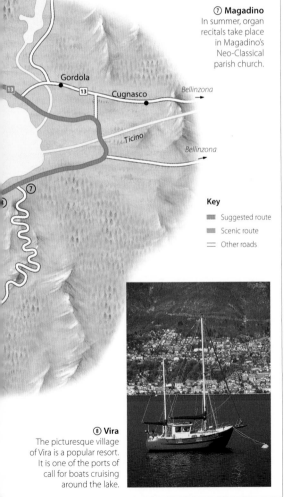

Gordola

Cugnasco

Bellinzona

Ticino

Bellinzona

### Key

▬ Suggested route

▬ Scenic route

═ Other roads

### ⑧ Vira
The picturesque village of Vira is a popular resort. It is one of the ports of call for boats cruising around the lake.

A narrow alley in Ascona's historic district

## ❺ Ascona

**Road map:** E5. 🏔 5,000. ℹ️ Via B. Papio 5, 0848 091 091. 🌐 **ascona-locarno.com**

A small fishing village for many centuries, Ascona developed in the early 20th century, when it became a fashionable health resort, attracting writers, painters and composers. Nearby Monte Verità (Hill of Truth) was established as a progressive colony around the same time, attracting some of Europe's leading thinkers, artists, revolutionaries and writers.

Ascona's exquisite Old Town (Centro Storico) is a maze of narrow cobbled streets lined with small craft shops and art galleries. Many of the most picturesque of Ascona's historic buildings, the oldest of which date from the 14th century, line Contrada Maggiore. Piazza San Pietro is dominated by the 16th-century Chiesa dei SS Pietro e Paolo, which has an altarpiece painted by Giovanni Serodine, a pupil of Caravaggio. Also notable are the Collegio Papio, a Renaissance building with an arcaded courtyard, and Santa Maria della Misericordia, a church with 15th-century frescoes. The Museo Comunale d'Arte Moderna, in a 16th-century *palazzo*, contains work by artists associated with the town, including Paul Klee. Piazza Motta, a pedestrianized lakefront promenade, is lined with cafés and restaurants.

The village of Lionza, in the Centovalli

## ❻ Centovalli

**Road map:** E5. ℹ️ Intragna; 091 780 75 00.

The stunning Centovalli (Valley of a Hundred Valleys) is so named for the many side valleys that cut into it. The **Centovalli Railway**, from Locarno to Domodossola in Italy, takes a spectacularly scenic route up the Centovalli. On this journey of about 40 km (25 miles), the train crosses 79 bridges or viaducts over deep canyons and passes through 24 tunnels. The first part of the journey leads along the vineyard-covered Val Pedemonte and then enters more rugged country, with forests of chestnut trees.

The train stops at several villages along the route. At **Verscio**, 4 km (2.5 miles) from Locarno, there is a school of circus art, run by the famous Swiss clown Dimitri. Nearby **Intragna** has a Baroque church. **Palagnedra** has a small Gothic church decorated with 15th-century frescoes.

🚂 **Centovalli Railway**
Via Franzoni 1, Locarno. **Tel** 091 751 87 31. 🆆 centovalli.ch

## ❼ Valle Maggia

**Road map:** E5. ℹ️ 091 753 18 85. 🆆 vallemaggia.ch

This deep valley runs for about 50 km (30 miles) northwest of Ascona up to Cevio. At its lower levels, the valley is wide, though as it ascends it becomes increasingly rugged, with forests of pine and larch. The valley is also dotted with historical buildings and churches amongst chalets and villages.

At **Maggia**, the largest village in the valley, is the 15th-century Chiesa Santa Maria delle Grazie. The exterior of this church is unremarkable but the interior is decorated with dazzling 16th- and 17th-century frescoes.

Past **Giumaglio**, where there are dramatic waterfalls, the road leads further up the valley to **Cevio**. A notable feature of this village is the 17th-century Palazzo Pretorio, its façade featuring the coats of arms of the bailiffs who successively occupied the building. Nearby stands the Palazzo Franzoni (1630), which houses a museum of regional history.

The hamlet of **Mogno** contains the serenely beautiful Chiesa di San Giovanni Battista. Designed by the Ticinese architect Mario Botta and completed in 1996, this extraordinary church is built of local stone. The interior is lined with white marble and grey granite arranged in stripes and chequer patterns. Their effect is enhanced by the play of light entering through the translucent ceiling.

## ❽ Val Verzasca

**Road map:** E5. ℹ️ Via ai Giardini, Tenero; 091 745 16 61. 🆆 tenero-tourism.ch

Washed by the emerald waters of the River Verzasca, Val Verzasca is the smallest of the valleys lying north of Locarno. A gigantic dam near the mouth of the valley has created the Lago di Vogorno, a large artificial lake. The valley is lined with villages, whose stone houses cling to the mountainsides.

**Vogorno** has a small church decorated with Byzantine frescoes. Near **Lavertezzo**, the river is spanned by the Ponte

Detail of a fresco in the church at Brione-Verzasca

Chiesa di San Giovanni Battista at Mogno, in Valle Maggia

The Ponte dei Salti, a medieval bridge near Lavertezzo, in Val Verzasca

dei Salti, a medieval double-arched bridge. A modern art trail, running for 4 km long (3 miles) between Lavertezzo and Brione, is lined with works by 34 Italian, Swiss and German sculptors.

At **Brione-Verzasca** is a church whose origins go back to the 13th century. Its façade is decorated with a painting of St Christopher and the interior features 15th-century frescoes. At the head of the valley lies the village of **Sonogno**, with stone houses typical of the Ticino. One of them, Casa Genardini, houses a regional museum.

## ❾ Bellinzona

*See pp224–5.*

## ❿ Val di Blenio

**Road map:** E4. 🛈 Olivone, 091 872 14 87. 🌐 blenio.com

This broad scenic valley, washed by the River Brenno, leads up to the Lucomagno Pass (1,916 m/6,286 ft). The road up the valley and over the pass leads into Graubünden. Val di Blenio lies in the heart of rural Ticino. It has magnificent scenery and is dotted with picturesque villages.

**Biasca**, at the foot of the valley, has a Romanesque church with Gothic frescoes. Just north of Biasca is **Malvaglia**. The 16th- to 17th-century church here has a Romanesque tower and its façade features a large painting of St Christopher.

**Negrentino** is notable for its early Romanesque church of St Ambrose, whose tall square belfry tower can be seen from afar. The interior of the church is decorated with frescoes dating from the 11th to the 16th centuries. **Lottinga** has an interesting museum of regional history. The villages higher up the valley, such as **Olivone**, are good bases for mountain hiking.

## ⓫ Airolo

**Road map:** E4. 🛈 091 869 15 33. 🌐 airolo.ch

Located just below the St Gotthard Pass, Airolo lies at the point where the motorway and railway line through the St Gotthard Tunnel emerge. As it is bypassed by these major routes, Airolo is a quiet town and, with several hotels, it is a convenient base for exploring the valley that stretches out below. A plaque in the town commemorates the 177 people who died during the tunnel's construction in the 1880s.

Commemorative plaque in Airolo

### Environs

Valle Leventina, below Airolo, carries the motorway and main railway line that run from Zürich to Bellinzona and Lugano. The valley is dotted with small towns and villages, many of which have interesting churches. While **Chiggiogna** has a church with 15th-century frescoes, **Chironico** has a 10th-century church with 14th-century frescoes. The 12th-century church in **Giornico** is one of the finest in the Ticino. The interior is decorated with frescoes dating from 1478.

## ⓬ St Gotthard Pass

**Road map:** E4. 🛈 091 869 12 35. 🌐 passosangottardo.ch

With the Reuss Valley in the canton of Uri to the north, and the Ticino valley to the south, the St Gotthard Pass lies at an altitude of 2,108 m (6,916 ft). It is on the principal route from northern Europe to Italy.

The pass has been used since the 13th century, when a bridge was built across a gorge near Andermatt. It was only in the 19th century, when a 15-km (9-mile) road and rail tunnel was built, that the route began to carry a large volume of traffic. Because of heavy snowfall, the pass is closed in winter, usually from November to April.

The 19th-century hospice on the pass houses the **Museo Nazionale del San Gottardo**. The museum documents the history of the pass and describes the plants and animals of this high Alpine region.

Marked trails lead up to the summit of many of the surrounding peaks, including Pizzo Lucendro, and to mountain terraces from which there are splendid views.

🏛 **Museo Nazionale del San Gottardo**
**Tel** 091 869 15 25 **Open** Jun–Oct: 9am–6pm daily. 🏛

# ● Bellinzona

Because of its location in a valley on the route over the great Alpine passes, Bellinzona was a fortress town from Roman times. During the Middle Ages, the dukes of Milan built three castles here, enabling them to defend this strategically placed town and control traffic passing through the valley. The Swiss Confederates seized control of Bellinzona in the 16th century, holding the town for 300 years. After gaining its independence in 1803, Bellinzona became the capital of Ticino. Its three castles, Castelgrande, Montebello and Sasso Corbaro, have together been declared a UNESCO World Heritage Site.

Chiesa Collegiata dei SS Pietro e Stefano

### Exploring Bellinzona
The best starting point for an exploration of Bellinzona is Castelgrande, which can be reached by taking a lift located to one side of Piazzella Mario della Valle. Steps from the castle platform wind down to Piazza Collegiata, in the heart of the Old Town, where there are several fine Renaissance buildings. A path east of the piazza leads up to Castello di Montebello. From here, a steep road leads on up to Castello di Sasso Corbaro.

Firework display over Castelgrande

### ⊞ Castelgrande
**Tel** 091 825 81 45. Museum: **Open** Apr–Oct: 10am–6pm daily; Nov–Mar: 10am–5pm daily. Castle: 10am–6pm Mon, 9am–10pm Tue–Sun. ▨

Set on a high plateau on the west side of the Old Town, this is the oldest and most impressive of Bellinzona's three castles. In the 12th century, the Roman fortress that already stood on the site was rebuilt and enlarged by the bishops of Como. The castle underwent a further phase of rebuilding after 1242, when Bellinzona was conquered by the dukes of Milan. The fortress was extended on several occasions until the late 15th century.

Today Castelgrande's main features are two square towers, the Torre Bianca (White Tower) and Torre Nera (Black Tower), which are joined by crenellated walls forming inner baileys.

The museum, in the south wing of the castle, documents the history of Bellinzona. Also on display here is a set of 15th-century painted panels from the walls and ceiling of a villa in Bellinzona.

Renaissance arcades around the courtyard of the Palazzo Civico

### ▦ Old Town
Bellinzona's Old Town nestles in the wide Ticino valley, in the shadow of its great medieval castles. With Italianate squares, Renaissance buildings and red cobblestones in its winding alleys, it is a typical Lombard town.

Among Bellinzona's many fine buildings is the Palazzo Civico, an elegant town hall with an arcaded courtyard in the Renaissance style. Other notable buildings are the **Chiesa Santa Maria delle Grazie**, a church with 15th-century frescoes depicting the Passion and Crucifixion, and the **Chiesa di San Rocco**, a Gothic church with a Baroque interior.

On Saturday mornings the Old Town is filled with colourful market stalls heaped with fresh produce, cheeses, bread, wines and local crafts.

### ⊞ Chiesa Collegiata dei SS Pietro e Stefano
This Renaissance monastery church, whose imposing façade is pierced by a rose window, stands at the foot of the ramparts of Castelgrande. Built originally in the Gothic style, it was rebuilt in the first half of the 16th century to plans by Thomas Rodari, the architect of Como's cathedral. The interior, in

which the earlier Gothic arches are preserved, is decorated with elaborate stuccowork and frescoes in a lavish Baroque style. Over the high altar is a depiction of the Crucifixion, painted by Simone Peterzano in 1658.

### 🏰 Castello di Montebello

**Tel** 091 825 13 42. Castle: **Open** Apr–Nov: 8am–8pm daily. Museum: **Open** Apr–Oct: 10am–6pm daily.

Consisting of a 13th-century keep and a 15th-century residential palace surrounded by walls, this fortress is the most complex of Bellinzona's three castles. The crenellated walls linking Castello di Montebello, to the east of the town, and Castelgrande, to the west, created a formidable defence system across the valley.

The museum, in the keep, contains an interesting collection of archaeological artifacts from the vicinity of Bellinzona, as well as weapons and armour.

Doorway, Chiesa Collegiata dei SS Pietro e Stefano

### 🏰 Castello di Sasso Corbaro

**Tel** 091 825 59 06. Castle: **Open** 10am–6pm Mon, 10am–10pm Tue–Sun. Museum: **Open** Apr–Oct: 10am–6pm daily.

Castello di Sasso Corbaro is the most recent of Bellinzona's three fortresses. It was built in 1479 on the orders of the Duke of Milan, after the Swiss had defeated the Milanese at the Battle of Giornico, thus posing an increased threat to Ticino.

The fortress consists of a tall quadrilateral residential tower and square ramparts defended by a corner tower. The fortress is set on an elevated headland on the east side of the town, and commands wide views across the Ticino valley all the way to the northern tip of Lake Maggiore in the southwest (*see pp220–21*).

The museum, which is in the keep, contains displays illustrating the folk art and traditional crafts of Ticino.

### 🏛 Villa dei Cedri

Piazza San Biagio. **Tel** 091 821 85 20. **Open** 2–6pm Tue–Fri, 11am–6pm Sat & Sun. 🖥 villacedri.ch

Set in extensive grounds, with a vineyard, this late 19th-century Neo-Renaissance villa is the town's art gallery. Its collection consists of 19th- and 20th-century paintings mainly by Swiss and Italian artists of Ticino and Lombardy, including works by the Swiss Symbolist artist Giovanni Segantini. Also on display is a collection of prints, including examples by Oskar Kokoschka and Alfonse Mucha.

### Environs

Less than 2 km (1 mile) south of Bellinzona is **Ravecchia**. In this town is an attractive Romanesque church, the Chiesa di San Biagio, which is decorated with Gothic frescoes.

## Bellinzona Town Centre

① Castelgrande
② Old Town
③ Chiesa Collegiata dei SS Pietro e Stefano
④ Castello di Montebello
⑤ Castello di Sasso Corbaro
⑥ Villa dei Cedri

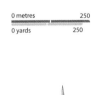

| 0 metres | 250 |
| 0 yards | 250 |

# ⑬ Three Passes

The circular route over the Uri Alps traverses some of the most spectacular high Alpine scenery in Switzerland. On the route are three mountain passes, the Susten Pass, Grimsel Pass and Furka Pass, each of which mark cantonal borders. A feat of 19th-century engineering, the road twists and turns, makes tightly winding ascents and descents, crosses bridges over dramatically plunging valleys, and passes through tunnels cut into the rock. All along the route are spectacular views of snow-capped mountains, majestic glaciers and beautiful mountain lakes.

**⑤ Susten Pass**
On the border between the cantons of Bern and Uri, the Susten Pass lies at an altitude of 2,264 m (7,428 ft).

**⑥ Innertkirchen**
This small town lies at the point where routes leading down from the passes join the road heading north towards Meiringen and Interlaken.

**⑦ Grimsel Pass**
At an altitude of 2,165 m (7,103 ft), the pass marks the border between the cantons of Bern and Valais. On the pass is the Totensee (Dead Lake).

**⑧ Furka Pass**
Lying between the cantons of Valais and Uri, the pass lies at 2,431 m (7,976 ft), with the Bernese and Pennine Alps on either side.

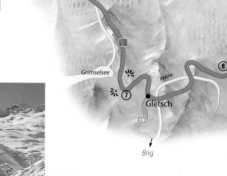

Gadmen

Interlaken ← 6-11

⑥

Guttannen

Aare

Älplibach

Grimselsee

Rhône

⑦ Gletsch

⑧

19

Brig

**⑨ Furkastrasse**
Built in the 1860s, this route over the Furka Pass offers spectacular views of high Alpine scenery. The Glacier Express passes through a tunnel beneath the pass.

### ④ Meienreuss Pass
Here a bridge spans a deep gorge in the Meien valley. From Wassen, near the foot of the valley, a road leads to Susten.

### ③ Wassen
The terrace in front of Wassen's Baroque church is a good vantage point for spectacular views of the valley below.

## Tips for Drivers

**Tour length:** 120 km (75 miles).
**Stopping-off points:** Both Andermatt and Göschennen have small hotels and restaurants.
**Other attractions:** The Handeggfall, between the Grimsel Pass and Guttannen, are impressive waterfalls at the confluence of the Aare and the Arlenbach.

### ② Göschenen
This town, at the northern end of the tunnel beneath the St Gotthard Pass, is a good base for hiking in the surrounding mountains.

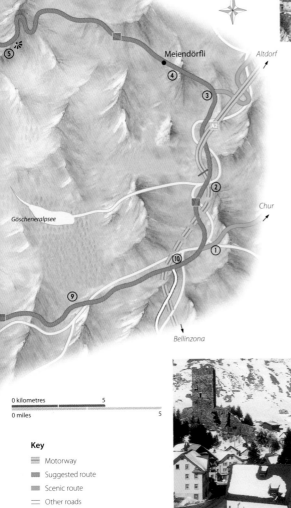

Meiendörfli

*Altdorf*

*Chur*

*Bellinzona*

Göscheneralpsee

### ① Andermatt
A skiing resort in winter and hiking centre in summer, Andermatt lies in the heart of the St Gotthard massif. Andermatt's church contains a beautiful Gothic font.

### ⑩ Hospental
Hospental lies at the convergence of roads from the north, south and west. The 13th-century castle that once guarded this crossroads still stands, although it is now in ruins.

0 kilometres 5
0 miles 5

### Key
▬ Motorway
▬ Suggested route
▬ Scenic route
═ Other roads

**For keys to symbols** *see back flap*

Frescoes on the ceiling of the chapel in Bürglen

the **Historisches Museum**, which illustrates the history and traditions of the canton of Uri.

🏛 **Historisches Museum**
Gotthardstrasse 18. **Tel** 041 870 19 06.
**Open** May & Jun, mid-Aug–mid-Oct & Dec–early Jan: 1–5pm Wed & Sat–Sun.
🚾 ⓦ hvu.ch

## ⓰ Urnersee

**Road map:** E3. 🚌 🚢 ℹ Brunnen, Bahnhofstrasse 15; 041 825 00 40.
ⓦ brunnentourismus.ch

## ⓮ Bürglen

**Road map:** E3. 🚠 3,600. 🚌

This small town at the mouth of the Schächen valley is reputed to be the birthplace of William Tell, hero of Swiss legend. The supposed site of his house is marked by a chapel built in 1582. Its façade and interior are decorated with frescoes illustrating the legend of William Tell. A figure of the hero also graces an 18th-century fountain in the town.

The legend of William Tell and the place it occupies in Swiss culture and national pride are the subject of the displays in the **Tell Museum**. Consisting of chronicles and other documents, as well as paintings, sculptures and other pieces, the exhibits illustrate the legend over the 600 years of its existence.

Also of interest in Bürglen are a 17th-century wooden tavern, the **Adler Inn**, and an early Baroque church with a stucco-decorated interior and a Romanesque tower.

**Environs**
At **Riedertal**, 3 km (2 miles) southeast of Bürglen, is a beautiful pilgrimage chapel in the Gothic-Renaissance style. It is decorated with Gothic frescoes and contains a 14th-century Pietà, which is the object of local veneration.

🏛 **Tell Museum**
Postplatz. **Tel** 041 870 41 55. **Open** May & Jun: 10–11:30am & 1:30–5pm daily; Jul & Aug: 9:30am–5pm daily; Sep & Oct: 10–11:30am & 1:30–5pm daily. 🚾 📷 ⓦ tellmuseum.ch

## ⓯ Altdorf

**Road map:** E3. 🚠 8,000. 🚌 🚢
ℹ Tellspielhaus; 041 874 80 00.
ⓦ uri.info 🎭 Dorffest (1 Aug), Chilbi (Nov).

The capital of the canton of Uri, Altdorf is supposed to be the town where William Tell shot the apple from his son's head. The **Telldenkmal**, a 19th-century statue of Tell and his son, stands on Rathausplatz. Plays based on the Tell legend are regularly performed in the Tellspielhaus here.

Also of interest in Altdorf is the town's historic arsenal and

Altdorf's Rathausplatz, with the Telldenkmal

The stunningly beautiful Urnersee forms the south-eastern arm of Lake Lucerne. Surrounded on all sides by high, steep-sided mountains, the Urnersee resembles a Norwegian fjord.

On an elevated promontory below Seelisberg, on the west side of the lake, is **Rütli Meadow** (Bergwiese Rütli), where the alliance between the cantons of Uri, Schwyz and Unterwalden was sworn in 1291 *(see p39)*.

The village of **Seedorf**, at the southern extremity of the Urnersee, has a picturesque Gothic-Renaissance castle. It was built in 1556–60 and now houses a small geological museum. **Flüelen**, nearby, is the farthest port of call for the boats that sail across the lake from Luzern.

About 3 km (2 miles) north of Flüelen, on the road to Sisikon, is the **Tellsplate**, a flat rock. According to legend,

### William Tell

The legendary hero who freed Switzerland from Habsburg oppression, William Tell is supposed to have lived in the 13th century (though some historians dismiss him as a myth). Having refused to bow to imperial power, Tell was seized by the bailiff Hermann Gessler and, as a punishment, was ordered to shoot an arrow through an apple balanced on his son's head. Tell shot the apple but, after declaring his intention to kill Gessler, was condemned to prison. During the boat journey across the Urnersee, Tell escaped and later killed Gessler.

Statue of William Tell and his son in Altdorf

The Urnersee, seen from its southern shore

this is where William Tell leaped to freedom during his boat journey across Lake Lucerne, on his way to imprisonment in Hermann Gessler's castle at Küssnacht. Near the rock stands the **Tellskapelle**, a 16th-century chapel that was remodelled in the 19th century.

**Brunnen**, at the northern extremity of the Urnersee, is one of Lake Lucerne's largest resorts. It commands a sweeping panorama of the Urnersee, with views across the water to Rütli Meadow, on the opposite shore. Brunnen has a small Baroque chapel, the Bundeskapelle, with an altarpiece painted by Justus van Egmont, a pupil of Rubens, in 1642.

## ⑰ Schwyz

**Road map:** E3. 🗻 14,000. 🚌 🚌
🛈 Zeughausstrasse 10; 041 855 59
50. 🌐 schwyz-tourismus.ch

This quiet town, capital of the canton of the same name, lies at the foot of the twin peaks of the Mythen. It has immense importance in Swiss history and culture.

The canton of Schwyz gave Switzerland both its name and its flag. Having sworn their mutual allegiance in 1291, the joint forces of Schwyz, Uri and Unterwalden united to defeat the Habsburgs at the Battle of Morgarten (1315). Thereafter they were known collectively as Schwyzers, and Helvetia (*see p39*) became known as Schwyzerland.

The **Bundesbriefmuseum** (Museum of Federal Charters) in Schwyz preserves a number

of documents relating to important events in Swiss history. The most highly prized exhibit is the Charter of Confederation, written on parchment and stamped with the seals of the three Forest Cantons in 1291.

Schwyz's Old Town contains many 17th- and 18th-century buildings. Hauptplatz, the central square, is dominated by Pfarrkirche St Martin, a Baroque church, and by the Rathaus, the 17th-century town hall whose façade features a depiction of the Battle of Morgarten painted in 1891. The **Ital-Reding-Haus**, a mansion built in 1609, contains a suite of rooms with 17th- and 18th-century furnishings and decoration. Nearby is Haus Bethlehem, a wooden house built in 1287.

A former granary dating from 1711 houses the **Forum der Schweizer Geschichte**. This museum of daily life is now part of the Swiss National Museum.

Arms of Uri on the Rathaus in Schwyz

**🏛 Bundesbriefmuseum**
Bahnhofstrasse 20. **Tel** 041 819 20 64.
**Open** May–Oct: 9–11:30am, 1:30–5pm Tue–Fri, 9am–5pm Sat & Sun; Nov–Apr: 9–11:30am & 1:30–5pm Tue–Fri, 1:30–5pm Sat & Sun. 🈂
🌐 bundesbriefmuseum.ch

**🏛 Ital-Reding-Haus**
Rickenbachstrasse 14. **Tel** 041 811 45 05. **Open** May–Oct: 2–5pm Tue–Fri, 10am–noon & 2–5pm Sat & Sun. 🈂

**🏛 Forum der Schweizer Geschichte**
Zeughausstrasse 5. **Tel** 058 466 80 11. **Open** 10am–5pm Tue–Sun.

## ⑱ Vitznau

**Road map:** D3. 🗻 1,000. 🚌 🚌
🛈 Bahnhofstrasse 1; 041 227 18 18.
🌐 wvrt.ch

Backed by the Rigi massif, this small resort lies in a sheltered bay on the north shore of Lake Lucerne. Besides its watersports facilities, Vitznau's main attraction is as a base from which to hike through the woods and Alpine pastures of the Rigi massif.

Vitznau is also the base station of the oldest rack railway in Europe. It opened in 1871 and leads up to just below the summit of Rigi-Kulm (1,798 m/5,900 ft), the highest peak in the Rigi massif. The view from this vantage point is breathtaking. Surrounded by the waters of Lake Lucerne, and the Zugersee, the Rigi massif appears to be an island, and in clear weather the distant snowcapped peaks of the Alps are visible in the far southwest.

The northwestern shore of Lake Lucerne, between Vitznau and Weggis

# ⑲ Kloster Einsiedeln

The Benedictine abbey at Einsiedeln is one of the finest examples of Baroque architecture in the world. Its history goes back to 835, when Meinrad, a monk, chose the spot for his hermitage (einsiedeln). In 934 a monastery was founded on the site. When, according to legend, a miracle occurred during the consecration of the church, the abbey became a place of pilgrimage. The church and monastery were rebuilt from 1704 to 1735, to a lavish Baroque design by Brother Kaspar Moosbrugger. Most of the paintings, gilding and stuccowork in the church are by the Bavarian brothers Cosmas Damian and Egid Quirin Asam.

**Library**
The abbey library is a fine example of the Baroque style. Only a part of the abbey's extensive collection of manuscripts is housed here.

**The confessional**, a chapel where pilgrims gather to make their confessions, is located in the north wing of the transept.

**Interior of the Church**
The spacious interior of the church is impressive. The nave is decorated with Baroque frescoes by Cosmas Damian Asam.

**Well of Our Lady**
As they arrive at the church, pilgrims traditionally drink the water from this well. It is crowned by a statue of the Virgin.

**★ Black Madonna**
A chapel inside the church contains the statue of a Black Madonna. This 15th century wooden figure of the Virgin with the infant Jesus is reputed to have miraculous powers.

★ **Wall Paintings**
The walls, ceiling and domes of the church are covered with frescoes and gilt stuccowork. This extraordinarily rich scheme is typical of the late Baroque style.

## VISITORS' CHECKLIST

**Practical Information**
**Road map:** E3. 🛈 Hauptstrasse 85; 055 418 44 88. Kloster Einsiedeln: **Tel** 055 418 62 70. Church: **Open** 6am–8:30pm (to 9pm Easter–Nov). Grosser Saal: **Open** 1:30–6pm. 🏛 Library: **Open** 2pm daily or by appointment. 🎉 Feast of the Miraculous Dedication (14 Sep).

**Transport**
🚌 🚃

**Organ**
Bedecked with figures of putti playing instruments, the organ occupies a gallery beneath the central dome.

★ **Grosser Saal**
Lavishly decorated with paintings and stuccowork, the Grosser Saal, or Great Hall, is still used for grand receptions and official ceremonies.

**Pulpit**
Figures of angels and the symbols of the Four Evangelists decorate the gilt pulpit. It was designed by Egid Quirin Asam and completed in 1726.

Lake Lucerne and the towns of Küssnacht am Rigi and Bürgenstock, seen from the summit of Pilatus

## ⓴ Zug

**Road map:** E3. 🚠 24,000. 🚌 🚃 🚢
🛈 Bahnhofstrasse, 041 723 68 00.
🌐 zug-tourismus.ch

Zug is set on the northeastern shore of the Zugersee, in the wooded foothills of the Zugerberg. It is the capital of its namesake, Zug, the smallest but the richest of all Swiss cantons. Having the lowest taxation in Switzerland, Zug has become the headquarters of many multinational companies.

Substantial parts of the walls, set with towers, still encircle Zug's medieval Old Town. The focal point of the Old Town is Kolinplatz. At the centre of this square is a fountain with a statue of the knight Wolfgang Kolin, a standard-bearer of the Swiss army. Nearby stands the Gothic Rathaus, built in 1509. Also of interest is the 15th- to 16th-century Kirche St Oswald, whose portal has figures of the Virgin, St Oswald and St Michael.

The former bailiff's castle houses the **Museum in der Burg**,

a museum with permanent collections of local history as well as special exhibitions. Nearby is a 16th-century granary now converted into the **Kunsthaus**, a gallery with an important collection of Viennese modern art. The **Museum für Urgeschichte** concentrates on prehistory and antiquity.

Cruises on the Zugersee depart from the harbour jetty.

### 🏛 Museum in der Burg
Kirchenstrasse 11. **Tel** 041 728 29 70.
**Open** 2–5pm Tue–Sat, 10am–5pm Sun. 📷

### 🏛 Kunsthaus
Dorfstrasse 27. **Tel** 041 725 33 44. **Open** noon–6pm Tue–Fri, 10am–5pm Sat & Sun. 📷
🌐 kunsthauszug.ch

### 🏛 Museum für Urgeschichte
Hofstrasse 15. **Tel** 041 728 28 80.
**Open** 2–5pm Tue–Sun. 📷

RIGI-FIRST
NEUER WINTERKURORT U. SPORTPLATZ

Poster advertising winter sports on Rigi

## ⓶① Küssnacht am Rigi

**Road map:** D3. 🚠 9,500. 🚃 🚢
🛈 Unterdorf 15; 041 850 33 30.
🌐 hohlgassland.ch

The small town of Küssnacht am Rigi lies at the foot of the Rigi. This massif rises to the east of the Küssnachtersee, the northern arm of Lake Lucerne.

The town is a good base for hiking in the mountains and for exploring Lake Lucerne. It also offers a wide range of sports facilities.

Buildings of interest in Küssnacht's historic district include the Baroque town hall and the Kirche St Peter und St Paul. Another is the Engel Hotel, a half-timbered building dating from 1552 that has been an inn for over 400 years.

## ⓶② Luzern
See pp236–43.

## ⓶③ Pilatus

**Road map:** D3. Pilatus Cable Car Co: Kriens/Lucerne Schlossweg 1, 041 329 11 11. 🌐 pilatus.ch

The rugged outlines of Pilatus, whose highest peak reaches an altitude of 2,132 m (7,000 ft), rise on the southwestern side of Lake Lucerne. Various legends are associated with the mountain. According to

Houses on the waterfront in Zug's medieval Old Town

one, the body of Pontius Pilate was thrown into a lake on the mountain, and his spirit continues to haunt its heights, unleashing violent storms.

There are several convenient ways of reaching the summit of Pilatus. The first stage is a boat or train ride from Luzern to Alpnachstad, near the foot of Pilatus. From here a rack railway climbs a gradient of 48 per cent, making it the steepest cog railway in the world. From Pilatus-Kulm, the upper station, a walking trail, leads up to a viewing platform on one of the mountain's peaks. In good weather it offers views of the Säntis, in the Alpstein, and of the Glarner and Berner Alps. The descent down from Pilatus-Kulm can be made either by the cog railway to Alpnachstad (runs in summer only), or by cable car down to Kriens.

**Ibex on the rugged slopes of Pilatus**

## ❷ Hergiswil

**Road map:** D3. 🏔 5,600. 🚗 🚌 🚢
ℹ️ Seestrasse 54; 041 630 12 58
**W** hergiswil.ch

The small lakeside village of Hergiswil, on the rail route from Luzern to Stans, is worth a visit for its glassworks, the Glasi Hergiswil. The factory was established in 1817 and was saved from closure in the late 1970s by the Ticinese glassmaker Roberto Niederer. It now employs about 100 people and is the focus of Hergiswil's life.

The factory is open to visitors, who can watch glass-blowers at work. Also on the premises is the **Glasi Museum**, which documents the history of the glassworks, with many photographs and hundreds of different examples of its glassware.

🏛 **Glasi Museum**
Seestrasse 12. **Tel** 041 632 32 32.
**Open** 9am–6pm Mon–Fri,
9am–4pm Sat. **W** glasi.ch

## ❷ Stans

**Road map:** D3. 🏔 7,300. 🚗 🚌
ℹ️ Bahnhofplatz 4; 041 610 88 33.
**W** tourismusstans.ch

Capital of the half-canton of Nidwalden, Stans is a small town on the banks of the River Engelberger Aa. Above the town rises the Stanserhorn (1,900 m/6,234 ft), the summit of which can be reached from Stans by funicular and the world's first double-decker cable car with an open top.

The town's charming historic district revolves around Dorfplatz. This square is dominated by a Baroque parish church, **Pfarrkirche St Peter und St Paul**, with a Romanesque tower, the remains of an earlier church. In the centre of Dorfplatz stands a 19th-century monument to Arnold von Winkelried who sacrificed his life to help his Confederate comrades defeat the Austrians at the Battle of Sempach in 1386.

Also of interest in the town are the Höfli, a medieval turreted house that contains a museum of local history, and the Winkelriedhaus, a late Gothic building that houses a museum of local folk crafts and traditions.

## ❷ Engelberg

**Road map:** D3. 🏔 3,400. 🚗 🚌
ℹ️ Klosterstrasse 3, 041 639 77 77.
**W** engelberg.ch

Within easy reach of both Luzern and Zürich, Engelberg is one of central Switzerland's main mountain resorts. It lies at an altitude of 1,000 m (3,280 ft), at the foot of Titlis, whose rocky peak reaches 3,239 m (10,627 ft) to a glacier.

The village nestles around the **Kloster**, a Benedictine monastery. Founded in the 12th century and rebuilt in the mid-18th, it has an exquisite Rococo church, built in 1735–40. The monastery, and its working cheese dairy, are open to visitors.

Engelberg has about 80 km (50 miles) of skiing pistes. It also offers tobogganing and ice-skating facilities. Marked trails in the vicinity lead past small mountain lakes and up to the summits of Titlis, Urirotstock, Schlossberg and Hutstock. There are also many cycling routes and facilities for summer sports such as paragliding. The Rotair cable car, which rotates as it travels so as to give passengers an all-round view, runs from Stand, above Engelberg, over the Titlis glacier.

The Rotair cable car from Engelberg up to Klein Titlis

# ㉒ Luzern

Central Switzerland's largest town, Luzern (Lucerne in French) lies on the western shore of Lake Lucerne. From its origins as a small fishing village, it grew into an important staging point when the St Gotthard Pass was opened in 1220. During the Reformation, Luzern led the Catholic resistance in Switzerland, and was long embroiled in political and religious disputes. Since the 19th century, tourism has underpinned Luzern's economy. Still attracting large numbers of visitors, the town also hosts the renowned Lucerne Festival.

Chapel Bridge, with the Wasserturm in the background

Luzern seen from the west, with Mount Rigi in the background

## Central Luzern

Luzern is a compact town that is easily explored on foot. The medieval Old Town *(see pp238–9)* lies on the north bank of the River Reuss and, from the train station on the south bank, it can be reached by crossing the medieval Chapel Bridge. The best view of Luzern is from the towers in the medieval fortifications that encircle the Old Town to the north. Luzern's main shopping districts are on the south bank, southwest of the train station, and in the Old Town, on the north bank.

## 🏛 KKL

Europaplatz 1.
With its cantilevered roof, the KKL building, or Kultur- und Kongresszentrum Luzern (Luzern Culture and Convention Centre), is a strikingly modernist glass and steel building that juts out over Lake Lucerne. It was designed by the French architect Jean Nouvel and was opened in 1998. The building contains conference halls, concert halls and theatres, and the Kunstmuseum *(see below)*.

## 🏛 Kunstmuseum

KKL, Europaplatz 1. **Tel** 041 226 78 00.
**Open** 10am–5pm Tue & Fri–Sun, 10am–8pm Wed–Thu.
The collections of the Kunstmuseum are displayed in about 20 rooms on the topmost floor of the KKL building *(see above)*. The gallery has a permanent collection of 18th- and early 20th-century Swiss painting, and also presents a rotating programme of exhibitions of the work of international contemporary artists.

## 🏛 Rosengart Collection

Pilatusstrasse 10. **Tel** 041 220 16 60.
**Open** Apr–Oct: 10am–6pm daily; Nov–Mar: 11am–5pm daily.
**W** rosengart.ch

The Rosengart Collection (Sammlung Rosengart) is a private collection of over 300 modernist paintings that was formed over several decades by the art dealers Siegfried Rosengart and his daughter, Angela. As well as 125 works by Paul Klee, the museum also has a fantastic collection of watercolours and sculptures by Pablo Picasso, many of them from the former Picasso Museum. The collection also includes Impressionist paintings, with canvases by Cézanne and Monet, and work by Chagall, Matisse and Kandinsky.

## 🌉 Chapel Bridge

This 14th-century covered footbridge spanning the Reuss at an angle formed part of the town's fortifications, protecting it against attack from the direction of the lake. Near the centre of the river, the bridge joins the Wasserturm, an octagonal tower that has served as a lighthouse, a prison and a treasury. In the 17th century, the bridge's roof panels were painted with scenes from the history of Luzern and episodes in the lives of St Leodegar and St Mauritius, martyrs who became the town's patron saints.

The oldest wooden bridge in Europe, Chapel Bridge (Kapellbrücke) has become the symbol of Luzern. It was partly destroyed by fire in 1993 but was rebuilt and most of its paintings restored.

The KKL building, on Luzern's waterfront

◄ The Rathausplatz in Altdorf, with the statue of William Tell and his son

## Jesuit Church

A major landmark on the south bank of the Reuss, the great Jesuitenkirche, the Jesuit church of St Francis Xavier, was built in 1666–73, although its onion-domed twin towers were not completed until the 19th century. The Baroque interior is richly decorated with stuccowork and the ceiling paintings depict the apotheosis of St Francis Xavier.

## Franziskanerkirche

Franziskanerplatz.

Dating from about 1270, this Franciscan church was built in the Gothic style, but has been much altered over the centuries. The Renaissance choir stalls,

Interior of the Franziskanerkirche

17th-century pulpit and Baroque ceiling paintings are among notable features of the interior.

## Historisches Museum

Pfistergasse 24. **Tel** 041 228 54 24. **Open** 10am–5pm Tue–Sun. **W** hmluzern.ch

Luzern's history museum occupies the former arsenal, a Renaissance building dating from 1597. Also named the Depot, the museum has been brought up to date with interactive displays, barcodes and hand-held scanners in place of traditional information boards and audio guides.

Thousands of fascinating historical objects on display include weaponry, costumes, and folk art and crafts, as well as early advertising material from the Swiss manufacturing and tourism industries. Actors in period costume dramatize scenes from history in daily performances.

In the adjacent building is the Naturmuseum. Its displays focus on various

### VISITORS' CHECKLIST

**Practical Information**
Road map: D3. 60,000.
Zentralstrasse 5; 041 227 17 17. **W** luzern.com Fasnacht Carnival (Feb or early Mar), Luzerner Fest (Jun), Lucerne Festival (Aug–Sep).

**Transport**

aspects of natural history, in particular zoology, palaeontology and geology.

## Spreuerbrücke

This wooden covered bridge spans the Reuss at the western edge of the Old Town. It was built in 1408 and incorporates a small chapel. The bridge's roof is lined with panels painted by Kaspar Meglinger in 1626–35. Depicting the Dance of Death, they run in sequence from the north bank and culminate with Christ's triumph over Death at the south bank.

Downstream is the Nadelwerk, a 19th-century flood-control device.

---

## Luzern Town Centre

① KKL
② Kunstmuseum
③ Rosengart Collection
④ Chapel Bridge
⑤ Jesuit Church
⑥ Franziskanerkirche
⑦ Historisches Museum
⑧ Spreuerbrücke
⑨ Weinmarkt
⑩ Naturmuseum
⑪ Rathaus
⑫ Kapellplatz
⑬ Museggmauer
⑭ Hofkirche
⑮ Bourbaki Panorama
⑯ Löwendenkmal
⑰ Gletschergarten

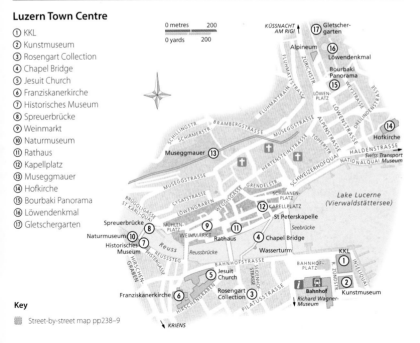

**Key**

Street-by-street map pp238–9

For hotels and restaurants see pp248–55 and pp264–75

# Street-by-Street: Old Town

Luzern's historic Old Town (Altstadt) is set on a shallow bend of the Reuss at the point where the river leaves Lake Lucerne. From the Middle Ages the town was defended by ramparts on its northern side and by Chapel Bridge, which spans the river on its eastern side. The Old Town's ancient layout survives, and the façades of its fine historic houses, particularly around Hirschenplatz and along Weinmarktgasse, are painted with frescoes or covered with sgraffito decoration. This historic district of Luzern is also a bustling urban centre, with plenty of shops, restaurants and cafés.

**Weinmarkt**
This central square, where wine was once sold, has several fine houses, many of which were guildhalls.

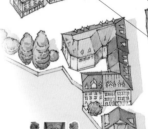

**Alley near Weinmarkt**
The narrow alleys off this square are lined with tall houses, some with colourfully painted shutters. Many of these houses have been converted into hotels, or contain boutiques and restaurants.

WEGGISGASSE

EISENGASSE

ROSSLIGASSE

WEINMARKTGASSE

WEINMARKT

KORNMARKT-PLATZ

UNTER DER EGG

★ **Rathaus**
Completed in 1606, the late Renaissance town hall has an ornate façade. The main entrance is flanked by double columns.

**Key**

 Suggested route

**Sternenplatz**
Many of the paintings on the façades of the houses in Luzern's Old Town are full of symbolism and allusions.

**St Peterskapelle**
A relief of 1513, showing Christ and his disciples in the Garden of Gethsemane, is set into the chapel's south wall.

**Kapellplatz**
The fountain in this square is crowned by a figure of Fritschi, a legendary character associated with spring and joy. He is celebrated at Fasnacht, Luzern's great spring festival.

STERNEN-PLATZ

KAPELL-PLATZ

KAPELLGASSE

FURRENGASSE

RATHAUSQUAI

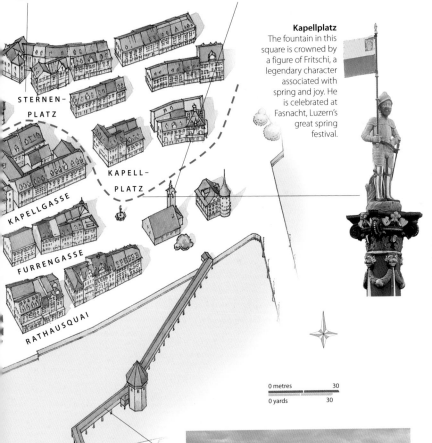

0 metres 30
0 yards 30

★ **Chapel Bridge**
This covered footbridge has become the symbol of Luzern. Originally built in the 14th century, it was partly destroyed by fire in 1993 and has been reconstructed.

# Exploring Luzern

One of the best views over the picturesque squares, churches, chapels and patrician houses of Luzern's Old Town is from the ramparts to the north. A pleasant walk eastwards from the Old Town leads to several other interesting buildings and museums, including the grand Renaissance Hofkirche and the Wagner Museum, dedicated to the Romantic composer. On the lakeshore further east is the fascinating Swiss Transport Museum, one of Switzerland's greatest attractions *(see pp242–3)*.

## 🏛 Weinmarkt

Lined with historic houses, this square is one of the most attractive features of Luzern's Old Town. The Weinmarktbrunnen, a Gothic fountain in the square, is a copy of the original, which now stands in the courtyard of the Rittersreher Palast, on Bahnhofstrasse. The houses around both this square and the adjacent Hirschenplatz have painted façades, ornate doorways and oriel windows. Many of these buildings were guildhouses.

Detail of fountain in Weinmarkt

## 🏛 Naturmuseum

Kasernenplatz 6. **Tel** 041 228 54 11.
**Open** 10am–5pm Tue–Sun.
🌐 **naturmuseum.ch**

The Natural History Museum is an easy ten-minute stroll from the Old Town, southwest across the Spreuerbrücke. With a variety of live animals and interactive displays, this is a popular choice with children and is one of the country's most family-friendly museums. Hallways are lined with stuffed animals and there is a full-time guide on hand to explain exhibits in detail. There is plenty to keep adults engaged, too, such as the topographical representation of the Alps in prehistoric times. Flora and fauna from central Switzerland, including a colourful exhibit of butterflies, are displayed on rotating panels.

## 🏛 Rathaus

Kornmarkt 3. **Tel** 041 227 17 17.
**Open** by arrangement.

The present town hall, built in a grand Renaissance style, was completed in 1606. Of the 14th-century town hall that stood on the same site, only a tower remains. The council chamber inside is lined with finely carved wood panelling.

## 🏛 Museggmauer

**Open** Easter–Oct: 8am–7pm.
The Museggmauer, the well-preserved northern section of Luzern's medieval fortifications, runs for about 850 m (2,800ft), from the north bank of the Reuss almost to the north shore of Lake Lucerne. The walls are set with nine towers, which were built in the second half of the 14th century. The wall walk commands fine views of the town, the river and the lake.

## 🏛 Kapellplatz

St Peterskapelle: **Open** 7:30am–6:15pm Mon–Wed & Fri, 7:30am–9pm Thu, 7:30am–5pm Sat, 8:30am–8pm Sun.

This picturesque square buzzes with life, particularly on market days. It takes its name from the Peterskapelle. This 18th-century chapel stands on the site of a 12th-century church, the earliest to be built in Luzern. The chapel contains a 14th-century Gothic crucifix.

Heraldic shield on one of the towers of the Museggmauer

## 🏛 Hofkirche

St. Leodegarstrasse. **Open** daily.
This collegiate church is a fine example of late Renaissance Swiss architecture. The original church, dating from the 12th century, was almost completely destroyed by fire in 1633. Only the twin towers, with pointed domes, remain and are incorporated into the present building.

The magnificent interior is decorated in Renaissance style. Notable features include the high altar, with statues of St Leodegar and St Mauritius, patron saints of Luzern. The altar in the north aisle is graced by a depiction of the Dormition (or Death) of the Virgin painted in 1500. The church also has elaborate pews, pulpit and font, and a huge organ, built in about 1640.

Painted façades of houses in the Weinmarkt square

*For hotels and restaurants see pp248–55 and pp264–75*

The altar in the north aisle of the Hofkirche

A niche in the north tower frames a depiction of Christ in the Garden of Gethsemane.

### 🏛 Bourbaki Panorama

Löwenplatz 11. **Tel** 041 412 30 30.
**Open** Apr–Oct: 9am–6pm daily;
Nov–Mar: 10am–5pm daily.
🔳 bourbakipanorama.ch

One of the world's few surviving panoramas, this giant circular mural depicts the march of the French army through Switzerland under General Bourbaki, during the Franco-Prussian War (1870–71). In a stone building now housed in a glass shell, it is 112 m (370 ft) long and 10 m (33 ft) high, and was painted by Edouard Castres. Sound effects and a narrative (in several languages) help bring the events depicted to life.

The building also contains a museum, art galleries, a cinema, bars and a restaurant.

### 🏛 Löwendenkmal

Denkmalstrasse.

This massive figure of a dying lion pierced by a spear is a startling monument to the Swiss Guards of Louis XVI of France. On 10 August 1792, the guards defended the Palais des Tuileries, in Paris, when it was stormed by revolutionaries. Those who survived the attack were arrested and guillotined on the night of 2–3 September.

The Löwen-denkmal, or Lion Monument, was carved out of the sandstone cliff face by the Danish sculptor Bertel Thorwaldsen, and it was unveiled in 1821. Reflected in the waters of a small pond, the monument has great drama and pathos.

The Löwendenkmal

### 🏛 Gletschergarten

Denkmalstrasse 4. **Tel** 041 410 43 40.
**Open** Apr–Oct: 9am–6pm daily;
Nov–Mar: 10am–5pm daily.
🔳 gletschergarten.ch

This attractive garden is an oasis of tranquillity, as well as being the setting for a fascinating natural phenomenon. In 1872 an enormous rock, complete with 32 potholes and well-sized holes, was excavated here. Formed by glacial abrasion, research showed it dated from the Ice Age. The garden was created to conserve this geological feature, which is protected by a tent-roof that allows visitors to view the rock from the sides.

The site includes an exhibition on the geological processes involved in creating the holes, a museum and the fascinating Mirror Maze of more than 90 mirrors in the style of Granada's Alhambra.

### 🏛 Richard Wagner-Museum

Richard Wagner-Weg 27. **Tel** 041 360 23 79. **Open** 10am–noon & 2–5pm Tue–Sun.

The German Romantic composer Richard Wagner was a regular visitor to Luzern. It was here that he wrote the third act of his opera *Tristan and Isolde*. Two complete operas, *The Mastersingers of Nuremberg* and *Siegfried*, date from this period, and while he was in Luzern Wagner also started work on *The Twilight of the Gods*.

The tranquil Villa Tribschen, where Wagner and his wife and son lived from 1866 to 1872, is devoted to this particularly happy period. Its rooms, with original furniture, are filled with memorabilia of the composer's life, including paintings, letters and musical instruments.

### Environs

The Museum im Bellpark in **Kriens**, 3 km (2 miles) southwest of Luzern and reachable by bus, contains a collection of objects relating to photography, video and the media.

The glass pavilion of the Bourbaki Panorama

# Swiss Transport Museum

Almost every mode of mechanized transport, from the earliest bicycle to the latest spacecraft, is displayed and explained at the Swiss Transport Museum (Verkehrshaus der Schweiz) in Luzern. Vintage cars and steam locomotives are part of the sections on road and rail transport, and the section on tourism showcases the ingenuity of rack railways and cable cars. Water transport, aviation and space travel are also documented. Among the museum's interactive features are three flight simulators; there are also many indoor and outdoor activities for younger visitors.

**Rail Transport Halls**
These halls have exhibits showing the history of Swiss rail transport, from the horse-drawn tram through to steam trains, cog trains and electric railways.

**Krokodil**
The elongated shape of this electric locomotive led to its being dubbed the *Crocodile*. Built in 1920, it served the route leading through the St Gotthard Tunnel.

Main entrance

**Gotthardmodell**
One of the most fascinating of the museum's displays is a model that re-creates the rail route through the St Gotthard Tunnel.

★ **Filmtheatre**
Viewers are taken on a 40-minute film experience of new worlds, enlarging the minute and showing the large at full size.

★ **Swiss Chocolate Adventure**
This themed area allows visitors to learn more about the discovery, origins, production and transport of chocolate, one of Switzerland's principal exports.

## Gallery Guide

*The rooms to the left of the main entrance are devoted to rail transport. Opposite the main entrance is the Road Transport Hall. The other main rooms contain aviation and space travel exhibits. The Filmtheatre has the largest screen in Switzerland, while the Planetarium and the Swiss Chocolate Adventure are educational and fun.*

### VISITORS' CHECKLIST

**Practical Information**
Lidostrasse 5. **Tel** 041 370 44 44.
**Open** Apr–Oct: 10am–6pm daily;
Nov–Feb: 10am–5pm daily.
📺 🏠 ♿
W verkehrshaus.ch

**Hans-Erni-Museum**
A section of the museum is devoted to the abstract paintings of Hans Erni (b.1909), a native of Luzern.

**Road Transport Hall**
Visitors press a buzzer to select the vehicle they want to see, and a robot conveys it on to a turntable for closer inspection.

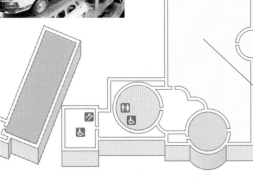

### Key

- 🟦 Railways
- 🟦 Road Transport Hall
- 🟦 Telecommunications
- 🟦 Planetarium
- 🟦 Aviation Hall
- ⬜ Air transport
- 🟦 Navigation Hall
- 🟦 Hans-Erni-Museum
- ⬜ Filmtheatre
- 🟦 Swiss Chocolate Adventure

**★ Aircraft**
This Fokker F. VII A, the oldest Swiss passenger plane still in existence, forms part of the museum's aviation section. The aircraft on display here range from microlights to supersonic military jets.

**For keys to symbols** *see back flap*

# TRAVELLERS'
# NEEDS

# WHERE TO STAY

Whether you are looking for a hotel in a city centre, at a leading winter resort, on the edge of a lake or in unspoiled countryside, Switzerland offers accommodation to suit all tastes and budgets. Across all categories and price ranges, Swiss hotels provide high quality and value for money, even though their prices tend to be relatively high. Cheaper options include guesthouses,

to be found in some of the country's most attractive towns and villages, and welcoming mountain inns, where you will be treated to warm Swiss hospitality. For those who enjoy the great outdoors, Switzerland has a host of well-equipped campsites in unforgettable scenery. Many farms also have rooms to let, and even give visitors the opportunity to sleep in barns, on pristine straw.

An opulent suite with views of the Alps at the splendid Gstaad Palace (see p248)

## Choosing a Hotel

The best source of information on hotels in Switzerland is the **Swiss Hotel Association**, which covers most types of accommodation, from luxury hotels to remote mountain inns. It also grades hotels on a scale of one to five stars, which correspond to well-defined standards of comfort.

Average prices range from 70 CHF for a double room without a bath in a one-star hotel to at least 1,200 CHF for a comfortable suite in a five-star establishment. Except in the very cheapest and the most expensive hotels, prices generally include breakfast, taxes and service. Some hotels, particularly those that are family-run, are not subject to official classification, but they are generally clean and comfortable. While many hotels have restaurants, a *hôtel garni* is an establishment that serves breakfast but no other meals.

In popular resorts, hotel prices are subject to seasonal

variations. According to their location, most hotels charge the highest prices during the winter sports season or at the height of the summer season, although discounts sometimes apply for longer stays. At city hotels, prices generally stay constant throughout the year, although special weekend rates are often available.

Hotels in many resorts offer guest cards (*Gästekarte*, *Kurkarte*, *carte des visiteurs* or *tessera di soggiorno*), which entitle holders to substantial discounts ranging from travel in the locality to admission to museums.

## Hotel Chains

Many hotels in Switzerland belong to international or national chains or associations. **Best Western** has around 30 three- and four-star hotels, while **Swiss Quality Hotels International** has over 70 three- to five-star establishments in the country's larger towns and cities and in the major holiday

resorts. Hotels in this chain offer discounts to holders of the Swiss Travel Pass (see p297).

The **Minotel Suisse** chain is an association of some 50 traditional family-run hotels with a rating of two to four stars. These hotels have restaurants that serve Swiss food and wine. In a less expensive price bracket are the 160 accommodation options with **Swiss Budget Hotels**, which range from one to three stars. These hotels tend to be off the main routes or outside the main tourist regions, which is why they offer such good value for money.

The 27 **Romantik** hotels are independently run establishments in fine historic buildings, such as châteaux. All offer exceptionally high standards of comfort, and most are in outstanding locations.

## Rooms/B&B

Guesthouses and private houses advertise rooms for rent with signs reading *Zimmer frei*, *Chambres à louer* or *Affitasi*

Terrace at the Grand Resort Bad Ragaz, famous for its sweeping views (see p253)

◀ Cheeses in the cellar at La Maison du Gruyère, in Fribourg

The marble-floored reception area at the Victoria-Jungfrau, in Interlaken *(see p248)*

*camere*. They are most likely to be found in resorts and in areas frequented by visitors.

Bed-and-breakfast accommodation is also becoming more widely available in Switzerland. At an average price of 40 CHF per night, both these types of accommodation offer excellent value.

## Hostels

Switzerland has more than 80 hostels, many with a range of double rooms, family rooms and dormitories. Prices average about 15 to 25 CHF per night, including breakfast, but there may be an extra charge if you don't bring your own sleeping bag. Most hostels have a television room, and some also serve evening meals.

## Sleeping in Straw

From May until late October, some farms allow visitors to sleep on freshly laid straw in their barns. Charges are about 20 CHF per night, which usually includes breakfast and the use of a shower. Visitors should bring their own sleeping bags.

Staying on a working farm is another way of experiencing rural Switzerland at first hand. Rooms or apartments can be rented by the night or the week.

## Mountain Inns

Picturesque mountain inns *(Berghausen* or *auberges de montagne)* offer convenient overnight accommodation to hikers. As well as dormitories, many have individual rooms. Most inns also serve hot meals.

## Campsites

Switzerland's campsites are graded on a scale of one to five stars. There are about 450 of them, many in outstandingly beautiful locations. Most campsites are closed in winter, and many of those at higher altitudes are open only for the warmest months of the year. Advance booking is recommended at any time.

## Recommended Hotels

The lodgings listed on the following pages include all manner of accommodation, from luxurious lakeside retreats to simple hostels. They are listed by area and then by price.

Much of the accommodation, particularly outside of the cities, has been chosen with location in mind. Included are good-value options affording great views of lakes and mountains. Serving hikers and skiers, these rooms can often be minimally furnished and functional in design. Alternatively, historic hotels, particularly those in popular Alpine resorts, offer rooms full of charm and a range of fantastic facilities.

Those featured as DK Choices have been chosen because they offer something special, be it exceptional service, beautiful interiors, top-notch amenities or a unique hotel experience.

---

# DIRECTORY

## Hotels

**Swiss Hotel Association**
Monbijoustrasse 130, Bern.
**Tel** 031 370 41 11.
w **swisshotels.com**

## Hotel Chains

**Best Western**
Monbijoustrasse 130, Bern.
**Tel** 0800 55 23 44.
w **bestwestern.ch**

**Minotel Suisse**
Avenue de Montchoisi 35,
1006 Lausanne.
**Tel** 021 310 08 00.
w **minotel.com**

**Romantik**
w **romantikhotels.com**

**Swiss Budget Hotels**
Monbijoustrasse 130, Bern.
**Tel** 084 880 55 08.
w **rooms.ch**

**Swiss Quality Hotels International**
Spittelstrasse 4, 8712 Stäfa.
**Tel** 044 928 27 27.
w **swissqualityhotels. com**

## B&B

**Bed and Breakfast**
Sonnenweg 3,
4144 Arlesheim.
w **bnb.ch**

## Hostels

**Swiss Backpackers**
Alpenstrasse 16,
3800 Interlaken.
**Tel** 033 823 46 46.
w **swissbackpackers.ch**

**Swiss Youth Hostels**
Schaffhauserstrasse 14,
8042 Zürich.
**Tel** 044 360 14 14.
w **youthhostel.ch**

## Sleeping in Straw

**Schlaf im Stroh**
**Tel** 041 678 12 86.
w **schlaf-im-stroh.ch**

## Holiday Farms

w **bauernhof-ferien.ch**

**Reka-Ferien**
Neuengasse 15, 3001
Bern. **Tel** 031 329 66 33.
w **reka.ch**

## Campsites

**Camping and Caravanning**
Bahnhofstrasse 5,
3322 Schönbühl.
**Tel** 031 852 06 26.
w **swisscamps.ch**

**CampingNET**
Grundhaldenstrasse 60,
8303 Bassersdorf.
w **camping.ch**

# Where to Stay

## Bern

### Glocke F
Hostel **Map** C3
*Rathausgasse 75, 3011*
**Tel** *031 311 37 71*
**w** bernbackpackers.com
Only a short walk from the train station, the Glocke offers a good range of amenities, including kitchen and laundry facilities and an Internet café. Great value.

### Landhaus F
Hostel **Map** C3
*Altenbergstrasse 4, 3013*
**Tel** *031 348 03 05*
**w** albertfrida.ch
The Landhaus is situated close to the River Aare, right across from the new Bear Park, on a quiet residential street. Rooms are simply decorated but modern and full of light.

### National F
Hostel **Map** C3
*Hirschengraben 24, 3011*
**Tel** *031 552 15 15*
**w** nationalbern.ch
Located in the vicinity of the train station, and with easy access to the Old Town, this family-run hotel offers spacious rooms. It also houses a popular Slow Food restaurant.

### Pension Marthahaus F
Bed and Breakfast **Map** C3
*Wyttenbachstrasse 22a, 3013*
**Tel** *031 332 41 35*
**w** marthahaus.ch
Rooms are of a good size at this inexpensive guesthouse in a 19th-century building. Guests enjoy free Internet access and the use of a kitchen.

The fairy-tale building housing the exclusive Gstaad Palace

### Belle Époque FF
Boutique Hotel **Map** C3
*Gerechtigkeitsgasse 18, 3011*
**Tel** *031 311 43 36*
**w** belle-epoque.ch
Rooms in this unique hotel in Bern's Old Town are furnished with Art Nouveau or *belle époque* antiques and paintings, creating a splendidly decadent atmosphere.

### Waldhorn FF
Modern Hotel **Map** C3
*Waldhöheweg 2, 3013*
**Tel** *031 332 23 43*
**w** waldhorn.ch
This modern pension is located slightly away from the city centre, in a quiet suburb with good tram connections. Free parking and free Wi-Fi, too.

## DK Choice

### Bellevue Palace FFF
Historic Hotel **Map** C3
*Kochergasse 3–5, 3000*
**Tel** *031 320 45 45*
**w** bellevue-palace.ch
Renowned for its luxury and high standards of service, this is a veritable Bern landmark. Larger-than-average rooms are generously furnished with great attention to detail. The terrace offers memorable views of the River Aare, with the Bernese Oberland mountain peaks in the distance.

## Mittelland, Bernese Oberland & Valais

### BRIG: Victoria FF
Historic Hotel **Map** D4
*Bahnhofstrasse 2, 3900*
**Tel** *027 923 15 03*
**w** hotel-victoria-brig.ghix.com
Featuring excellent views of the Valaisan Alps, the rooms at this historic and imposing hotel are large and modern. A good base for exploring the surrounding area.

### CRANS-MONTANA: Royal FF
Modern Hotel **Map** C4
*10 Rue de l'Ehanoun, 3963*
**Tel** *027 485 95 95*
**w** hotel-royal.ch
This Swiss chalet-style hotel offers comfortable bedrooms and a spa. The staff can arrange activities such as golf and hiking in the summer, and skiing and sledging in the winter.

### CRANS-MONTANA:
Grand Hotel du Golf FFF
Luxury Hotel **Map** C4
*7 Allée Elysée-Bonvin, 3963*
**Tel** *027 485 42 42*
**w** ghgp.ch
Located in Switzerland's premier golf resort, this hotel boasts excellent facilities, plus views of the Valaisan Alps.

### GRINDELWALD:
Grand Regina FFF
Historic Hotel **Map** D4
*Dorfstrasse 80, 3818*
**Tel** *033 854 86 00*
**w** grandregina.ch
This imposing hotel offers spa facilities and a sauna, plus indoor and outdoor pools. Rooms are luxuriously comfortable.

### GSTAAD: Gstaad Palace FFF
Luxury Hotel **Map** C4
*Palacestrasse, 3780*
**Tel** *033 748 50 00*
**w** palace.ch
A majestic hotel set in a private park. Amenities include full beauty and spa facilities, tennis courts and several restaurants.

### INTERLAKEN: Hotel du Lac FF
Historic Hotel **Map** C4
*Höhenweg 225, 3800*
**Tel** *033 822 29 22*
**w** dulac-interlaken.ch
This riverside hotel in the centre of Interlaken has splendid views and large, comfortable rooms.

### INTERLAKEN:
Victoria-Jungfrau FFF
Luxury Hotel **Map** C4
*Höhenweg 41, 3800*
**Tel** *033 828 28 28*
**w** victoria-jungfrau.ch
Expect opulent furnishings and generously sized bedrooms at this elegant hotel with extensive spa, fitness and beauty facilities.

### KANDERSTEG: Belle Epoque
Hotel Victoria FF
Historic Hotel **Map** C4
*Äussere Dorfstrasse 2, 3718*
**Tel** *033 675 8000*
**w** hotel-victoria.ch
A renovated grand hotel in the village centre, with an indoor swimming pool and tennis courts. Children are welcome.

**KANDERSTEG: Landgasthof
Ruedihus** **FFF**
Historic Hotel **Map** C4
*Hauptstrasse, 3718*
**Tel** *033 675 81 81*
**w** ruedihus.ch
Old iron and wood are used
extensively at this historic
farmhouse surrounded by
nature. Some of the rooms
have four-poster beds.

**LAUTERBRUNNEN: Silberhorn** F
Chalet **Map** D4
*Alte Isenfluhstrasse, 3822*
**Tel** *033 856 22 10*
**w** silberhorn.com
A delightful inn close to the
train station and set in a large
private garden. In winter, a ski
piste descends all the way to
the hotel grounds.

**LEUKERBAD: Lindner** **FF**
Spa Complex **Map** C4
*Dorfplatz, 3954*
**Tel** *027 472 10 00*
**w** lindnerhotels.ch
A tunnel connects this luxurious
hotel to the main Leukerbad
spa complex, which offers
sauna, steam rooms and all
sorts of treatments. Bedrooms
are graded by luxury.

## DK Choice

**LEUKERBAD: Les Sources
des Alpes** **FFF**
Spa Complex **Map** C4
*Tuftstrasse 17, 3954*
**Tel** *027 472 20 00*
**w** sourcesdesalpes.ch
A charming, romantic
establishment tucked away at
the edge of the old village, this
hotel has its own hot springs
and an impressive array of
beauty and spa facilities. Each
room is uniquely decorated,
and each guest receives
personalized stationery. The
outdoor pool provides views
of the surrounding peaks.

**MÜRREN: Alpenruh** **FF**
Chalet **Map** D4
*Hinter der Egg, 3825*
**Tel** *033 856 88 00*
**w** alpenruh-muerren.ch
Clean modern rooms and
outstanding views of the Alps in
a quiet area close to the ski lifts.

**SAAS FEE: Jägerhof** **FF**
Chalet **Map** D5
*Obere Gasse 16, 3906*
**Tel** *027 957 13 10*
**w** hotel-jaegerhof.ch
Situated just outside the village
centre, this friendly hotel offers
a hot tub, sauna and solarium.

The indoor pool at the Bella Tola hotel, in St-Luc, in Val d'Anniviers

**SION: Du Rhône** **FF**
Modern Hotel **Map** C5
*10 Rue du Scex, 1950*
**Tel** *027 322 82 91*
**w** durhonesion.ch
This well-equipped hotel in
a quiet neighbourhood has a
modern, functional interior.
It offers complimentary Wi-Fi
and cable TV in all rooms.

**SOLOTHURN: Baseltor** **FFF**
Luxury Hotel **Map** C3
*Hauptgasse 79, 4500*
**Tel** *032 622 34 22*
**w** baseltor.ch
Located close to the cathedral,
the Baseltor is run by its friendly
and welcoming owners. The
restaurant is of an extremely
high standard.

**VAL D'ANNIVIERS: Bella Tola** **FF**
Romantic Hotel **Map** C5
*Rue Principale, St-Luc, 3961*
**Tel** *027 475 14 44*
**w** bellatola.ch
This award-winning hotel with
period furnishings, spacious
rooms and stunning views
also boasts an extremely loyal
clientele. The ski bus stops
right outside.

**VERBIER: Les Touristes** **F**
Budget Hotel **Map** C5
*134 Route de Verbier, 1936*
**Tel** *027 771 21 47*
**w** hoteltouristes-verbier.ch
Good value for money, the rooms
at this hotel are small and basic
but not without character. There
is ample free parking.

**VERBIER: Verbier Central** **FF**
Boutique Hotel **Map** C5
*Place Centrale, 1936*
**Tel** *027 771 50 07*
**w** centralhotelverbier.com
Rooms here are small but very
modern; some have balconies
with excellent views. Situated in
the animated centre of Verbier.

**VISP: Visperhof** **FF**
Modern Hotel **Map** D4
*Bahnhofstrasse 2, 3930*
**Tel** *027 948 38 00*
**w** visperhof.ch
Rooms, all non-smoking, come
with free Wi-Fi access, as well as
a complimentary basket of fruit.
There is also an independent,
self-catering apartment.

**WENGEN: Belvedere** **FF**
Historic Hotel **Map** D4
*Galliweidli, 3823*
**Tel** *033 856 68 68*
**w** belvedere-wengen.ch
Rooms are comfortable at this
large Art Nouveau-style hotel in
the centre of Wengen. Ski lifts are
close by, and a cable car takes
you to Männlichen mountain,
from where you can enjoy views
of the Eiger and the Jungfrau.

**WENGEN: Regina** **FF**
Historic Hotel **Map** D4
*Schonegg 1347a, 3823*
**Tel** *033 856 58 58*
**w** hotelregina.ch
This grand period hotel in a quiet
area of Wengen offers charming,
old-fashioned bedrooms and a
well-regarded restaurant.

**ZERMATT: Bahnhof** **F**
Historic Hotel **Map** C5
*Bahnhofstrasse 54, 3920*
**Tel** *027 967 24 06*
**w** hotelbahnhof.com
A Zermatt landmark offering
inexpensive dormitories and
doubles, the Bahnhof is popular
with climbers and skiers.

**ZERMATT: Romantica** **FF**
Chalet **Map** C5
*Chrum 21, 3920*
**Tel** *027 966 26 50*
**w** reconline.ch/romantica
This hotel has small but
comfortable rooms with majestic
views, plus two cottages that
sleep two people. Lovely garden.

**For more information on types of hotels** *see pages 246–7*

# Geneva

**Comédie** F
Modern Hotel **Map** A5
*12 Rue de Carouge, 1205*
**Tel** *022 322 23 24*
w hotel-comedie.ch
An inexpensive, friendly hotel
with easy access to the Old
Town. Modern, clean interiors
and free Wi-Fi throughout.

**Hôtel de la Cloche** F
Boutique Hotel **Map** A5
*6 Rue de la Cloche, 1201*
**Tel** *022 732 94 81*
w geneva-hotel.ch/cloche
This popular hotel is surprisingly
peaceful, despite its central
location. Elegant furnishings,
fireplaces and parquet flooring
throughout create a cosy vibe.

**Hotel Cornavin** FF
Business Hotel **Map** A5
*23 Boulevard James-Fazy, 1201*
**Tel** *022 716 12 12*
w fassbindhotels.com/en-hotel-
cornavin.html
This is a quiet hotel despite its
location next to the train station.
The top floors offer magnificent
views of the city.

**Royal Manotel** FF
Business Hotel **Map** A5
*41 Rue de Lausanne, 1201*
**Tel** *022 906 14 14*
w hotelroyalgeneva.com
A centrally located hotel with
Neo-Classical architecture and
elegant furnishings. Excellent
attention to detail.

## DK Choice

**L'Auberge d'Hermance** FFF
Boutique Hotel **Map** A5
*12 Rue du Midi, 1248*
**Tel** *022 751 13 68*
w hotel-hermance.ch
Tucked away in a pretty hamlet
within walking distance of
Lake Geneva, this cosy inn
has just six rooms, three of
which are suites. The decor is
a mix of traditional and
contemporary, with beamed
ceilings alongside modern
furniture. Free Wi-Fi.

**Hôtel Beau-Rivage** FFF
Luxury Hotel **Map** A5
*13 Quai du Mont-Blanc, 1201*
**Tel** *022 716 66 66*
w beau-rivage.ch
A lakeside family-run hotel of
architectural note, the Beau-
Rivage offers both elegant rooms
and apartments with music and
video libraries, plus free Wi-Fi.

Room with a view at the historic Lausanne Palace & Spa *(see p251)*

**Kipling** FFF
Design Hotel **Map** A5
*27 Rue de la Navigation, 1201*
**Tel** *022 544 40 40*
w manotel.com/kipling
The elegant interiors, in raspberry
and coffee hues, have an Oriental
touch. Some rooms come
complete with kitchenettes.

# Western Switzerland

**AIGLE: Du Nord** F
Modern Hotel **Map** B4
*2 Rue Colomb, 1860*
**Tel** *024 468 10 55*
w hoteldunord.ch
Situated in a traffic-free area of
the village, the hotel Du Nord
has comfortable rooms with
tea- and coffee-making facilities.

**AVENCHES: Hotel de la
Couronne** F
Modern Hotel **Map** B3
*20 Rue Centrale, 1580*
**Tel** *026 675 54 14*
w lacouronne.ch
Expect generously sized and
elegantly furnished rooms with
interesting architectural features.
Wine tastings are a bonus.

**BALLAIGUES: Hôtel Croix d'Or** F
Basic Hotel **Map** A3
*1 Place du Château, 1338*
**Tel** *021 843 26 09*
w lacroixdor.ch
This small hotel in the village
centre offers basic clean rooms
with shared bathrooms.

**LA CHAUX-DE-FONDS:
Hôtel de la Fleur-de-Lys** F
Business Hotel **Map** B3
*13 Avenue Léopold-Robert, 2300*
**Tel** *032 913 37 31*
w fleur-de-lys.ch
Tastefully decorated rooms and a
renowned Italian restaurant at this
hotel close to the train station.

**DELÉMONT: Le National** F
Modern Hotel **Map** C2
*25 Route de Bâle, 2800*
**Tel** *032 422 96 22*
w lenational-hotel.ch
Conveniently situated next to
the historic district, this chic
hotel offers ample parking
and a restaurant of note.

**LES DIABLERETS: Mon Séjour** F
Guesthouse **Map** B4
*34 Rue du Pillon, 1864*
**Tel** *024 492 14 08*
w hotel-mon-sejour.ch
Hikers and skiers flock to this
place, where inexpensive
accommodation is in dormitories
or double rooms. There are no
en-suite rooms, though there
are facilities on each floor.

**LES DIABLERETS:
Eurotel Victoria** FF
Family Hotel **Map** B4
*Chemin du Vernex, 1865*
**Tel** *024 492 37 21*
w eurotel-victoria.ch
A family-run hotel in the village
centre. Rooms are classically
furnished and comfortable.

**ESTAVAYER-LE-LAC:
Le Rive Sud** F
Historic Hotel **Map** B3
*16 Rue de l'Hôtel de Ville, 1470*
**Tel** *026 663 92 92*
w lerivesud.ch
This hotel within a stone house
offers several attractive features
and tastefully furnished rooms,
some with Jacuzzi bathtubs.

**FRIBOURG:
Hôtel du Sauvage** FF
Boutique Hotel **Map** B3
*12 Planche-Supérieure, 1700*
**Tel** *026 347 30 60*
w hotel-sauvage.ch
Conveniently situated in central
Fribourg, this hotel has tastefully
furnished rooms and ancient
wooden ceilings.

**GRUYÈRES:**
**L'Hôtel de Gruyères** FF
Historic Hotel **Map** B4
*1 Ruelle des Chevaliers, 1663*
**Tel** *026 921 80 30*
W gruyeres-hotels.ch
On the outskirts of the Old Town,
this peaceful hotel has period
farmhouse decor and views of
the countryside and mountains.

**LAUSANNE: Hôtel AlaGare** F
Basic Hotel **Map** B4
*14 Rue du Simplon, 1006*
**Tel** *021 612 09 09*
W hotelalagare.ch
Set in a pedestrianized area, this
hotel has bright, comfortable
rooms. Smaller rooms with
shared bathrooms are on offer
for those with tighter budgets.

**LAUSANNE: Elite** FF
Boutique Hotel **Map** B4
*1 Avenue Sainte-Luce, 1003*
**Tel** *021 320 23 61*
W elite-lausanne.ch
Not far from Lausanne's train
station and shopping areas, this
townhouse boasts large gardens
and a relaxed atmosphere.

**LAUSANNE:**
**Lausanne Palace & Spa** FFF
Historic Hotel **Map** B4
*7–9 Rue du Grand-Chêne, 1002*
**Tel** *021 331 31 31*
W lausanne-palace.com
A luxurious belle époque hotel in
the city centre. Guests enjoy spa
facilities, large bedrooms and a
Michelin-starred restaurant.

**LE LOCLE:**
**Auberge de Prévoux** F
Guesthouse **Map** B3
*10 Le Prévoux, 2400*
**Tel** *032 931 23 13*
W aubergeduprevoux.ch
Renowned for its cuisine, this
family-run inn has just four
clean and spacious rooms with
good views of the countryside.

**LEYSIN: Classic Hotel** F
Modern Hotel **Map** B4
*4 Route de la Cité, 1854*
**Tel** *024 493 06 06*
W classic-hotel.ch
A large, centrally located hotel
with a complimentary shuttle
service to the ski pistes.

**LUTRY: Le Bourg 7** FF
Boutique Hotel **Map** B4
*7 Rue du Bourg, 1095*
**Tel** *021 796 37 77*
W lebourg7.com
An elegant hotel with a modern,
bright interior, Le Bourg 7 is set in
a quiet village in the Lake Geneva
wine-growing area. All the
furniture in the rooms is for sale!

**MONT-PELERIN: Le Mirador**
**Kempinski** FFF
Luxury Hotel **Map** B4
*5 Chemin du Mirador, 1801*
**Tel** *021 925 11 11*
W mirador.ch
Set in the heart of Swiss wine
country, this idyllic hotel is
surrounded by vineyards. It
also boasts a Givenchy spa
with wide-ranging facilities.

## DK Choice

**MONTREUX: Fairmont**
**Le Montreux Palace** FFF
Historic Hotel **Map** B4
*2 Avenue Claude Nobs, 1820*
**Tel** *021 962 12 12*
W montreux-palace.ch
One of the grandest hotels
in Switzerland, with elegant
*belle époque* architecture, set on
the banks of Lake Geneva.
Guest rooms boast the latest
technology, but the decor harks
back to a more opulent age.

**MONTREUX: Hôtel**
**Villa Germaine** FFF
Historic Hotel **Map** B4
*3 Avenue Collonge, 1820*
**Tel** *021 963 15 28*
W en.mymontreux.ch/tourisme-
hebergement/hotels/villa-germaine
A fairy-tale villa providing
exceptional views and a private
garden. Attractive exterior and
comfortable rooms.

**MORGES: Mont-Blanc au Lac** FF
Historic Hotel **Map** A4
*Quai du Mont-Blanc, 1110*
**Tel** *021 804 87 87*
W hotel-mont-blanc.ch
In an attractive lakeside setting
(so expect great views) a short
walk from the town centre, this
hotel has pleasant rooms and a
gourmet restaurant.

The opulent *belle époque* interiors of the
Fairmont Le Montreux Palace

**MURTEN/MORAT:**
**Le Vieux Manoir** FFF
Luxury Hotel **Map** B3
*18 Rue de Lausanne, 3280*
**Tel** *026 678 61 61*
W vieuxmanoir.ch
An exclusive hotel set in fabulous
surroundings with breathtaking
views. Comfortable bedrooms
and highly rated restaurants.

**NEUCHÂTEL: La Maison**
**du Prussien** FF
Historic Hotel **Map** B3
*11 Rue des Tunnels, 2000*
**Tel** *032 730 54 54*
W hotel-prussien.ch
Originally a brewery, this large
stone house oozes romantic
charm. The gourmet restaurant
is an added bonus.

**NEUCHÂTEL: Beau-Rivage** FFF
Luxury Hotel **Map** B3
*1 Esplanade du Mont-Blanc, 2000*
**Tel** *032 723 15 15*
W beau-rivage-hotel.ch
This sumptuous hotel enjoys a
beautiful lakeside setting and
stunning views. Elegant
furnishings and full spa facilities.

**NYON: Hotel Real** FF
Modern Hotel **Map** A4
*1 Place de Savoie, 1260*
**Tel** *022 365 85 85*
W hotelrealnyon.ch
Rooms are spacious at this
contemporary lakeside hotel
constructed with Carrara marble
and other precious materials.

**ST-URSANNE: La Couronne** F
Historic Hotel **Map** C2
*3 Rue de 23 Juin, 2882*
**Tel** *032 461 35 67*
W hotelcouronne.ch
Close to the Old Town, this inn
has plenty of character and
pleasant outside areas. The
restaurant serves local food.

**VEVEY: Hôtel des Trois**
**Couronnes** F
Historic Hotel **Map** B4
*49 Rue d'Italie, 1800*
**Tel** *021 923 32 00*
W hoteltroiscouronnes.ch
A grand lakeside hotel with
splendid interiors and friendly
staff. The views are breathtaking.

**VEVEY: Vevey Hotel &**
**Guesthouse** F
Hostel **Map** B4
*5 Grande Place, 1800*
**Tel** *021 922 35 32*
W veveyhotel.com
Close to the train station and the
lake, this hostel offers bunk beds
and private rooms, bathrooms on
each floor and Wi-Fi, as well as
discounts on regional transport.

**For more information on types of hotels** *see pages 246–7*

**YVERDON-LES-BAINS:**
**Grand Hôtel des Bains** FF
Spa Complex **Map** B3
*22 Avenue des Bains, 1400*
**Tel** *024 424 64 64*
W grandhotelyverdon.ch
A grand hotel by name and by
nature, with luxurious rooms and
many health and beauty facilities.

# Northern Switzerland

**AARAU: Sorell Hotel Argovia** F
Business Hotel **Map** D2
*Kasernenstrasse 24, 5001*
**Tel** *062 823 21*
W hotelargovia.ch
A comfortable, modern hotel
close to the train and bus
stations. Family rooms available.

**BADEN: Atrium Hotel Blume** FF
Historic Hotel **Map** D2
*Kurplatz 4, 5400*
**Tel** *056 200 02 00*
W blume-baden.ch
A majestic atrium and fountain
dominate this 15th-century hotel
with a thermal spring and spa
centre. Expect comfortable,
tastefully decorated bedrooms.

**BADEN: Limmathof** FF
Historic Hotel **Map** D2
*Limmatpromenade 28, 5400*
**Tel** *056 200 17 17*
W limmathof.ch
A contemporary hotel with
designer furnishings. Health and
beauty facilities, plus a hot spring.

**BASEL: Dorint** F
Business Hotel **Map** C2
*Schoenaustrasse 10, 4058*
**Tel** *061 695 70 00*
W hotel-basel.dorint.com
Situated close to the trade-show
centre, but with good transport
links to the city. Apartments are
available, too.

**BASEL: Rochat** F
Historic Hotel **Map** C2
*Petersgraben 23, 4051*
**Tel** *061 261 81 40*
W hotelrochat.ch
The Rochat is in a building with
great architectural character in
the city centre. Rooms are
functional and simply furnished.

**BASEL: Au Violon** FF
Historic Hotel **Map** C2
*Im Lohnhof 4, 4051*
**Tel** *061 269 87 11*
W au-violon.com
A modern hotel converted from
an old prison, with a quiet inner
courtyard. Wooden floorings and
comfortable rooms, all ensuite.

**BASEL: Bildungszentrum** FF
Historic Hotel **Map** C2
*Missionsstrasse 21, 4003*
**Tel** *061 260 21 21*
W bildungszentrum-21.ch
This hotel is housed in an
imposing stone building set in
private grounds. Spacious rooms
have Internet access, and there
are also two restaurants, a gym
and two lounge areas. Guests
are given a complimentary
Basel Mobility Ticket to use
trams and buses for free.

**BASEL: Hotel Krafft** FF
Design Hotel **Map** C2
*Rheingasse 12, 4058*
**Tel** *061 690 91 30*
W krafftbasel.ch
Idyllically located on the banks of
the Rhine, this hotel has wooden
floors and soft furnishings, plus a
gourmet restaurant.

**BASEL: Radisson Blu** FF
Business Hotel **Map** C2
*Steinentorstrasse 25, 4001*
**Tel** *061 227 27 27*
W radissonblu.com/hotel-basel
This hotel with stylish, modern
furnishings and conference
facilities is located a short walk
from the train station.

**BASEL: Teufelhof** FF
Design Hotel **Map** C2
*Leonhardsgraben 47–49, 4051*
**Tel** *061 261 10 10*
W teufelhof.com
The Teufelhof offers two hotels –
the Art Hotel and the Gallery
Hotel – united by a passion for
the arts. Both are redecorated
every two years by local artists.
There are also a good restaurant
and an in-house theatre.

**BASEL: Euler** FFF
Historic Hotel **Map** C2
*Centralbahnplatz 14, 4002*
**Tel** *061 275 80 00*
W hoteleuler.ch
Conveniently close to Basel train
station, but peaceful and quiet,
with elegant rooms and terrace
dining in the summer.

## DK Choice

**BASEL: Les Trois Rois** FFF
Luxury Hotel **Map** C2
*Blumenrain 8, 4001*
**Tel** *061 260 50 50*
W lestroisrois.com
Refurbished in 2006, this
grand old hotel's Art Deco
furnishings and stunning
interiors hark back to a time
gone by. Many of the rooms
have balconies overlooking the
river and Basel's Old Town.

**MURI: Ochsen** F
Historic Hotel **Map** D2
*Seetalstrasse 16, 5630*
**Tel** *056 664 11 83*
W ochsen-muri.ch
This well-established hotel is
set in its own grounds and has
a covered garden restaurant.
Bedrooms are light and modern.

**WINTERTHUR: Banana City** FF
Business Hotel **Map** E2
*Schaffhauserstrasse 8, 8400*
**Tel** *052 268 16 16*
W bananacity.ch en
Named after its unique structure,
this modern glass-and-steel hotel
has large, well-soundproofed
rooms that are full of light.

**WINTERTHUR: Wartmann** FF
Modern Hotel **Map** E2
*Rudolfstrasse 15, 8400*
**Tel** *052 260 07 07*
W wartmann.ch
Close to the train station and the
shopping areas, the Wartmann
has clean and functional rooms.

# Zürich

**City Backpacker/**
**Hotel Biber** F
Hostel **Map** E2
*Niederdorfstrasse 5, 8001*
**Tel** *044 251 90 15*
W city-backpacker.ch
Clean and comfortable rooms in
the heart of the Old Town. Free
Wi-Fi and communal facilities.

**Otter** F
Design Hotel **Map** E2
*Oberdorfstrasse 7, 8001*
**Tel** *044 251 22 07*
W hotelotter.ch
A central hotel with comfortable
rooms; none is ensuite. Popular
café and restaurant on site.

The spa complex at the Grand Resort Bad
Ragaz *(see p253)*

**Sorell Hotel Rütli**            F
Design Hotel            Map E2
*Zähringerstrasse 43, 8021*
**Tel** *044 254 58 00*
W rutli.ch
The traditional exterior of this
seemingly old-fashioned hotel
hides 58 comfortable rooms
with all mod cons; 12 of them
have been decorated by local
graffiti artists.

**X-tra Hotel**            F
Basic Hotel            Map E2
*Limmatstrasse 118, 8005*
**Tel** *044 448 15 95*
W x-tra.ch
A short hop from the city
centre, this well-known hostel
is popular with young travellers.
The music venue on site hosts
regular events.

**Lady's First**            FF
Design Hotel            Map E2
*Mainaustrasse 24, 8008*
**Tel** *044 380 80 10*
W ladysfirst.ch
This is an unusual fashion hotel
aimed at a female clientele.
Although men are welcome
as guests, the spa facilities and
recreation rooms are available
for women only.

---

### DK Choice

**Romantik Hotel Florhof**   FF
Boutique Hotel            Map E2l
*Florhofgasse 4, 8001*
**Tel** *044 250 26 26*
W hotelflorhof.ch
Housed in a renovated
aristocratic mansion, the
Florhof has an evocative
garden featuring an 18th-
century fountain and a fig tree.
Centrally located in a quiet area
close to the university. Expect
high standards of service and
traditional, cosy rooms.

---

**Baur au Lac**            FFF
Design Hotel            Map E2
*Talstrasse 1, 8001*
**Tel** *044 220 50 20*
W bauraulac.ch
Located in the heart of Zürich,
yet secluded in its own private
park, the Baur au Lac feels
homely despite the opulence.
No two rooms are alike, but
expect luxury in every one.

**Eden au Lac**            FFF
Luxury Hotel            Map E2
*Utoquai 45, 8008*
**Tel** *044 266 25 25*
W edenaulac.ch
An imposing lakeside hotel with
deluxe rooms and spacious suites
furnished in a variety of styles.

The elegant Baur au Lac hotel, on the River Limmat in Zürich

# Eastern Switzerland & Graubünden

**APPENZELL:**
**Romantik Hotel Säntis**   FF
Chalet            Map F2
*Landesgemeindeplatz 3, 9050*
**Tel** *071 788 11 11*
W saentis-appenzell.ch
Located in the town centre,
close to the River Sitter, this
hotel has a captivating exterior
in the style of a Swiss chalet
and comfortable rooms.

**AROSA: Quellenhof**   FF
Country Hotel            Map F4
*Aussere Poststrasse, 7050*
**Tel** *081 377 17 18*
W quellenhof-arosa.ch
Just outside the town, this hotel
is famous for its equestrian
holidays. Inside, stripped pine
dominates, and rooms are cosy
and comfortable.

**BAD RAGAZ: Grand Resort**
**Bad Ragaz**            FFF
Spa Complex            Map F3
*Pfäferserstrasse 8, 7310*
**Tel** *081 303 30 30*
W resortragaz.ch
This resort comprises two
luxury hotels, the Quellenhof
and the Hof Ragaz, which share
an immense park near the golf
course and one of the largest spa
complexes in Europe. Both hotels
are housed in listed buildings,
with breathtaking views.

**BIVIO: Post**            FF
Historic Hotel            Map F4
*Julierstrasse 64, 7457*
**Tel** *081 659 10 00*
W hotelpost-bivio.ch
Ideally located for ski touring,
this former coaching inn offers
comfortable accommodation in
rooms and suites. There is also a
sauna and the convivial Chimney
Room, with a cosy fireplace.

**CHUR: Romantik Hotel**   FF
Historic Hotel            Map F3
*Reichsgasse 11, 7000*
**Tel** *081 258 57 57*
W stern-chur.ch
A hotel with a history and
plenty of character. Rooms
have been renovated to a
high standard, and the on-site
restaurant is noteworthy for its
regional specialities.

**DAVOS: National**            FF
Modern Hotel            Map F3
*Obere Strasse 31, 7270*
**Tel** *081 415 10 10*
W national-davos.ch
A luxury hotel set in its own
private park, the National is close
to the town centre and only a
bus ride from the ski lifts. Note
that it is open only in winter.

**DAVOS: Schatzalp**   FF
Historic Hotel            Map F3
*Bobbahnstrasse 23, 7270*
**Tel** *081 415 51 51*
W schatzalp.ch
This luxury hotel boasts a
spectacular location 300 m
(1,000 ft) above Davos and is
accessible only by funicular. The
views are, naturally, exceptional.

**KLOSTERS: Bargis**            F
Guesthouse            Map F3
*Kantonstrasse 8, 7252*
**Tel** *081 422 55 77*
W bargis.ch
Enjoy home-cooked food and
a tranquil location at this small
farmhouse-style establishment
with a homely feel.

**KLOSTERS: Vereina**   FFF
Luxury Hotel            Map F3
*Landstrasse 179, 7250*
**Tel** *081 410 27 27*
W hotelvereina.ch
The Vereina provides its guests
with plush, comfortable rooms
and extensive spa facilities.
Spacious suites are also available.

**For more information on types of hotels** *see pages 246–7*

The Badrutt's Palace, enjoying a breathtaking lakeside location in St Moritz

**RAPPERSWIL: Jakob**     **F**
Modern Hotel     Map E3
*Hauptplatz 11, 8640*
**Tel** *055 220 00 50*
w jakob-hotel.ch
Centrally located, the Jakob has
light and airy rooms, a cigar
lounge, a wine bar and a bistro.

**ST GALLEN: Einstein**     **FF**
Business Hotel     Map F2
*Berneggstrasse 2, 9001*
**Tel** *071 227 55 55*
w einstein.ch
Marble is used extensively
throughout this elegant hotel
with splendid views of the abbey.

**ST MORITZ: Laudinella**     **FF**
Family Hotel     Map F4
*Via Tegiatscha 17, 7500*
**Tel** *081 836 00 00*
w laudinella.ch/en
Impressively decorated public
rooms. The wellness area on the
fifth floor offers spectacular views.

## DK Choice

**ST MORITZ:**
**Badrutt's Palace**     **FFF**
Luxury Hotel     Map F4
*Via Serlas 27, 7500*
**Tel** *081 837 10 00*
w badruttspalace.com
One of the world's most famous
hotels. The distinctive tower,
with a box of rooms stuck to
the side, is unique. Rooms are
opulently decorated, and formal
dress is required after sundown.
The hotel has its own ski school.

**ST MORITZ: Grand**
**Hotel Kronenhof**     **FFF**
Luxury Hotel     Map F4
*Pontresina, 7504*
**Tel** *081 830 30 30*
w kronenhof.com
A historic hotel with grandiose
public areas, two restaurants and
extremely comfortable rooms.

**SCHAFFHAUSEN: Parkvilla**     **FF**
Family Hotel     Map E2
*Parkstrasse 18, 8200*
**Tel** *052 635 60 60*
w parkvilla.ch
A turreted manor house with a
glass elevator on the outside of
the building. Elegant rooms and
apartments, too.

**SCHAFFHAUSEN:**
**Fischerzunft**     **FFF**
Luxury Hotel     Map E2
*Rheinquai 8, 8200*
**Tel** *052 632 05 05*
w fischerzunft.ch
On the banks of the River Rhine,
this hotel has ten individually
decorated rooms. A restaurant
serves Asian specialities, and
there's an extensive wine cellar.

**SCHWÄGALP: Berghotel**     **F**
Chalet     Map F3
*Schwägalp, 9107*
**Tel** *071 365 66 00*
w saentisbahn.ch/hotel-
schwaegalp.html
The Berghotel is situated at
more than 1,300 m (4,300 ft)
above sea level. Access is by ski
lift, and in winter you can ski to
and from the hotel.

**SCUOL: Crusch Alba**     **F**
Chalet     Map G3
*Clozza 246, 7550*
**Tel** *081 864 11 55*
w crusch-alba.ch
Rooms are decorated in Swiss
storybook style at this hotel
in an old stone house. Good
access to ski lifts.

**STEIN AM RHEIN: Rheinfels**     **FF**
Historic Hotel     Map E2
*Rhigass 8, 8260*
**Tel** *052 741 21 44*
w rheinfels.ch
The hotel boasts its own boat
dock and a garden terrace. Some
rooms have antique furniture,
and there is a fish restaurant.

**VADUZ: Park Hotel**
**Sonnenhof**     **FF**
Romantic Hotel     Map F3
*Mareestrasse 29, 9490*
**Tel** *00423 239 02 02*
w sonnenhof.li
In addition to large, individually
furnished rooms with sumptuous
fabrics and paintings, this hotel
boasts a gourmet restaurant and
beautiful views.

## Central Switzerland & Ticino

**AIROLO: Forni**     **F**
Basic Hotel     Map E4
*Via Stazione 19, 6780*
**Tel** *091 869 12 70*
w forni.ch
The Forni has been a family-run
hotel for a century. It has small
but pleasantly furnished rooms,
some with balconies providing
views of the mountains. Guests
can relax on the large sun terrace.

**ALTDORF: Höfli**     **F**
Historic Hotel     Map E3
*Hellgasse 20, 6460*
**Tel** *041 875 02 75*
w hotel-hoefli.ch
The Höfli provides clean,
functional rooms in a convenient
location, and it is great value for
money. It also has a Swiss
restaurant and a pizzeria.

**ANDERMATT (HOSPENTAL):**
**St Gotthard**     **F**
Historic Hotel     Map E4
*Gotthardstrasse 15, 6493*
**Tel** *041 887 12 66*
w hotel-gotthard.ch
Built in 1722, this picture-
postcard hotel has plenty of old
guesthouse charm. Some rooms
are traditionally decorated with
carved ceilings and panelling.

**ANDERMATT:**
**Drei Könige & Post**     **FF**
Family Hotel     Map E4
*Gotthardstrasse 69, 6490*
**Tel** *041 887 00 01*
w 3koenige.ch
This historic coaching inn on the
mountain pass is within walking
distance of both the ski lifts and
the train station.

**ASCONA: Romantik Hotel**
**Castello Seeschloss**     **FF**
Romantic Hotel     Map E5
*Via Circonvallazione 26, 6612*
**Tel** *091 791 01 61*
w castello-seeschloss.ch
There are lovely views over
Lake Maggiore from the pretty
garden of this hotel. Rooms are
individually furnished and varied.

**Key to Price Guide** *see page 248*

**BECKENRIED: Boutique
Hotel Schlussel** FF
Boutique Hotel **Map** D3
*Oberdorfstrasse 26, 6375*
**Tel** *041 622 03 33*
🔲 schluessel-beckenried.ch
Bright rooms decorated in
neutral tones feature free-
standing baths at this charming
hotel in a 19th-century building.

**BELLINZONA: Hotel
Internazionale** FF
Modern Hotel **Map** E5
*Viale Stazione 35, 6500*
**Tel** *091 825 43 33*
🔲 hotel-internazionale.ch
Despite its location opposite the
train station, this hotel offers
quiet, functional rooms, some
with castle views.

**BRUNNEN: Seehotel
Waldstätterhof** FF
Historic Hotel **Map** E3
*Walstätterquai 6, 6440*
**Tel** *041 825 06 06*
🔲 waldstaetterhof.ch
A magnificent five-storey hotel
with its own boat dock, stunning
views and spa facilities.

**CENTOVALLI (INTRAGNA):
Stazione "Da Agnese"** F
Family Hotel **Map** E5
*Via Cantonale, 6655*
**Tel** *091 796 12 12*
🔲 daagnese.ch
Popular for its cuisine, this inn
provides small but cheerful
rooms with rustic furnishings.
Lovely views, too.

**EINSIEDELN: Sonne** F
Family Hotel **Map** E3
*Hauptstrasse 82, 8840*
**Tel** *055 412 28 21*
🔲 hotel-sonne.ch
Rooms are reasonably sized,
if a little old-fashioned, at this
perfectly located hotel with a
friendly, welcoming atmosphere.

**ENGELBERG: Schweizerhof** FF
Historic Hotel **Map** D3
*Dorfstrasse 42, 6390*
**Tel** *041 637 11 05*
🔲 schweizerhof-engelberg.ch
Exuding quirky charm, most
rooms here have fabulous views
of the monastery or the lake.

**KUSSNACHT AM RIGI:
Du Lac Seehof** F
Historic Hotel **Map** D3
*Seeplatz 6, 6403*
**Tel** *041 850 10 12*
🔲 hotel-restaurant-seehof.ch
Expect beautiful views of the
mountains from this lakeside
hotel. There's a boat dock and
a large garden, and rooms are
comfortable and sunny.

**LOCARNO: Belvedere** FFF
Historic Hotel **Map** E5
*Via ai Monti della Trinita 44, 6600*
**Tel** *091 751 03 63*
🔲 belvedere-locarno.ch
The Belvedere is situated on a
sunny hill overlooking Locarno
and the lake. Features include
marble floors and frescoed
ceilings, a large garden, several
restaurants and a spa.

**LUGANO: Villa Castagnola** FFF
Historic Hotel **Map** E5
*Viale Castagnola 31, 6906*
**Tel** *091 973 25 55*
🔲 villacastagnola.com
Set in a lush private park, this
elegant establishment is a
throwback to the days of old
grand hotels. The estate boasts
restaurants, a swimming pool
and a beauty spa.

---

## DK Choice

**LUZERN: Art Deco
Hotel Montana** FFF
Luxury Hotel **Map** D3
*Adligenswilerstrasse 22, 6002*
**Tel** *041 419 00 00*
🔲 hotel-montana.ch
A historic spa hotel with
panoramic views over Lake
Lucerne. Public areas are
furnished in Art Deco style,
though most rooms have
contemporary furnishings.
A funicular delivers guests
from the lakeside right into
the hotel lobby.

---

**SCHWYZ: Wysses Rössli** FF
Historic Hotel **Map** E3
*Hauptplatz 3, 6430*
**Tel** *041 811 19 22*
🔲 roessli-schwyz.ch
Perfectly located for hiking the
Swiss Trail and exploring the
Muota Valley, this hotel in a
17th-century building offers
individually decorated rooms.

**STANS: Engel** F
Modern Hotel **Map** D3
*Dorfplatz 1, 6370*
**Tel** *041 619 10 10*
🔲 engelstans.ch
Each room at this hotel is
individually decorated and
unique, even in colour scheme,
and each comes with fabulous
mountain views.

**STANSTAAD: Hotel Rössli** F
Basic Hotel **Map** D3
*Dorfplatz 9, 6362 Stansstad*
**Tel** *041 619 15 15*
🔲 roessli-stansstad.ch/hotel.html
A practical choice, the family-
friendly Rössli is ideally located
for those who wish to go hiking
and bike riding (bikes are
provided free).

**VITZNAU:
Hotel Vitznauerhof** FFF
Luxury Hotel **Map** D3
*Seestrasse 80, 6354*
**Tel** *041 399 77 77*
🔲 vitznauerhof.ch
Beautiful views are a signature
of this luxury hotel, which is
ideally located for hiking up
Mount Regis. Rooms are elegant
and well furnished.

**WEGGIS: Seehof du Lac** FF
Historic Hotel **Map** D3
*Gotthardstrasse 4, 6353*
**Tel** *041 390 11 51*
🔲 hotel-du-lac.ch
Situated right on the lake,
with bright and modern guest
rooms, some with balconies.
Public areas are more traditional.

**ZUG: Ochsen** FF
Modern Hotel **Map** E3
*Kolinplatz 11, 6301*
**Tel** *041 729 32 32*
🔲 ochsen-zug.ch
A stunning flower-festooned
building with whitewashed
and wooden-floored rooms,
some with lovely views.

Contemporary furnishings at the Art Deco Hotel Montana, Luzern

**For more information on types of hotels** *see pages 246–7*

# WHERE TO EAT AND DRINK

The great variety of restaurants in Switzerland reflects the country's cultural and regional diversity. While large cities such as Zürich and Geneva have top-class eateries that serve international cuisine, the majority of Swiss restaurants are fairly small and family-run establishments, offering wholesome, filling dishes that reflect rural traditions and that are made with local farm produce. Many lakeside and riverside restaurants specialize in dishes featuring locally caught fish.

Switzerland also has many small, informal dining spots. While German-speaking Switzerland has the *Stübli*, French-speaking Switzerland has the rôtisserie and the brasserie. In Ticino the choice ranges from the classic pizzeria to the *osteria*. South of the Alps, you may also dine alfresco in the warmer months.

## Types of Restaurants

In Switzerland, restaurants serving international cuisine are located almost exclusively in the larger cities. The typical Swiss restaurant, by contrast, is a homely establishment serving a range of local dishes that vary according to the region.

In the German-speaking regions of Switzerland, a restaurant is sometimes called a *Beiz* or *Gasthaus*. Pleasant meals can also be enjoyed in a *Kneipe*, which serves a small selection of hot dishes in addition to beer. A rustic *Stübli* often specializes in just one type of dish, such as the hearty and warming *rösti*, fondue or *raclette (see p258)*.

In addition to restaurants, French-speaking regions of Switzerland have rôtisseries, which specialize in grilled food. Its more humble version is the brasserie, which serves buffet meals at lunchtime and turns into a restaurant with waiter service in the evenings.

Some wine bars, called *caveaux* in French and *Weinstübli* in German, also serve meals, as do some beer taverns *(Bierstübli)*. *Spunte*, or bars, in German-speaking Switzerland serve mainly beer. *Bars*, their counterparts in French-speaking Switzerland, serve coffee and alcoholic drinks, but they rarely offer food.

In the Italian-speaking canton of Ticino, one of the most popular establishments is the pizzeria. Other types of Italian restaurants include the simple *osteria* and the *grotto*, meaning "cave", a cosy rustic tavern where meals are usually served outdoors. Ticino is also

The splendid Art Nouveau exterior of Hanselmann's, in St Moritz *(see p273)*

well-endowed with ice-cream parlours *(gelaterie* or *cremerie)*.

Inexpensive meals, which are of excellent quality for the price, are offered in the self-service buffets of chain supermarkets and department stores, including Migros, Coop and Manor. These buffets, with filling soups, freshly made salads, pasta dishes and vegetarian fare, are open all day. Once found only in larger towns, fast-food outlets and

even sushi bars are now making inroads, though the Swiss tend to prefer their own cuisine and remain slow to adopt foreign tastes.

Smoking in restaurants is banned in all of Switzerland's cantons, as is smoking in public places, including bars and shopping malls. Smoking is also prohibited on trains throughout the country.

Many restaurants are closed one day a week. This is their rest day *(Ruhetag, jour de repos, jour de fermeture* or *giorno di chiusura)*.

## Meals

Depending on the region, breakfast may either be quite substantial or consist simply of a light, appetizing snack. In Ticino, for example, it may be only coffee and a croissant. Elsewhere, particularly in German-speaking Switzerland, breakfast can be considerably more filling, consisting of muesli, rye bread or crusty bread, salami and cured meats,

Tables set up for alfresco dining at Restaurant Suder, in Bern *(see p264)*

The panoramic terrace at Vaduz Sonnenhof *(see p274)*

cheese and eggs, washed down with fruit juice, tea or coffee.

All over Switzerland, lunch is served between noon and 2pm (most restaurants stop serving by 2:30pm). For many Swiss people, this is the main meal of the day. Most restaurants offer a hearty dish of the day (*Tagesteller, plat du jour* or *piatto del giorno*), and they are usually great value for money.

Evening meals are served between 6:30 and 9pm, depending on the region. The more expensive restaurants, particularly those in large towns, stay open until 10pm or later.

## Menus

In restaurants in larger towns, as well as in holiday resorts and areas that attract large numbers of foreign visitors, the menu (*Karte, carte* or *carta*) is written in French or German (or both), and often also in English. A few restaurants have separate menus printed in English. In smaller towns and in rural or remote areas, menus are written in German, French or Italian only.

Menus are often presented with an additional list of seasonal dishes. Most places display their menus, with prices, outside the premises.

## Prices and Tipping

Restaurant meals in Switzerland tend to be relatively expensive. The average price of a dish of

the day with salad is 12–22 CHF. A fish main course can cost around 35–45 CHF. A bowl of soup or a salad costs around 8 CHF. The average price of a fondue for two people is about 30 CHF. By contrast, the price of a meal in the self-service restaurant of a department store is typically no more than 15–20 CHF.

The price of a glass of local wine ordered with a meal is 3–4 CHF. A third of a litre of beer costs roughly the same. The price of a cup of coffee or a soft drink is rarely less than 3 CHF.

Restaurants in the most popular tourist spots or in particularly attractive locations generally charge a little more for their services.

Most restaurants also add a cover charge per person, which includes bread. At all restaurants, a 15 per cent service charge is included in the final total. Tipping is therefore officially unnecessary. However, it is still customary to round up the bill or to add a few francs to the total.

## Children

In Switzerland, a meal out is treated as a family occasion, and it is not unusual to see small children in restaurants, even late at night. Most restaurants provide highchairs and offer a special children's menu. Many restaurants also have toilets with baby-changing facilities.

## Vegetarians

Although meat features rather prominently in Swiss cuisine, menus in restaurants sometimes include a selection of vegetarian dishes, as well as a variety of vegetables and salads. Self-service restaurants often include a range of vegetable-based dishes.

Food allergies and intolerances are generally less well understood in rural areas.

## Recommended Restaurants

With more than 100 Michelin-starred restaurants and countless family-run establishments, it's easy to eat very well in Switzerland, and the listings that follow are representative of a country with a somewhat eclectic cuisine. To sample the gastronomic highlights of each area, try fondue and *raclette* when in the French-speaking west; savour fresh fish and polenta when in the Italian south (not forgetting an indulgent ice cream); and look for *rösti* in the German-speaking regions.

The eateries labelled as a DK Choice come highly recommended. Often these restaurants combine exceptional cuisine with breathtaking locations, while others serve hearty, simple and wickedly calorific dishes and are often good value in an otherwise expensive country.

Tse Yang, with its enviable location overlooking Geneva's Jet d'Eau *(see p267)*

# The Flavours of Switzerland

With a few notable exceptions, the traditional recipes of most Swiss regions are "borrowed" from the adjoining countries to which they are linguistically linked. This makes for very distinctive local cuisines – dishes and palates change every dozen miles travelled. With no coastline, a shortage of flat arable land and a short growing season, Swiss cuisine does a great deal with limited resources. Healthy eating has become a prime consideration. Freshwater fish, such as trout and perch, appear on many menus, and organic foods are in high demand. Cheese, of course, features prominently in many dishes.

Swiss chocolate

Restaurant in the Valais offering traditional wood-fired *raclettes*

open pastry cases. Game, from roasted wild boar to stewed rabbit, fills the autumn table. Winter foods are filling, and long and convivial meals of fondue and *raclette* help to while away the dark evenings. Cheese and dried meat dishes are served with a flat bread that can be kept in attics for months at a time. In Alpine villages, loaves of dense rye

bread suited to this long storage were baked in communal ovens. The Swiss claim to have around 300 varieties of bread.

## German-speaking Switzerland

Until recent times by far the most prosperous region of Switzerland, the Teutonic cantons (administrative

## French-speaking Switzerland

Influenced by France, but creatively independent, Francophone Switzerland has a distinctive cuisine. Summer foods celebrate the short but intense growing season. Apricots are a particular speciality of the Rhône valley. Berries of all types abound, preserved in jams or baked in

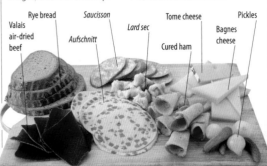
Valais air-dried beef · Rye bread · Aufschnitt · Saucisson · Lard sec · Tome cheese · Cured ham · Bagnes cheese · Pickles

Generous platter of a typical *Assiette Valaisanne*

## Regional Dishes and Specialities

Switzerland has produced several very simple dishes of enormous appeal. All are consumed daily by the Swiss, and devoured with gusto by millions of tourists. The French regions are the homeland of hearty cheese dishes such as fondue and *raclette*. *Rösti* is the national dish of the German-speaking regions, its popularity defining the linguistic and culinary border (called the *Röstigraben*). Müsli was invented by Swiss-German Dr Bircher-Benner. *Birchermüsli* uses plenty of chopped

*Birchermüsli*

fresh fruits and nuts and is softened with water, juice or milk. It is often eaten as an evening meal, as well as for breakfast, in the north. Nuts, as well as top-quality Swiss chocolate, feature in desserts and cakes.

**Fondue** is a bubbling pot of Emmental, Gruyère and white wine sauce into which bread cubes are dunked.

Visitors to a bakery stall in Lugano Market, Ticino

regions) favoured a cuisine heavy in meats, especially pork and sausages; hearty soups; savoury and sweet dumplings; and delicious, calorie-laden cakes and pies. Swiss-German bread tends to be darker and saltier than breads in French- or Italian-speaking cantons. Soft pretzels are sold everywhere in German-speaking areas, yet are almost impossible to find elsewhere in the country. Portion sizes, at home and in restaurants, are noticeably more generous in the north of the country. Offal, pigs' knuckles and trotters, and plates with six different kinds of meat, topped with sauerkraut and potatoes, make a Swiss-German diner very happy indeed, whereas French-speakers and visitors might be overwhelmed.

## Ticino

Everything that's missing in the mountains and cold plains that dominate most of Switzerland is to be found in sunny Ticino, and many Swiss take their holidays here. The cuisine is heavily

Cow in the lush summer pastures of the Swiss Alps

influenced by that of Lombardy and Piedmont, the closest Italian provinces. Fresh fish from the lakes, pasta, polenta, gnocchi and risotto are typical Ticino dishes. The diet is rich in fresh fruits and vegetables. Porcini mushrooms are commonly used in risotto, while braised beef accompanies polenta. Beef, pork and veal are the main meats. On a more indulgent note, this is one of the best places in Switzerland to eat ice cream and, unique to the region, *torta di pane* is a rich, cake-like dessert made from stale bread, grappa, amaretti (almond biscuits), dried fruits and pine nuts.

### ON THE MENU

**Bernerplatte** Smoked meats, sausages, bacon and pork with sauerkraut.

**Croûte au fromage (Käseschnitte)** Bread, soaked in white wine, covered with cheese, then baked. May be topped with fried egg or ham.

**Filet de cerf** Swiss mountain deer (served only in autumn).

**Filets de perche** Lake perch fillets, fried in butter, with lemon and parsley.

**Gelato alla farina bona** Ice cream made with roasted maize flour, speciality of Ticino.

**Zupfa** Braided bread served at breakfast on Sundays.

**Raclette** cheese is melted by the fire or under a grill, then scraped onto boiled potatoes; it is served with pickles and onions.

**Rösti** uses grated potatoes fried in butter and firmed into a cake, which is then fried again on both sides.

**Engadiner Nusstorte** is a shortcrust pastry pie filled with pieces of walnut mixed with caramel and honey.

# Swiss Cheeses

Switzerland is justly renowned for its cheeses, which range in taste from mild and nutty to rich and spicy. Cheese is a way of life in Switzerland. Thinly sliced, it is eaten for breakfast and is the basic ingredient or garnish of many dishes. It is also tossed into salads and is savoured at lunch or dinner as a delicacy in its own right. Half of Switzerland's milk yield goes into the making of cheese. One of the country's greatest exports, it is also an important part of the Swiss economy.

Poster for Appenzeller cheese

Cheeses in cold storage

## Origin of Cheese

Cattle have been raised and pastured in Switzerland since about 2,000 BC. In this mountainous country, expanses of arable land are naturally very limited. By contrast, Switzerland's lush Alpine meadows are ideal for keeping livestock. Milk and milk products formed the basis of the staple diet of Switzerland's mountain-dwellers, and in winter were necessary for their survival.

With the advent of roads, and more importantly of railways, linking the villages of remote mountain regions with the rest of the country, Alpine cheeses

found new markets. Cheese-making also spread to the lower valleys.

Until the 15th century, most Swiss cheeses were soft. Hard cheeses gradually became more popular. Being riper, they kept better than soft cheeses, and could therefore be transported over longer distances.

## Cheese Production

The cheese-making process involves five basic stages. First the milk is poured into large steel vats and heated to 30–36° C (86–96° F). A starter-culture, a liquid containing bacteria, is added to the milk. This causes the milk to turn sour. With the addition of an enzyme, such as rennet or pepsin, the milk forms a curd, a custard-like substance containing whey. When the curd is heated to 39–54° C (102–130°F), the whey separates from the curd. The whey is

drained off and the curd is salted, packed into moulds and pressed to extract more whey. The curd is then shaped into blocks or circular slabs and left to mature, first in brine, where a rind forms on the cheeses, and later in a cold store, where the cheeses are regularly turned to maintain an even texture and prevent the moisture content from pooling.

The maturing, or ripening, process ranges from a few days to several months, or even years, depending on the type of cheese. The longer the ripening period, the harder the cheese.

The cheese-making season starts in early spring and

Rounds of cheese

continues until late autumn, coinciding with the growth of the most nourishing grass. Most Swiss cheeses are produced by small family-run businesses, of which there are about 1,000. Most of them rely on mechanized methods and sophisticated modern equipment. However, in some high Alpine regions, cheeses are still handmade entirely by traditional methods. Such cheeses, known as *Bergkäse, Alpkäse, fromage des alpes* or *formaggio di alpe*, are highly acclaimed.

Some cheese dairies are open to visitors. Among them are the Appenzeller Schaukäserei in Stein *(see p192)* and La Maison du Gruyère, at Pringy, just outside Gruyères *(see p128)*.

Heating and stirring milk in a vat in a modern cheese factory

## Types of Cheese

There are more than 450 varieties of Swiss cheese, each with its own individual texture, flavour and aroma. Each also reflects German, French or Italian traditions, and is used in different ways: either eaten thinly sliced, made into fondue or *raclette*, or grated onto pasta dishes.

**Vacherin Fribourgeois** is a medium-soft cheese produced exclusively in the canton of Fribourg. It is used primarily to make fondue.

**Appenzeller** is a highly aromatic cheese produced in northeastern Switzerland. The length of time it is ripened affects its taste. A black label indicates a well-matured variety, with a strong taste.

**Gruyère** is a hard cheese with a distinctive texture and flavour. Whereas a young Gruyère has a mild flavour, described as *doux*, a highly matured one has an intense flavour and is described as *salé*. Gruyère is made in western Switzerland.

**Tête de Moine**, meaning "monk's head", was first made by monks in the 12th century. Soft and light, it has a strong flavour which is best appreciated when the cheese is cut into slivers. Tête de Moine, also known as Bellelay, is made in the Jura.

**Emmental**, the most popular of all Swiss cheeses, is mild, with a nutty flavour, and large holes. This cheese is made in Emmental and throughout the central lowlands of German-speaking Switzerland. Emmental, which is exported worldwide, is one of the best cheeses to use for making fondue.

**Raclette** has a rich, spicy flavour and, because it melts easily, it is widely used for making the dish known as *raclette*, hence its name. This is one of the most popular cheeses in Switzerland. Although it originated in Valais, *raclette* is now made throughout Switzerland.

**Sbrinz** is a dry cheese with an intense flavour, similar to Parmesan. It is grated and sprinkled over dishes, or thinly sliced and served as a dessert cheese. Originating in Brienz, in the Bernese Oberland, *Sbrinz* is now made throughout central Switzerland. It is matured for up to three years.

**Tilsiter** is a creamy cheese with a delicate flavour. It is named after Swiss émigrés in Tilsit, Prussia, who devised the recipe in the 19th century and returned with it to Switzerland. *Tilsiter* is now made in eastern Switzerland.

## Retail and Export

Switzerland's annual cheese production amounts to over 180,000 tonnes, some 35 per cent of which is exported. The most popular varieties worldwide are Emmental, known as the King of Cheeses, and Gruyère.

Many of Switzerland's cheese dairies have shops where their own cheeses are offered for sale. A wide range of locally produced cheeses, including some of the most highly prized varieties, can also be found on market stalls all over Switzerland.

Some larger towns have specialist cheese shops, which stock the widest range of Swiss cheeses. Supermarkets also sell good-quality cheeses, either pre-packed or cut to order from a chilled counter.

Most Swiss cheeses are made with raw milk, which gives them their distinctive flavour. Those made with pasteurized milk are labelled accordingly. The more mature a cheese, the more expensive it is likely to be.

A variety of cheeses on display in a shop window, Stein am Rhein

# What to Drink in Switzerland

Swiss wines are almost unknown outside their country of origin as they are rarely exported. Although vineyards are found throughout Switzerland, the best are those in the cantons of Valais and Vaud, particularly on the sheltered hillsides around Lake Geneva. Switzerland also has over 100 large and small breweries, which between them produce dark beers, light ales and lagers, also mostly for domestic consumption. Coffee, sometimes served with cream, and tea, which is usually served black, are popular hot drinks. Unique to Switzerland is Rivella, a soft drink made with whey.

Poster advertising Swiss wines

Rivella, made with whey

Valser mineral water

Caotina, a chocolate drink

## Non-alcoholic Drinks

Meals are frequently accompanied by still or sparkling mineral water from Switzerland's own mineral springs. The best-known brands include Valser, Henniez, Fontessa, Passugger and Aproz. A popular sweet, fizzy and refreshing drink is Rivella, which is made with lactoserum, a by-product in the cheese-making process (see p260). Four different kinds of Rivella are available: original (with a red label), with a reduced sugar content (a blue label), with green tea (a green label) and dairy-free (a yellow label). Caotina is a smooth, flavoursome chocolate drink.

## Hot Drinks

Coffee, served in many guises, from creamy cappuccino to pungent espresso, is the most popular hot drink in Switzerland. Coffee served with a dash of liqueur or fruit-flavoured vodka is known in both German and French as *Kaffe fertig*, and in Italian as *caffé corretto*. Tea is less widely drunk than coffee but, served ice-cold (as *Eistee, thé froid* or *te freddo*), it is particularly refreshing on hot summer days. Mint tea and Alpine herb infusions are also popular. Ovomaltine, a malted powder added to hot milk, and hot chocolate make warming and restorative winter drinks. Ovo Drink is a ready-mixed Ovomaltine and milk drink.

A malted drink, made with hot milk

Ovomaltine and milk drink

Bottled beer from Chur

Canned lager

Bottled beer from Basel

## Beer

The most popular type of beer in Switzerland is a light, German-style beer with an alcohol content of 4.2 to 5.5 per cent. Strong beers, with a 6 per cent alcohol content, include *weizen* (wheat) and *alt* (dark) varieties. Dominant brands include Feldschlösschen, made in the Basel region, Calanda from Chur, Rugenbräu from Interlaken and Cardinal from Fribourg. Draught beer is usually served in measures ranging from 1 to 5 decilitres. The most common are the 3-decilitre *Stange* (about half a pint) and the 2-decilitre *Herrgöttli* (just over a third of a pint).

Label of the dark Calanda beer

## White Wine

The most popular Swiss white wine is the delicate, freshly-scented Fendant from Valais, traditionally served with fondue and *raclette* or drunk as an apéritif. From around Lake Geneva come the well-balanced wines of the Lavaux region, the delicate and refreshing wines of La Côte, and the intensely aromatic wines of the Chablais. This region, as well as Neuchâtel, also produces the light and subtle Chasselas wine, which is served with white meat and cheese and as an apéritif.

Sylvaner, in eastern Switzerland, is also renowned for its white wines. Having a subtle aroma and intense flavour, they are served with fish or asparagus. Chardonnay is produced mainly around Geneva and in Valais. It is served with fish and seafood.

Swiss Blanc from Rheinau Abbey

Pinot Gris from Neuchâtel

Fendant, a Chasselas from Valais

Mont-sur-Rolle Grand Cru de La Côte

## Red Wine

One of the most common Swiss red wines is the subtle Dôle, made from a blend of Gamay and Pinot Noir grapes. This is closely followed by the Pinot Noir wines. Both often come from Valais and are ideal with red and white meats and cheese. The vineyards around Lake Geneva produce the light Salvagnin and Gamay wines, which are often served with red meat and hot hors-d'oeuvres. The Lake Neuchâtel region also produces Gamay, which goes well with poultry, veal and cheese. From eastern Switzerland comes Blauburgunder, a fine accompaniment to poultry. Typical of Ticino is Merlot, a ruby-red wine with a subtle aroma. It is excellent with red meat or risotto.

Syrah from the Geneva region

Merlot from Ticino

Pinot Noir from Zürich

Dôle from the Sion region

## Spirits and Liqueurs

A proportion of the fruit grown in Swiss orchards is used to make a variety of spirits and fruit liqueurs. The most popular spirits include Kirsch, made from cherries, and Williams, made from William pears. In the French-speaking regions of Switzerland, *pruneau* is distilled from plums, and in Ticino, grappa is distilled from the skins, stalks and pips of grapes. *Betzi*, made in German-speaking regions, is a brandy made from a mixture of fruit. Other Swiss spirits and liqueurs are made from apples, quinces, plums, apricots, cherries, raspberries or herbs. A meal often ends with a glass of brandy, to aid digestion, and a dash of spirits may be added to coffee. Liqueur, such as Kirsch, is often added to fondue.

Williamine pear brandy

Grundbacher plum spirit

Grappa from Ticino

Apple spirit from Zug

# Where to Eat and Drink

## Bern

### Altes Tramdepot
**Brauerei Restaurant**    **F**
Regional Speciality    **Map** C3
*Grosser Muristalden 6, 3006*
**Tel** *031 368 14 15*
Enjoy a meal in the unique
atmosphere of a former tram
depot. There is an on-site brewery
with traditional beers, and bench
seating inside and out.

### Le Mazot
Regional Speciality    **F**
   **Map** C3
*Bärenplatz 5, 3011*
**Tel** *031 311 70 88*
Popular with both locals and
tourists, this Valais speciality
restaurant is renowned for its
*raclette* and *rösti*. Friendly service.

### Okra
Indian    **F**
   **Map** C3
*Lorrainestrasse 9, 3013*
**Tel** *031 332 18 44*    **Closed** *Mon*
In a quiet part of town, Okra
serves delicious Indian cuisine,
including some lesser-known
dishes. Pleasant outside area.

### DK Choice

**Restaurant Beaulieu**    **F**
Regional Speciality    **Map** C3
*Erlachstrasse 3, 3012*
**Tel** *031 331 25 25* **Closed** *Easter–Pentecost*
This old-fashioned restaurant
serves traditional Swiss and
Bernese cuisine. The *rösti*
is considered a speciality.
Although the menu is
strictly in German, the staff
are more than happy to
translate.

### Restaurant Muesmatt
Asian    **F**
   **Map** C3
*Freiestrasse 65, 3012*
**Tel** *031 508 22 02*    **Closed** *Mon*
A traditional neighbourhood
eatery in a quiet location, with
freshly prepared sushi and wok
dishes, plus an all-you-can-eat
offer on Saturday evenings.
Takeaway service also available.

### Schmiedstube
Regional Speciality    **F**
   **Map** C3
*Schmiedenplatz 5, 3011*
**Tel** *031 311 34 61*    **Closed** *Sun*
Enjoy the atmosphere of an old
Bernese inn in a modern building
near the Clock Tower. Fresh
ingredients dictate the daily
specials. Outdoor tables in good
weather, and a children's menu.

### Tibits
Vegetarian    **F**
   **Map** C3
*Bahnhofplatz 10, 3011*
**Tel** *031 312 91 11*
A Swiss fast-food chain serving
healthy, seasonal vegetarian
food priced by weight *(see p270)*.

### The Beef
**Steakhouse & Bar**    **FF**
Steakhouse    **Map** C3
*Kramgasse 74, 3011*
**Tel** *031 311 64 00*    **Closed** *Sun*
A restaurant for carnivores, with
all manner of meat dishes – from
tartare to Canadian bison. Try the
Swiss dried and aged beef.

### Brasserie Bärengraben
Regional Speciality    **FF**
   **Map** C3
*Grosser Muristalden 1, 3006*
**Tel** *031 331 42 18*
Reservations are advised at this
eatery serving brasserie-style
food and regional Bernese
dishes. It has a popular summer
garden with great city views.

### Frohegg
International    **FF**
   **Map** C3
*Belpstrasse 51, 3007*
**Tel** *031 382 25 24*    **Closed** *Sun &
holidays*
A bistro-style restaurant with
great service. Look out for their
monthly menus featuring
international dishes (especially
Indian) and their fixed-price
lunch menus.

### Klösterli Weincafe
International    **FF**
   **Map** C3
*Klösterlistutz 16, 3013*
**Tel** *031 350 10 00*
Award-winning food and a
friendly atmosphere, perfect for a
relaxed conversation. Sample the
Bernese dried meats and cheeses.

Chesery, housed in a Swiss mountain chalet
in Gstaad *(see p265)*

**Price Guide**

Based on the cost of a three-course
meal for one, with half a bottle of house
wine, and including tax and service.

| | |
|---|---|
| **F** | up to 60 CHF |
| **FF** | 60 to 120 CHF |
| **FFF** | over 120 CHF |

### Restaurant Harmonie
Regional Speciality    **FF**
   **Map** C3
*Hotelgasse 3, 3011*
**Tel** *031 313 11 41*    **Closed** *Sat & Sun*
Popular with tourists and locals
alike, this restaurant specializes
in local dishes, in particular
fondue. Friendly service and a
pleasant, light interior.

### Restaurant Suder
Traditional    **FF**
   **Map** C3
*Weissensteinstrasse 61, 3007*
**Tel** *031 371 57 67*    **Closed** *Sun
& Mon*
Housed in a former train station,
and featuring a beautifully lit
conservatory, Suder serves
delicious dishes prepared with
seasonal and local ingredients.

### Ristorante Luce
Italian    **FF**
   **Map** C3
*Zeughausgasse 28, 3011*
**Tel** *031 310 99 99*
A popular venue specializing in
the food of the Emilia-Romagna
region in Italy. Diners enjoy pasta
dishes and pizzas, as well as meat
and fish delicacies.

### Zebra
Mediterranean    **FF**
   **Map** C3
*Schwalbenweg 2, 3012*
**Tel** *031 301 23 40*    **Closed** *Sun
& Mon*
A small, cosy restaurant serving
fresh and mostly organic local
produce. There is a pleasant
garden for alfresco dining.
No credit cards.

### Zimmermania
French    **FF**
   **Map** C3
*Brunngasse 19, 3011*
**Tel** *031 311 15 42*    **Closed** *Sun
& Mon*
French-style bistro cuisine with
an old-fashioned vibe and good
service. Try the onion soup or
the duck liver terrine.

### Restaurant Essort
International    **FFF**
   **Map** C3
*Jubilaumsstrasse 97, 3005*
**Tel** *031 368 11 11*    **Closed** *Sun
& Mon*
Modern cuisine and attentive
service in a simple but stylish
interior where the owners'
passion for photography is
displayed on the walls.

**Restaurant Kornhauskeller** **FFF**
International Map C3
*Kornhausplatz 18, 3000*
**Tel** *031 327 72 72*
One in a large chain of Swiss
Italian-themed restaurants,
Kornhauskeller boasts an
impressive, elegant interior
in a former corn house. It
is particularly popular at
lunchtime.

**Wein&Sein** **FFF**
International Map C3
*Münstergasse 50, 3011*
**Tel** *031 311 98 44* **Closed** *Sun
& Mon*
A gourmet restaurant offering
fixed-price menus at lunch and
dinner, Wein&Sein provides
creative food at reasonable
prices. Reservations advised.

## Mittelland, Bernese Oberland & Valais

**BREITEN OB MOREL:**
**Restaurant Taverne** **FF**
Traditional Map D4
*Breitenstrasse 1, 3983*
**Tel** *027 927 10 22*
This simple mountain
guesthouse has a reputation for
serving excellent food. Gourmet
dishes are prepared using local
produce. Evening meals only.

**BRIG: Walliser Weinstube** **F**
Traditional Map D4
*Bahnhofstrasse 9, 3900*
**Tel** *027 923 14 28* **Closed** *Sun
& Mon; 2 weeks Jul/Aug*
A wine bar serving hearty Swiss-
French cuisine from the Valais,
including *raclette* and cheese
fondue. International clientele.

**CHERMIGNON D'EN HAUT:**
**Café Cher-Mignon** **FF**
Traditional Map C4
*Tsanveulle 16–18, 3971*
**Tel** *027 483 25 96* **Closed** *Sun
& Mon; Jun*
The ambitious menu at this
popular restaurant with a simple
interior offers a range of excellent
options. Weekend dinners are
limited to 30 patrons, so
reservations are strongly advised.

**CRANS-MONTANA:**
**Pas de l'Ours** **FFF**
French Map C4
*41 Rue Pas de l'Ours, 3963*
**Tel** *027 485 93 33*
Dine on superbly presented
cuisine prepared with locally
sourced ingredients at this
Michelin-starred restaurant
offering Provençale/Swiss fusion.
There is also a less formal bistro.

Panelled walls and fresh flowers at Restaurant Suder, in Bern *(see p264)*

### DK Choice

**GSTAAD: Michel's Stallbeizli** **F**
Traditional Map C4
*Gsteigstrasse 41, 3780*
**Tel** *033 744 43 37*
The dining room is separated
from the cows by a glass wall at
this working farm that is popular
with families. Groups only from
May to September; cash only.

**GSTAAD: Chesery** **FFF**
Traditional Map C4
*Alte Lauenstrasse 7, 3780*
**Tel** *033 744 24 51* **Closed** *Mon*
Boasting 18 Gault Millau points
and a Michelin star, chef Robert
Speth serves up superb, seasonal
food in a chalet-style setting.

**INTERLAKEN:**
**Gasthof Hirschen** **F**
Traditional Map C4
*Hauptstrasse 11, 3800*
**Tel** *033 822 15 45*
Three separate restaurants
serve excellent local produce,
including cheese fondue, *raclette*
and venison. A children's menu
is also available.

**INTERLAKEN: Restaurant**
**Goldener Anker** **FF**
International Map C4
*Marktgasse 57, 3800*
**Tel** *033 822 16 72*
Enjoy an extensive menu of
local and international dishes
at this restaurant that excels
in fine dining and live music.
Very friendly service.

**INTERLAKEN: West End** **FF**
Italian Map C4
*Rugenparkstrasse 2, 3800*
**Tel** *033 822 17 44* **Closed** *Sun*
A classic Italian restaurant with
ingredients imported directly
from Parma. Try the home-made
pasta, plus truffles and wild
mushrooms when in season.

**INTERLAKEN: WineArt** **FF**
Traditional Map C4
*Jungfraustrasse 46, 3800*
**Tel** *033 823 73 74* **Closed** *Sun*
Run by a wine association, this
place has more than 600 wines
available by the glass and a
menu with a Mediterranean
vibe. Modern decor.

**KANDERSTEG:**
**Nico's Restaurant** **FF**
Traditional Map C4
*Äussere Dorfstrasse 99, 3718*
**Tel** *033 675 84 80*
Dine in a welcoming room with
a roaring fire in the winter. The
focus at Nico's is on bringing
the mountain to the table.
Local, seasonal produce and
impeccable presentation.

**LAUTERBRUNNEN: Schützen** **FF**
Traditional Map D4
*Fuhren 439, 3822*
**Tel** *033 855 50 50*
Enjoy a range of *Flammenkuchen*
(*tartes flambées*) and fondues
served by staff in traditional
costume at this traditional
wooden chalet. Mountain views
and a summer garden.

**MARTIGNY: Café National** **FF**
French Map B5
*Route du Bourg 25, 1920*
**Tel** *027 722 53 90* **Closed** *Sun in
summer*
Everything except the food is
understated at this popular café
with an informal atmosphere
and friendly staff. Located in
the old Bourg area.

**RIEDERALP: Danys Restaurant** **F**
Traditional Map D4
*Haus Westside, 3987*
**Tel** *027 927 14 44*
This is the place for excellent
simple dishes prepared using
local produce: fondues, both
cheese and *chinoise*, plus *raclettes*
and grilled meats.

For more information on types of restaurants *see page 256*

**RIEDERALP: Derby**      F
Traditional      **Map** D4
*Sportplatzweg, 3987*
**Tel** *027 927 10 33*   **Closed** *Fri dinner*
Dine on traditional food
accompanied by local wines.
There is live music each evening
during the skiing season, and a
bright and cheerful bar area.

**SAAS FEE: Dü Saas-Fee**    FF
Traditional      **Map** D5
*Untere Gasse 3 , 3906*
**Tel** *079 356 40 92*   **Closed** *summer*
Located in a wooden barn, this
place specializes in cured cold
meats, fondue and *raclette*. Clean,
elegant interior, and a superb
local wine list.

**SAAS FEE: Essstube**     FF
Traditional      **Map** D5
*Hannigstrasse 47, 3906*
**Tel** *027 957 15 53*   **Closed** *Sun*
Traditional food is served with a
personalized twist at this popular
eatery with a minimalist interior
and food photography lining the
walls. Good value for money.

**SAAS FEE: Waldhotel**
**Fletschhorn**      FFF
French      **Map** D5
*Oberdorf, 3906*
**Tel** *027 957 21 31*
A highly rated French restaurant
in a Relais Château hotel, with
18 Gualt Millau points and a
Michelin star. Cooking seminars
and an extensive wine cellar.

**SCHILTHORN:**
**Restaurant Piz Gloria**    FF
Traditional      **Map** C4
*Schilthorn, 3825*
**Tel** *033 856 21 56*
Piz Gloria was the first revolving
restaurant in the Alps and is still
the second highest at 2,970 m
(9,744 ft). The views of the Eiger,
Monch and Jungfrau are superb.

**SIERRE: Café Restaurant**
**de La Contree**      FF
Traditional      **Map** C4
*1 Rue de la Vanire, 3960*
**Tel** *027 455 12 91*   **Closed** *Mon & Tue*
Come for the renowned steak
tartare and the unusual fish
tartare, washed down with local
wines. A terrace overlooks the
vineyards and the Alps.

**SION: Le Baroque**
**Tartare House**      FF
French      **Map** C5
*24 Avenue de France, 1950*
**Tel** *027 322 72 00*   **Closed** *Sun & Mon*
As the name suggests, all manner
of tartare can be found on the
menu here – including tartare
of fish, vegetables and fruit.
Fixed-price lunch menus.

**SION: Brasserie Grand Pont**   FF
Brasserie      **Map** C5
*6 Rue du Grand-Pont, 1950*
**Tel** *027 322 20 96*   **Closed** *Sun*
The menu at this restaurant
in the heart of the Old Town is
imaginative, fusing European and
Asian flavours. Laid-back service.

**SOLOTHURN: Thai Sunshine**   F
Thai      **Map** C3
*Berntorstrasse 13, 4500*
**Tel** *032 530 18 98*
Excellent service complements
a menu of authentically spicy
cuisine. While the decor is dated,
the food is of good quality.

**SOLOTHURN: Zum Alten**
**Stephan Stadtbeiz**     FFF
Traditional      **Map** C3
*Friedhofplatz 10, 4500*
**Tel** *032 622 11 09*   **Closed** *Sun & Mon*
With a Michelin star and an
attractive setting in the Old
Town, this place serves elegant
and creative dishes.

**THUN: Essen und Trinken**    FF
Traditional      **Map** C3
*Untere Hauptgasse 32, 3600*
**Tel** *033 222 48 70*   **Closed** *Tue & Wed*
This pretty, romantic restaurant is
renowned for its bar, which offers
cocktails and good wines. The
menu is small but well executed.

**TORBEL: Bergrestaurant**
**Moosalp**      FF
Traditional      **Map** C5
*Törbel, 3923*
**Tel** *027 952 14 95*   **Closed** *May*
An isolated mountain restaurant,
worth visiting for its authentic
preparation of fondues and
*raclettes*. Great dried local meats.

**VERBIER: Brasserie Le Bec**    FF
Traditional      **Map** C5
*77 Rue de Medran, 1936*
**Tel** *027 775 44 04*
Verbier's hottest spot is just at the
bottom of the slopes, at the huge
hotel/shopping complex at
Medran. Snacks and meals all day.

**VERBIER: Le Carrefour**     FF
Traditional      **Map** C5
*95 Route du Golf, 1936*
**Tel** *027 771 55 55*   **Closed** *May & Jun*
Enjoy traditional fare like *rösti* with
eggs alongside views of Verbier
from the sheltered terrace, which
has a cosy pinewood interior.

**VERBIER: La Marlenaz**     FF
Traditional      **Map** C5
*Route de Marlenaz, 1936*
**Tel** *027 771 54 41*
Regional and international dishes
are served all day at this rustic,
charming restaurant with a sunny
terrace at 1,850 m (6,070 ft).

Zum Alten Stephan Stadtbeiz, on a cobbled
square in Solothurn

**VISP: Restaurant Pizzeria**
**Buon Gusto**      F
Italian      **Map** D4
*Allmei 5, 3930*
**Tel** *027 946 61 61*   **Closed** *Sun*
A wide variety of Italian dishes,
including an interesting range of
pizzas and pasta, are served in a
spacious, simply decorated room.

**ZERMATT: Café du Pont**    F
Regional Speciality    **Map** C5
*Oberdorfstrasse 7, 3920*
**Tel** *027 967 43 43*
Often very busy, this traditional
place is reputed to have some
of the best fondues in Zermatt,
plus regional and Swiss dishes.

**ZERMATT: Sparky's Bar**
**and Restaurant**      F
Indian      **Map** C5
*Schluhmattstrasse 32, 3920*
**Tel** *027 968 19 18*   **Closed** *May & Oct*
A wide selection of Asian dishes
is served up by Sparky himself.
The place for a casual, no-frills,
value-for-money experience.

**ZERMATT: Zum See**     FF
Traditional      **Map** C5
*Wichieweg 44, 3920*
**Tel** *027 967 20 45*
Popular with skiers, this is one
of the most highly regarded
mountain restaurants in the Alps,
offering an ever-changing menu.

# Geneva

**Bistrot du Boeuf Rouge**    F
French      **Map** A5
*17 Rue Alfred-Vincent, 1201*
**Tel** *022 732 75 37*   **Closed** *Sat & Sun*
Booking is recommended at
this restaurant specializing
in dishes from France, in
particular Lyon. Noteworthy
French wine list.

### Café de Paris F
**Steakhouse** Map A5
*26 Rue Mont Blanc, 1201*
**Tel** *022 732 84 50*
A venerable Geneva institution, famous for its one-item menu: entrecôte steak with chips, green salad and secret butter sauce!

### Café du Soleil F
**Traditional** Map A5
*6 Place du Petit-Saconnex, 1209*
**Tel** *022 733 34 17*
Popular with the international community of Geneva, this place has a warm atmosphere. On the menu are traditional Swiss dishes, with fondue a speciality.

### Chez Ma Cousine Vieille Ville F
**Chicken Speciality** Map A5
*6 Place du Bourg de Four, 1204*
**Tel** *022 310 96 96*
Only chicken is served here, either grilled or in a Thai or Indian style. Takeaway available.

### Inglewood Plainpalais F
**Fast Food** Map A5
*44 Boulevard du Pont-d'Arve, 1205*
**Tel** *022 320 38 66* **Closed** *Sun*
This award-winning burger joint uses good-quality, locally sourced meat cooked to order. Reservations recommended.

### Le Radar de Poche F
**Italian** Map A5
*8 Rue des Chaudronniers, 1204*
**Tel** *022 311 36 68* **Closed** *Sun*
Serving food at lunchtime only, this bar/café has a small, simple menu and a nice vibe. Very popular with the locals.

### Le Thermomètre F
**French** Map A5
*22 Rue Neuve-du-Molard, 1204*
**Tel** *022 310 25 35* **Closed** *Sat & Sun*
This family restaurant with American diner-style decor has a basic menu. Reservations are advised at lunchtime.

### Les Armures FF
**Traditional** Map A5
*1 Rue du Puits-Saint-Pierre, 1204*
**Tel** *022 310 34 42*
Suits of armour and swords adorn the walls here, creating a medieval feel. Come for fondue, and traditional Swiss-French and French cuisine.

### Brasserie des Halles de l'Île FF
**Regional Speciality** Map A5
*1 Place de l'Île, 1204*
**Tel** *022 311 08 88*
This charming restaurant serves tapas or dishes from the à la carte menu. An all-you-can-eat brunch is available at weekends.

### L'Entrecôte Couronnée FF
**French** Map A5
*5 Rue des Pâquis, 1201*
**Tel** *022 732 84 45* **Closed** *Sat lunch, Sun & Mon.*
A charming small bistro serving award-winning local meats and produce. The steak with butter sauce is particularly good.

### La Gondola FF
**Italian** Map A5
*4 Rue Muzy, 1207*
**Tel** *022 736 12 12* **Closed** *Sun*
A family-owned Italian restaurant/ pizzeria with a real wood-burning oven. It also serves good pasta and fish and meat dishes.

### Le Rouge et Le Blanc FF
**Mediterranean** Map A5
*27 Quai des Bergues, 1201*
**Tel** *022 731 15 50*
At lunch this is a restaurant; at dinner, a tapas bar. The food is as good as the riverside location, with a view of the Jet d'Eau.

### Thai Phuket FF
**Thai** Map A5
*33 Avenue de France, 1202*
**Tel** *022 734 41 00* **Closed** *Sat lunch*
This is said to be the best Thai restaurant in the region so expect tasty Thai dishes. An extensive wine list.

## DK Choice

### Le Vieux Bois FF
**French** Map A5
*12 Avenue de la Paix, 1202*
**Tel** *022 919 24 26* **Closed** *Sat & Sun*
Le Vieux Bois is the working laboratory of Switzerland's famous hotel school L'École Hôtelière de Genève. Cooks and waiters are attentive and keen, and prices are reasonable. There is a lovely summer garden.

### Hôtel d'Angleterre – Windows Restaurant FFF
**French** Map A5
*17 Quai du Mont-Blanc, 1201*
**Tel** *022 906 55 14*
Splash out on exquisite, five-star international cuisine that comes complete with breathtaking views of Lake Geneva and the mountains beyond.

### Du Parc des Eaux-Vives FFF
**Brasserie** Map A5
*82 Quai Gustave Ador, 1211*
**Tel** *022 849 75 75*
Exceptional views over Lake Geneva and the Jura mountains accompany your meals here. The restaurant A l'Étage offers elegant seasonal dining; the Brasserie offers simple Mediterranean dishes and a more informal vibe.

### Rasoi by Vineet FFF
**Indian** Map A5
*1 Quai Turrettini, 1201*
**Tel** *022 909 00 00* **Closed** *mid-Jul– mid-Aug*
Geneva's first fine-dining Indian restaurant boasts a Michelin star, a chic interior and suitably innovative cuisine.

### La Table du 9 FFF
**French** Map A5
*9 Rue Verdaine, 1204*
**Tel** *022 310 25 50* **Closed** *Sun*
This restaurant in Geneva's Old Town offers a short but varied menu of European dishes. Portion size is good, and the service is friendly.

### Tse Yang FFF
**Chinese** Map A5
*19 Quai du Mont-Blanc, 1201*
**Tel** *022 732 50 81*
This Chinese restaurant is held in very high esteem in Geneva. The Szechuan dishes are particularly recommended. Attentive service.

Tse Yang, arguably the best Chinese restaurant in Geneva

**For more information on types of restaurants** *see page 256*

### Vertig'O
French      FFF      Map A5
*11 Quai du Mont-Blanc, 1211*
**Tel** *022 909 60 73*    **Closed** *Sat lunch, Sun & Mon*
Classic French and Swiss-French cuisine is served at this Michelin-starred restaurant run by chef Jérôme Manifacier. The wine list is exclusively French and Swiss.

# Western Switzerland

### AIGLE: La Pinte Communale   FF
Italian and French      Map B4
*4 Place du Marché, 1860*
**Tel** *024 466 62 70*    **Closed** *Sun*
Home-made pasta and delicious main courses are prepared with fresh local produce. A children's menu is available.

### LES AVANTS: Auberge de la Cergniaulaz
Traditional      FF      Map B4
*18 Route de la Cergniaule, 1833*
**Tel** *021 964 42 76* **Closed** *Mon & Tue; Jan–Mar*
Enjoy lovely views from the terrace or the country-cosy interior while savouring local produce and well-executed food.

### AVENCHES: Restaurant des Bains
International      FF      Map B3
*1 Route de Berne, 1580*
**Tel** *026 675 36 60*    **Closed** *Sun & Tue eve; Mon*
A child-friendly place serving a range of international dishes. Although the food is not always consistent, it is often excellent.

### BRENT: Le Pont de Brent   FFF
French      Map B4
*4 Route de Blonay, 1817*
**Tel** *021 964 52 30* **Closed** *Sun & Mon*
A Michelin-starred gourmet restaurant providing exceptional French cuisine, a first-class wine list and impeccable service.

### BULLE: L'Ecu   FF
Traditional      Map B4
*5 Rue Saint-Denis, 1630*
**Tel** *026 912 93 18* **Closed** *Mon & Tue*
L'Ecu has earned a reputation for using locally sourced produce – wild mushrooms, waterfowl and lake fish. Good value for money.

### CAUX: Plein-Roc   FF
Traditional      Map B4
*Aux Rochers de Naye, 1824*
**Tel** *021 989 83 74*
In an extraordinary location overlooking Lake Geneva, Plein-Roc is reached by cog-wheel railway from Montreux. Good Swiss and French cuisine.

### CHAMBESY: Plage du Reposoir   FF
Traditional      Map A4
*222 Route de Lausanne, 1292*
**Tel** *022 732 42 65*
A lakeside beach restaurant with plenty of activities for children. On the menu is a variety of pasta dishes, pizza and local fish.

### LA CHAUX-DE-FONDS: Crêperie Poivre et Sel   F
Crêperie      Map B3
*2 Rue des Terreaux, 2300*
**Tel** *032 968 10 74*    **Closed** *Sun*
There are excellent pancakes with all types of fillings – savoury or sweet – in this modern eatery. Quick and friendly service, too.

### LA CHAUX-DE-FONDS: Brasserie La Fontaine   FF
Traditional      Map B3
*17 Avenue Léopold-Robert, 2300*
**Tel** *032 534 49 85*
Regulars come here for the simple but solid brasserie food. The place is also famous for the beers brewed on the premises.

### CRISSIER: Restaurant de l'Hôtel de Ville   FFF
French      Map B4
*1 Rue d'Yverdon, 1023*
**Tel** *021 634 05 05* **Closed** *Sun & Mon*
With a long-standing reputation for quality, this restaurant is now run by chef Benoit Violier. Diners enjoy exquisite French cuisine and impeccable service.

### CULLY: Auberge du Raisin   FF
Traditional      Map B4
*1 Place de l'Hôtel-de-Ville, 1096*
**Tel** *021 799 21 31*    **Closed** *Sun*
This charming restaurant serves fish from the lake and other local specialities, alongside a good choice of local Lavaux wines.

The exterior of the Hotel du Raisin in Cully, housing the Auberge du Raisin

### DELÉMONT: Hotel Restaurant du Midi   FF
French      Map C2
*10 Place de la Gare, 2800*
**Tel** *032 422 17 77* **Closed** *Tue dinner & Wed*
This establishment offers a choice of bistrot, restaurant or gourmet dining. Seafood and shellfish feature heavily in the gourmet restaurant. Good wines.

### DELÉMONT: Le Mexique   FF
Traditional      Map C2
*142 Route du Vorbourg, 2800*
**Tel** *032 422 13 33*    **Closed** *Mon*
Contrary to its name, Le Mexique specializes in Italian and Ticino cuisine. The large garden is a bonus for children.

### LES DIABLERETS: Auberge de la Poste Restaurant   FF
Traditional      Map B4
*8 Rue de la Gare, 1865*
**Tel** *024 492 31 24*    **Closed** *Wed*
Good choice of regional dishes: fondues, *croutes au fromages* (melted cheese on wine-soaked bread) and grilled steaks to name just a few. Splendid views.

### FRIBOURG: Crêperie Sucré Salé   F
Crêperie      Map B3
*50 Rue de Lausanne, 1700*
**Tel** *026 321 32 50*    **Closed** *Mon*
Sweet, savoury and vegetarian pancakes are on offer in the central pedestrianized area of the city. Salads, soups and waffles complete the range.

### FRIBOURG: L'Aigle-Noir   FF
Brasserie      Map B3
*10 Rue des Alpes, 1700*
**Tel** *026 322 49 77* **Closed** *Sun & Mon*
The summer terrace at this restaurant offers superb views over the Old Town. On the menu is good regional fare, including fondues and meats.

### FRIBOURG: Café Restaurant Le Jura   FF
Traditional      Map B3
*20 Route du Jura, 1700*
**Tel** *026 466 32 28*    **Closed** *Sun*
Housed in the hotel of the same name, this café is particularly popular at lunchtime. The menu is biased towards French and Swiss-French food.

### GRUYÈRES: Le Chalet de Gruyères   F
Traditional      Map B4
*53 Rue du Bourg, 1663*
**Tel** *026 921 21 54*
In an attractive former mill, this place specializes in fondues made from Gruyère cheeses. *Raclettes* and grilled meats are also served.

The outdoor dining area at Pinte de Pierre-a-Bot, in Neuchatel

## LAUSANNE:
**Luncheonette Café**     **F**
Vegetarian     **Map** B4
*5 Rue Grand St-Jean, 1003*
**Tel** *078 912 55 10*    **Closed** *Sun*
A vegetarian café serving creative
organic wraps, salads and soups
alongside fair trade teas and
coffees. The atmosphere is laid-
back and friendly.

## LAUSANNE: Le Tramway    FF
Bistro     **Map** B4
*6b Rue de la Pontaise, 1018*
**Tel** *021 646 39 72*    **Closed** *lunch;*
*Sun & Mon*
It is worth making reservations
well in advance at this superb,
relaxed bistro in the old tram
depot, since it fills up quickly.
The menu offerings are simple
but exquisite.

## LAUSANNE:
**La Table d'Edgard**     **FFF**
French     **Map** B4
*7 Rue du Grand-Chene, 1003*
**Tel** *021 331 31 31*    **Closed** *Sun*
*& Mon*
The Michelin-starred restaurant
of the luxurious Lausanne Palace
& Spa Hotel provides diners with
elegant traditional French cuisine
and a superb wine list.

## MONTREUX: Beijing Town    F
Asian     **Map** B4
*50 Avenue du Casino, 1820*
**Tel** *021 961 38 83*
This small, bustling restaurant
serves affordable Chinese food
along with Malaysian and Thai
dishes. Takeaway available, too.

## MONTREUX: Delifrance
**Montreux**     **F**
Fast Food     **Map** B4
*Place de la Paix, 1820*
**Tel** *021 961 35 94*    **Closed** *Sun*
A café, French bakery and
sandwich shop with an emphasis
on top-quality ingredients. Nice
outside terrace area.

## MONTREUX:
**Caveau du Museum**     **FF**
Traditional     **Map** B4
*40 Rue de la Gare, 1820*
**Tel** *021 963 16 62*
Lots of wood and timber create
a warm, cosy atmosphere here.
Food specialities include the
famous potato gratin with ten
cheeses and, on Wednesdays
only, the *Charbonnade Trilogy*,
a tableside BBQ of three meats
(beef, turkey, ostrich), served
with five home-made sauces.

## DK Choice

**MURTEN: La Pinte du**
**Vieux Manoir**     **FF**
Traditional     **Map** B3
*18 Rue de Lausanne, 3280*
**Tel** *026 678 61 80*    **Closed** *Mon &*
*Tue; mid-Dec–mid-Feb*
Chef Franz W Faeh presents
superbly executed regional and
national dishes, adding the
occasional Asian twist here and
there and faultless presentation.
In warm weather, it is possible
to dine on the terrace with
views of Lake Murten.

## NEUCHATEL:
**Pinte de Pierre-a-Bot**     **F**
Traditional     **Map** B3
*106 Route de Pierre-à-Bot, 2000*
**Tel** *032 725 33 80*
Set in the open countryside
outside Neuchâtel, this place
offers a simple, honest and
inexpensive menu of grilled
meats, seafood and fondues.

## NEUCHATEL: Brasserie
**Le Cardinal**     **FF**
Traditional     **Map** B3
*9 Rue du Seyon, 2000*
**Tel** *032 725 12 86*    **Closed** *Sun*
A popular brasserie with an Old
World atmosphere. The food is
French-inspired and of a high
standard; the service, impeccable.

## LE NOIRMONT:
**Georges Wenger**     **FFF**
French     **Map** B2
*2 Rue de la Gare, 2340*
**Tel** *032 957 66 33*    **Closed** *Mon*
*& Tue*
Two Michelin stars, two elegant
dining rooms and a solid
reputation for superb gourmet
cuisine. Excellent wine list, too.

## NYON: Café du Marché    FF
International     **Map** A4
*3 Rue du Marché, 1260*
**Tel** *022 362 49 79*    **Closed** *Sun*
*& Mon*
The Café du Marché offers simple
international food with seasonal
specialities. Brunch is available
on Saturdays.

## PAYERNE: Auberge de Vers
**Chez Perrin**     **FF**
Mediterranean     **Map** B3
*1 La Foule d'En-Haut, 1551*
**Tel** *026 660 58 46*    **Closed** *Sat lunch,*
*Sun dinner; Mon; 1–14 Aug & mid-*
*Dec–early Jan*
Renowned for meats grilled
over an open fire, this place
also has Mediterranean dishes
from Italy, France and Spain.

## PERREFITTE:
**Restaurant de L'Etoile**     **FF**
Traditional     **Map** C2
*4 Gros Clos, 2742*
**Tel** *032 493 10 17*    **Closed** *Sun*
*& Mon lunch*
The extensive menu features
both traditional dishes and
brasserie-style fare made with
fresh, seasonal produce.

## PORRENTRUY: Des Trois
**Tonneaux**     **F**
Traditional     **Map** B2
*16 Rue des Baiches, 2900*
**Tel** *032 466 13 17*    **Closed** *Tue & Sun*
This old-fashioned bistro is
renowned for its home-made
savoury speciality, the *gâteau au*
*fromage* (savoury cheesecake).
Vegetarian dishes also available.

## SAIGNELEGIER: Café du Jura   F
Regional Speciality     **Map** B2
*2 Rue Bel-Air, 2350*
**Tel** *032 950 11 43*    **Closed** *Sun*
A simple place serving hearty
fare such as beef bourguignon
and local specialities. Meat dishes
tend to predominate.

## ST-URSANNE: La Couronne   F
Regional Speciality     **Map** C2
*3 Rue du 23 Juin, 2882*
**Tel** *032 461 35 67*    **Closed** *Wed; Thu*
*Oct–Apr*
Cheese dishes feature heavily
on the menu at La Couronne,
with some unusual variations.
Fresh trout is also a speciality.

**For more information on types of restaurants** *see page 256*

**ST-URSANNE: Hôtel
du Boeuf**　　　　　　**FF**
Traditional　　　　**Map** C2
*60 Rue du 23 Juin, 2882*
**Tel** *032 461 31 49*
A simple country inn with a
local reputation for hospitality
and good home cooking at
moderate prices. Vegetarian
dishes are also available.

**YVERDON-LES-BAINS:
Crêperie l'Ange Bleu**　　　**F**
Crêperie　　　　**Map** B3
*11 Rue du Collège, 1400*
**Tel** *024 426 09 96*
A small and popular creperie –
two factors that can affect the
service. Also on the menu are
snacks, salads and hot dogs.

# Northern Switzerland

**AARAU: Panini Cultura Caffe**　**F**
Italian　　　　**Map** D2
*Laurenzentorgasse 14, 5000*
**Tel** *062 822 22 20*　　**Closed** *Mon*
Tasty sandwiches and *piadine*
(Italian flatbread) are available for
lunch and dinner at this coffee
bar. In the summer, ice cream is
served on a large terrace.

**AARAU: Meat's**　　　　**FF**
Traditional　　　　**Map** D2
*Bahnhofstrasse 4, 5000*
**Tel** *062 822 52 23*
In the heart of the Old Town, this
is a steakhouse, grill and wine
bar. In good weather, you can sit
on the terrace or in the garden.

**BADEN (DÄTTWIL): Pinte**　**FF**
Traditional　　　　**Map** D2
*Sommerhaldenstrasse 20, 5405*
**Tel** *056 493 20 30*　**Closed** *Sat & Sun*
Patrick Troxler and Nina Bhend
head a team devoted to local
produce and seasonal specialities.
Only European wines are served.
Cooking seminars available.

**BADEN: Restaurant Baldegg**　**FF**
Traditional　　　　**Map** D2
*Baldegg 1, 5400*
**Tel** *056 222 57 35*　　**Closed** *Mon*
Enjoy views over the Alps from
the terrace while dining on
local and Swiss fare that varies
according to seasonal availability.

**BASEL: Blindekuh**　　　**F**
European　　　　**Map** C2
*Dornacherstrasse 192, 4053*
**Tel** *061 336 33 00*　**Closed** *Sun & Tue*
Run by partially sighted or blind
staff, at Blindekuh you dine in
complete darkness. Go for the
surprise menu and try to identify
your food.

The cosy oak-furnished interior of Kohlmanns

**BASEL: Tibits**　　　　**F**
Vegetarian　　　　**Map** C2
*Stänzlergasse 4, 4051*
**Tel** *061 205 39 99*
Tibits is a Swiss vegetarian and
vegan chain that serves soups,
salads and an eclectic range
of hot dishes – all priced by
weight. Healthy fruit juices,
too. Self-service.

**BASEL: Kohlmanns Basel**　**FF**
French　　　　**Map** C2
*Steinenberg 14, 4001*
**Tel** *061 225 93 93*
Located in the Old Town,
Kohlmanns offers a varied
menu of regional specialities.
Try the *tarte flambée* or the
Basel smoked sausage.

**BASEL: Restaurant Schnabel**　**FF**
Traditional　　　　**Map** C2
*Trillengässlein 2, 4051*
**Tel** *061 261 21 21*　　**Closed** *Sun*
One of the oldest restaurants in
the Old Town, Schnabel serves
local specialities with a nod to
the Mediterranean. Good venison
dishes, plus a respectable list of
fish and vegetarian options.
Popular with the locals.

**BASEL: Rhywyera**　　　**FF**
Traditional　　　　**Map** C2
*Unterer Rheinweg 10, 4058*
**Tel** *061 683 32 02*　　**Closed** *Sun*
Innovative, contemporary
cuisine specializing in local fare
is on offer here. Rhywyera has a
beautiful terrace overlooking the
Rhine. Reservations advised.

**BASEL: Stucki**　　　　**FFF**
French　　　　**Map** C2
*Bruderholzallee 42, 4059*
**Tel** *061 361 82 22*　　**Closed** *Sun
& Mon*
Exquisite French cuisine can be
savoured in one of three dining
rooms at this highly regarded,
award-winning restaurant. Try
the halibut with a juniper glaze.

**DORNACH: Restaurant
Schlosshof**　　　　**FF**
European　　　　**Map** C2
*Schlossweg 125, 4143*
**Tel** *061 702 01 50*　　**Closed** *Mon;
Sep–Apr*
The menu varies with the
seasons, from autumn game
to winter *rösti* and summer
barbecues in the leafy garden.
Superb views.

## DK Choice

**EGLISAU: La Passion
Gasthof Hirschen**　　　**FFF**
French　　　　**Map** E2
*Untergass 28, 8193*
**Tel** *043 411 11 22*　**Closed** *Sun &
Mon*
Chef Christian Kuchler has
already earned one Michelin
star and is tipped as one of
Switzerland's upcoming stars.
At this restaurant, he offers
classic French haute cuisine
with a creative twist in the
elegant La Passion room.
There is also a more informal
menu in the folksy Bistro.

**KAISERSTUHL:
Fischbeiz Alte Post**　　**FF**
Seafood　　　　**Map** D2
*Rheingasse 6, 5466*
**Tel** *044 858 22 03*　**Closed** *Tue & Wed*
This award-winning restaurant
serves both sea and freshwater
fish, accompanied by beautiful
views of the River Rhein, best
enjoyed from the pretty terrace.

**KAISERSTUHL: Landgasthof
Kaiserstuhl**　　　　**FF**
Traditional　　　　**Map** D2
*Brünigstrasse 232, 6078*
**Tel** *041 678 11 89*
A relaxed, hospitable, family-run
restaurant on the lake, with
simple fare and scenic views.
Fish is the speciality, and you
can even catch your own.

**LIESTAL: Bad Schauenburg** **FF**
French **Map** C2
*Schauenburgerstrasse 76,4410*
**Tel** *061 906 27 27* **Closed** *Sun dinner*
Housed in the hotel of the same name, this is a well-regarded restaurant serving classic European and Swiss food with a creative twist. There are lovely views from the terrace.

**MURI: Café Moospintli** **FF**
Traditional **Map** D2
*Murimoos 897, 5630*
**Tel** *056 675 53 73*
Pastries, sandwiches and desserts make up the completely alcohol-free menu at this friendly and casual café with a large garden. Child-friendly.

**RHEINFELDEN:**
**Feldschlosschen Restaurant** **FF**
Traditional **Map** D2
*Feldschlösschenstrasse 32, 4310*
**Tel** *061 833 99 99*
Tucked into a brewery, this restaurant serves a range of beer-friendly, good-quality dishes. Friendly staff.

**WETTINGEN: China City** **F**
Chinese **Map** D2
*Alberich Zwyssigstrasse 81, 5430*
**Tel** *056 426 95 91*
This elegantly decorated Chinese restaurant offers a good selection of dishes and efficient service. There's also a terrace for summer eating.

**WETTINGEN: Schloss**
**Schartenfels** **FF**
Traditional **Map** C2
*Schartenfelsstrasse 51, 5430*
**Tel** *056 426 19 27* **Closed** *Tue*
Creative Mediterranean-based fare is on the menu at this restaurant housed in a castle. Crisp and elegant decor, plus splendid views from the terrace.

**WINTERTHUR: Tibet Bistro** **F**
International **Map** E2
*Neuwiesenstrasse 14, 8400*
**Tel** *052 534 16 56* **Closed** *Mon*
Not a large menu, but the Tibetan dishes are good quality and authentic. Try the freshly steamed *momos* (Nepalese dumplings). A small restaurant with a casual atmosphere.

**WINTERTHUR: Sporrer** **FF**
International **Map** E2
*Im Sporrer 1, 8408*
**Tel** *052 222 27 08* **Closed** *Mon & Tue*
Renowned for its home-style gourmet cuisine, Sporrer boasts an excellent location with views over the city. Children's play area.

**ZOFINGEN:**
**Federal Restaurant** **FF**
International **Map** D2
*Vordere Hauptgasse 57, 4800*
**Tel** *062 751 88 10* **Closed** *Sun & Mon*
A high-quality European-Asian fusion menu is on offer at this compact restaurant located in the Old Town. Federal is a restaurant for gourmets.

**ZOFINGEN: Ristorante**
**La Lupa** **FF**
Italian **Map** D2
*Kirchplatz 10, 4800*
**Tel** *062 751 12 36* **Closed** *Mon*
This small Italian restaurant in the Old Town serves pizza, pasta dishes and other Italian fare. La Lupa gets busy, and it can then suffer from slow service.

# Zürich

**Fribourger Fonduestuebli** **F**
Traditional **Map** E2
*Rotwandstrasse 38, 8004*
**Tel** *044 241 90 76* **Closed** *Jun–Aug*
A good value and highly popular fondue restaurant. The menu is traditional, with a range of unmissable desserts and cold starters available. Reservations recommend.

### DK Choice
**Haus Hiltl** **F**
Vegetarian **Map** E2
*Sihlstrasse 28, 8001*
**Tel** *044 227 70 00*
Reputedly the world's oldest vegetarian restaurant, Haus Hiltl is also a Zurich institution. There is both a buffet system, where you pay by weight, and an à la carte restaurant. The food features both Asian and Italian influences.

**Holy Cow!** **F**
Fast Food **Map** E2
*Zähringerstrasse 28, 8001*
**Tel** *021 323 11 66* **Closed** *Sun*
Only local and seasonal produce is used at Holy Cow! Innovative and creative relishes and sauces accompany good-quality burgers.

**Josef** **F**
International **Map** E2
*Gasometerstrasse 24, 8005*
**Tel** *044 271 65 95* **Closed** *Sat lunch & Sun*
At this young and relaxed place, there is no distinction between starters and main courses: diners can pick and mix as they please.

**Lily's Stomach Supply** **F**
Fast Food **Map** E2
*Langstrasse 197, 8005*
**Tel** *044 440 18 85*
A fast-food restaurant with ambition, this place emphasizes organic and fresh ingredients and is popular with young locals. The menu offers dishes from the Indian subcontinent and the Far East. Delivery service available, too.

**Raclette Stube** **F**
Traditional **Map** E2
*Zahringerstrasse 16, 8001*
**Tel** *044 251 41 30*
This popular *raclette* and fondue restaurant is situated in the heart of the Old Town. The menu features a good range of desserts and Kirsch.

**Reithalle** **F**
International **Map** E2
*Gessner-Allee 8, 8001*
**Tel** *044 212 07 66*
Housed in a former stable, this popular eatery serves a varied traditional menu. Customers sit at long, communal tables, which encourages socializing with fellow diners.

The dining room at Reithalle, in Zürich, with its communal tables

**For more information on types of restaurants** *see page 256*

**Thali Indian Restaurant**    F
Indian      **Map** E2
*Schaffhauser Strasse 32, 8006*
**Tel** *043 541 85 10*
A simple Indian restaurant serving good, authentic fare, including tasty *pakoras* (fried vegetables) and *thalis* (set meals in little bowls).

**Wirtschaft Neumarkt**    F
European      **Map** E2
*Neumarkt 5, 8001*
**Tel** *044 252 79 39*    **Closed** *Sun*
Enjoy traditional regional dishes in the elegant tranquillity of a historic building in the Old Town. There's also a pretty back garden.

**Ban Song Thai**    FF
Thai      **Map** E2
*Kirchgasse 6, 8001*
**Tel** *044 252 33 31*    **Closed** *Sun*
Reservations are highly recommended at Ban Song Thai, said to be Switzerland's best Thai restaurant. Every dish is MSG-free.

**Bodega Española**    FF
Mediterranean      **Map** E2
*Münstergasse 15, 8001*
**Tel** *044 251 23 10*
A Spanish wine bar established in 1874. Tapas is served on the lower floor, and a more formal restaurant can be found upstairs.

**Brasserie Lipp**    FF
French      **Map** E2
*Uraniastrasse 9, 8001*
**Tel** *043 888 66 66*
A lively brasserie where shellfish, seafood and steaks are house specialities. There are inspiring views of the city from the Jules Verne Panoramabar.

**Hotel Restaurant Helvetia**    FF
Traditional      **Map** E2
*Stauffacherquai 1, 8004*
**Tel** *044 297 99 99*    **Closed** *Sun dinner*
A lively bar/meeting place that serves classic French and Swiss dishes. Reservations advisable.

**Pizzeria Scala**    FF
Italian      **Map** E2
*Rotbuchstrasse 1, 8006*
**Tel** *044 363 85 50*    **Closed** *Sun*
Enjoy pizzas and pasta dishes at this popular, attractive trattoria in a quiet residential area.

**Sala of Tokyo**    FF
Asian      **Map** E2
*Limmatstrasse 29, 8005*
**Tel** *044 271 52 90* **Closed** *Sun & Mon*
Zürich's prized sushi bar, the first such restaurant to open in the country, remains well regarded.

**Key to Price Guide** *see page 264*

---

**Haus zum Rueden**    FFF
International      **Map** E2
*Limmatquai 42, 8001*
**Tel** *044 261 95 66*    **Closed** *Sat & Sun*
Choose to dine in one of three air-conditioned rooms in this guild house dating from 1295. The Gothic Room is the most impressive. Market-fresh cuisine.

**Kronenhalle**    FFF
Traditional      **Map** E2
*Rämistrasse 4, 8001*
**Tel** *044 262 99 11*
Original works by Picasso and Matisse hang in the Kronenhalle, making it a unique location to enjoy some classic French cuisine.

**Mesa**    FFF
International      **Map** E2
*Weinbergstrasse 75, 8006*
**Tel** *043 321 75 75* **Closed** *Sat lunch; Sun*
Mesa boasts a Michelin star and 17 Gault Millau points. Be prepared for exceptional, creative cuisine, a good wine list and excellent service.

**Rico's Kunststuben**    FFF
International      **Map** E2
*Seestrasse 160, 8700*
**Tel** *044 910 07 15*    **Closed** *Sun & Mon*
This restaurant has two Michelin stars and 18 Gault Millau points. Savour innovative dishes of a superior standard in a modern interior. Relaxed service.

**Spice**    FFF
International      **Map** E2
*Germaniastrasse 99, 8044*
**Tel** *043 255 15 70*    **Closed** *Sun & Mon*
Reserve a seat at the Chef's Table to watch Michelin-star creations unfold up close, or learn to do it yourself at one of the cooking courses. Affordable business lunches available.

---

# Eastern Switzerland & Graubünden

**APPENZELL: Hôtel Appenzell**    F
Traditional      **Map** F2
*Hauptgasse 37, 9050*
**Tel** *071 788 15 15*
Simple and modestly priced dishes are made using market-fresh ingredients. There is a good vegetarian range. Breakfast and afternoon tea are also available.

**ARBON: Braukeller Frohsinn**    F
Traditional      **Map** F2
*Romanshornerstrasse 15, 9320*
**Tel** *071 447 84 84*    **Closed** *Sun*
This large restaurant boasts an on-site brewery and a beer cellar. The menu ranges from steaks and snacks to fresh fish.

**AROSA: Gspan**    F
Traditional      **Map** F4
*Gspanstrasse, 7050*
**Tel** *081 377 14 94*
Interesting Graubünden specialities, grilled meats and other traditional dishes all feature on the menu here. Superb views.

**BAD RAGAZ: Gasthof Loewen**    F
Traditional      **Map** F3
*Löwenstrasse 5, 7310*
**Tel** *081 302 13 06*    **Closed** *Sun & Mon*
A riverside restaurant where you can enjoy seasonal and locally sourced produce in a white-and-wood interior from the 1800s. Reasonably priced wine list.

**CELERINA: Restorant Uondas**  FF
Traditional      **Map** F4
*Via San Gian 7, 7505*
**Tel** *081 837 01 01*    **Closed** *Apr–mid-Jun*
Uondas has elegant, modern decor and a laid-back, child-friendly ambience. Try the grilled meats and the delicious home-made ice cream. Good service.

The understated interior of Sala of Tokyo, Switzerland's first sushi bar

## CHUR: Café Ratushof F
Traditional **Map** F3
*Bahnhofstrasse 14, 7000*
**Tel** *081 252 39 55*
A modest eatery where friendly staff serve hearty fare, including filling dishes like *rösti*, to loyal hungry folks.

## DAVOS: Montana Stube F
Traditional **Map** F3
*Bahnhofstrasse 2, 7260*
**Tel** *081 420 71 77* **Closed** *Sun, Mon & Tue*
Try the delicious spring chicken cooked on the fire, one of the house specialities at this traditional mountain *Stube* with spectacular views.

## GLARUS: Schützenhaus F
Traditional **Map** E3
*Schützenhausstrasse 55, 8750*
**Tel** *055 640 10 52* **Closed** *Mon & Tue*
A menu of unpretentious and inexpensive home-cooked food includes some tasty local specialities at this restaurant housed in a historic building.

## KLOSTERS: Rustico FF
Traditional **Map** F3
*Landstrasse 194, 7250*
**Tel** *081 410 22 88* **Closed** *Wed; 9–30 Jun*
Two hotel restaurants: Rustico offers local dishes like *rösti* and meatballs, while Prättiger Hüschi does fondue and *raclette*. There is also a tapas bar.

## KREUZLINGEN: Zum Blauen Haus FF
Event Bar **Map** F2
*Hauptstrasse 138, 8280*
**Tel** *071 688 24 98* **Closed** *Mon & Sun*
The house specialities are meat or prawns, grilled over an open wood fire. Extensive collection of single-malt whiskies.

## NEUHAUSEN AM RHEINFALL: Schlössli Wörth FF
Traditional **Map** E2
*Rheinfallquai 30, 8212*
**Tel** *052 672 24 21* **Closed** *Wed, Sep–Mar*
Located in an old customs house in sight of the largest waterfall in Europe. Outstanding cuisine and a playroom for children.

## POSCHIAVO: Hotel Albrici F
Italian **Map** G4
*Piazza da Cumün, 7742*
**Tel** *081 844 01 73*
This 17th-century building with a wood-burning pizza oven also serves regional specialities such as *pizzoccheri*, ribbon pasta made from buckwheat flour.

The chocolate counter at Hanselmann's, a café-patisserie in St Moritz

## RAPPERSWIL: Villa Aurum FF
French **Map** E3
*Alte Jonastrasse 23, 8640*
**Tel** *055 220 72 82* **Closed** *Sun & Mon*
This city-centre villa has an atmospheric dining area in a cellar with high-vaulted ceilings. The focus is on local, organic and seasonal produce.

## RORSCHACH: Aqua Fine Dining FF
Traditional **Map** F2
*Churerstrasse 28, 9400*
**Tel** *071 858 39 80*
Theme evenings, such as Italian Night or Retro 1960s, are typical at this restaurant. There is also a brewery and a summer beer garden on the lakeshore.

## ST GALLEN: Tres Amigos F
Mexican **Map** F2
*Hechtgasse 1, 9004*
**Tel** *071 222 2506*
A lively and inexpensive fast-food franchise serving Mexican fare. Varied wine list and a good choice of Mexican beers.

## ST GALLEN: Level Schoren FF
Mediterranean **Map** F2
*Dufourstrasse 150, 9000*
**Tel** *071 999 09 09* **Closed** *Sun & Mon*
There are several dining areas with an elegant, cosy feel and a winter terrace at this place known for its hearty roasted meats.

## DK Choice

## ST MORITZ: Hanselmann's FF
Tea Room **Map** F4
*Via Maistra 8*
**Tel** *081 833 38 64*
As famous as the Cresta Run, and almost as old, this café draws snowboarders and royalty alike with its Engadine Nusstorte, probably the best in the world.

## ST MORITZ: Ecco on Snow FFF
Gourmet **Map** F4
*Via Maistra 3, 7512*
**Tel** *081 836 63 00* **Closed** *Mon & Tue; summer*
Open only during the winter months, Ecco on Snow is part of the Giardino Mountain hotel complex outside St Moritz. Chef Rolf Fliegauf, who has been awarded two Michelin stars, creates culinary masterpieces in truly opulent surroundings.

## ST MORITZ: La Marmite FFF
Gourmet **Map** F4
*Corviglia, 7500*
**Tel** *081 833 63 55*
Haute cuisine at high altitude was invented here, and La Marmite is still the highest gourmet restaurant in the Alps, at 2,486 m (8,156 ft). Expect excellent standards of service, linen and crystal, caviar, truffles and a sublime wine list.

## ST MORITZ: Talvo by Dalsass FFF
Gourmet **Map** F4
*Via Gunels 15, 7512*
**Tel** *081 833 44 55* **Closed** *Mon & Tue; Apr–Jun; Oct & Nov*
The menu here changes frequently according to the seasons, and there are daily deliveries of fresh fish from Italy. Talvo boasts a Michelin star and 18 Gault Millau points.

## SCHAFFHAUSEN: Die Fischerzunft FF
Seafood **Map** E2
*Rheinquai 8, 8200*
**Tel** *052 632 05 05* **Closed** *Mon & Tue*
Diners flock to this restaurant for the impeccable service and the superb cuisine from chef André Jaeger, who serves classic dishes with an Asian influence. A Michelin star and 19 Gault Millau points.

**For more information on types of restaurants** *see page 256*

**SCHAFFHAUSEN: Zum Adler**   FF
Traditional              Map E2
*Vorstadt 69, 8200*
**Tel** *052 625 55 15*    **Closed** *Mon*
Fish, meat and vegetarian dishes
are served with the famous
house sauce. Reasonably priced
wines and a comfortable
atmosphere. Much loved by locals.

**SCUOL: Crusch Alba**       FF
Traditional              Map G3
*Pütvia 246, 7550*
**Tel** *081 864 11 55*
A warm and cozy eatery offering
hearty specialities from
Graubünden. Dishes are mostly
based on cheese and potatoes.

**SPLUGEN: Bodenhaus**        F
Traditional              Map F4
*Bodaweg 1, 7435*
**Tel** *081 650 90 90*
Built in 1722, this renovated
building maintains its original
character. The cuisine is seasonal,
light and creative. Good wine list.

**STEIN AM RHEIN: Adler**    FF
Traditional              Map E2
*Rathausplatz 2, 8260*
**Tel** *052 742 61 61*
The decorated façade makes for
an impressive entrance. On the
menu is delicious regional food.

**STEIN AM RHEIN:**
**Rheingerbe**               FF
Traditional              Map E2
*Schifflandi 5, 8260*
**Tel** *052 741 29 91*    **Closed** *summer:*
*Tue; winter: Mon & Tue*
Housed in a 16th-century tannery
with a riverbank terrace. Book
ahead for quality regional food
and locally sourced ingredients.

## DK Choice

**VADUZ:**
**Vaduz Sonnenhof**         FFF
International            Map F3
*Mareestrasse 29, FL-9490*
**Tel** *423 239 02 02*    **Closed** *Sat*
*lunch*
Run by chef Hubertus Real, this
Michelin-starred restaurant is
one of the best in Liechtenstein.
Food is seasonal modern
European, and daily lunch
menus are priced competitively.
Spectacular mountain views.

**WEINFELDEN:**
**Pulcinella im Schwert**    FF
Italian                  Map E2
*Wilerstrasse 8, 8570*
**Tel** *071 622 12 66*    **Closed** *Sun & Mon*
This is the place for lovingly
prepared Italian and local
specialities, including home-
made pasta. Good local wine list.

Vaduz Sonnenhof, surrounded by green meadows and breathaking views

**ZUOZ: Dorta**              FF
Traditional              Map G4
*Via Dorta 73, 7524*
**Tel** *081 854 2040*   **Closed** *Mon–Wed*
In a characteristic farm dating
from the 16th century, this
restaurant specializes in local
dishes. Try their hay soup.

# Central Switzerland & Ticino

**ALTDORF:**
**Goldener Schlüssel**       FF
Traditional              Map E3
*Rathausgasse 72, 3011*
**Tel** *031 311 02 16*    **Closed** *Sun*
Located in a small hotel,
this restaurant is particularly
renowned for its steak and pork
dishes. Children's menu available.

**ASCONA: Al Piazza**         F
Traditional              Map E5
*Piazza G Motta 29, 6612*
**Tel** *091 791 11 81*
Just a few steps from Lake
Maggiore, Al Piazza serves a
range of Italian and Ticino dishes
– pasta, pizza and polenta.

**BECKENRIED: Panorama**
**Klewenalp**                FF
Traditional              Map D3
*Klewen 1, 6375*
**Tel** *041 620 29 22*
A mountain restaurant with
sun terraces in summer and
winter. On the menu is mountain
fare, from fondues to meat
platters. Regular music events.

**BELLINZONA:**
**Cantinin del Gatt**         F
Traditional              Map E5
*Vicolo al Sasso 4, 6500*
**Tel** *091 825 27 71*    **Closed** *Mon*
*& Sun dinner; end Jul–mid-Aug*
Local dishes featuring seasonal,
locally sourced ingredients are
served in a vaulted room. Try
the rabbit with wild garlic.

**BURGENSTOCK: Taverne 1879**  F
Traditional              Map D3
*Burgenstock, 6363*
**Tel** *041 619 16 05*    **Closed** *Sat & Sun*
Enjoy superb views of the
lake from the terrace and the
elevated dining room at this
restaurant serving Swiss food
and regional specialities.

**CAVIGLIANO: Tentazioni**   FF
Mediterranean            Map E5
*Via Cantonale, 6654*
**Tel** *091 780 70 71*    **Closed** *varies*
*according to the season*
Mediterranean-style cuisine in a
boutique hotel dating from the
1950s. Tentazioni won first prize
at the Best of Swiss Gastro 2014
awards, in the Gourmet category.
Close to the village of Verscio.

**EINSIEDELN: Linde**        FF
International            Map E3
*Schmiedenstrasse 28, 8840*
**Tel** *055 418 48 48*
Dine on handmade pasta and
fresh fish dishes in a lovely
room with wooden floors
covered in Oriental rugs.

**ENGELBERG:**
**Hotel Bänklialp**          FF
Traditional              Map D3
*Bänklialpweg 25, 6390*
**Tel** *041 639 73 73*
There are five dining rooms
here, each with a different
character but all serving Swiss
specialities like fondues and *rösti*.
Frequent musical evenings.

**KUSSNACHT AM RIGI: Engel**  FF
Regional Speciality      Map D3
*Hauptplatz 1, 6403*
**Tel** *041 850 92 17*    **Closed** *Sun*
*& Mon*
The building housing Engel
is a museum of antiques and
carved wood. One dining room
dates back more than 660 years.
Menus are geared to the seasons
and the food is imaginative and
strikingly presented.

**LOCARNO:**
**Casa del Popolo** F
Italian Map E5
*Piazza Corporazioni, 6600*
**Tel** *091 751 12 08* **Closed** *Sun*
This trattoria in the Old Town is popular with locals, who come for the steak tartare, the pizzas and the liver and onions. Credit cards not accepted.

**LOCARNO:**
**La Cittadella Trattoria** FF
Italian Map E5
*Via Cittadella 18, 6600*
**Tel** *091 751 58 85* **Closed** *Mon*
Downstairs is a trattoria with a wood-burning pizza oven, while upstairs is a more elegant dining room serving fish and shellfish.

**LUGANO: Colibrí** F
Italian Map E5
*Via Aldesago 91, 6974*
**Tel** *091 971 42 42*
This restaurant is on Monte Brè, 15 minutes by tram or car from downtown Lugano. Panoramic views from the outdoor terrace overlooking the lake.

**LUGANO: Arté** FFF
French Map E5
*Viale Castagnola 31, 6906*
**Tel** *091 973 48 00* **Closed** *Sun & Mon*
Lugano's only Michelin-starred restaurant. Chef Frank Oerthle specializes in lake fish and seafood. Excellent wines and views over Lake Lugano.

**LUZERN: La Cucina** F
Italian Map D3
*Pilatusstrasse 29, 6002*
**Tel** *041 226 88 88*
A point of reference for Italian cuisine. Specialities include home-made pasta and pizza. There is a beautiful wooden interior and candlelit tables.

**LUZERN: Hofgarten** F
Traditional Map D3
*Stadthofstrasse 14, 6006*
**Tel** *041 410 88 88*
A vegetarian menu features home-made pasta stuffed with organic vegetables and cheese and polenta. Books and drawing materials are available to keep children entertained.

**LUZERN: Old Swiss House** FF
Traditional Map D3
*Löwenplatz 4, 6002*
**Tel** *041 410 61 71*
Located near the famous lion statue, this half-timbered house with an old-fashioned wooden interior draws rave reviews from tourists from around the world. Standard Swiss fare and a 30,000-bottle wine cellar.

**LUZERN: La Terrazza** FF
Italian Map D3
*Metzgerrainle 9, 6400*
**Tel** *041 410 36 31*
Specialities at this popular and good-value riverside restaurant include pizza, risotto, bruschetta and pasta dishes. The decor is modern, with high ceilings and vaulted alcoves.

**MENDRISIO: Grotto Bundi** F
Traditional Map E5
*Viale alle Cantine 24, 6850*
**Tel** *091 646 70 89* **Closed** *Mon*
Grotto Bundi is the place for traditional Ticino fare. Try the polenta cooked over the fire, and a range of game, cheese and meat specialities. There is also local produce for sale.

**PILATUS: Queen Victoria** FFF
Traditional Map D3
*Schlossweg 1, 6010*
**Tel** *041 329 11 11*
Situated right at the top of the mountain, this Victorian dining room has marbled pillars and breathtaking views over the Alps.

**RIGI KALTBAD: Bergsonne** FFF
International Map D3
*Fyrabigweg 1, 6356*
**Tel** *041 399 80 10*
Enjoy tremendous views of the lake and the mountains from the wide terraces at Bergsonne. The food is prepared with fresh ingredients from local farms, and there is a fine wine list. Four dining areas, all with an elegant yet relaxing atmosphere.

**STANS: Cubasia** F
International Map D3
*Stansstaderstrasse 20a, 6370*
**Tel** *041 619 71 71* **Closed** *Mon*
An unusual restaurant offering a spicy mix of hearty Chinese and Cuban fare. The Havana noodles are especially great. Lively music.

**STEINEN: Adelboden** FFF
Traditional Map E3
*Schlagstrasse, 6422*
**Tel** *041 832 12 42* **Closed** *Sun & Mon; end Jul–mid-Aug*
In a historic 18th-century family guesthouse. The French cuisine is of the highest standard, with two Michelin stars.

**VAL DI BLENIO: Centro**
**Pro Natura** F
Traditional Map E4
*Via Lucomagno Acquacalda, 6718*
**Tel** *091 872 26 10*
The restaurant of the Ecological Centre has basic decor but serves good, healthy dishes made from locally sourced farm produce.

**VERSCIO: Grotto Pedemonte** F
Traditional Map E5
*Stradón, 6653*
**Tel** *091 796 20 83* **Closed** *Wed; Nov–Mar*
A popular eatery serving regional fare in a tiny stone building. Outside there are granite tables, fig trees and mountain views.

## DK Choice

**WEGGIS: Annex** FFF
Traditional Map D3
*Hertensteinstrasse 34, 6353*
**Tel** *041 392 05 05* **Closed** *Mon & Tue*
The restaurant of the Relais et Châteaux Park Hôtel Weggis boasts one Michelin star for its French menu with Asian and Mediterranean inspiration. Great attention to detail.

**ZUG: AnaCapri Ristorante** FF
Italian Map E3
*Fischmarkt 2 Am See, 6300*
**Tel** *041 710 24 24*
Good-value pasta dishes, plus meat and fish made with seasonal produce. Superb views.

The rustic stone dining room of Dorta, in Zuoz *(see p274)*

**For more information on types of restaurants** *see page 256*

# SPORTS AND OUTDOOR ACTIVITIES

The Swiss are among the fittest, healthiest and most active people in the world. There is something in the Swiss air that makes you want to go outside and play. The first winter tourists (Brits in St Moritz in 1864) did exactly that – they grabbed sledges local farmers used for hauling wood and invented the sports that have evolved into luge and bobsleigh Olympic events. Swiss sports are all about participating, rather than watching. Whatever you do there is almost always a spectacular view of cool pine forests, tiny Alpine lakes or the sun glistening on a glacial tier of ice, and you can feel secure knowing that Swiss guides are at the top of their professions.

Sledging near Klosters village in Graubünden

## Winter Sports

Sledging (sledding) is the oldest winter sport in Switzerland, and still one of the most popular with Swiss families. Even resorts with no skiing have sledge runs, some open at night. Grindelwald has a sledge run 15 km (9 miles) long *(see p86)*. Variations on traditional sledging include snowtubing, where oversized inner tubes are used, and snow rafting, where a rubber boat slides down a prepared piste.

Snowshoeing has become a popular sport, especially among families and with hikers who can now access winter paths and pastures. Mountain guides also lead more ambitious treks, often to remote valleys. Snowshoers should always check local avalanche conditions before heading off marked trails.

Almost every Swiss village has an outdoor ice-skating rink, with shrieks of children conveying a winter carnival atmosphere.

Most resorts also have spacious indoor rinks used for figure skating and hockey games. Curling, a kind of bowls on ice, is taken seriously, especially since the Swiss won a gold medal at the 1998 Winter Olympics. In resorts like Davos and Wengen, holidaymakers are encouraged to join in hockey and curling matches with pick-up teams.

Switzerland is not short on spectator sports, either. And naturally St Moritz, the birthplace of winter holidays, leads the world. Nowhere else has an annual gourmet festival with banquets on ice, as well as horse racing, cricket, polo and golf tournaments, all conducted on the frozen lake *(see p37)*. Children especially love the dog-sled races, held across Switzerland, where teams of huskies mush through snowy forest trails.

Climbing artificial ice towers or frozen waterfalls, an ice axe in each hand and crampons to kick out footholds, is burgeoning in Switzerland. The world championships have been held in Saas Fee on several occasions *(see p94)*.

Uniquely refreshing is the sport of ice diving at Lake Lioson, 1,900 m (6,232 ft) above Lake Geneva, in canton Vaud. Here, divers in wet suits and scuba tanks drop through a hole in the frozen lake, and swim with the fish.

## Climbing

With mountains like the Matterhorn and the Eiger, Switzerland attracts climbers of every ability from all over the world. Rock climbers, in their skimpy shorts and ballet-slipper-like shoes, are relative newcomers compared to mountain climbers with their mania for "bagging" summits higher than 4,000 m (13,000 ft). It was actually the British, not the Swiss, who were the first mountain climbers. Edward Whymper famously conquered the Matterhorn in 1865 *(see p94)*.

Rock climbing in the Swiss Alps, with clear blue skies and sunshine

Summer hiking along a beautiful Alpine lake

Rock climbing (also called free climbing), with its technical bias for inching up sheer walls with almost invisible finger- and toe-holds, has spawned a fad for indoor climbing walls, now found everywhere in Switzerland.

Summit-seekers, in all weathers and seasons, will find Swiss guides ready to teach and accompany them on routes from Ticino to the Jura to the famous peaks of the Bernese Oberland, Valais and Graubünden. Crampons, ice axes, harnesses and other gear are all available for hire in mountaineering resorts.

## Hiking

No nation offers such a variety of hiking environments, so well signposted and integrated into the national system of postal buses (see p299), which reach even the remotest hamlet. Tourist offices organize theme hikes, such as identifying mushrooms, collecting butterflies, touring vineyards and walking from gourmet restaurant to gourmet restaurant. On some hikes, mules or llamas will carry your baggage.

From flat strolls through parkland to risky ledges (often with steel cables for attaching a safety harness) and glacier crossings, Switzerland has over 60,000 km (38,000 miles) of marked trails. In summer, resorts operate ski lifts to provide easy access to high pastures, from where many hikes begin.

In summer it is possible to walk right across the rooftop of the Alps, from Saas Fee in Switzerland to Chamonix in France, even taking in Aosta in Italy. First accomplished by the British in the early 20th century, this itinerary is called the *Haute Route*. Hikers sleep in high altitude refuges built by the Swiss Alpine Club (see p281). Each one is a day's march apart.

Hikers should ensure their insurance covers helicopter rescue, and leave word with innkeepers or the local tourist office of their route and estimated return time.

## Sky Sports

The only way to fully appreciate the vast size and splendour of Switzerland's wilderness of glaciers, peaks and blue ice crevasses is to see it from the air. Hour-long sightseeing flights in small planes or helicopters, from Bern, Zürich or Sion airports, are surprisingly inexpensive.

Hot-air balloons cannot fly over the higher peaks, but the views are still enchanting, as is the flying experience itself. There are more than 500 balloons and 50 flight centres in Switzerland. Château d'Oex has a microclimate ideal for balloon flights (see p37). Crans-Montana, Verbier and Davos have all held balloon festivals.

Paragliding in the Alpine air is unique, both because of the exceptional thermal lift and the enormous vertical descents that are possible. Flying as a passenger is also tremendous fun, and no experience is required. Various schools also offer holiday courses in which you can work towards the internationally recognized Swiss paragliding licence.

## Water Sports

With its Alpine lakes, glacier-fed rivers and majestic waterfalls, Switzerland is a natural playground for water sports. Swiss sailors stunned the world in 2003 and 2007, when the Swiss yacht *Alinghi* won the America's Cup. Sailing boats, steam-powered paddle-wheel excursion boats, dinghies, canoes and kayaks all set forth on the lakes of Geneva, Constance and Neuchâtel, and down the rivers Rhône and Rhine.

Paragliding over snow-covered mountains in the Bernese Oberland

Windsurfing – a popular sport on Swiss lakes

Every lake has its summer swimming *plage* (beach). The rivers host innovative water sports like "hydro-speed" (a hybrid of free swimming and rafting) as well as traditional rafting, water-skiing and floating down quiet stretches in oversized inner tubes.

Windsurfing is also popular, the smaller lakes providing ideal learning centres. Aqua parks with slides and spouts also abound. In Bern, each summer evening the burghers hike a few miles up the River Aare, then plunge into the swift current to float back to town, a tradition dating back to medieval times.

## Cycling

Both mountain bikes and racing cycles are available for rent almost everywhere in Switzerland, not least at many train stations *(see p299)*. There are nine long-distance national bike routes adding up to a total of 3,300 km (2,000 miles). In addition there are numerous off-road routes over mountain passes and through deserted hamlets.

For pure fun, especially for the less fit and family groups, there is downhill-only mountain biking. In summer, Swiss ski resorts modify the ski lifts to carry cycles up to 3,000 m (10,000 ft) or more. From these heights dirt roads and grassy tracks meander down through fields of wildflowers to the valley floor below. More adventurous cyclists can take the specially prepared hard-core

itineraries with jumps and expert-only trails skirting cliffs. To protect the environment and separate family hikers from cyclists, some resorts limit cyclists to specially marked trails.

## Adventure Sports

Bungee jumping and canyoning (descending ravines by jumping cliffs and sliding over rocks) remain popular high-adrenaline sports. The bungee jump from the Verzasca Dam near Locarno is cited as one of the biggest in the world, at 220 m (722 ft). But now there are new ways to fly down canyons, tethered at all times to a steel security cable.

At Saas Fee's Fairy Gorge and Grindelwald's Spider Highway holidaymakers with no experience can zip across networks of steel cables and swing out over dizzying heights

in perfect safety. A similar experience flying across a lake near Engelberg is called the "flying fox". Many resorts also have networks of rope bridges strung high in the treetops called *sentiers suspendus* or suspended pathways.

Exploring caves with a professional guide is also fun. Two of the world's ten biggest caves are in Switzerland: the Hoelloch system in Schwyz and the Muttee in canton Bern.

## Leisure Sports

Among the many reasons for golfing in the scenic Swiss Alps, consider that any drive on the high altitude championship course at Crans-Montana, home of the European Masters tournament, will travel 20 m (65 ft) further than at home. Many courses offer spectacular views of lakes and mountains.

Tennis courts (both outdoor and indoor) are dotted all over Switzerland, as you would expect in the home country of Roger Federer, the Swiss ace. Most surfaces are red clay or "synthetic grass", both much easier on the knees than the hard courts commonly found in North America.

Horse riding is an ideal way to see parts of the Swiss countryside that are otherwise ignored. A unique breed of horse, the Franches-Montagnes from Jura, is exceptionally easy to ride and train, the perfect horse for excursions *(see p137)*.

Mountain biking in the Swiss Alps

# DIRECTORY

## Winter Sports

**Cresta Tobogganing Club**
Via Ruinatsch 9,
7500 St Moritz.
**Tel** 081 832 20 52.
W cresta-run.com

**Ice Diving Lake Lioson**
Restaurant du Lac Lioson,
1862 Les Mosses.
**Tel** 024 491 11 44.
W lesmosses.ch

**Pradaschier Toboggan Ride**
Postfach, 7075
Churwalden.
**Tel** 081 356 22 07.
W lenzerheide.com

**Snowtubing**
Tourist Office,
1862 La Lécherette.
**Tel** 024 491 14 66.
W lesmosses.ch

**St Moritz Polo Club**
Via Maistra 24,
7500 St Moritz.
**Tel** 081 839 92 92
W stmoritz.ch

**Swiss Alpine Guides**
Postfach 29,
3800 Interlaken.
**Tel** 033 822 60 00.
W swissalpineguides.ch

**Swiss Guides**
Case Postale, 1936 Verbier.
**Tel** 079 446 22 89.
W swissguides.com

**Swiss Ice Skating Instructors Association**
In der Brunnmatt 1,
8103 Unterengstringen.
**Tel** 079 679 03 17.
W selv.ch

**Swiss Skating Association**
Haus des Sportes,
Postfach 606,
3000 Bern 22.
**Tel** 031 359 73 60.
W swissiceskating.ch

**Swiss Sled Dog Association**
Lenggstrasse 10,
5322 Koblenz.
**Tel** 079 401 71 03.
W schlittenhundesport klub.ch

## Climbing

**Bergschule Uri Mountain Reality**
Postfach 141,
6490 Andermatt.
**Tel** 041 872 09 00.
W bergschule-uri.ch

**Swiss Alpine Club**
Monbijoustr. 61,
3000 Bern 23.
**Tel** 031 370 18 18.
W sac-cas.ch

**Swiss Indoor Climbing Walls**
W indoorclimbing.com

**Swiss Mountain Guides Association**
Hadlaubstrasse 49,
8006 Zürich.
**Tel** 044 360 53 66.
W 4000plus.ch

**Swiss Rock Guides**
W swissrockguides.com

## Hiking

**Adrenaline Mountain Guides**
CP 54, 1936 Verbier.
**Tel** 079 205 95 95.
W guides-verbier.com

**Eurotrek**
Dörflistrasse 30, 8057
Zürich. **Tel** 044 316 10 00.
W eurotrek.ch

**Swiss Hiking Association**
Monbijoustr. 61, 3007 Bern.
**Tel** 031 370 10 20.
W swisshiking.ch

**Trekking Team**
Casa Rossina, 6652 Tegna.
**Tel** 091 780 78 00.
W trekking.ch

## Sky Sports

**Air Glaciers Helicopters**
Sion Airport, 1951, Sion.
**Tel** 027 329 14 15.
W air-glaciers.ch

**Fly Time Paragliding**
La Gare, 1934 Le Chable.
**Tel** 079 606 12 64.
W fly-time.ch

## Scenic Air Flights
Postfach 412,
3800 Interlaken.
**Tel** 033 821 00 11.
W scenicair.ch

**Swiss Balloon Association**
Bannstrasse 1, 4124
Schönenbuch, Basel.
**Tel** 061 481 32 22.
W sbav.ch

## Water Sports

**Aqua Park**
Route de la Plage,
1897 Le Bouveret.
**Tel** 024 482 00 11.
W aquaparc.ch

**Swiss Adventures**
Alpinzentrum, 3780 Gstaad.
**Tel** 033 748 41 61.
W swissadventures.ch

**Swiss Canoe Federation**
Rüdigerstrasse 10,
8045 Zürich.
**Tel** 043 222 40 77.
W swisscanoe.ch

**Swiss Sailing Federation**
Talgutzentrum 27,
3063 Ittigen.
**Tel** 031 359 72 66.
W swiss-sailing.ch

**Swiss Windsurf Association**
W windsurf.ch

**Swissraft**
Punt Arsa Promenade 19,
7013 Domat/Ems.
**Tel** 081 911 52 50.
W swissraft.ch

## Cycling

**Alpen Cross Mountain Biking**
Hirzlistrasse 7,
8638 Goldingen.
**Tel** 055 412 88 44.
W alpencross.ch

**Bike Switzerland**
22 Rue des Grottes,
1201 Geneva.
**Tel** 078 601 69 57.
W bikeswitzerland.com

**Veloland Schweiz**
Spitalgasse 34, 3011 Bern.
**Tel** 031 318 01 28.
W veloland.ch

## Adventure Sports

**Alpin Center Zermatt**
Bahnhofstrasse 58,
3920 Zermatt.
**Tel** 027 966 24 60.
W alpincenter-zermatt.ch

**Caving and Canyoning**
Casa Rosina,
6652 Tegna.
**Tel** 091 780 78 00.
W trekking.ch

**Garbely Adventure**
In den Lussen,
3999 Oberwald.
**Tel** 027 973 25 75.
W garbely-adventure.ch

**Outventure**
Mühlebachstrasse 5,
6370 Stans.
**Tel** 041 611 14 41.
W outventure.ch

**Sentier Suspendu**
1944 La Fouly.
**Tel** 027 783 25 45.
W sentier-suspendu.ch

## Leisure Sports

**Swiss Equestrian Association**
Papiermühlestrasse 40H,
3000 Bern 22.
**Tel** 031 335 43 43.
W fnch.ch

**Swiss Franches-Montagnes Horse Association**
Les Longs Prés,
1580 Avenches.
**Tel** 026 676 63 43.
W fm-ch.ch

**Swiss Golf Association**
Place de la
Croix-Blanche 19,
1066 Epalinges.
**Tel** 021 785 70 00.
W asg.ch

**Swiss Golf Network**
Sandrainstrasse 17,
3007 Bern.
**Tel** 044 586 98 66.
W swissgolfnetwork.ch

**Swiss Tennis Federation**
Solothurnstrasse 112,
2501 Biel.
**Tel** 032 344 07 07.
W swisstennis.ch

# Skiing in Switzerland

Snowsports holidays were invented in Switzerland in the 19th century, and for that unmistakeable Swiss hotel or chalet experience, as well as unrivalled infrastructure both on and off piste, Switzerland remains the world's premier winter sports destination. Only here can you board a train right at the airport terminal (Zürich or Geneva), with connections to any of the country's major ski resorts. Nowhere else will you find so many car-free resorts, the most famous of these being Zermatt, Saas Fee, Wengen and Mürren. Switzerland has more 4,000-m (13,000-ft) peaks than any other alpine nation, the highest ski lifts and ski fields, and superb conditions.

Snowboarder in mid-jump with a stunning backdrop at Leysin

Young skiers riding a "magic carpet" ski lift at Wengen

## Skiing

There are more than 250 skiing areas and some 2,400 cable cars and ski lifts, transporting more than 310 million passengers a year. "Magic carpet" conveyor-belt ski lifts transport beginners and children uphill. Zermatt and Saas Fee have underground "metro" trains, protected from weather and applauded by environmentalists, as they require no pylons.

Swiss resorts do not use chemicals in their snowmaking, and most have drastically reduced salt on the roads. Forests, and the animals that spend winter in them, are protected by fenced-off no-skiing zones. Free buses within resorts, some solar-powered, are part of the strong pro-environmental policies.

Swiss ski passes are more expensive than elsewhere in Europe, though cheaper than in North America. Family discounts are the best in the world. Children under nine, for example, ski free in Zermatt and at all Lake Geneva region resorts.

## Snowboarding

The distinction between skiers and snowboarders is all but extinct now. For years the trend has been to shorter, fatter skis. Two such skis are about the same width as a snowboard. Skiers and boarders now share techniques: "carving" (making deep cuts in the piste), "freeride" (long, fast turns in deep snow) and "freestyle" (jumps or tricks).

No Swiss resorts ban snowboarders or restrict them to certain areas. Indeed, what used to be called "snowboard parks" are now renamed "terrain parks", where both skiers and boarders make jumps side by side.

## When to Go

Swiss resorts with glaciers, like Zermatt and Saas Fee, are open summer and winter alike. High resorts like Verbier traditionally open at the start of November and close in May. But it is a fact of life that, for the past decade, early

season skiing has lacked sufficient snowfall. The most expensive and crowded periods are Christmas, Easter and the entire high-season month of February. By contrast, most hotels and resorts offer tremendous bargains during the quiet month of January. March is the best month for a combination of reduced prices, most sunshine and deepest snowpack (see pp34–5).

## Choosing a Resort

Switzerland has skiing areas for all price ranges and abilities. **Zermatt**, **St Moritz**, **Davos**, **Gstaad** and **Verbier** are the most fashionable. High resorts with glaciers have the best guarantee of snow. In addition to Zermatt, Verbier and **Saas Fee**, these include the more family-oriented resorts of **Les Diablerets** and **Engelberg**.

Intermediates, who want to cruise long, well-groomed pistes, will find endless variety in resorts that have joined

The view from Blatten village looking towards Breithorn mountain

together on a single ski pass. The **Portes du Soleil** straddling the Swiss-Franco border has 650 km (404 miles) of marked trails. Zermatt, joined with its Italian neighbour Cervinia, boasts 360 km (224 miles) of cross-border skiing.

For chalet charm and views, the small resorts of Mürren, **Wengen**, **Andermatt** and **Saas Fee** are unbeatable. For families, the pace and price of resorts like **Val d'Anniviers**, **Adelboden** and **Kandersteg** are particularly attractive.

## Accommodation

One of the most memorable parts of a Swiss skiing holiday is staying in an authentic chalet or a grand old hotel. But there is also a wide choice of budget accommodation, including guesthouses. Self-catered apartments are a popular alternative; holiday costs can be cut considerably by buying groceries at chain supermarkets like Migros. Another possibility is staying in a Swiss city and driving each day to a different resort (*see pp246–7*).

Off-piste skiing in pristine, powdery snow in Uri canton

## Off-piste Skiing

It is estimated that more than half of all skiers (tourists and locals) in Switzerland now ski off piste, defined as skiing off marked trails in natural snow which has not been packed down by machines.

There has been a consequent explosion in tours to the "back-country" by qualified mountain guides. Visitors should make sure their insurance covers such activities explicitly, including rescue by helicopter (common in Switzerland, even for minor accidents on piste).

## At the Top

Switzerland has 42 authorized landing zones where helicopters may deposit skiers searching for the best-quality untracked snow. Mountain guides are always required, and groups are chosen according to ability level, which need not be expert.

Amazingly popular is the oldest way of getting to the top, sliding uphill on skis fixed with "skins" that prevent backward slippage. At high altitudes the Swiss have erected hundreds of "huts", really small hotels with food and wine served by a "guardian". These huts are spaced a day's tour apart. The most famous ski tour across the glaciers starts in Saas Fee and ends a week later in Chamonix (France).

# DIRECTORY

## Practical Info

### International Ski Federation
w fis-ski.com

### Meteo Swiss
w meteoswiss.ch

### Piste maps
w alpineskimaps.com

### Switzerland Tourism
w myswitzerland.com

### Valais Tourism
Tel 027 327 35 70.
w valais.ch

## Guides, Gear & Schools

### Air Glaciers Helicopters
Tel 033 856 05 60.

### Mountain Air Sports
Tel 027 771 62 31.
w mountainairverbier.com

### Swiss Alpine Club
Tel 031 370 18 18.
w sac-cas.ch

### Swiss Mountain Guides
Tel 044 360 53 66.
w 4000plus.ch

### Swiss Rent a Sport
Tel 081 410 08 18.
w swissrent.com

### Swiss Ski Schools
Tel 031 810 41 11.
w snowsports.ch

### Swiss Snowboard
w swisssnowboard.ch

### Terrain Parks
w worldsnowboardguide.com

## Resorts

### Adelboden
Tel 033 673 80 80.
w adelboden.ch

### Andermatt
Tel 041 888 71 00.
w andermatt.ch

### Davos
Tel 081 415 21 21.
w davos.ch

### Engelberg
Tel 041 639 77 77.
w engelberg.ch

### Gstaad
Tel 033 748 81 81.
w gstaad.ch

### Kandersteg
Tel 033 675 80 80.
w kandersteg.ch

### Les Diablerets
Tel 024 492 00 10.
w diablerets.ch

### Portes du Soleil
Tel 024 477 23 61.
w portesdusoleil.com

### Saas Fee
Tel 027 958 18 58.
w saas-fee.ch

### St Moritz
Tel 081 837 33 33.
w stmoritz.ch

### Val d'Anniviers
Tel 0848 848 027.
w valdanniviers.ch

### Verbier
Tel 027 775 38 88.
w verbier.ch

### Wengen
Tel 033 856 85 85.
w wengen.ch

### Zermatt
Tel 027 966 81 00.
w zermatt.ch

# SPA RESORTS IN SWITZERLAND

With its pure Alpine air and therapeutic hot springs, Switzerland has always been a favoured destination for those recovering from illness or seeking to improve their health or lifestyle. With the help of relaxing treatment courses using physiotherapy and natural spa resources, such as hot mineral springs and therapeutic muds, countless people have regained their health and strength. Modern Swiss spas lead the world, not only in their standards of comfort and care, but with their pioneering treatments. Few other countries offer such a diverse choice of spa experiences, from traditional "cures" in thermal pools to the latest health and beauty treatments.

Therapeutic massage at Clinique La Prairie, near Montreux

## Thermal Spas

Switzerland has an abundance of hot springs but just 20 thermal resorts. These spa towns are a pleasant mix of ancient traditions and 21st-century comforts, with public thermal baths, shops, gardens, sports amenities and a full calendar of cultural events. Spa "cures" are carried out in modern treatment centres following a medical consultation and include hydrotherapy, physiotherapy, mud treatments, massage and balneotherapy (therapeutic bathing).

In **Bad Ragaz**, mineral-rich water is piped down from a hot spring in a nearby gorge and used in the treatment of rheumatic, circulatory and neurological disorders. Aesthetic and cosmetic procedures are also offered in the town's medical clinics.

The strong sulphur waters in **Lenk** are good for treating respiratory disorders. The modern spa and health centre has a specialist inhalation clinic with physiotherapy, lymph drainage and other lung-related treatments. Traditional spa rheumatism cures, dietary advice, slimming and beauty treatments are also available.

The village of **Leukerbad** is Europe's largest alpine spa, with 65 thermal springs, 22 thermal baths and a large hydrotherapy/ balneotherapy treatment centre. The hot mineral-rich waters are used to treat rheumatic conditions, metabolic diseases and hormonal disorders, for rehabilitation after accidents, surgery or strokes and in sports medicine.

The sparkling carbonated springs of **St Moritz** are the highest in Switerland. The waters are used by doctors and therapists in the medical centre, combining traditional spa therapies with the latest medical advances.

The hot springs of **Yverdon-les-Bains** have eased rheumatic pain and respiratory conditions since Roman times. Today, spa treatments are carried out in the public Centre Thermale – a large modern spa complex with indoor and outdoor thermal pools, fitness facilities, saunas, Turkish baths, solaria, mud baths and massages.

## Medical Spas

Swiss medical spas are known for their rejuvenating treatments and clinical excellence. The exclusive **Clinique La Prairie** near Montreux specializes in rejuvenating treatments. A recent expansion has provided a dedicated spa floor with state-of-the-art amenities and new equipment in the medical centre, which carries out general as well as cosmetic surgery. Also in Montreux is **La Clinic**, a hospital with the luxury of a five-star hotel, offering rejuvenating treatments, cosmetic surgery, dentistry and hair replacement. The sumptuous **Kempinski Grand Hotel des Bains** in St Moritz has a medical spa as well as a lavish wellness facility with treatments and access to the town's medical centre.

Taking the fresh Alpine air and the hot thermal waters in the small village of Leukerbad, in the Valais

## Hotel Spas

Many four- and five-star hotels offer outstanding spa facilities. The new ESPA spa has transformed Interlaken's **Victoria Jungfrau Grand Hotel & Spa** into a spa destination with state-of-the-art treatment rooms, thermal and relaxation areas and an extensive menu of fabulous treatments.

At **Le Mirador Kempinski Lake Geneva**, the spa adjoins the hotel and has a swim-through indoor/outdoor pool and an extensive spa menu that includes massage, hydrotherapy, wellness treatments and weight-loss programmes.

Grindelwald's **Grand Regina-Alpin Well & Fit Hotel** offers spa treatments, massage and hairdressing. Facilities include pools and a thermal circuit with caves, baths, steam rooms, saunas and ice showers.

Vals' dramatic **Therme Vals** has thermal pools and a wellness centre with aromatherapy, kelp wraps, acupressure, manicures, pedicures and facials.

**La Réserve**'s opulent spa on Lake Geneva provides indoor and outdoor pools, sauna, hammam and 17 treatment rooms for massages, personalized treatments and facials.

ESPA spa at the Victoria Jungfrau Grand Hotel & Spa in Interlaken

The Tschuggen Bergoase at Arosa's **Tschuggen Grand Hotel** is built into a mountain over four levels and linked to the hotel by a glass bridge. Spring water flows throughout the spa and the spectacular open-plan design encompasses thermal and relaxation areas, indoor and outdoor pools, treatment rooms and spa suites. A wide range of spa treatments are available.

At Lausanne's **Beau Rivage Palace Hotel**, the Spa Cinq Mondes offers Asian healing traditions and holistic health rituals. There are pools, tropical shower promenade and nine treatment rooms, some with Japanese flower baths.

The **Grand Hotel Bellevue** in Gstaad has a well-equipped spa with a thermal suite and spa menu that includes holistic rituals, Kneipp therapies, aromatherapy, body massages and wraps, spa baths and Shiseido treatments.

In Zermatt, **Hotel Mirabeau's** new Alpine Wellness Refuge uses natural products made from local mountain flowers, honey and herbs. Connected to the hotel by a tunnel, the spa has a warm indoor pool and a thermal circuit with scented hay mattress, Kneipp bath, mountain-flowers steam bath, sauna with open sky shower and relaxation room with waterbeds.

# DIRECTORY

### Thermal Spas

**Bad Ragaz**
Valens.
Tel 081 300 40 20.
spavillage.ch

**Lenk**
Simmental.
Tel 033 736 35 35.
lenk.ch

**Leukerbad**
Valais.
Tel 027 472 71 71.
leukerbad.ch

**St Moritz**
Engadin.
Tel 081 837 33 33.
stmoritz.ch

**Yverdon-les-Bains**
Vaus.
Tel 024 423 61 01.
yverdonlesbains region.ch

### Medical Spas

**La Clinic**
Montreux.
Tel 021 966 70 00.
laclinic.ch

**Clinique La Prairie**
Clarens-Montreux.
Tel 021 989 33 11.
laprairie.ch

**Kempinski Grand Hotel des Bains**
St Moritz.
Tel 081 838 38 38.
kempinski.com/stmoritz

### Hotel Spas

**Beau Rivage Palace Hotel**
Lausanne.
Tel 021 613 33 33.
brp.ch

**Grand Hotel Bellevue**
Gstaad.
Tel 033 748 00 00.
bellevue-gstaad.ch

**Grand Regina-Alpin Well & Fit Hotel**
Grindewald.
Tel 033 854 86 00.
grandregina.ch

**Hotel Mirabeau**
Zermatt.
Tel 027 966 26 60.
hotel-mirabeau.ch

**Le Mirador Kempinski Lake Geneva**
Vevey.
Tel 021 925 11 11.
kempinski.com/en/montreux

**La Réserve**
Lake Geneva.
Tel 022 959 59 59.
lareserve.ch

**Therme Vals**
Vals.
Tel 081 926 80 80.
therme-vals.ch

**Tschuggen Grand Hotel**
Arosa.
Tel 081 378 99 99.
tschuggen.ch

**Victoria Jungfrau Grand Hotel & Spa**
Interlaken.
Tel 033 828 28 28.
victoria-jungfrau.ch

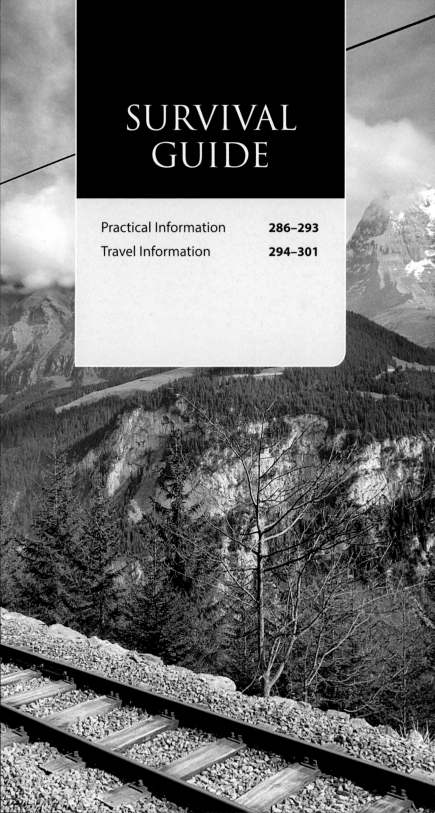

# SURVIVAL GUIDE

# PRACTICAL INFORMATION

A prime tourist destination, Switzerland attracts large numbers of visitors, both during the winter sports season and at other times of the year. As tourism is an important part of Switzerland's economy, the country has a highly developed tourist infrastructure and a positive attitude towards helping foreign visitors make the most of their stay.

Museums and other places of interest are well-maintained, with helpful information in several languages, usually including English. English is also spoken at most tourist offices, as well as in almost all the larger hotels and major winter sports resorts.

Having one of the most efficiently run and convenient public transport systems in Europe, Switzerland is also a very easy country to travel around, whether by road or rail, or at a more leisurely pace by boat on Switzerland's larger lakes.

### When to Go

The best time of year to visit Switzerland depends on how you plan to spend your time here. The winter sports season runs from mid-December to late spring. The most crowded periods are the Christmas and Easter holiday weeks, and the entire "high season" month of February.

Summertime in Switzerland is pleasantly warm. The height of the summer season runs from the beginning of July to late August. Accommodation then tends to be harder to find, and visitor attractions are at their most crowded.

Spring and autumn are much quieter, and are excellent seasons for exploring the countryside. The mountains are particularly beautiful in spring, when wild flowers start to bloom, and in autumn, when leaves begin to turn. In the countryside, spring and autumn are also the time of year when you are most likely to witness folk festivals.

### Visa and Customs Regulations

Citizens of the EU, the United States, Canada, Australia, New Zealand and South Africa need a valid passport to visit Switzerland and Liechtenstein but do not require a visa. However, individual visits are limited to three months, and

Information board in Parc Mon Repos, Geneva

total visits per year should not exceed six months. Visitors planning a longer stay (to work or study in Switzerland, for example) should contact the Swiss embassy in their own country. Switzerland is a member of the Schengen Agreement, which abolishes border controls on travel within member states.

Customs regulations are straightforward. Visitors from Europe may import 2 litres of wine and 1 litre of spirits, and 200 cigarettes or 50 cigars, or 250g of pipe tobacco. Visitors from other countries may import 400 cigarettes, 100 cigars and 500g of pipe tobacco. However, no visitors under the age of 17 may bring alcohol or tobacco into Switzerland. Visitors may also bring in a variety of items for their own use while in Switzerland, such as camping and sports equipment, cameras and laptop computers, and gifts up to a value of 300 CHF.

### Opening Hours

Most museums and visitor attractions are open six full days a week. Many close on Mondays and some on Tuesdays. Shops, post offices, banks and tourist offices are generally open from Monday to Friday, 8am–6:30pm. Shops also open on Saturdays, 8am–4pm, while post offices open until 11am or noon. However, shops in smaller towns and villages may close for lunch and those in smaller towns may be closed on Mondays. In many resorts, shops stay open all day on Sunday. Shops on station concourses have longer opening hours and are also open on Sundays.

The tourist information centre at the Bärengraben in Bern

◀ The funicular train linking Lauterbrunnen to Mürren

News kiosk with publications in German, French and Italian

## Languages

German is the most widely spoken language in Switzerland, after which are French and Italian. German-speakers, followed by French-speakers, are most likely to speak English as well. Many organizations that have contact with foreign visitors speak English and most tourist offices have English-speaking staff.

Swiss German differs from the standard, or High, German of Germany and Austria. Swiss German *(Schwyzer-tütsch)*, which has several regional dialects as well as its own syntax and vocabulary, is used in everyday speech and is hardly ever written. High German *(Hochdeutsch)* in Switzerland is primarily a written language, being used for public signs and notices and in the media but also in education and in formal situations such as public speaking.

Pillar with news and information

## Newspapers

Switzerland's national press is dominated by French- and German-language titles. Among the leading dailies are the conservative *Neue Zürcher Zeitung*, the more liberal *Tages-*

*Anzeiger* and the progressive *Le Temps*. Swiss weeklies include *Die Weltwoche* and *Wochen-zeitung*. The daily *Corriere del Ticino* is widely read in Ticino.

British and American newspapers, such as *The Times*, *The Guardian, New York Times* and *USA Today*, are sold in large towns and cities and in most major resorts. *The Economist, Time* and *Newsweek* are also available.

## Time

Switzerland is one hour ahead of Greenwich Mean Time (GMT) in winter and two hours ahead of GMT in summer. The Swiss use the 24-hour clock. In German *halb* (half) refers to the half-hour before the hour; for example, *halb zwei* means 1:30, not 2:30.

## Electricity

The current in Switzerland is 220v AC 50 cycles. Sockets are of the three-pin type, and they accept the two- or three-pin round-pronged plugs used elsewhere in continental Europe. Although many hotels provide adaptors on request, it can be more convenient to bring your own. For equipment designed for use in the USA, you will need a transformer.

# Personal Security and Health

With efficient public services and one of the lowest crime rates in the industrialized world, Switzerland is generally a safe country for foreign visitors. The Swiss are helpful, polite and welcoming, so travelling anywhere in their country is a pleasant experience. With a temperate climate, clean water and few natural hazards, Switzerland poses virtually no health risks to visitors. However, those who enjoy the more strenuous outdoor activities, particularly at high altitudes, should be aware of potential dangers.

Patrol car of Geneva police

## Personal Safety

Despite Switzerland's deserved reputation for safety, visitors should be vigilant, particularly when walking in unlit streets late at night, withdrawing cash at an ATM, travelling on public transport, or among large crowds of people in public places. Pickpockets in search of wallets and credit cards sometimes operate in the streets and squares of large towns, as well as at airports,

Policeman patrolling the streets on a bicycle

train stations and other transport hubs. Thieves may be on the lookout for opportunities to grab handbags and jewellery from unwary visitors. It is also wise to make use of hotel safes to store valuable items and never to leave valuables in cars, which should always be left locked. If you intend to stay in hostels, it is worth taking a padlock to secure a locker.

Generally, caution and common sense are the best defences. However, if you are the victim of theft, report it at once to the police. Obtaining a police report will enable you to make an insurance claim. Loss or theft of credit cards should also be reported as soon as possible to the issuing company (see p290).

Women travelling alone are unlikely to experience problems, but it is best to follow the same safety precautions you would usually and to keep away from lonely, unlit areas at night.

## Police

The Swiss are scrupulously law-abiding and expect the same of foreign visitors. Simply crossing the street on a red pedestrian light may result in a police caution or a fine. More serious transgressions, such as the possession of drugs, may lead to imprisonment or deportation. At all times, you should carry your passport or ID, which the police will ask to see if they have reason to stop you.

Each of the country's 26 cantons has its own armed police force, as do individual towns and cities. Each canton also has its own laws, although the differences between them are minimal.

## Health

No vaccinations are required for visitors entering Switzerland, except for those who have visited a high-risk region in the two weeks preceding their arrival in the country.

Tap water is safe to drink everywhere in Switzerland, and the water gushing from fountains in towns and villages is also safe, unless otherwise indicated by the words *kein Trinkwasser*, *eau non potable*

Municipal police patrol car

or *acqua non potabile*. It is, however, best not to drink from streams and springs, however pure they may appear to be.

At altitudes over about 3,000 m (10,000 ft), visitors should be aware of the risk of altitude sickness. Aspirin and bed rest may alleviate mild symptoms, which include nausea, headache and fatigue but which usually pass after 48 hours. If symptoms persist, the only effective remedy is to descend to a lower altitude.

Sunstroke is also more likely at high altitudes, where the air is thinner, or where snow or water reflect the sun's rays. To prevent sunstroke, drink plenty

Rescue helicopter in action in Crans-Montana

of water, wear a hat and sunglasses and use a sunblock with a high UV-protection factor. The best prevention, however, is to limit the amount of time you spend in the sun, especially in the first few days of your stay.

At any time of the year, the weather in the mountains can be very changeable, with cold wind, rain and sudden snow-storms posing the greatest danger. Skiers and hikers should wear several layers of warm clothing, a hat and waterproofs, and carry supplies of high-energy food and water. The best precaution of all is the decision to turn back when weather conditions threaten to deteriorate.

Entrance to a pharmacy in St Gallen

## Medical Care

There is no national health service in Switzerland, so medical treatment of any kind must be paid for. Switzerland has a reciprocal agreement with all EU countries. Visitors must obtain a European Health Insurance Card (EHIC) – the form is available from post offices. However, taking out health insurance before your trip is still recommended. This is particularly important if you are planning a skiing, mountaineering or hiking holiday, or intend to practise any extreme sports. Insurance should also cover the cost of helicopter rescue. Helicopters are increasingly used in the mountains, even for minor injuries, and without insurance helicopter rescue is expensive.

In case of illness or injury, lists of local doctors can be obtained from the more expensive hotels, the consulate of your own country (see p287) or from tourist information offices (see p279). Almost every hospital (Spital, hôpital, ospedale) has a 24-hour accident and emergency department. However, before receiving hospital treatment, you are advised to contact your insurer or your country's embassy (see p287).

## Pharmacies

All pharmacies (Apotheke, pharmacie or farmacia) are denoted by a sign in the form of a green cross. Pharmacies have helpful and knowledge-able staff who are able to give advice on minor health problems. Many pharmacies close on Saturday afternoon.

Duty pharmacies are open outside normal shopping hours, and their address is posted in the windows of pharmacies that are closed. In larger towns and cities, duty pharmacies stay open round the clock.

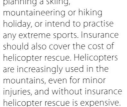

An auxiliary services vehicle

## Emergencies

If you are involved in, or witness, an emergency, immediately call the police by dialling 117, or the ambulance (144), fire brigade (118), road rescue (140) or helicopter rescue service (1414). If you are asked to sign a police document, do not do so unless you understand its content. Ask to have it translated. If you hold an insurance policy issued in your home country, you should immediately contact the insurer's central office, by ringing the number given on the policy document. Should you need legal assistance, your embassy can offer advice (see p287).

# Banking and Local Currency

You may bring any amount of currency into Switzerland, but for any amount over 10,000 CHF the source must be declared. Travellers' cheques are the safest way to carry money abroad, but credit and debit cards, both of which can be used to withdraw local currency, are the most convenient. The unit of currency in Switzerland and in Liechtenstein is the Swiss franc (CHF).

### Payment

The preferred payment is the Swiss franc. However, euros are now widely accepted in shops, hotels and restaurants, though the rate of exchange is usually less advantageous than at a bank.

Ticket offices of SBB, the Swiss federal railway (see pp296–7), accept payment in euros. Throughout Switzerland euros can often be used at airports as well as to pay motorway tolls. Some coin-operated telephones will accept euro coins (see p292).

### Banks and Bureaux de Change

Most banks are open Monday to Friday from 9am to 5pm, although in smaller towns they may close from noon to 2pm. Currency can be exchanged over the counter at banks, or cash withdrawn with a credit or debit card at cash machines (ATMs).

Even the banks in small towns have cash machines, and these can of course also be found at all airports and at major railway stations. Cash machines generally dispense both euros and Swiss francs.

The least favourable rates of exchange are usually those offered by hotels. Always check the rate, whether using a bureau de change, hotel or bank, to get the best rate.

Basler Kantonalbank cash machine

### Credit Cards

The use of credit cards is less widespread in Switzerland than in the United Kingdom and United States. Visitors should bear in mind that some shops, hotels and restaurants ask for payment to be made in cash. In general MasterCard and Visa have the widest use in Switzerland, with American Express and Diners Club less widely accepted.

### Tax-free Goods

Value-added tax (VAT) is levied at 8 per cent, with some basic items rated at 2.5 per cent. Visitors to Switzerland can reclaim sales tax, or VAT, on individual purchases of 300 CHF or more made at a single store. Obtain a VAT refund form at the time of purchase and take the goods out of the country (unopened) within 30 days. The form should be presented to

## DIRECTORY

### Swiss Banks

**Banque Cantonale de Genève**
17 Quai de l'Ile,
1204 Geneva.
**Tel** 022 317 27 27.

**Credit Suisse Group**
Paradeplatz 8,
8001 Zürich.
**Tel** 044 333 11 11.
W credit-suisse.com

**Raiffeisen Bank**
Brandschenkestrasse 110d,
8002 Zürich.
**Tel** 0844 88 88 08.
W raiffeisen.ch

**UBS AG**
Bahnhofstrasse 45,
8001 Zürich.
**Tel** 044 234 11 11.
W ubs.com

**Zürcher Kantonalbank**
Bahnhofstrasse 9,
8001 Zürich.
**Tel** 0844 843 823.
W zkb.ch

### Lost/Stolen Credit Cards & Travellers' Cheques

**American Express**
**Tel** +44 (0) 1273 69 69 33.

**Diners Club**
**Tel** 0870 190 00 11.

**Mastercard**
**Tel** 0800 96 47 67.

**Thomas Cook/Travelex Worldwide Refund Service**
**Tel** 0800 62 21 01.

**Visa**
**Tel** 0800 89 4732 (cards).

A branch of Credit Suisse, one of Switzerland's largest banks

customs when you leave the country. To obtain your refund, either take the form to the refund counter or send it back to the store when you are home. For a fee, **Global Refund**, a Europe-wide refund service, will handle all the paperwork for you.

## Currency

The Swiss unit of currency is the Swiss franc, which is abbreviated as CHF and known as *Schweizer Franken* in German, *franc suisse* in French and *franco svizzero* in Italian. The franc is divided into 100 *centimes*, which are known as *Rappen* in German and as *centesimi* in Italian.

Because of the customs union that exists between Switzerland and the principality of Liechtenstein, the Swiss franc is also the official currency of Liechtenstein.

## Banknotes

*Swiss banknotes are issued in denominations of 10, 20, 50, 100, 200 and 1,000 francs. The different banknotes are distinguished by their size and colour. The smallest, both in terms of size and value, is the 10-franc note. The largest is the 1,000-franc note.*

10 francs

20 francs

50 francs

100 francs

200 francs

1,000 francs

5 francs

2 francs

1 franc

50 centimes

20 centimes

10 centimes

5 centimes

## Coins

*Swiss coins are issued in denominations of 1, 2 and 5 francs, and of 5, 10, 20 and 50 centimes. All Swiss coins are silver-coloured, except the 5-centime coin, which is gold-coloured.*

# Communications and Media

Like the country's other services, Switzerland's telephone, Internet and postal systems are efficient and reliable. Swisscom's modern public telephones have built-in electronic directories and also built-in facilities for sending emails and text messages. Switzerland's post office, known as Die Post in German, La Poste in French and La Posta in Italian, offers an equally modern and comprehensive mail service, as well as other useful services. Neighbouring Liechtenstein has its own separate telephone and postal systems.

## Useful Numbers

- Country code for Switzerland: 41 Liechtenstein: 423
- Useful country codes: Australia: 61 Ireland: 353 New Zealand: 64 South Africa: 27 UK: 44 US & Canada: 1
- Directory enquiries for Switzerland and Liechtenstein: 111 All other countries: 11 59

A Swisscom telephone box

## International and Local Telephone Calls

Switzerland's principal telecommunications company is **Swisscom**. It has 4,800 public telephones, most of which are located outside post offices and in train stations. Instructions on how to use the telephone system are given in four languages, including English.

Some public telephones are coin-operated. Those that are accept Swiss francs and euros. The easiest way of using a public telephone is with a prepaid phonecard, known as a taxcard. Taxcards, in denominations of 5, 10, 20 and 50 CHF, are sold at post offices and train stations as well as in news kiosks.

Calls within Switzerland are cheapest at weekends, and on weekdays between 7pm and 7am. Inland calls to 0800 numbers are free. Calls from hotels, which set their

own phone tariffs, always cost more than from public telephones.

Swisscom alone has over 2,000 wireless LAN (local area network) hot spots, from which VOIP (voice over Internet protocol) telephone services like Skype, for example, can be used.

All Swiss telephone numbers now consist of ten digits. This means that you must always include the three-digit area code, even when dialling a local number.

## Mobile Phones

There are three main mobile telephone providers in Switzerland: Swisscom (the largest), Sunrise and Orange. Coverage varies across the country, so some background research is a good idea if you're staying in the country for a while. Eastern Switzerland, for example, is not a good area

to make calls for Orange customers, whereas the company claims it provides the fastest data connection.

Ready-to-use mobile phones with prepaid cards can be bought at department stores or electrical shops. Charges for Swiss mobile phone users are comparatively high, while roaming charges are some of the highest in Europe, so be careful if you're travelling in neighbouring countries with a prepaid Swiss phone.

## Internet

There are numerous **cafés**, special terminals and Wi-Fi hot spots throughout Switzerland. Many hotels offer free Wi-Fi, as do restaurants and fast-food outlets. Train stations and Intercity trains have Wi-Fi (for a fee) in first class, while Swiss

An Internet booth in Lugano, southern Switzerland

Sign for a Post Office in a German-speaking region of Switzerland

postbuses offer it for free. Note that Swiss telephone providers charge for a hot-spot service.

## Postal Services

In large towns post offices are open from 8am to 6.30pm Monday to Friday, and from 8am to 11am or noon on Saturdays. In smaller towns, they close between noon and 2pm. In large cities, including Zürich, Geneva, Bern and Basel, post offices situated near railway stations have counters that remain open until 9–10pm. A small extra charge is made for using their services, but be aware that they don't handle the more complicated transactions, such as money transfers.

Many post offices also have fax machines as well as shops selling books, confectionery and writing and packaging materials.

## Stamps and Mail

Postage stamps are available at post offices, newsagents and online. They can also be purchased from machines, which are located within post offices and also beside some postboxes.

The Swiss postal system operates a two-tier delivery system. Inland letters sent by A-Post are delivered the next day. Those sent by B-Post, which is cheaper, reach their destinations in two to three days. For international letters there are two categories, Prioritaire and Économique. Prioritaire mail is delivered in two to four days within Europe and up to seven days everywhere else. Économique mail is delivered in four to eight days within Europe and up to 12 days elsewhere.

A Die Post postbox in Switzerland

## Poste Restante

A convenient way of receiving mail if you are travelling in Switzerland is by using Poste Restante. By this system, mail is sent to any post office in the country that you designate, and is kept there until you come to collect it. Mail should be addressed with your name, the words "Poste Restante", the letters "CH" (for "Switzerland") and the four-digit postcode of the relevant town. A full list of Swiss postcodes is published in phone directories. The Poste Restante fee for a short break of two weeks is approximately 8 CHF, if the account is set up online.

## Liechtenstein

Liechtenstein has its own telephone company, **Telecom FL**, and its own postal service, **Liechtensteinische Post**. It also issues its own postage stamps, which are coveted by collectors. Swisscom and Telecom FL cards can be used in both countries. Calls from Switzerland to Liechtenstein are treated as international, and you should dial 00, then the country code (423). A call from Liechtenstein to Switzerland is treated as national.

---

### DIRECTORY

**Telephones**

**Yellow Pages (business & services)**
🔲 local.ch

**Internet**

**Charly's Multimédia**
7 Rue de Fribourg,
1201 Geneva.
**Tel** 022 901 13 13.

**Internetcafe Zürich**
Urainiastrasse 3,
8001 Zürich.
**Tel** 044 210 33 11.

**Postal Services**

**Die Post/La Poste/La Posta**
🔲 post.ch

**Swisscom**
🔲 swisscom.ch

**Liechtenstein**

**Telecom FL**
🔲 telecom.li

**Liechtensteinische Post**
🔲 post.li

---

Display indicating value of the deposited coins

Coin slot

Button for selecting number of stamps

Operating instructions in three languages

Stamp dispenser knob

Table of stamp prices

Stamps delivered here

Postage-stamp vending machine

# TRAVEL INFORMATION

Lying at the crossroads of major European routes, Switzerland has excellent transport connections. The country has air links with all major European cities, as well as frequent intercontinental flights.

The country's internal transport system is also highly efficient, pleasant and easy to use, and a panoply of travel passes offer substantial discounts. Swiss trains and passenger postal buses together cover almost every corner of the country, offering visitors some of the best views of Switzerland's dramatic mountain scenery. Well-maintained roads make driving in Switzerland a pleasure and allow motorists either to cover long distances quickly or to explore the country's remoter regions at a more leisurely pace.

Sign indicating Zürich airport

### By Air from the UK

Several airlines operate frequent daily direct flights between the United Kingdom and Switzerland. The main carriers are **British Airways** and **SWISS**, the national airline. Several low-cost airlines, including **easyJet**, also operate flights between the United Kingdom and Switzerland.

SWISS flies daily direct from London City Airport to Geneva and from Heathrow to Geneva and Basel. Daily flights from Birmingham, Manchester and Heathrow to Zürich connect onward to Geneva and Basel.

Cheaper air fares can sometimes be obtained if you buy your plane ticket as part of a package from a tour operator. The London-based Swiss company **Switzerland Travel Centre**, which specializes in travel to and holidays in Switzerland, can advise on every type of requirement.

### By Air from the US

Flights between the United States and Switzerland are provided by **SWISS, American Airlines**, **United Airlines**, US Airways and **Delta**. Flights to Zürich and Geneva depart from New York, Boston, Atlanta, Miami, Philadelphia, San Francisco, Washington DC and Los Angeles.

The duration of flights is about seven or eight hours from the east coast of the United States, about 10 hours from the Midwest and about 14 hours from the west coast.

### Special-Interest Packages

Tour operators both in the United Kingdom and in the United States offer many special-interest package holidays in Switzerland. Most of them revolve around winter sports; however, there are a range of other options, including birdwatching and botanical tours led by specialists, and independent walking or cycling holidays, as well as rail tours and cultural explorations of the country.

### Swiss Airports

Switzerland's three main international airports are Basel, Zürich and Geneva. Both of the latter conveniently house train stations within the air terminal complex.

Basel is served by EuroAirport. Split into Swiss and EU sectors, it is located on French territory and also serves Mulhouse (in France) and Freiburg (in Germany). In addition to internal flights, EuroAirport provides links to several European cities.

Switzerland also has three smaller airports – Bern-Belp, Sion and Agno in Lugano – which provide a limited number of package and holiday flights, as well as internal connections. Most of the flights at Bern-Belp are to or from France, Germany and Italy, while Sion is ideally placed for access to the largest ski resorts, as well as the thermal resorts.

Zürich's Kloten airport, the busiest in Switzerland

Zürich's international airport

## Fly Rail Baggage

When flying to Switzerland via Zürich or Geneva from any airport in the world, you can make use of the convenient **Fly Rail Baggage** service. From the check-in desk at your home airport, you can send your luggage direct to any one of 81 train stations in Switzerland, where you can collect it at your convenience. Some hotels will collect your luggage for you.

To use Fly Rail Baggage you must obtain a special luggage tag from SWISS or a Swiss tourist office. The service costs about 22 CHF per piece of luggage. It is not, however, available if you are flying with a low-cost airline, and bulky items such as bicycles are not carried. As security concerns may also limit the availability of this service, you are advised to check with the airline or your travel agent.

## Station Check-in

Passengers flying from Zürich or Geneva with certain scheduled airlines and charter flights can make use of the convenient station check-in service. This costs around 22 CHF per item of luggage and can make for a more leisurely journey to the airport without having to carry heavy bags. You can check in your luggage from 24 hours before your flight at any one of 57 of the larger Swiss train stations. You will be given your boarding pass with your requested seat, and your luggage is transported to the airport and loaded onto your flight. You can then forget about your luggage until you collect it from the carousel at your destination airport.

A list of some 80 participating airlines can be found on the Swiss Federal Railways (SBB) website (www.sbb.ch).

## DIRECTORY

**American Airlines**
Tel 1-800-433-7300 (US).
W aa.com

**British Airways**
Tel 0844 493 0787 (UK); 1-800-247-9297 (US); 0848 845 845 (Switzerland). W ba.com

**Delta**
W delta.com

**easyJet**
W easyjet.com

**Fly Rail Baggage**
W sbb.ch

**SWISS**
Tel 0845 601 0956 (UK); 1-877 359-7947 (US); 0848 700 700 (Switzerland). W swiss.com

**Switzerland Travel Centre**
Tel 0207 420 4934 (UK).
W stc.co.uk

**United Airlines**
W united.com

## Tour Operators

**Alphorn Tours**
Tel 877 257 4676 (US).
W alphorntours.com

**Great Rail Journeys**
Tel 01904 521 936 (UK).
W greatrail.com

**Inn Travel**
Tel 01653 617 001 (UK).
W inntravel.co.uk

**Naturetrek**
Tel 01962 733 051 (UK).
W naturetrek.co.uk

Bus for passenger transfer at Zürich airport

| Airport | ℹ Information | Distance from City | Journey Time by Taxi | Journey Time by Public Transport |
|---------|---------------|--------------------|-----------------------|-----------------------------------|
| Basel | 061 325 31 11 | 5 km (3 miles) | 20 minutes | Bus: 15 minutes |
| Bern | 031 960 21 11 | 9 km (6 miles) | 30 minutes | Bus: 20 minutes |
| Geneva | 022 717 71 11 | 5 km (3 miles) | 20 minutes | Train: 6 minutes<br>Bus: 20 minutes |
| Lugano | 091 610 12 82 | 20 km (12 miles) | 40 minutes | Bus: 10 minutes |
| Zürich | 043 816 22 11 | 10 km (6 miles) | 25 minutes | Train: 9 minutes |

# Travelling by Train

The comprehensive Swiss rail network provides an excellent means of transport. Trains are modern, clean and comfortable, and services are frequent and dependably punctual. Because the railway timetable is efficiently integrated with other forms of public transport, connections are very convenient. The train is also one of the best ways to see the country. Special excursions by train and boat enable visitors to enjoy exceptionally beautiful scenery on several routes through mountains and over passes, across lakes and along valleys.

An Intercity train

### Arriving by Train

The most direct rail route from London to Switzerland is via the Channel Tunnel to Paris Gare du Nord. Transferring to Paris Gare de Lyon, three separate TGV (high-speed) train lines lead directly to

A moden train station with blue information boards

Geneva, Lausanne, Basel and Bern. There are a number of TGV connections into Switzerland, although TGV trains do not travel at their maximum speeds within Switzerland, due to lack of suitable rails.

The quickest journey (from London to Geneva) takes at least eight hours and, although all these routes are scenic, passing through the French Alps, reaching Switzerland by train from the United Kingdom is not as cheap, quick and convenient as flying (see pp294–5).

Switzerland has good links with European high-speed-train networks, among which are Germany's ICE, France's TGV and Italy's Cisalpino. Comprehensive Swiss public transport timetables, including international connections, can be consulted on the website www.sbb.ch/timetable.

### Trains

Switzerland's main train operator is Swiss Federal Railways, or SBB/CFF/FFS (Schweizerische Bundes-bahnen/Chemins de Fer Fédéraux/Ferrovie Federali Svizzere). SBB covers almost all the country, and over a dozen smaller operators run certain routes.

Most trains run from 6am to midnight, with hourly services operating between major towns. Smoking is forbidden on all trains at all times. Long-distance trains, including InterCity (IC), Eurocity (EC) and Interregio (IR) trains, have restaurant cars and trolleys serving drinks and snacks.

Trains also carry unacc-ompanied luggage. You can send your luggage ahead from almost any station to another station or bus terminal. This is very useful if you are on the move, and want to spend the day unencumbered by baggage (see p295).

### Travel Passes

A range of travel passes are available. Offering substantial discounts for rail travel, these passes can also be used on other modes of public transport, such as buses, trams, funiculars and boats.

## DIRECTORY

**SBB Timetable**
Tel 0900 300 300. w sbb.ch

**Travel Passes**
w swisstravelsystem.com
w raileurope.com

### Scenic Journeys

**Glacier Express**
Tel 0848 642 442.
w glacierexpress.ch

**Golden Pass Line**
Tel 0900 245 245.
w goldenpass.ch

**Bernina Express**
Tel 081 288 65 65.
w rhb.ch

**William Tell Express**
Tel 0900 300 300.
w sbb.ch

The Swiss Travel Pass allows unlimited rail travel on almost all train, bus and boat services, and on trams and buses in 75 towns. It allows reductions of up to 50 per cent on many railways, funiculars and cable cars. The Swiss Travel Pass is available for periods of 3, 4, 8 or 15 consecutive days. It also gives free entry to 470 museums.

The Swiss Travel Pass Flexi buys unlimited travel on any 3, 4, 8 or 15 days within a month. Further discounts apply to those under 26. The Swiss Transfer Ticket covers one round trip from the Swiss border or any Swiss airport to anywhere in the country. The Swiss Half Fare Card entitles you to one month's half-price travel. The Family Card allows children up to the age of 16 to travel free when accompanied by an adult. Regional passes are also available.

To see the full range of travel passes, visit www.swisstravel system.com. Most national travel passes can be purchased from travel agencies and Swiss tourist offices in your own country.

## Scenic Journeys

Special trains take visitors on panoramic journeys

The concourse of Winterthur railway station

through Switzerland's most spectacular scenery. Some trains have glass-roofed carriages that enable travellers to enjoy views in all directions.

Among the most popular of these rail journeys are the **Glacier Express**, which travels from St Moritz or Davos over the Oberalp pass to Zermatt; the **Golden**

Double-decker carriage of an SBB train

**Pass Line**, from Montreux over the Brünig Pass to Luzern; the **Bernina Express**, from Davos, Chur or St Moritz over the Bernina Pass and down to Tirano, in Italy; and the **William Tell Express**, which starts with a cruise on Lake Lucerne, then cuts through the St Gotthard tunnel and descends to Lugano.

Tickets for these scenic journeys can be bought at any station. Most require reservation at least 24 hours in advance.

## Switzerland's Main Rail Network

### Key

— Major railway
— Minor railway
····· Rail tunnels

# Travelling by Car, Bus, Bicycle and Boat

Motorway links provide swift means of road transport the length and breadth of the country, and well-maintained roads link Switzerland's major towns. Scenic routes also lead to high mountain passes and down Alpine valleys. Travelling through Switzerland by car is only one means of exploring the country. A fleet of passenger-carrying postbuses traverse spectacular landscape to reach remote Alpine towns and villages. A slower but equally rewarding alternative is to travel by bicycle, using convenient bus and rail links. Switzerland can also be appreciated at a slower pace, by taking a cruise on any of its breathtakingly beautiful lakes.

Multistorey car park in Geneva

Road sign in western Switzerland

## Arriving by Car

Fast car-carrying train services through the Channel Tunnel and good motorway routes eastwards across France make driving to Switzerland from the United Kingdom a viable alternative to flying. Frequent car ferries also cross the Channel from Dover to Calais and from Hull to Rotterdam or Zeebrugge. From Calais the quickest route is by motorway eastwards through France, entering Switzerland via the A40 to Geneva.

From Zeebrugge or Rotterdam, there are fast motorways across Belgium, Luxembourg, France and Germany, from where the A5 leads to Basel. By either route, the journey from the Channel coast to the Swiss border is unlikely to take less than eight hours.

If you drive on French *autoroutes* remember that motorway tolls may add considerably to the cost of your journey.

## Rules of the Road

In Switzerland, as in the rest of mainland Europe, driving is on the right. Overtaking on the right is prohibited and at junctions priority is given to drivers on the right, except when you are entering a roundabout. Unless road signs indicate otherwise, the speed limit is 120 km/h (75 mph) on motorways, 100 km/h (60 mph) on main highways, and 80 km/h (50 mph) on other roads. In built-up areas it is 50 km/h (30 mph) but can sometimes be as low as 30 km/h (20 mph). Speed cameras and radar are in widespread use.

The driver and passengers of a car must wear seatbelts. Children under 12 years old must travel in the back seat, and those under seven must be strapped into a child seat. All vehicles must also carry a breakdown warning triangle. Headlights must be on at all times, day or night. Any infringement of traffic regulations is likely to incur an on-the-spot fine, for which drivers should request a receipt.

The use of mobile phones while driving is considered to be a serious infringement, as is driving under the influence of alcohol. The blood-alcohol content limit is 0.05 per cent. Drivers should also carry their driving licence and the vehicle's registration document, which may be checked by the police.

## Driving on Motorways

To use Swiss motorways, which are indicated by green signs, drivers require a sticker, or *vignette*. Costing 40 CHF, a *vignette* is valid until the end of January of the following year and can be purchased at border crossings, petrol stations, in post offices and at tourist offices. A *vignette* is also required for motorcycles and trailers. Driving on a motorway without a valid *vignette* incurs a fine.

## Driving in the Alps

Drivers are required by law to use snow tyres and/or chains on mountain roads when indicated

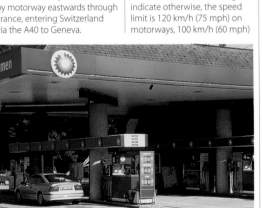

BP petrol station

by special warning signs. Road signs on routes leading into the Alps inform drivers of conditions ahead and whether passes are closed. The road tunnels beneath the Gotthard, San Bernardino and Great St Bernard passes are open year-round, and some operate a toll system. The Lötschberg, Furka, Albula and Vereina tunnels have rail links, and cars are carried on trains.

Most of the country's high Alpine passes are generally open from June until October, although this is subject to weather conditions.

Drivers must always yield to postbuses, which may swing wide on narrow curves.

## Car Hire

The major international car-hire companies offer services in Switzerland, with offices in the

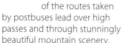

Sign to a motorway

main airports and in the town centres. Swiss Railways also offer a short-term Click and Drive car hire service. Cars are booked online and collected at one of 390 selected railway stations. Local firms usually offer cheaper rates, but for the cheapest deals it is best to pre-book in your own country. To hire a car in Switzerland, a driver must be over 20 years of age (in some cases 25) and must show a valid driving licence.

A postbus on one of many Alpine routes inaccessible by rail

## Buses and Postbuses

Outside of the towns and cities, public transport can be provided by local bus companies or the yellow-coloured postbuses. Most bus stations are located very near train stations, and bus and rail services are well coordinated, so that bus departures coincide with train arrivals and vice versa.

Alpine routes that are inaccessible by rail are also served by postbuses (known as *postautos* or *postcars*), which are yellow and bear the Die Post, La Poste or La Posta logo. As well as carrying mail and passengers, postbuses also carry unaccompanied luggage, which is convenient for hikers. Some of the routes taken by postbuses lead over high passes and through stunningly beautiful mountain scenery.

Bus stop sign for the postbus

## Bicycles

Switzerland has a very cyclist-friendly infrastructure. **PubliBike** is a nationwide bike-sharing scheme. Bicycles (*velos*) can also be hired at some 100 train stations (follow signs indicating *Mietvelos, Location de Vélos* or *Bici da Noleggiare*), and need not be returned to the same station. Rental information is available from Swiss Federal Railways *(see p296)*. For a fee, bicycles can be carried on postbuses and on trains (unless otherwise indicated in the timetables). Reservations for cycles are mandatory on all InterCity tilting trains from March to October.

Recommended cycle routes are marked by red signs with a white bicycle symbol. Cycling maps are obtainable from local tourist offices. Several long-distance cycle routes traverse the country. The North–South

Route runs for 360 km (225 miles) from Basel to Chiasso, in southern Ticino.

## Lake Cruises

Taking a cruise on one of Switzerland's lakes is a relaxing way to explore. A fleet of paddle steamers ply Lake Lucerne and many other lakes, and there are scenic cruises of Lake Geneva, Bodensee and Lake Lugano. Most cruises run only from April to October.

All Swiss travel passes are valid for cruises on the lakes, except for Lake Maggiore. The **Swiss Pass** gives free travel on many cruises and journeys by public transport, as well as 50 per cent off most mountain railways.

## DIRECTORY

### Car-Hire Companies

**Avis**
Tel 0848 81 18 18.
W avis.com

**Europcar**
Tel 0848 80 80 99.
W europcar.com

**Hertz**
Tel 0848 82 20 20.
W hertz.com

### Postbuses

**Swiss Post**
W swisspost.ch

### Cycling

**PubliBike**
W publibike.ch

**Veloland**
W veloland.ch

### Lake Cruises

**Lake Lucerne Navigation Company**
W lakelucerne.ch

**Schweizerische Bodensee-Schiffahrtsgesellschaft AG**
W sbsag.ch

**Swiss Pass**
W swisstravelsystem.com

# Getting Around in Towns

Most Swiss towns, particularly the historic districts of larger cities, are compact, making them easy to explore on foot. Some major historic town centres are also pedestrianized, or barred to almost all motorized traffic. To reach outlying attractions, visitors will sometimes need to take buses, trams, suburban trains or in certain cases funiculars. These are all easy to use, especially as tickets and travel passes are valid for every mode of public transport. Taxis are also available, although they are expensive. Bicycles, which can be hired from many rail stations, are an alternative means of getting around. For unforgettable views of Switzerland's great lakeshore towns, visitors should take a boat cruise.

A conducted sightseeing tour of a town centre

## Taxis

Because the Swiss public transport system is so efficient, taking a taxi is rarely worth the extra expense. Although they vary from town to town, taxi fares are uniformly high, consisting of a flat rate and an additional charge for every kilometre (just over half a mile) travelled. These charges are higher at night and at weekends.

Taxis can be any colour and are identifiable by a "taxi" sign on the roof. They can be hired from ranks, which are almost always located in front of railway stations. They can also be booked by telephone.

## Buses and Trams

The quickest and easiest way of getting around in towns is by hopping on a bus, trolleybus or tram. These run at frequent intervals from about 5am until midnight. Night buses run only

at weekends. Inside buses and trams are maps showing the itinerary travelled, and the stops along the route. Each stop is announced by the driver, or by a recording. To request a stop, press the button next to the door. The doors of buses open automatically. Tram doors are opened by passengers pressing a button.

## S-Bahn and Metro

Zürich, Bern, Geneva and other cities are served by S-Bahn, or suburban, trains (known as RER in French). The hubs of these networks are the cities' main stations, from where you can travel not only to the suburbs but to neighbouring towns. Bicycles can be carried on almost all S-Bahn trains. The S-Bahn network map is displayed inside the carriages.

Some towns built on steep cliffs or clinging to hillsides, such as Lausanne and Fribourg, also have funicular railways. Lausanne's funicular trains run from the main train station, in two directions. One line leads up to the town centre, and the other leads down to Ouchy, the suburb on the shores of Lake Geneva. Lausanne is also the only Swiss town to have a metro.

## Tickets

Information on the various types of tickets available is displayed at bus and tram stops. In most towns, the public transport network is divided into zones, and the more zones you intend to traverse the more a ticket will cost. Also, tickets are valid for a limited period, ranging from an hour to a full day or more, and can be used on any mode of transport. In Zürich, for example, one ticket can be used on buses, trams, S-Bahn trains and boats.

In towns and cities there is an automatic ticket machine at every bus and tram stop. The machines accept coins (Swiss francs and sometimes euros) and special cards that are sold in all newsagent kiosks. When you board a bus or tram, you should validate your ticket by stamping it at a machine on board the vehicle. Ticket inspectors (some in uniform) regularly carry out checks. The penalty for travelling without a valid ticket is 40–60 CHF.

The Swiss Travel Pass and Swiss Travel Pass Flexi (see pp296–7) are valid on all modes of public transport in 75 Swiss towns (listed on the ticket). The Swiss Travel Pass also gives free entry to 470 museums. Some towns issue special passes for visitors. The ZürichCard (24 CHF for 24 hours, 48 CHF for 72

Button for confirming payment in cash

Slot for inserting the CASH smartcard

Buttons for selecting parking stand number

Coin slot

Tickets are dispensed from here

Coin- and card-operated parking-ticket machine

An SBB bus bound for Bülach, in the suburbs of Zürich

hours), for example, offers reduced rates for guided tours, free entry to 38 museums and a free drink at some 20 restaurants.

## Parking

Using a car in city centres can be quite inconvenient. It is far easier to leave your car in an out-of-town car park (signposted "P&R", for "Park and Ride") and switch to a bus or tram to reach the town centre.

On-street parking and urban car parks are usually very expensive, especially in large towns and cities. Parking bays are colour-coded, or delineated with coloured lines. Those in a White Zone are usually pay-and-display. To use those in a Blue Zone you need a parking disc, which limits the parking time allowed. Discs are available from tourist offices, banks and other points. Bays in a Red Zone allow free parking for 15 hours, and the parking disc must be displayed. Illegal parking is likely to result in a fine. Most parking-ticket machines accept coins but do not accept cards other than CASH, a Swiss smartcard.

## Bicycles

Switzerland's zealous anti-pollution and anti-congestion ethic means that the use of bicycles is actively encouraged. Many towns have cycle lanes, filter lights at crossings and ubiquitous cycle racks. Bicycles can be hired at many main railway stations (see p299). Some towns offer free bicycle rental. To hire a bicycle under this scheme, all you need to do is show your passport and pay a deposit of 20–50 CHF, which is refunded when you return the bike. Details can be obtained from local tourist information offices or by visiting www.rentabike.ch or www.publibike.ch.

Sign for metered car parking

## Sightseeing on Foot

Many of the oldest and best-preserved town centres have been partly or wholly pedestrianized, restoring their historic atmosphere and making them very pleasant to explore on foot. Suggested itineraries are usually marked with a continuous line or a succession of painted footprints, and major historic buildings and other features of interest along the route have information panels.

The tourist offices in some towns organize guided tours, which are often led by English-speaking guides. Most tourist information offices also provide town maps and helpful information in English.

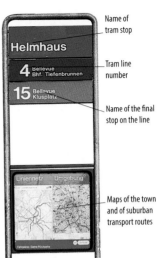

Name of tram stop

Tram line number

Name of the final stop on the line

Maps of the town and of suburban transport routes

Information board at a tram stop in Zürich

## Ferries

Ferry trips can offer quite a different perspective of Switzerland's lakeshore towns. Ferries operate from Zürich, Geneva, Lugano, Locarno, Thun, Luzern and other towns, whose beautiful lakeshore buildings may be seen to their best advantage when viewed from the water.

Most ferry companies run cruises only from early April to the end of October. Steamer services operate on Lake Geneva and Lake Lucerne. Longer cruises, on Lake Maggiore, depart from Locarno or Ascona for Stresa in the Italian part of the lake.

Tickets can usually be bought either from the ticket windows at the boat landings or directly on the boat – the price is the same. The Swiss Travel Pass (see pp296–7) is valid for travel on all lakes except Lake Maggiore. Full details are available from tourist offices.

A tram on Zürich's network

# General Index

# Acknowledgments

Dorling Kindersley and Hachette Livre Polska would like to thank the following people and institutions, whose contributions and assistance have made the preparation of this guide possible.

**Publishing Manager**
Kate Poole

**Managing Editors**
Helen Townsend, Jacky Jackson

**Publisher**
Douglas Amrine

**Cartography**
Uma Bhattacharya, Mohammad Hassan, Jasneet Kaur, Casper Morris

**DTP**
Vinod Harish, Vincent Kurien, Jason Little, Azeem Siddiqui

**Revisions Team**
Namrata Adhwaryu, Hilary Bird, Andrew Bishop, Julie Bond, Louise Cleghorn, Kati Clinton, Caroline Elliker, Karen Fitzpatrick, Anna Freiberger, Priya Kukadia, Rahul Kumar, Jude Ledger, Carly Madden, Kate Molan, George Nimmo, Reetu Pandey, Susie Peachey, Rada Radojicic, Catherine Richards, Sands Publishing Solutions, Jaynan Spengler, Hollie Teague, Nicky Twyman, Conrad Van Dyk, Vinita Venugopal, Antoinette Verlan, Ed Wright

**Factchecker**
Doug Sager

**Picture Research**
Rachel Barber, Rhiannon Furbear, Ellen Root

**Proofreader**
Stewart Wild

**Index**
Helen Peters

**Additional Contributors**
Catherine Beattie, Doug Sager

**Additional Photographers**
Ian O'Leary

**Special Assistance**
Appenzellerland Tourismus; Artothek, Baud V Maydell; Bellinzona Turismo; Biel/Bienne Seeland Tourismus; Burgerbibliothek, Bern; Corbis; Enteturistico Lago Maggiore; Furrer Jakob (photograph of beers, p262); Historisches Museum, Basel (Therese Wollmann); Kunsthaus, Zürich (Cécile Brunner); Kunstmuseum, Basel; Kunstmuseum, Bern (Regula Zbinden); Alicja Kusch (photograph of Bomi shop in Klif); André Locher (photographs of Yverdon-les-Bains and Mesocco); Lugano Turismo; Katarzyna and Wojciech Medrzak; Grzegorz Mościbrocki (World of Alcoholic Drinks); Mövenpick Wein, Zug (Brigitte auf der Maur); Musée d'Art et d'Histoire, Geneva (Isabelle Brun-Ilunga, Marc-Antoine Claivaz); Musée d'Art et d'Histoire, Neuchâtel (Marie-Josée Golles); Musée Romain, Avenches (Anne Hochuli-Gysel); Offentliche Kunstsammlung Basel, Kunstmuseum und Museum für Gegenwartskunst (Maria-Theresa Brunner); Schweiz Tourismus, Zürich (Fred Schreiber); Schweizerisches Landesmuseum (Angelica Condrau, Andrea Kunz); Swiss Embassy, Warsaw; Gerry Thönen (photograph of an orchard); Tourist Information Centre, Geneva (Frédéric Monnerat); Verkehrshaus, Luzern (Hans Syfrig, Martin Sigrist); Wistillerie Etter Soehne Ag, Zug (Eveline Etter); Zentralbiliothek, Zürich (Kristin Steiner).

## Picture Credits

37bl; Kelly-Mooney Photography 30tr; Francis G Mayer 42bc; Richard T Nowitz 31tr; Gianni Dagli Orti 43bl; José F. Poblete 26–7c, 138; Annie Poole/Papilio 27tl; Christian Sarramon 87br; Leonard de Selva 45br; Ted Spiegel 40tr; Ink Swim 45tc, 232c; Tim Thompson 27br; Vittoriano Rastelli 25tr; Ruggero Vanni 31c; Jean Bernard Vernier/Sygma 47crb, 47bl, 110cla, 111tl; Scott T Smith 26cl; Sandro Vanini 31br, 56bl, 218cla; Pierre Vauthey/Sygma 31cr, 35bl; Patrick Ward 31bl; Werner Forman 145tl; Nik Wheeler 1; Adam Woolfitt 26tr; Zefa/Uli Wiesmeier 281tr.

**Dorta:** 275br.

**Dreamstime.com:** Steve Allen 14tl; Arocas 13br; Astra490 139cb, 194bl, 211bc; Eva Bocek 15bl; Cosmopol 97cb; Exinocactus 194tc; Georgesixth 232tc; Hai Huy Ton That 101br; Sang Lei 11tl; Mathes 58tr; Olegmit 180; Arseniy Rogov 10cla; Sergiyn 75br; Spunky1234 14cr; Victor Torres 55tr; Travelpeter 113cb; Tupungato 54bl; Tosca Weijers 278br; John Wollwerth 12bl.

**Enteturistico Lago Maggiore:** T Krueger 218tr.

**Fairmont Le Montreux Palace:** 251bc.

**Familie Grolimund:** 292cl, 293tl.

**Fondation du Chateau de Chillon:** 126cl/bl.

**Geneve Tourism:** 108br.

**Getty Images:** LOOK/Bernard van Dierendonck 277tl; Stephen Studd 239br.

**Grand Resort Bad Ragaz:** 246br, 252br.

**Gstaad Palace:** 246cla, 248bl.

**Cafe Hanselmann:** 256ca, 273tr.

**Robert Harding Picture Library:** Werner Dieterich 13tr.

**Historisches Museum Basel:** 145br.

**Oldrich Karasek:** 5tr, 72clb.

**Piotr Kiedrowski:** 110crb, 111tr.

**Kohlmanns Basel** 270tr.

**Kunsthaus Zürich:** 38, 45cra, 174bl, 174cla, 175cb; Dadaist work, Hans Arp © DACS, London 2012 171tr; Au-dessus de Paris, 1968, Marc Chagall ©ADAGP, Paris and DACS, London 2012 175cr; Bird in Space, 1925, Constantin Brancusi ©ADAGP, Paris and DACS, London 2012 175tc; Guitar on a Pedestal Table, 1915, Pablo Picasso ©Succession Picasso/DACS 2012 175cra.

**Kunstmuseum Basel:** 150clb, 150bl, 151ca, 151cra, 151crb, 151bc; Senecio, 1922, Paul Klee ©DACS 2012 150tr; Burning Giraffe, 1936–7, Salvador Dalí © Kingdom of Spain – Gala-Salvador Dalí Foundation, DACS, London 2012 150bl.

**Kunstmuseum Bern:** 60cla, 60cl; Peter Lauri 60br, 61crb; Dans un Jardin Meridional, 1914 Pierre Bonnard ©ADAGP, Paris and DACS, London 2012 61tc; Ad Parnassum, 1932, Paul Klee ©DACS 2012 61cra; Drunken Doze, 1902, Pablo

Picasso ©Succession Picasso/DACS 2012 61bc.

**Landesmuseum Zürich:** (2003) 39br, 40bc, 41tc, 41cra, 43tl.

**Lausanne Palace & Spa:** 250tr.

**Lugano Turismo:** 214tr.

**Musée d'Art et d'Histoire, Neuchâtel:** 44–5c.

**Musée d'Art et d'Histoire, Geneva:** MAH 43crb,106tr; Jean Marc Yersin 106ca, 106cb, 107cra; Yves Siza 106bl, 107bl; Bettina Jacot-Descombes 107tc; Le Bain Turc, 1907, Félix Edouard Vallotton 107clb.

**Museum für Gestaltang/Fleck Balagh:** 168tl.

**Öffentliche Kunstsammlung, Basel:** Martin Bühler 40cl.

**Małgorzata Omilanowska:** 30cl, 30cr, 51tr, 51bl, 55br, 57tc, 62cl, 62tr, 62bl, 63tl, 164cla, 165cr, 169br, 170bc, 172tr, 178bc, 179tl, 301tr, 301b.

**Park Hotel Sonnenhof:** Vaduz Sonnenhof 257tl, 274tr.

**Photolibrary:** imagebroker.net/Meinrad Riedo 240bl; Mauritius Die Bildagentur Gmbh/Beuthan Beuthan 259tl.

**Pinte de Pierre-a-Bot:** 269tl.

**Police of Geneve:** 288crb/bl.

**Reithalle:** 271br.

**Sala of Tokyo, Zurich:** Doris Staub 272br.

**photo SBB:** 296cl, 296bl.

**Schweizerishes Landesmuseum, Zürich:** 166–7 all.

**Schweiz Tourismus:** 4br, 73tr, 115cra, 195tc, 195bl; U. Ackermann 24bl; D. Brawand 229br; R. Brioschi 176br; L. Degonda 28tr, 123cra, 123tr; S. Eigstler 27ca; S. Engler 34br, 36br, 109cr, 121br, 123bl, 176bl; Höllgrotten Baar 213tr; P. Maurer 22c, 33tl, 236cla; F. Pfenniger 28cl; M. Schmid 21b, 29tl, 123tl, 229tl; H. Schwab 27cr, 33br, 213br, 232bl; C. Sonderegger 22b, 23tr, 23br, 25bl, 32tr, 32cl, 32bl, 32br, 33tr, 33bl, 34cla, 35cla, 36ca, 37cla, 123br, 173b, 182cl, 183tr/br, 212cla, 218br, 224bl, 233br, 236tr, 236bl; W. Storto 219cr; K. Richter 24tr.

**Restaurant Suder:** Renate Fankhauser 256br, 265tr.

**Superstock:** age fotostock 284-6; Yoko Aziz/age fotostock 101cla; Higuchi Hitoshi/Prisma 228bc.

**Swiss Transport Museum:** 242tr/cla/clb/bc, 243cra/br; Photopress/Sigi Tischler 242br; Photopress/Alexandra Wey 243cl.

**Thun-Thunersee Tourismus:** 78ca.

**Tse Yang:** 257br, 267br.

**Victoria-Jungfrau Grand Hotel & Spa:** 247tl; 283tr.

**Paweł Wroński:** 92clb, 94br, 120bl, 299bl.

**Zentral Bibliothek, Zürich:** 40–41c, 42crb.

**Zum Alten Stephan Stadtbeiz:** 266tr.

Front endpaper: **Alamy Images:** age fotostock Spain, S.L. Ltc; Joana Kruse Rtr; Photo Patricia White 2 Lbl; **AWL Images:** Peter Adams Ltl; Jon Arnold Lbc; Walter Bibikow Rbc; **Corbis:** Jose F. Poblete Rtc; **Dreamstime.com:** Olegmit Rbr

Jacket: Front and spine– **4Corners:** Giovanni Simeone.

**All other images © Dorling Kindersley**
**For further information see www.dkimages.com**

## Special Editions of DK Travel Guides

DK Travel Guides can be purchased in bulk quantities at discounted prices for use in promotions or as premiums. We are also able to offer special editions and personalized jackets, corporate imprints, and excerpts from all of our books, tailored specifically to meet your own needs.

To find out more, please contact:
*in the United States* **SpecialSales@dk.com**
*in the UK* **travelspecialsales@uk.dk.com**
*in Canada DK Special Sales at* **general@ tourmaline.ca**
*in Australia* **business.development@pearson. com.au**

# Phrase Book

German is the most widely spoken language in Switzerland, followed by French and Italian. Swiss German, which is used in everyday speech, differs from standard High German (*see p287*). Because it consists of several local dialects, each of which are almost impossible to transcribe, the phrases given below are in High German, with some of the most commonly used expressions in Swiss German marked by an asterisk.

## In Emergency

| English | German | French | Italian |
|---|---|---|---|
| Help! | Hilfe! | *Au secours!* | *Aiuto!* |
| Stop! | Halt! | *Arrêtez!* | *Alt!* |
| Call a doctor! | Holen Sie einen Artz! | *Appelez un médecin!* | *Chiami un medico!* |
| Call an ambulance! | Holen Sie einen Krankenwagen! | *Appelez une ambulance!* | *Chiami una ambulanza!* |
| Call the police! | Holen Sie die Polizei! | *Appelez la police!* | *Chiami la polizia!* |
| Call the fire brigade! | Holen Sie die Feuerwehr! | *Appelez les pompiers!* | *Chiami i pompieri!* |
| Where is a telephone? | Wo finde ich ein Telefon? | *Ou y a-t-il un téléphone?* | *Dov'è il telefono?* |
| Where is the hospital? | Wo finde ich das Krankenhaus? | *Ou est l'hôpital?* | *Dov'è l'ospedale?* |

## Communication Essentials

| | | | |
|---|---|---|---|
| Yes | Ja | *Oui* | *Sì* |
| No | Nein | *Non* | *No* |
| Please | Bitte | *S'il vous plaît* | *Per favore* |
| Thank you | Danke vielmals | *Merci* | *Grazie* |
| Excuse me | Entschuldigen Sie *Äxgüsi | *Excusez-moi* | *Mi scusi* |
| Hello | Grüss Gott *Grüezi | *Salut* | *Salve/Ciao* |
| Goodbye | Auf Widersehen *Ufwiederluege | *Au revoir* | *Arrivederci* |
| Bye! | Tschüss! | *Salut!* | *Ciao!* |
| here | hier | *ici* | *qui* |
| there | dort | *là* | *là* |
| What? | Was? | *Quel/Quelle?* | *Quale?* |
| Where? | Wo/Wohin? | *Oé?* | *Dove?* |

## Useful Phrases and Words

| | | | |
|---|---|---|---|
| Where is ...? | Wo befindet sich...? | *Oé est ...?* | *Dov'è...?* |
| Where are ...? | Wo befinden sich...? | *Oé sont...?* | *Dove sono...?* |
| Do you speak English? | Sprechen Sie Englisch? | *Parlez-vous anglais?* | *Parla inglese?* |
| I understand | Ich verstehe | *Je comprends* | *Capisco* |
| I don't understand | Ich verstehe nicht | *Je ne comprends pas* | *Non capisco* |
| I'm sorry | Es tut mir leid | *Je suis désolé* | *Mi dispiace* |
| big | gross | *grand* | *grande* |
| small | klein | *petit* | *piccolo* |
| open | auf/offen | *ouvert* | *aperto* |
| closed | zu/geschlossen | *fermé* | *chiuso* |
| left | links | *à gauche* | *a sinistra* |
| right | rechts | *à droite* | *a destra* |
| near | in der Nähe | *près* | *vicino* |
| far | weit | *loin* | *lontano* |
| up | auf/oben | *en haut* | *su* |
| down | ab/unten | *en bas* | *giù* |
| early | früh | *de bonne heure* | *presto* |
| late | spät | *en retard* | *tardi* |
| entrance | Eingang/Einfahrt | *l'entrée* | *l'entrata* |
| exit | Ausgang/Ausfahrt | *la sortie* | *l'uscita* |
| toilet | WC/Toilette | *les toilettes/les WCs* | *il gabinetto* |

## Making a Telephone Call

| | | | |
|---|---|---|---|
| I'd like to place a long-distance call. | Ich möchte ein Fernsgespräch machen. | *Je voudrais faire un interurbain.* | *Vorrei fare una interurbana.* |
| I'd like to make a reverse charge call/call collect. | Ich möchte ein Rückgespräch machen. | *Je voudrais faire une communication PCV.* | *Vorrei fare una telefonata a carico del destinatario.* |
| I'll try again later. | Ich versuche es später noch einmal. | *Je rappellerai plus tard.* | *Ritelefono piè tardi.* |
| Can I leave a message? | Kann ich etwas ausrichten? | *Est ce que je peux laisser un message?* | *Posso lasciare un messaggio?* |

## Staying in a Hotel

| | | | |
|---|---|---|---|
| Do you have a vacant room? | Haben Sie ein Zimmer frei? | *Est-ce que vous avez une chambre libre?* | *Avete camere libere?* |
| double room | ein Doppelzimmer | *une chambre à deux* | *una camera doppia* |
| twin room | ein Doppelzimmer mit zwei Betten | *une chambre à deux lits* | *una camera con due letti* |
| single room | ein Einzelzimmer | *une chambre à une personne* | *una camera singola* |
| with a bath/shower | mit Bad/Dusche | *avec salle de bains/douche* | *con bagno/doccia* |
| How much is the room? | Wievel kostet das Zimmer? | *Combien coûte la chambre?* | *Quanto costa la camera?* |
| Where is the bathroom? | Wo ist das Bad? | *Oé est la salle de bains?* | *Dov'è il bagno?* |